# THE JUDGE

*Thomas Mellon, by Théobald Chartran, 1895.*
*Courtesy of the Richard King Mellon Foundation.*

# THE JUDGE

*A Life of Thomas Mellon,
Founder of a Fortune*

JAMES MELLON

Yale UNIVERSITY PRESS
*New Haven and London*

Published with assistance from the Kingsley Trust Association Publication Fund
established by the Scroll and Key Society of Yale College.

Yale University Press books may be purchased in quantity for educational, business, or promotional use.
For information, please e-mail sales.press@yale.edu (U.S. office) or sales@yaleup.co.uk (U.K. office).

Designed and set in Adobe Garamond Premier Pro with Requiem display
by Princeton Editorial Associates Inc., Scottsdale, Arizona.
Printed in the United States of America.

Library of Congress Cataloging-in-Publication Data

Mellon, James, 1942–
The judge : a life of Thomas Mellon, founder of a fortune / James Mellon.
    p.    cm.
  Includes bibliographical references and index.
  ISBN 978-0-300-16714-6 (cloth : alk. paper)
  1. Mellon, Thomas, 1813–1908.   2. Capitalists and financiers—United States—
Biography.   3. Mellon family.   I. Title.
  HC102.5.M377M35     2011
  332.092—dc22
  [B]                                                    2010043321

A catalogue record for this book is available from the British Library.

This paper meets the requirements of ANSI/NISO Z39.48–1992 (Permanence of Paper).

10 9 8 7 6 5 4 3 2 1

*For my mother,*
*Gertrud Altegoer Mellon*

# Contents

*Preface*

T HE PHARAOHS LEFT THEIR PYRAMIDS," John D. Rockefeller
his Center, Henry Ford his Foundation; and Andrew Carnegie
sowed the Earth with libraries that bear his name. That Thomas
Mellon left only his sons points to a striking difference between him
and the conspicuous megagnomes of his day. Because neither monuments nor philanthropy appealed to him, he had little choice but to
leave his wealth to family members. Yet nothing could shake his
conviction that inherited wealth normally contains the germs of its
own dissolution—that, like a living creature, it is programmed for
death; that heirs who are relieved, by the accident of birth, from the
necessity of struggle tend to degenerate mentally and physically.

Thomas Mellon established his family in business and was the
founder of a historic fortune. At a glance, his life seems to chronicle
the familiar ascent from rags to riches that intrigues and strikes a
chord with most Americans. But the man whose passage from farmer
to financier is chronicled here differed refreshingly from the thundering herd of self-made men. He was a brilliant, quirky, driven auto-
didact who read Greek and Latin, who served as the classics professor of
his university before becoming a lawyer and as a judge before founding the Mellon family's bank and launching its early businesses. He
pondered deeply about life. His hunger for knowledge was insatiable,

and his reading ranged from Herodotus to Karl Marx. He was also a man of action who charged in and out of politics, leaving a wide path of destruction; was a founder of the Republican Party; served for ten years as a judge; and sent four people to the gallows.

More important, Mellon's life lays bare the bundle of attitudes, systematic repressions, and prejudices that make up the "Protestant work ethic"—that unsparing mindset that trumpets individualism at the expense of community but which lent wings to the economic development of America and secured its industrial supremacy. He exemplified a mentality that facilitated the vast accumulations of wealth needed to secure America's industrialization. How this wealth would be divided was left for the future to decide.

Though Thomas Mellon's wife insisted on calling him "Pa," Pittsburghers referred to him as "Judge Mellon," and his numerous descendants still speak fondly of "the Judge." He had earned that title by virtue of his ten-year term on the Court of Common Pleas, but there is a more compelling reason for the nickname. In his unvarnished autobiography, *Thomas Mellon and His Times,* he passes withering judgment on the controversial issues of his day in fields as disparate as business, religion, democracy, taxation, the role of government, marriage, morality, trial by jury, education, military service, the death penalty, the Irish, and loss of identity in a progressively more industrialized and impersonal world—all subjects that continue to agitate the public mind. He even proposes a revolutionary form of courtship. The reader will find a refreshing absence of political correctness here. Mellon was an uncanny observer of life, a pitiless critic of men and women, and an irreverent arbiter of ideas; it would be difficult to imagine anyone with stronger judgmental tendencies.

The most cogent argument for writing a life of Thomas Mellon (1813–1908) is that none exists, even though it was he who established the Mellon family in finance and who tinctured his children and grandchildren with the values that propelled them to excel. He was also the father, and, more important, the teacher of Andrew W. Mellon, who would build a massive segment of America's industrial base, would give the country the National Gallery of Art—its most valuable donation to date—and, as secretary of the treasury, would direct the finances of the world's most powerful nation under three presidents.

Thomas Mellon wrote a delightfully engaging autobiography, but he wrote it too soon: he lived for twenty-two more years after its publication. These were the consequential years when he faced down and overthrew the nefarious ring that was misgoverning Kansas City, when he concluded his political life, plunged headlong into an ill-considered final business venture, relinquished his fortune, and became infatuated with the supernatural.

There are also some intriguing omissions in his memoir. While acknowledging that he sentenced both men and women to death, he neglects to identify these criminals, remains silent about their crimes, and leaves us to wonder whether they were in fact executed. By searching the voluminous collections of nineteenth-century newspapers in various Pittsburgh libraries, I was able to reconstruct these chilling cases and to amass a trove of additional intelligence about Thomas Mellon that previous writers failed to discover. This treasury of information revealed the principal reason why he was drafted for the bench by three of Pittsburgh's most eminent lawyers, as well as the saga of his head-on collision with organized labor in the Waverly coal strike and the record of his attempt to bankrupt the *National Labor Tribune.* From the forgotten minutes of Pittsburgh's two city councils emerges a portrait of Mellon the opinionated and focused (yet awkward and reluctant) politician, the man who maneuvered to prevent Allegheny County from building Henry Hobson Richardson's mammoth courthouse, and who stridently opposed the erection of Andrew Carnegie's free library for Pittsburgh.

That Thomas Mellon happens to have been my great-great-grandfather counted for nothing in persuading me to write this biography. It was his riveting uniqueness that fascinated me, and I have worked hard to present a balanced portrait of him, rather than one that is sanitized by familial piety.

That said, my own relationship to this subject did give me an advantage: I had access to the Mellon family's private collections of letters, diaries, photographs, and other intimate material. These yielded some gems—among them Thomas Mellon's university correspondence and a jarring eyewitness account of how Mellon's deceased son George "appeared" and "spoke" to him at a séance in the presence of numerous witnesses.

The outstanding original source for this book was a manuscript collection of recorded conversations between the journalist Boyden Sparkes and my grandfather, William L. Mellon. "W.L.," as he was called, knew his own grandfather, Thomas Mellon, intimately; he was also a close business associate of Andrew W. Mellon for forty-eight years. Late in life he hired Sparkes to ghostwrite his autobiography, and the two engaged in a series of lengthy conversations that were taped and then transcribed. That these recorded interviews took place while Sparkes was houseguesting in the Mellon homes or boat-guesting on one of their yachts may explain why they came to occupy more than a thousand pages.

While a cornucopia of original material was utilized to complete this meditation on Thomas Mellon's life, the traditional sources were scrutinized anew: I have rigorously reevaluated Mellon's autobiography for unrecognized insights and have reexamined in full depth the collection of starkly revealing letters that he exchanged with his son James, who was my great-grandfather and namesake.

Above all, I have attempted to provide a critical viewpoint from which to judge "the Judge."

# THE JUDGE

# I

Beginnings in Ulster,
the Crossing, and the Fourth R

*This remained my home for fifteen years, during that period of life which is by far the most important to a young man—the period when he is a "hobble-de-hoy," neither a man nor a boy; the vealy stage of existence, when sentiments and habits are emerging out of chaos and crystallizing into form. It is the period when slight influences produce lasting effects for good or evil. Here were implanted in my nature those root principles of right and duty, tenacity of purpose, patient industry and perseverance in well doing which have accompanied me through life.*

Thomas Mellon, *Thomas Mellon and His Times, 1885*

FOUR MILES NORTH OF OMAGH, in the ancient province of Ulster, currently known as Northern Ireland, the river Strule swings to the east and then back again before resuming its northward course through County Tyrone. The resulting loop encompasses 183 acres of the town land of Castletown, and it was there that Thomas Mellon began the journey of life on February 3, 1813. His birthplace, Camp Hill Cottage, is a traditional thatch-roofed farmhouse with walls made of field stones mortared together and whitewashed. It was built by Thomas's father, Andrew Mellon, in 1812, when he married Rebecca Wauchob, and it is still to be seen on the twenty-three acres of arable land that Thomas's grandfather had detached from his own lease and assigned to Andrew as a wedding present. The farmhouse is now protected by the Scotch-Irish Trust of Ulster and is part of the Ulster-American Folk Park at Omagh.

"Mellon" is a surname derived from the Gaelic O'Mellain, which means "of the pleasant people." A small number of Scottish and Irish families, most of them unrelated, still share this surname today.

Family tradition holds that the first of Thomas Mellon's ancestors to settle in Ireland was Archibald Mellon. He and his wife, Elizabeth, apparently left Scotland shortly after 1660 and began to farm on the townland of Castletown, in the parish of Cappagh, near Omagh.[1] These early Mellons rented land from the viscounts Mountjoy and earls of Blessington, and their freehold leases, like many in Ulster, were of such lengthy duration that they almost amounted to ownership.[2]

Rebecca Wauchob's forebears, who were also of Scottish origin, rented the townland of Kinkit, in the parish of Urney, on favorable terms from the earls and marquesses of Abercorn. The Wauchobs' Scottish ancestor initially leased Kinkit around 1690,[3] shortly after the Great Siege of Derry, and bearers of their curious surname are still to be found in that region. The Mellon and Wauchob families were not neighbors, but Andrew and Rebecca appear to have found no difficulty in traversing the twelve miles of hilly farmland that separated them.

At Castletown, the early Mellons were never a clan in the strict sense, but their cottages did form an enclave where individual families, domiciled in close proximity, shared some of the farm work, dug peat from the same bog, and frequently ate meals together. Their numbers must also have allowed the Presbyterian Mellons to worry less about the long-standing tension with the local Catholics. They planted the oats and wheat from which their bread was baked, raised turnips and potatoes, cultivated fruit trees by the Strule, and grew hay for their livestock. Pigs, chickens, ducks, and geese, foraging in the farmyards, maintained a murmur of grunting, clucking, and quacking around the individual cottages. A typical Mellon family at Castletown would have raised sheep for wool and mutton, owned a milk cow, and kept at least one horse for riding, plowing, and pulling the market wagon.

Flax was cultivated as a cash crop and was spun and woven by candle-light.[4] Mellon men as well as women labored at the looms to weave the durable cloth from which British military uniforms were cut during the American Revolution and the subsequent Napoleonic Wars.

The lives of these early Mellon families were inseparably inter-mingled, like the patterns in the linen cloth they wove. Their common efforts strengthened their loyalty to one another and forged a bond that would be tempered by their early struggles in America and would endure among the Mellons of Pittsburgh until well into the twentieth century. But the family enclave at Castletown never func-tioned as a commune. Its inhabitants were spiritual descendants of the Reformation—Presbyterians, puritans, Calvinists—and their fierce commitment to individualism and personal enrichment was un-shakable. Each family leased its own land and kept its own accounts.[5] Worldly success outweighed every other measure of self-esteem, for the Mellons were Scotch-Irish.

Protestant settlers like the Mellons and the Wauchobs had come to Ireland as the result of a royal decision decades before. In 1607 the Protestant king James I of England, who was also the king of Scotland and Ireland, took a giant step toward bringing his unruly Irish subjects under control. He decided to divide and subjugate the overwhelmingly Catholic population of Ireland by settling large numbers of Protestant immigrants in the cluster of northern Irish counties known as Ulster. The last two native Irish rulers, the Catholic earls of Tyrone and Tyrconnel, were harassed into exile, and their holdings in Ulster—over 3.7 million acres—reverted to the Crown by escheat.[6]

King James granted most of the repossessed land to English and Scottish Protestants. With few exceptions, the new landlords roughly evicted their Catholic tenants and left them to farm on stony, infertile ground, often in the woods or on barren hillsides. These brutal evictions engendered an enduring hatred and violence between the Protestants and the Catholic Irish that indelibly tinctured the views of the early Mellons. While the dispossessed Catholics grappled with starvation, successive waves of Protestant immigrants contrived to

*Land encompassed by a loop in the river Strule, Lower Castletown,
near Omagh, Northern Ireland, was farmed by Thomas Mellon's
ancestors and relatives from the seventeenth until the nineteenth century.*

rent the most arable farmland in Ulster. Like the Mellons, most of these newcomers were Presbyterians from the Scottish Lowlands—a people toughened by poverty, internecine strife, and recurring warfare with England. These hardy immigrant Scots came to be known as the Scotch-Irish.[7]

There were sound reasons for Lowland Scots to settle in Ulster. The Irish soil was superior to that of Scotland. But equally important, the new Ulster landlords would rent out land on long leases that frequently remained in force for the tenant's entire lifetime. These leases could normally be bought, sold, and bequeathed; and if the landlord repossessed a property, he had to pay for any improvements that the tenant had made. Under these conditions, the Scotch-Irish tenants were often able to accumulate a small amount of capital and improve their condition.[8]

Unlike the feudal Scots, who were enthralled to a particular landlord, the immigrant Scotch-Irish could search for the most favorable plot of farmland to rent and bargain with the owners. This enabled them to feel independent and gave them self-respect—qualities which would come to define the Scotch-Irish character and that of the early Mellons. Also, unlike the Catholic Irish, who were denied most civil liberties, the immigrants from Scotland were intermittently permitted to engage in free trade and manufacture, to hold office, and to be represented in government. But they had to struggle for these rights, as a willful and capricious England repeatedly attempted to extend its religious, economic, and political hegemony over all the Irish factions. Monarchs attempted to force their Presbyterian subjects to accept the spiritual authority of bishops, but no attempt was made to alter the actual rites of Presbyterian worship. Thus the Scotch-Irish enjoyed a large measure of religious freedom. They were also permitted to give their children the rigorous elementary education that the Presbyterian faith demanded and strictly supervised. Not surprisingly, the early Mellons, as far as we know, could read and write.[9]

But the Scotch-Irish lived uneasily in Ulster. A hill or a stream was frequently all that separated their cottages from a community of

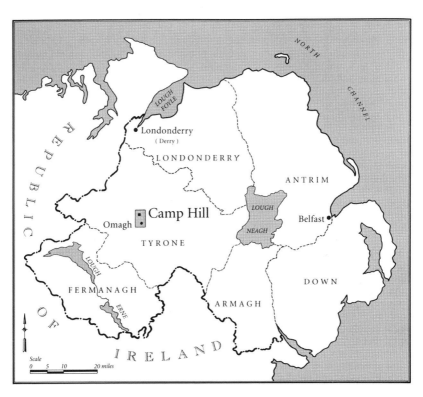

*Ireland and Northern Ireland, or Ulster. Courtesy University of Pittsburgh Press; maps by Christopher H. Marston.*

dispossessed and vengeful Irish Catholics. Indeed, segregated communities of Catholics and Presbyterians are still common in Northern Ireland.

In 1641, while King James's successor, Charles I, was warring with his recalcitrant parliament, the native Catholic Irish slaughtered thousands of Scotch-Irish immigrants and reestablished their control over most of Ireland. Their acts triggered a fearsome retribution. When Parliament prevailed in the Civil War and King Charles was beheaded, the new English ruler, General Oliver Cromwell, invaded Ireland in 1650 and drowned the Irish rebellion in blood. An estimated 600,000 Irish, most of them Catholic natives, were put to the sword, succumbed to disease, or starved to death. Most of Ulster was laid waste and depopulated.[10] Archibald Mellon must have found only desolation when he arrived from Scotland in the 1660s.[11]

A spirit of lively but amicable competition would prevail among the Mellons for generations after their immigration from Ireland to America. This healthy rivalry was typical of the Scotch-Irish. Whether in the Old World or the New, they were individualistic, ambitious, committed to education, and adamant in their belief that with hard work and a smidgen of learning, people could improve their lot. They were also notably aggressive. In Ulster, they had displaced the native Irish and had clung tenaciously to the usurped land. In America, they would routinely encroach on Indian land and then prevail in the resulting conflicts. Viewing the native Irish with fear and contempt, the Scotch-Irish were strident supporters of British rule in Ireland, but in the New World, most of them would fervently support the American Revolution.[12]

Nowadays, those who visit the Ulster-American Folk Park and stoop to enter Camp Hill Cottage by the low front door are likely to conclude that the former occupants were poor. But census figures for the early nineteenth century tell us that one-third of the cottages in Ulster boasted only a single room, and the occupants frequently shared their living space with farm animals.[13] Thousands of poor and working folk raised large families in what twenty-first-century readers would

*Camp Hill Cottage, where Thomas Mellon was born in 1813;*
*1875 photograph.*

see as exceedingly cramped and unsanitary cottages; the ruins of many such "shanties" can still be seen in Ireland today. Whoever owned a three-room cottage like Camp Hill was regarded as "generally well-off," or "comfortably fixed," as Thomas Mellon wrote. The Mellons at Castletown viewed themselves as having something to lose, and also a lot to gain.[14]

In the parish of Cappagh, which encompassed Castletown, Presbyterians, Catholics, and Anglicans lived in close proximity and suffered each other like incompatible spouses. Church attendance was heavy, for it determined one's social position in the here and now as well as one's destination in the Hereafter. The Mellons and Wauchobs clung tenaciously to the Presbyterian faith. Though they farmed in Ireland for at least five generations, not a single member of either family is known to have made an interfaith marriage. To proclaim their ascendancy over the Catholics, the Mellons worshipped with sullen defiance in the austere Presbyterian meetinghouse, while across the river, the regional Anglican landlords conspicuously attended the local congregation of their own church, the Church of Ireland, to proclaim their ascendancy over the other denominations.[15]

By the later years of Mellon tenancy in Ulster, the time had passed when a strange noise at night would send Scotch-Irishmen scrambling from their beds shouting, "To arms! The Catholics are coming!" But the native Irish were still viewed with scorn by Presbyterians and Anglicans alike. Excluded from most civil liberties, Catholics were even prohibited from building their own churches. Often they worshipped in each other's homes, in farm buildings, or simply under a shady tree.

Thomas Mellon was not yet six when he journeyed to the New World, but idyllic recollections of Ireland would remain etched in his prodigious memory. On revisiting the land of his birth after an absence of sixty-four years, he could still recall the route from Omagh to the Crossroads Meeting House, to the very pew where he had squirmed through many a sermon and must have learned that the Mellons were Presbyterians, whatever that meant. The same tenacious memory would lead him back to Camp Hill Cottage and the little room with the fireplace where he had eaten his meals by candlelight, wedged into a circle of neighbors and relatives, around the rough wooden table. There he had come to view himself as a farmer's son and had learned that the trivial chores he performed as a small boy would eventually be replaced by more strenuous obligations, such as plowing. The sight of his parents and relatives laboring in the fields and by the cooking fire must have quietly persuaded him that man is a working creature and that farming is the right kind of work.

Thomas Mellon would later recall his early childhood in Ireland with affection and would relate to his numerous great-grandchildren many humorous anecdotes and blissful memories of life at Camp Hill.[16] But the pastoral Irish overture to his life ended abruptly in 1818, when he and his parents emigrated to America and settled in western Pennsylvania. Between 1796 and 1817, a total of seventeen Mellons had already left Ireland forever. That so many of the family left the land of their birth suggests a somewhat less idyllic reality.

In the late 1700s, before Thomas Mellon's birth, the Mellon families at Castletown faced a critical and worsening predicament. More than thirty people in three or four families survived on less than ninety acres of arable land. There was cousin Mark Mellon, his wife, and their numerous descendants, along with Thomas Mellon's grandparents, Archibald and Elizabeth, whose seven sons and two daughters were approaching marriageable age. It was obvious that many of the Mellons would soon be compelled to abandon the ancestral turf. But where were they to settle? Ireland was more densely populated than any other region of the United Kingdom or, for that matter, of Europe; and Ulster was the most densely populated part of Ireland. Moreover, Irish farmers were being crushed by taxation as Britain fought for its life against Napoleon. The Scotch-Irish are fiercely impatient with conditions that prevent them from improving their lot, and so many decided to emigrate rather than settle elsewhere in Ireland.

Because theirs would be a journey of no return in cramped quarters on a sailing ship, immigrant families had to dispose of whatever they could not carry. Horses, cattle, furniture, the plow and wagon—all had to be sold or given away. By square-rigger, the voyage to America lasted many weeks, depending on wind and weather. Today, visitors can tour a reconstruction of one such vessel at the Ulster-American Folk Park.

Conditions aboard these ships were crowded and woefully unsanitary, with the food frequently rotten and many passengers retching from seasickness. Water was rationed, and the smell of people living shoulder to shoulder could be overpowering. Medical attention, for what it was worth, was often unavailable, and the immigrants were crammed together in such close proximity that diseases could sweep the entire ship. The bodies of those who died at sea were wrapped in a sheet of sailcloth or sewn into a sack with some heavy object, like a cannonball, and thrown overboard.

The multitude of Scotch-Irish immigrants who settled in America between 1790 and 1820 included twenty Mellons. Because Thomas and his parents were the last of these to immigrate, the sorrow of leaving their home was mitigated by the prospect of reunion with family members who were already established in Pennsylvania. The first to settle there had been John Mellon (1750/51–1841), the elder brother of Thomas's grandfather, Archibald.[17] Some time between 1796 and 1798, John and his family had journeyed to Westmoreland County, which was already filling up with Scotch-Irish settlers. They had farmed for a decade near the present-day Unity Church, two miles west of Latrobe, and had then resettled at Conneaut Lake, in Crawford County, where some of their descendants are still to be found.

Archibald Mellon (1756–1835), John Mellon's brother and Thomas Mellon's grandfather, sold part of his freehold lease at Lower Castletown in 1808 and apparently used the receipts to help two of his sons, Armour and Thomas, emigrate to America the same year.[18] In 1816, two more of Archibald's six sons, William and Archibald ("Archy"), arrived and settled in Westmoreland County.

Also in 1816, the sixty-year-old Archibald Mellon, the acknowledged chief of the Mellons still living in Ireland, crossed to America with his wife, Elizabeth, son, John, and daughters, Annie and Margaret. These Mellons disembarked at Baltimore, traversed the Alleghenies by Conestoga wagon, and descended into the Ligonier Valley, reaching Laughlintown (near present-day Rolling Rock Club), on November 8.[19] The following day, they arrived at Crabtree, in Unity Township. Archibald Mellon would farm there for the rest of his life.

The family's center of gravity had now shifted from Ireland to America, and by the following summer, thirty-three-year-old Andrew Mellon, his twenty-nine-year-old wife, Rebecca, and five-year-old Thomas were almost the last family members still occupying the Mellon enclave in Ireland. "Although it was a settled point when my grandparents left [for America] that we should remain permanently at the old place," Thomas would recall, "my father soon began to entertain thoughts of following his family. Letters from America were eagerly

*Abbreviated Genealogy of the Early Mellon Family*

ARCHIBALD

Emigrated from Scotland to County Tyrone, northern Ireland, settled at Lower Castletown near Omagh between 1660 and 1700. m. Elizabeth

SAMUEL

ARCHIBALD

Mark

Will registered in 1788, farmed on the Fairy Water, near the Poe Bridge, at Omagh, County Tyrone, m. _____ Semple

Some of his descendants emigrated to West Philadelphia, Pennsylvania, in the 1840s or '50s

John (1750/51–1841)

Emigrated to Westmoreland County, Pennsylvania, between 1796 and 1798, first of Mellon family to settle in America; moved to Crawford County, around 1806, married twice

The Mellon family of Crawford County, Pennsylvania

ARCHIBALD (1756–1835)

Emigrated to Westmoreland County, Pennsylvania, in 1816, immigrant ancestor of the Mellon family of Pittsburgh, m. Elizabeth (1760–1847), daughter of Samuel Armour, of Legnabraid, Parish of Ardstraw

ANDREW (1785–1856) emigrated 1818, m. Rebecca (1789–1868) daughter of Samuel Wauchob

Like their parents and uncle John, the following Mellons emigrated from Lower Castletown, County Tyrone, northern Ireland. With the exception of Thomas, they settled at first in Westmoreland County, Pennsylvania:

Armour, emigrated 1808

Thomas, emigrated 1808

Archibald, emigrated 1816

William, emigrated 1816

John, emigrated 1816

Margaret, emigrated 1816

Annie, emigrated 1816

Samuel, emigrated 1817

Though Thomas Mellon was born in Ireland, his siblings (see below) were all born at Poverty Point, near Murrysville, Westmoreland County, Pennsylvania:

Samuel (1825–79), m. Angeline Maund (1835–1920)

Elizabeth (1822–98), m. George Bowman (1820–79)

THOMAS (1813–1908), emigrated 1818, m. Sarah Jane (1817–1909), daughter of Jacob Negley

Six sons and two daughters

Margaret (1827–89), m. Robert Jack Shields (1829–1908)

Elinor (1819–84), m. David Stotler (1809–48)

looked for, and gazetteers and books of geography descriptive of the country and its resources eagerly read."[20]

One such publication that he names in his autobiography was *The American Gazetteer.* Compiled by Jedidiah Morse, this is an impressive work: a discussion of conditions, opportunities, and obstacles in the states and cities of North America, as well as in the Latin American and Caribbean colonies. The book depicts Pennsylvania in a favorable light with respect to farming, weather, political organization, and transportation. Andrew and Rebecca must have been gratified to read that there were eighty-six Presbyterian congregations, most of them concentrated in western Pennsylvania, and only eleven Catholic congregations. The town of Pittsburgh is depicted as "situated on a beautiful plain running to a point" and is touted to contain a Presbyterian church, an academy, a church for German Lutherans, a courthouse and jail, two breweries, and a distillery. This was actually an outdated description, for it pertained to the town as it had been in 1797, twenty years earlier. As Thomas recalls: "I well remember the long winter nights which were spent by my parents perusing and discussing descriptions of different parts of America, and the products of the land, and opportunities for bettering the condition of settlers there. In the course of two years they had fully made up their minds to leave."[21]

Early in 1818, Andrew Mellon sold the freehold lease on his farm at Castletown, disposed of all but the most portable belongings, and, after bidding farewell to his friends, neighbors, and a few relatives, prepared to leave Ireland forever. On June 10, the family set sail from Londonderry on the *Alexander,* a brig of the Buchanan Line, commanded by Captain Mackie.[22]

The social historian James Leyburn estimates that of the 200,000 Ulstermen who immigrated to America between 1717 and 1775, approximately half could not pay for the transatlantic passage and had to journey as indentured servants.[23] The Mellons embarked with no such obligations. The sale of their freehold lease on Camp Hill may have gained them the two hundred gold guineas with which Thomas claims they arrived in America.[24]

And so this family of three set sail in the wake of those who had gone before and embarked on the most perilous and courageous gamble of their lives—the Homeric journey in which they turned their backs forever on friends, neighbors, relatives, even their native land, and with only the chattels they could carry, abandoned forever the Old World to risk all in the New.

There is an ill-considered, oft-repeated myth that the immigrants who settled in America were the flotsam and jetsam of humanity—dropouts who had proved unfit for the harsher struggle of life in Britain, Ireland, and Europe. But precisely the opposite was true: As a rule, it was the brave, the strong, the industrious, and those who had acquired a well-founded belief in themselves who wagered everything in pursuit of elusive opportunities on a continent rife with dangers thousands of miles away. The old, the frightened, and the feckless remained behind and resigned themselves to suffer the evils that they knew.

In his memoirs, Thomas Mellon insists that the voyage to Saint John, New Brunswick, lasted twelve weeks instead of the usual five or six.[25] This is confirmed by the surviving records, which suggest that the *Alexander* arrived in port just prior to September 5.[26] "All I remember of St. John," Thomas writes, "is seeing fields covered with fish split open to dry. And here I first saw and tasted the cucumber, and saw negroes."[27]

From Canada, the family sailed on another vessel down the East Coast to Baltimore and disembarked at Fell's Point on or about October 1, 1818.[28] When Andrew had engaged a teamster, the family decamped for western Pennsylvania. Their Conestoga wagon, rumbling along the rutted roads at two miles per hour, took about three weeks to cover the 350 miles to Westmoreland County. On the latter part of this journey, Thomas and his parents found themselves traversing the military road that General John Forbes had built in 1758 to recapture western Pennsylvania from the French and their Indian allies. By this historic route, the family crossed Laurel Ridge in the Alleghenies, descended the Ligonier Valley, and arrived in Unity Township.

Thomas and his parents had heard at Youngstown that their American relatives were engaged in road work just beyond the village. They left their wagon, proceeded on foot, and soon came in sight of a roadside shanty near which a number of Mellons were variously occupied. Archibald and Elizabeth were among them, as were Thomas's uncles, Samuel and Archy. These Mellons had contracted to build two miles of the new Greensburg and Stoystown Turnpike and had erected the shanty to house their laborers.[29]

Thomas Mellon, who was twenty-two years old when his grandfather died, recalls Archibald as an affectionate family man, an accomplished storyteller, and an energetic companion who "was remarkably agile and active. Until near his death he invariably preferred walking to riding on horseback or otherwise. With cane in hand, a walk of twelve miles seemed but a recreation to him; and in his journeys the public road had no special attractions—he would make crooked paths straight by crossing fields and woodlands."[30]

No likeness of Archibald Mellon has survived, and the tangible evidence of the family's immigrant ancestor has dwindled to only his headstone, a knotted hickory cane, and two well-formed signatures on coarse brown paper. He died in 1835 at age seventy-nine, and his grave is still to be seen in Unity Cemetery, though rain, snow, and the passage of the seasons have all but obliterated his name.

Thomas wrote of his paternal grandmother, Elizabeth Armour Mellon, that she was "one of those devoted wives and mothers who are happy in self-sacrifice when promoting the happiness of husband and children; kind, intelligent and unceasing in attention to her family duties."[31] That he would one day angle for, and land, just such a wife was probably not coincidental.

Andrew, Rebecca, and Thomas spent their first winter in America living with numerous relatives on Archibald's farm at Crabtree. But in the second week of April 1819 they bought a farm of their own, just twelve miles away in Franklin Township, near Murrysville (close to present-day Export).[32] Four of Thomas's aunts and uncles soon began to farm in the same vicinity. That all of these relatives settled within riding distance of one another enabled them to maintain for a while longer the close ties that had bound them in Ireland. Three generations of a family who had lived side by side at Lower Castletown now found themselves forming a second Mellon enclave.

The neighborhood in which Andrew Mellon's family had settled was inauspiciously known as Poverty Point—with good reason, for the only building on their new farm was a dilapidated log cabin that required a week of intensive carpentry to refurbish. The property included a fine orchard, however, and the land itself, much of it already cleared for cultivation, totaled over 160 acres—seven times more than Andrew had been able to lease in Ireland.[33] Thomas would live here through his teenage years. His siblings would be born on this farm: Elinor in 1819, Elizabeth in 1822, Samuel in 1825, and Margaret in 1828.

The first five years at Poverty Point amounted to a grim struggle for survival. Andrew and Rebecca must have anticipated some hardships, but they could not have foreseen the Panic of 1819, a horrific depression that savaged the American economy, just as they acquired their farm. In western Pennsylvania, land values and commodity prices plunged by 80 percent, banks failed, and businesses foundered. Had Andrew been able to buy his farm without borrowing money, the family could have weathered 1819 and the lean years that followed with comparative ease. But lacking the wherewithal to pay in full, he had been forced to give the seller a five-year mortgage for most of the purchase price. Thus from 1819 to 1824, the family's life was blighted by a desperate struggle to meet mortgage payments.[34]

This struggle proved to be the first serious challenge that young Thomas faced. His share of the farm work was increased as rapidly as his growing strength and skill would permit. At the age of eight, he was helping to make brandy by picking up hundreds of apples and peaches in the orchard and drawing them downhill on a sled to a makeshift distillery his father had built between two boulders. At ten, he was caring for the farm animals, weaving three-bushel sacks out of tow linen at night, and transporting produce to market. At twelve, he was put behind the plow.[35]

It must have been with increasing dread that Thomas began to comprehend a truth that would do much to shape his destiny and that of our family—the power of debt. A faceless destroyer, debt could tear away the flimsy roof and walls which were all that stood between a child and the winter sky. In the worried voices of his parents he must have heard the frantic plight of the debtor. His appetite for the ensnaring power of the lender would come later. In old age, he would insist that aversion to debt was characteristic of the Mellon family. However true this may have been, his own aversion to debt was uncommonly powerful and must have resulted from his childhood experiences.

By casting a shadow over five years of Thomas's boyhood, the family's struggle to save the farm and home must have taught him that only by strict adherence to Scotch-Irish values, such as discipline, parsimony, hard work, self-denial, and tenacious family loyalty could life's inevitable disasters be overcome and survival snatched from the jaws of disaster. Conversely, Thomas would come to view pleasure, ease, luxury, and recreation as unnecessary, debilitating, and therefore dangerous indulgences that were to be strenuously avoided, especially by young men in their formative years. And it was probably this period of anxious trial that fostered in him an exaggerated craving for wealth as the one sure guarantee of safety, serenity, and human dignity.

Young Thomas learned a number of other lessons as well. That he and his parents had muddled through a near-fatal economic holocaust left him with a heightened sense of foreboding and a lifelong pessimism. He would conclude that economic depressions are inevitable, recurring disasters. And, more generally, he would come to perceive life itself as a perilous undertaking in which the individual is repeatedly tested by sudden, unanticipated misfortunes. The most brutal lesson he learned—that only the fit survive disaster—was the one that would most effectively and continuously guide his passage through life.

Thomas Mellon saw virtue in hard work and responsibility. At an early age, he discovered that his "energy, industry, determination, self-reliance and self-denial" brought him closer to his parents and gave him a head start in understanding affairs of business: "At meals or by the fireside, or in other intervals of leisure with my parents, we would hold free intercourse and discuss the conditions of the stock or plans of farm work and future prospects with eager gratification. In this way I was led to assume cares and enter into the spirit of our affairs."[36] Forty years later, he would contrive to foster precisely such a relationship with his own sons. He saddled each of them with weighty business responsibilities at an incredibly early age and attempted to arouse in them a thirst for accumulation. But most of all, he sought to retain their confidence and thus to be able to direct them at the various crossroads in their lives.

Through the years of anguish and struggle, what saved the Mellons from losing their farm and their dreams was Scotch-Irish tenacity—and a clause in Andrew's mortgage agreement allowing payments "in money and bags and oats at market prices."[37] Oats had slumped to 20 percent of their former value, and money had all but vanished from circulation; but the rough three-bushel bags that were used for sacking grain had miraculously retained their worth. By planting a field with flax and toiling deep into the night at the spinning wheel and loom, as they had done in Ireland, the beleaguered family, now encumbered with little Elinor and soon to be burdened with baby Elizabeth as well, somehow muddled through. That the earliest known Mellon debt instrument was funded with bundles of tow sacks and bags of oats, conveyed to Greensburg once a year on three pack horses, confirms that truth can be stranger than fiction.[38]

But overall, growing up at Poverty Point was a happy experience for Thomas. Even if Andrew would prove obdurate in one area of life, he cared deeply about his son, and Rebecca was a wise and affectionate mother. Raised on simple, wholesome food and toughened by farm work, the boy developed a robust constitution and was seldom sick. Though strenuously challenged on the farm and later in the classroom, he must also have been permitted some leisure, for he later interspersed his memoirs with delightful anecdotes of his early experiences.[39] Indeed, the emotional equilibrium that many associate with a happy childhood appears to have sustained him throughout life.

Notorious for their exterior severity, the Scotch-Irish hide a covert sentimentality about family, friends, home and hearth. As a young man, Thomas Mellon would look back on his boyhood at Poverty Point with a fondness that drove him to doggerel:

> It was here that my father and mother resided,
> When first they arrived from their own native land;
> It was here that their care and affection provided
> For health to my body and food to my mind;
> And yonder the stream and the wide spreading willow,
> Where often I wandered at evening and morn;
> And here is the house where she watched at my pillow,
> Who wept when I sighed with affliction's sharp thorn;
> Here the same room where when finished our labours,
> We gathered around the loved family hearth;
> And there, when on long winter nights with our neighbors,
> We assembled and tasted the fat of the earth.[40]

But Thomas later remembered his boyhood years on the farm primarily for their formative importance: "This remained my home for fifteen years, during that period of life which is by far the most important to a young man—the period when he is a 'hobble-de-hoy,' neither a man nor a boy; the vealy stage of existence, when sentiments and habits are emerging out of chaos and crystallizing into form. It is the period when slight influences produce lasting effects for good or evil. Here were implanted in my nature those root principles of right and duty, tenacity of purpose, patient industry and perseverance in well doing which have accompanied me through life."[41]

However, these were far from the only ethical axioms that he had absorbed from the grown-up conversation he had heard over the years.

At the hearth and around the dinner table, he had listened to his parents, neighbors, and visiting relatives judge all men by their facility for acquiring wealth. He must have heard little or nothing about beauty or worldly pleasures, for these were viewed by the Scotch-Irish as perilous distractions from the puritan ideals of righteousness and accumulation.

Because Mellons had always been tillers of the soil and were expected to remain so, farming was adverted to with respect. Moreover, Thomas came to understand that life on a farm required each to shoulder a fair share of the workload. In farming, building a close-knit cooperative family, cemented by ties of affection and loyalty, is not only admirable but vital to survival. That he grew up in just such a family can only have helped him to create similar conditions in the family he himself would raise.

Though an elementary education was not required by law in either Ireland or America, most Scotch-Irish parents sent their children to school until they could read, write, and cipher. The Presbyterian faith did not rest on apostolic succession or authority but on supposedly rational deductions from Scripture. Not only were parishioners exhorted to examine the biblical underpinnings of their faith, but they were expected to discuss and resolve apparent Scriptural contradictions. In America, as in Ulster, the Presbyterian meetinghouses demanded and promoted elementary education.

The rural one-room pay school was therefore a fixture of Scotch-Irish life in western Pennsylvania. Each year, the local teacher, who was frequently disabled, elderly, or otherwise unable to work in the fields, would junket from farm to farm soliciting pupils. Classes were held at his home, or else in a cabin or farm building placed at his disposal. Tuition was not always paid in cash; most teachers also accepted food.

The Mellon children at Lower Castletown had attended such schools, and Thomas would be expected to do so in America. His parents, uncles, aunts, and grandparents appear to have been educated to the level of basic literacy and numeracy, though one cousin, Patrick

Mellon, still signed his name with a mark in 1800.[42] Two signatures of Thomas's great-grandfather Samuel Mellon, which appear on legal documents, suggest that he too was literate.[43] But the first American Mellons were also heirs to a tradition that demanded an acquisitive rather than spiritual orientation toward life, that glorified the impulse to gather rather than spend and called for the vehement rejection of debt, risk, squandering, and especially taxation.

In 1819, during their first summer at Poverty Point, Rebecca guided the hand of her six-year-old son in forming the letters of the alphabet and then began to drill him in spelling. The following summer he attended two months at a pay school about three miles from the farm, but his mother continued to tutor him. By year's end, he had mastered simple reading and had memorized from the King James version of the Bible the rhetorical first chapter of the Gospel of John, which reverberates with the distant thunder of Creation: "In the beginning was the Word, and the Word was with God, and the Word was God. . . . All things were made by him. . . . In him was life; and the life was the light of men. And the light shineth in darkness; and the darkness comprehended it not."

Beginning in 1821, Thomas, who was then eight, received about four months of formal schooling per year. But because his share of the farm work had increased, he was compelled to snatch his education when farming was at a standstill or when his father could temporarily manage without him. Armed with the *Western Calculator,* by J. Stockton, and the *United States Spelling Book,* Thomas struggled to master the three Rs. He also read and reread the classic *Practical Arithmetic,* by John Gough of Dublin, using the copy that his father and grandfather had learned from.[44]

But there was also a fourth R in the curriculum: religion. For, in addition to reading the Old and New Testaments, Scotch-Irish pupils were drilled in the sulfurous dogma of Presbyterianism. Advanced students were expected to memorize the *Shorter Catechism,* and there were daily readings from the *New England Primer,* which was memorable for its gruesome illustration of John Rodgers being burned at the

## The Burning of

## JOHN RODGERS.

JOHN RODGERS, minister of the gospel in London, was the first martyr in queen Mary's reign, and was burnt at Smithfield, in the winter of 1554. His wife, with nine small children, and one at her breast, followed him to the stake : with which sorrowful sight, it is said, he was not in the least daunted, but with wonderful patience, died courageously for the gospel of Jesus Christ.

*John Rodgers burning at the stake, from the* New England Primer.
*Courtesy New York Public Library.*

stake.[45] From boyhood, Thomas Mellon's spiritual fare was the fiercest, harshest brand of Christianity:

> Born and reared as I was in the spirit of puritanism, religion was the first subject to which my attention was directed. The Old and New Testaments were my school books, and the *Westminster Catechism* and *Confession of Faith* my guides to opinion....
>
> My religious instructors led me to believe that all men were already condemned, their guilt predetermined, and an endless and horrible punishment awaiting them, with but slight chance of escape for the smallest possible number; and that this small number, according to the doctrines of election and predestination, were personally designated and foreordained from all eternity.
>
> If religion in this form was calculated to excite fear rather than devotion, it nevertheless presented problems which afforded admirable exercise for the intellect; and I was placed between two forces: religious teaching drawing one way, and the rational mind another.[46]

For him, the tug-of-war between faith and reason would never be resolved.

Thomas's early reading included the admonitory literature of puritanism: Joseph Alleine's *An Alarm to the Unconverted,* John Bunyan's *The Pilgrim's Progress,* Richard Baxter's *The Saints' Everlasting Rest,* and Thomas Boston's *Human Nature in the Fourfold State.* But hellfire and damnation would never persuade Thomas Mellon that any religious dogma merited his blind acceptance.

What he did accept blindly was the secular ethics of his faith. John Calvin, whose astringent theology forms the basis of Presbyterianism, insists that only a handful of mortals—the elect—will escape damnation and eternal torment. God chooses both the elect and the damned before they are born, and no earthly power can alter his choices. Man cannot know whether he is predestined for salvation or perdition, but he believes that God favors the elect in this life, not merely in the next, and so he strives to demonstrate his fitness for salvation by succeeding in his worldly endeavors. That wealth was perceived as a sign of divine preferment argued forcefully for competitive materialism among Presbyterians. Little wonder that when Thomas Mellon introduces a new character in his memoirs—a farmer or businessman—he frequently mentions in the next breath whether or not that individual was successful.

As to the role of religion among the early Mellons, Thomas recalled:

> My ancestors on all sides were Presbyterians as far back as I can trace them; not over zealous or fanatical, but sincere in their belief, and supporting the church as a proper duty, none of them taking a leading part in church affairs, however. . . . My father and my uncle Archy were each elected elder in their time in the different congregations to which they belonged, but declined to serve. Whilst their lives and actions were in conformity with conventional Christian morality and requirements, they possessed a freedom of thought and opinion which seemed to them inconsistent with the exercise of such an office: indeed I find a vein of rationalism cropping out occasionally in my forefathers, not, however, amounting to skepticism in essentials.[47]

There was a tent in the woods at Poverty Point where the Rev. Hugh Kirkland preached to Thomas and his family. He denounced the Catholic Church as "the Antichrist and the whore of Babylon," railed against "the desecration of the Sabbath by the Lutherans," and condemned "the damnable heresies of the Methodists in denying the doctrines of innate depravity and predestination." But Andrew Mellon, who attended church mainly as a social obligation and viewed the other Protestant sects with tolerant indifference, permitted the Methodists to worship in one of his disused farm buildings.[48]

Reflecting on the severity of Presbyterian ethics, Mellon notes that "if [these] doctrines were literally true as expressed, the consequences of disobedience were momentous. Yet I saw that the great majority of people lived in disregard of their requirements, and the minority yielded but a superficial conformity."[49] Religion was regularly discussed at home, and Thomas must have noticed at an early age that for the Scotch-Irish, religion served more as a rule of thumb for social classification than as a guiding authority in moral decisions or as an expression of spirituality. It was at Poverty Point, not in County Tyrone, that he learned his place in the pecking order of Irish society. He was Presbyterian, Ulster-born, and distantly of Scottish descent, and the Catholic Irish, whether in the Old World or the New, were not only his reviled social inferiors but his sworn enemies.

Thomas must have heard his parents and relatives demonize the Catholic Irish as slothful, ignorant, credulous drunkards, seething with hate for their Protestant betters, predisposed to violence, irresponsible, and blindly obedient to the exhortations of manipulative priests and political demagogues. He would accept their demonization and brand it into the minds of his own children. According to the author's father, Matthew Mellon, during his boyhood in Pittsburgh, if the name of a Catholic cropped up at mealtime, his grandfather James (one of Thomas Mellon's sons) would lean over and whisper, "Wrong church. Wrong church." Ulster stereotypes die hard, in part because these uncharitable caricatures did once contain a kernel of truth. But, more important, they formed the victory song of the winning side in a centuries-long struggle between Catholic natives and Protestant intruders for the farmland of Ulster.

Such were the social, ethical, religious, and historical prejudices that came to be seeded as commonsense truths in Thomas Mellon's thinking. His poignant description of life at the hearth in a western Pennsylvania cabin among Scotch-Irish immigrants affords a memorable glimpse of how Ulster ideals were handed down in a family—how they were *caught,* rather than *taught:* "The boisterous mirth and hilarity was such as can never be equaled under the restraints of more refined society; and the close communion into which it brought all the members of the family, old and young, at all leisure hours, so thoroughly inoculated the children with the views and sentiments of the parents that in thoughts, tastes and habits the coming generation exactly reproduced the one going out. There is no other family system wherein the young can be so thoroughly imbued with the nature and disposition of their parents."[50]

The mix of Scotch-Irish ideals and attitudes transmitted to young Thomas in this fashion include the suppression of natural frivolity in favor of a dour, calculating attitude toward life; secular, materialistic values favorable to the accumulation of wealth; worldly advancement through education and by personal rather than communal initiatives; individualism; self-reliance; tenacity of purpose restrained by caution; optimal control over one's destiny; a deep vein of covert sentimentalism relating to home and family; a fierce insistence on intellectual freedom; smoldering hostility toward Catholicism; a galloping Hiberniphobia [hatred of the native Irish]; a distrust of politics and contempt for professional politicians; revulsion at the thought of expressing intimate feelings overtly; and an implacable conservatism, or devotion to values and institutions perceived as having proved their worth.

That the Scotch-Irish had for generations lived as feared and resented intruders substantially accounts for the ferocity of their prejudices and for their fortress mentality. They had migrated in waves to northern Ireland and had settled there on land from which the native Irish had been driven like stray dogs. Later, as Scotch-Irish immigrants teemed into western Pennsylvania, they ousted the Indians by relentless encroachment and sometimes by force. With their aggressive resourcefulness, they also supplanted the less venturesome hegemony of the early German settlers. Wherever their yearning for a safer and more affluent life had carried them, these hardy, industrious, and occasionally ruthless intruders had displaced the natives and were duly resented for it. The Scotch-Irish became militantly ethnocentric and defiantly exclusionist. The massive walls of Londonderry, which had proved impregnable to the assaults of a besieging Catholic army, in 1689, are still the most poignant symbol of the Ulster fortress mentality. Their enduring presence is celebrated by the Scotch-Irish in song and story.

Thomas Mellon's removal to America in 1818 did nothing to halt the barrage of Scotch-Irish values and attitudes that assailed him right and left. In Westmoreland County, everyone had Ulster neighbors. Everyone dealt with Ulstermen in commerce, agriculture, and the professions. Because western Pennsylvania had become a cultural extension of northern Ireland, which in turn was a cultural extension of Scotland, Scotch-Irish morals, customs, and idiosyncrasies acquired the force of biblical commandments.

In Mellon's boyhood, the early German pioneers, misnamed the Pennsylvania Dutch, remained a tolerated minority west of the Alleghenies; indeed, at Poverty Point they were the majority. But the resourceful immigrants from Ulster had achieved dominance over the older German settlers in every sphere of life. The Scotch-Irish accorded a grudging measure of respect to pioneer Lutheran and Mennonite families like the Negleys, Winebiddles, Overholts, Roups, and Baums, some of whom had converted to Presbyterianism. But on the whole, they viewed the Pennsylvania Germans with aversion, because by Scotch-Irish standards they appeared to have no organized religion. Lacking the rigid moral discipline that Presbyterian meetinghouses imposed on their congregations, the Pennsylvania Germans were viewed as morally permissive and sexually promiscuous. Mellon notes that Scotch-Irish parents who had Pennsylvania German neighbors would frequently prohibit their children from playing with the ones next door.[51] He also concludes that in the German mind "there was more repose and contentment," in the Scotch-Irish "more earnestness and activity," and he adds that the Scotch-Irish apparently "possessed more general intelligence."[52]

# II

## From Plowboy to Professor

*It was about my fourteenth year, at a neighbor's house, when plowing a field we had taken on his farm for buckwheat, that I happened upon a dilapidated copy of the autobiography of Dr. [Benjamin] Franklin. It delighted me with a wider view of life and inspired me with new ambition. . . . The maxims of "poor Richard" exactly suited my sentiments. I read the book again and again, and wondered if I might not do something in the same line by similar means.*

THE EXTRAORDINARY CONFIDENCE THAT Andrew and Rebecca Mellon placed in their son is evidenced by their allowing him to visit Pittsburgh alone, in April 1823, when he was only ten years old. Rumor had it that many wonders were to be seen in the Scotch-Irish metropolis, from steam-powered factories and riverboats to mansions inhabited by rich people who lived almost unimaginably luxurious lives. Determined to experience these miracles, the boy extracted from his father a three-day leave of absence, which was to fall between the first and second corn hoeings. His pocket money for the journey was a sack of rye that he hoisted onto a packhorse and sold at Murrysville for ninety-nine cents. From there, Thomas set out on foot, "without satchel, comb or brush," following the "turnpike" to Pittsburgh.[1]

On the twenty-mile trek, he fell in with a farmer from his own neighborhood who told him as they were walking along that at Pittsburgh he would see more novelties in one day than at Poverty Point in a whole lifetime.[2] This remark so nettled Thomas Mellon that he would record it sixty years later in the pages of his autobiography. Mellon was no poorer than thousands of other farm boys in western Pennsylvania. It was his tendency to *regard* himself as poor that caused him to be irked by his condition and by the inauspicious name of his neighborhood.

Likewise, young Abraham Lincoln was not poor by the standards of a rural farming community on the western frontier. Yet he too *perceived* himself as having been raised in poverty. Clearly, both of these young men were predisposed to compare their early circumstances with those of wealthier, rather than less affluent, families. Both were shamed by what they perceived as the degrading austerity of their childhoods, and from shame sprang ambition.

Approaching Pittsburgh from the east, Thomas ambled down the Frankstown State Road (now Frankstown Avenue), passing houses that, compared to his own, looked like palaces. He entered the village of Negleytown and came to a general store that bore the Negley name emblazoned in gold letters. Nearby, a rhythmic chugging sound, accompanied by white puffs of steam, announced the presence of Jacob Negley's renowned mechanical gristmill, the first contraption of its kind to be constructed west of the Alleghenies. Thomas made bold to inspect this marvel at close range. Filled with wonder, he studied the grand, greasy engine, hissing and thumping with its menacing, alien beat. His mind, which would later show itself to be formidably analytical, may well have grasped the principle of steam power. But how fully did he comprehend its implications? Could this perceptive ten-year-old have recognized that he was witnessing the birth of a new age? If not, he would perceive it soon enough, as steam power implacably reduced his cozy, rural, small-town world to insignificance and supplanted it with an impersonal, mechanized industrial society that he would come to view with increasing alarm. A sudden, earsplitting shriek of the steam whistle ended his reveries and sent him fleeing.

The boy now seated himself on a hillside, just west of Negley Lane (now North Negley Avenue) and north of Penn Avenue. To the northeast lay a vast meadow that extended almost to the Allegheny River. He had learned that all of this land and the imposing yellow brick house that stood at its western edge belonged to Jacob Negley. As Thomas studied the so-called Negley Mansion, he permitted himself some Scotch-Irish daydreams: "I remember wondering how it could be possible to accumulate such wealth, and how magnificent must be the style of living and what pleasures they must enjoy who possessed it. I remember also of the thought occurring whether I might not one day attain in some degree such wealth and equality with such great people."[3]

He envisioned the Negley children decked out in their Sunday clothes, riding in a fancy carriage, and drew solace from imagining that he might in some way excel these effulgent creatures, if only at reading, writing, and arithmetic. It would have startled the boy if he had known the reality of the Negleys' lives. Just then, as he sat in wide-eyed contemplation of their "mansion" and meditated on what it stood for, financial ruin, with its deflated dreams and humiliations, was staring Jacob Negley and his family in the face. It would have startled Thomas even more to know that he would one day mix blood with one of the Negley children.[4]

Proceeding down Penn Avenue, Thomas now saw Pittsburgh for the first time. He was walking into a town of about seven thousand inhabitants, with an additional four thousand living in suburbs like Allegheny, Bayardstown, Lawrenceville, and Birmingham. Wedged between the Allegheny and Monongahela rivers where they join to form the Ohio River, were approximately a thousand houses, eight churches, a courthouse and jail, three banks, a Masonic hall, and even a university. Other marvels awaited him. His cousins the Dunfords, with whom he spent two nights, took him to a glassworks and an iron foundry and showed him a steam-powered cotton mill, which impressed

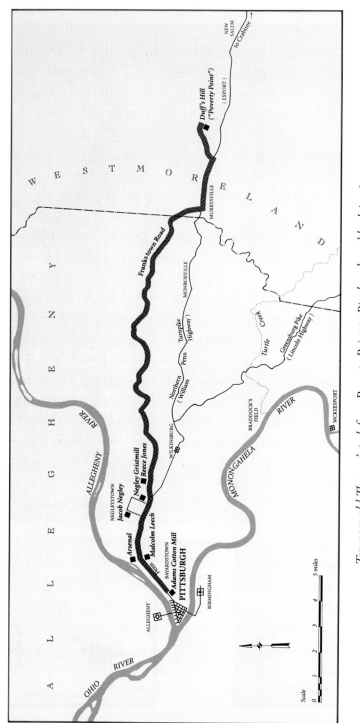

*Ten-year-old Thomas's trek from Poverty Point to Pittsburgh and back in 1823. Courtesy University of Pittsburgh Press; map by Christopher H. Marston.*

him even more than Jacob Negley's gristmill. He may even have seen one of the earliest paddle-wheeled steamboats on the fabled Forks of the Ohio. Walking through town, he would have passed along rows of houses that contrasted jarringly with his family's rudimentary cabin. But far from demoralizing him, these novelties churned his imagination and filled him with new dreams. As he tramped back to Poverty Point, his head was swimming with exhilarating thoughts.

By 1825, when Thomas was twelve years old, his parents had acquired the wherewithal to build a larger home. It took the family less than a year to erect a "square, log, two-story, shingle-roofed dwelling, with a one-story kitchen at the rear or end."[5] Thomas's duties included dragging the logs with a team from the woods and hauling the stone from the fields for the chimneys that his father would build with his own hands. The basic log construction reflected German tradition and was probably inspired by the neighboring Pennsylvania German farmhouses. The stone masonry of the fireplaces was in all likelihood traditionally Irish and resembled its counterpart at Camp Hill Cottage. Mellon recalled that "we had as fine a 6-roomed dwelling as the best of our neighbors, and that fall and winter as good a square log double barn as was to be seen thereabouts. And in less than seven years from the time of our possession we had the farm in first rate order and were beginning to accumulate money."[6] The house still stands at the corner of Cline Hollow and Hills Church roads, in present-day Export. It was weatherboarded in the 1880s and completely adulterated in style: of the original structure, all that remains are the beams.[7]

Thomas's boyhood consisted of farm work, tensely interspersed with education. Though his farm duties at first held precedence in the broadening arena of his life, education eventually prevailed. As the boy was reaching adolescence, he began to receive packets of books from his namesake uncle, Thomas Mellon. The familiar *English Reader* by Lindley Murray arrived in one such packet, as did an unnamed novel that Thomas read but found annoying because of its difficult vocabulary. His uncle included a resolute letter of encouragement in every packet, urging his nephew to keep striving for education.

*Precise reconstruction of the log farmhouse that Thomas Mellon
and his father built near Murrysville, Pennsylvania, in 1825.
Courtesy Ulster-American Folk Park, Omagh, Northern Ireland.*

The elder Thomas Mellon (1789–1866) was the first Mellon to cast
off farming and pursue a business career. From Ireland, he had journeyed to New Orleans via Pennsylvania and had secured a position
there in the counting house of a fellow Ulsterman. The two had become
partners, and Mellon had made a small fortune trading commodities
during the War of 1812. He had also fought in the final battle of that
war, at New Orleans, under General Andrew Jackson.

In 1819, he married Eliza Toby, of an established family in Philadelphia, and it was there that the couple settled permanently. With initiative, perseverance, and only a smidgen of education, Uncle Thomas Mellon had liberated himself from the constraints of a farming life. He was determined that his bright young nephew and namesake should do likewise.

The carefully chosen books that his uncle regularly sent him caught the fancy of young Thomas's sharp, inquisitive mind and speedily converted him into a voracious reader. By the age of fourteen, he was devouring almost any book he could find. When a teacher came to the farm recruiting pupils, Thomas found himself trying to determine whether he or the visitor was better read.[8]

His literary preferences were taking shape. Books that taught him new abilities or served as signposts for advancement riveted his attention. Seldom a reader for pleasure, he nonetheless fell in love with Robert Burns's poetry, to which his mother, a Burns enthusiast, had probably introduced him. The generous quotations from Burns that grace the pages of his autobiography confirm that the national bard of Scotland, and therefore also of Ulster, was not only Thomas Mellon's favorite poet but also a spiritual companion for life.

He snatched greedily at even the smallest opportunity for reading. At lunch, he would eat with a book on his lap. While plowing he would read a page or two as his horse rested at the end of each furrow. In this manner, he consumed a collection of Shakespeare's plays that his uncle had sent him. But surprisingly, the poet laureate of our language worked no magic on Thomas. "The fine sentiments of Shakespeare," he would complain, "seemed to cost too much sifting among the quarrels of kings and vulgar intrigues of their flunkies, and the obsolete manners of a rude age."[9] He preferred Oliver Goldsmith and Alexander Pope, but he was not enthusiastic about either. In literature, as in much else, he made no concessions to popular taste but relied on his own judgment.

The formative moment in Thomas's adolescent reading occurred when he discovered the book that would transform his destiny and

*The elder Thomas Mellon (1789–1866), young Thomas's uncle and namesake; painting by Bass Otis, 1826.*

that of the Mellon family. At the age of fourteen, Mellon was plowing a field for buckwheat when he happened upon a dilapidated copy of Benjamin Franklin's *Autobiography*. "It delighted me with a wider view of life and inspired me with new ambition," Mellon wrote. Reading Franklin, he questioned a life of farming for the very first time. "For so poor and friendless a boy to be able to become a merchant or a professional man had before seemed an impossibility; but here was Franklin, poorer than myself, who by industry, thrift and frugality had become learned and wise, and elevated to wealth and fame. The maxims of 'poor Richard' exactly suited my sentiments." Mellon read the book again and again, gradually coming to believe he could tread a similar path. "I had will and energy equal to the occasion, and could exercise the same degree of industry and perseverance. . . . After that I was more industrious when at school, and more constant than ever in reading and study during leisure hours. I regard the reading of Franklin's autobiography as the turning point of my life."[10]

One celebrated passage in the *Autobiography* must surely have caught young Thomas's attention: the point where Franklin famously enumerates the virtues and accompanying principles that lead to "moral perfection" and not coincidentally to worldly advancement. Those who would be "healthy, wealthy, and wise," are invited to reflect on the following:

1.   TEMPRANCE.
Eat not to dullness; drink not to elevation.

2.   SILENCE.
Speak not but what may benefit others or yourself; avoid trifling conversation.

3.   ORDER.
Let all your things have their places; let each part of your business have its time.

4.   RESOLUTION.
Resolve to perform what you ought; perform without fail what you resolve.

5.   FRUGALITY.
Make no expense but to do good to others or yourself; i.e., waste nothing.

6. INDUSTRY.
Lose no time; be always employ'd in something useful; cut off all unnecessary actions.

7. SINCERITY.
Use no hurtful deceit; think innocently and justly, and, if you speak, speak accordingly.

8. JUSTICE.
Wrong none by doing injuries, or omitting the benefits that are your duty.

9. MODERATION.
Avoid extremes; forbear resenting injuries so much as you think they deserve.

10. CLEANLINESS.
Tolerate no uncleanliness in body, cloaths, or habitation.

11. TRANQUILLITY.
Be not disturbed at trifles, or at accidents common or unavoidable.

12. CHASTITY.
Rarely use venery but for health or offspring, never to dullness, weakness, or the injury of your own or another's peace or reputation.

13. HUMILITY.
Imitate Jesus and Socrates.[11]

That the practice of these profitable virtues might become habitual, Franklin devises a system for daily examining and scoring himself. To help him acquire the habit of ORDER—"let each part of your business have its time"—he draws up a schedule for the entire day:[12]

| | 5 A.M. | Rise, wash and address |
| | 6 | *Powerful Goodness!* Contrive |
| THE MORNING. | | day's business and take |
| *Question.* What good | | the resolution of the day; |
| shall I do this day? | | prosecute the present study, |
| | | and breakfast. |
| | 7 | |
| | 8 | |
| | 9 | Work. |
| | 10 | |
| | 11 | |
| NOON. | 12 | Read, or overlook my |
| | 1 | accounts, and dine. |
| | 2 | |
| | 3 | Work. |
| | 4 | |
| | 5 | |
| EVENING. | 6 | Put things in their places. |
| *Question.* What good | 7 | Supper. Music or diversion, |
| have I done to-day? | 8 | or conversation. Examination |
| | 9 | of the day. |
| | 10 | |
| | 11 | |
| | 12 | |
| NIGHT. | 1 | Sleep. |
| | 2 | |
| | 3 | |
| | 4 | |

In middle-class values, Franklin had discovered a source of strength, and through their rigorous application he had charted a steep upward path to material well-being. Young Thomas was champing at the bit to follow that path. Self-mastery and the reduction of daily life to a strict discipline accorded entirely with Scotch-Irish values and with his personality. In fact, he had already learned the potency of resolution, frugality, and industry during the trying aftermath of 1819, when he and his family had struggled to save the Mellon farm. But Franklin was touting these virtues as tools not merely for survival but for advancement.

In another sphere of life, Thomas had come to question the dogmatic religion of his forebears, but refused to renounce his belief in God. Franklin had also grappled with this dilemma, and had found a solution that would satisfy both Mellon and himself: "I had been religiously educated as a Presbyterian," recalls the skeptical Philadelphian,

> and tho' some of the dogmas of that persuasion, such as *the eternal decrees of God, election, reprobation, etc.,* appeared to me unintelligible, others doubtful, and I early absented myself from the public assemblies of the sect, Sunday being my study day, I never was without some religious principles. I never doubted, for instance, the existence of the Deity; that he made the world, and govern'd it by his Providence; that the most acceptable service of God was the doing good to man; that our souls are immortal; and that all crime will be punished, and virtue rewarded, either here or hereafter. These I esteem'd the essentials of every religion.[13]

Because Franklin doubts the validity of an ethics based on biblical revelation, he devises a preponderantly secular morality, which is humanistic, pragmatic, godless, and surprisingly modern:

> I grew convinc'd that *truth, sincerity* and *integrity* in dealings between man and man were of the utmost importance to the felicity of life, and I form'd written resolutions, which still remain in my journal notebook, to practice them ever while I lived. [Biblical] Revelation had indeed no weight with me, as such; but I entertained an opinion that, though certain actions might not be bad *because* they were forbidden by it, or good *because* it com-

manded them, yet probably these actions might be forbidden *because* they were bad for *us*, or commanded *because* they were beneficial to *us*, in their own natures, all the circumstances of things considered.[14]

Hence, "honesty is the best policy" not because the Bible demands integrity, but because *dis*honesty is counterproductive: It triggers its own retribution by something akin to natural law and can therefore be viewed as a ruinous form of folly based on ignorance. For the most part, Thomas Mellon came to embrace Franklin's secular ethics, and he would find it easy to give an evolutionary interpretation to this pragmatic morality, when, in middle life, he discovered the social Darwinism of Herbert Spencer.

The literature of self-improvement was precisely what Thomas devoured. In Franklin's *Autobiography* he had discerned a battle plan for worldly advancement, a trajectory for material gain through disciplined initiative, leading to financial freedom. Determined to follow this course, he also pored over Isaac Watts's renowned treatise *The Improvement of the Mind.* To propose a rigorous system of "rules for the attainment and communication of useful knowledge, in religion, in the sciences, and in common life" was the author's stated purpose, and young Mellon found this mental regimen so edifying that he would send copies of "Watts on the Mind" to friends and relatives for the rest of his life.

As the son and grandson of farmers, he had been raised to view life not as a frivolous Epicurean adventure but rather as an earnest, arduous, carefully programmed undertaking. Yet this curiously self-possessed teenager had concluded at a surprisingly early age that he was free to choose his vocation. "From the time I was a very small boy, the question of future occupation was uppermost in my mind; and now this question pressed upon me with renewed force. I derived little pleasure from mingling with the young people around me at home: their tastes and purposes were not congenial. My source of pleasure was reading, which I resorted to at every spare moment."[15]

Thomas was beginning to distance himself from schoolboys who did not share his growing discontent and related ambition. It had dawned on him that beyond the barnyard lay a world in which many people lived more freely and fully than farmers. That with Franklin's guidance he should enter that world and become a professional or businessman accorded fully with the Scotch-Irish ideals of work and accumulation. But his father remained doggedly opposed. "My father's uniform advice was decidedly, indeed almost peremptorily in favor of farming. . . . He looked upon farming as the best, safest, most worthy and independent of all the occupations of men; and any one who forsook it for something else was regarded as led astray by folly and nonsense."[16]

In preindustrial America, a farmer would train his sons for agriculture and, if possible, leave each of them enough land to support a family. Andrew Mellon was eager to acquire a well-stocked farm for his son and took pride in being able to do so. He felt free, and also obliged, to direct his son's destiny, and for Thomas to become "a doctor or teacher or miserably dependent preacher, or what was in his eyes worst of all, to enter the tricky, dishonest profession of the law, was a proposition which seemed to him too preposterous to contemplate." When Thomas finally disclosed that he did not want to be a farmer and was determined to pursue his education in preparation for a more lucrative line of work, his worst fears were quickly realized: He recalls that his father

> could not be reconciled to it, and would not entertain the subject. It was grievous to me to give him so much evident annoyance; but the resolution he came to was, that if I could not continue a respectable, industrious young man, but would abandon my present course of well doing to run after some delusion of fancy, he would be no party to such folly. . . . Then if I failed, which he regarded as certain, there would be something for me to fall back on so long as he was possessed of property or means. . . . His firmness staggered my resolution; and for a year or so

I was wavering and undecided, almost indeed won over to his side.[17]

The foregoing may suggest that Andrew Mellon was an ignorant, narrow-minded occupational chauvinist and a domestic autocrat, but Thomas would remember his father as "a man of sound common sense and temperate habits . . . , popular with his neighbors and acquaintances. He read a good deal, and had fixed opinions on most subjects of the day; was an advanced thinker for one in his position, but quiet of manner, and with no disposition to obtrude his views on others. In politics he was what was known as an old line Whig." Andrew "was a Presbyterian, without any tincture of bigotry" and "a kind and provident husband and parent." Yet, Thomas wrote, "he could not enter into the plans and purposes or sympathize with the views of his children as our mother could."[18]

> As to my mother, . . . I can remember that as a wife she was a help-mate in all the qualities indicated by that forcible term; and as a mother she was all that tenderness and self-sacrifice could make her. With her, woman's wit served the purpose of much learning; and her strong common sense made her a valuable adviser even in the most important affairs. Her ability in this respect many times surprised me. She had a philosophy of her own by which she gauged everything that transpired, and believed in the wisdom of desiring neither poverty nor riches, but struggling for wealth and competence as affording independence. She shunned extremes and approved the middle course in life. Her favorite books were the Bible and Burns' poems. Although not entirely reconcilable, yet, with exceptional passages, she could find wisdom and piety in both.[19]

In 1828, the elder Thomas Mellon journeyed from Philadelphia to visit his relatives in western Pennsylvania. While at Poverty Point, he argued tenaciously for giving his nephew and namesake a higher edu-

*The elder Andrew Mellon (1785–1856), Thomas's father.*

*An 1860s daguerreotype of Rebecca Wauchob Mellon (1789–1868),
Thomas's mother. Courtesy Charles Mellon Lockerby.*

cation. If Andrew at first objected, which is likely, he permitted himself to be persuaded. Rebecca almost certainly concurred, for she
tended to sympathize with her son in his secret longings and had
become his confidant. Also, while refusing to pressure her son, for she
was too gentle for that, Rebecca clung vainly to the hope that Thomas
might become a clergyman, a calling for which a classical education
would be required.

Uncle Thomas prevailed, and that fall his fifteen-year-old nephew
was launched on a course of "higher studies" at the County Academy
in Greensburg. Of the many supportive letters that he received from
his uncle during this period of aching uncertainty and struggle, only
one has survived:

> Philadelphia, Pa.
>
> Jan. 8, 1829.
>
> Dear nephew:-
>
> A few days ago I received your Father's letter of the 19th.
> informing me he had placed you at school in Greensburg,
> according to my request, which I am glad to learn, but sorry he
> did not send you earlier in the season. You must remain at school
> in Greensburg at least six months this season, and I have no
> doubt, as you are so good a boy in everything else, that you will
> pay particular attention to your learning, and improve every
> moment of your time, while at school, and in future life you will
> reap the benefit. Learn to spell and read correctly, to write a plain
> and easy hand, and to understand arithmetic perfectly, which is
> nothing more than a suitable and fitting education for every
> farmer.
>
> Enclosed I send you a five dollar Bank of Pennsylvania note to
> furnish you with any little thing you may stand in need of, such
> as paper, books, shoes, etc. These long evenings, furnish yourself
> with good fire and candles to enable you to learn your lessons
> perfectly for the day, and on Sunday go to the different churches,

and visit often any genteel farmers you may be acquainted with, for the sake of information and learning manners.

I send . . . a parcel of interesting newspapers for you to read. After you are done with them, give them to Father's family to read. Write me occasionally, so that I may see how you improve.

. . . I remain your friend,

Thomas Mellon[20]

Feigning deference to the wishes of his brother Andrew, the elder Thomas Mellon pretends to acquiesce in a future of farming for his nephew. But what bulges out between the lines here is the writer's thinly veiled determination to free young Thomas from the thralldom of agriculture forever.

The boy continued to read for his life. He circumvented the biblical injunction against working on Sunday by employing the same ruse that Franklin had resorted to: he defined reading as a form of rest.[21]

Books that young Mellon would recall from his four-month term at the County Academy included a treatment of ancient history by Alexander Tytler, an *English Grammar* by Lindley Murray, *Rudiments of Geography* by William Woodbridge, and Simpson's *Euclid,* an introduction to plain geometry.

More important were his impressions of the Williams family, with whom he boarded at Greensburg. They were comfortably well-off but esteemed refinement over wealth. The teenage Thomas would remember them as "a sort of aristocracy, . . . dignified and stately in their manners, exclusive in their companionship, high toned in their honor and morality." In this family he perceived an alternative way of life, rich in thought and enlivened by the society of successful, ambitious, responsible people who were also cultivated. These impressions hastened his alienation from "the rude pursuits of farm life and the low sentiments and purposes of our neighbors at home. . . . After leaving the academy my heart was not in farm work, although I continued to execute it with due diligence for two or three years, until a final decision respecting my future course was arrived at."[22]

Agonizing over the farming question, he turned to his mother for sympathy and advice. "My mother had been from the beginning let into the secret of my new aspirations, and shared my hopes and fears. She was my most confidential adviser at all times."[23] They both saw a college education as vital to his dreams for a mercantile, professional, or literary life, and also for the ministry, which Rebecca continued to hope her son would consider.

In a letter to Uncle Thomas, he briefly contemplates "studying divinity, probably in Pittsburgh."[24] But on further reflection, he recoils from the prospect of becoming a "miserably dependent preacher."

"Two insuperable objections existed to the ministry: I could not give up the hope of bettering my condition by the acquisition of wealth, nor could I submit to become a pliant tool of any church organization, or be subject to the unreasonable prejudices and whims of those who rule in congregations."[25] He was coming to know himself—to discover the immutable core of his personality and the limits it imposed on him.

He dreamed of a college education as the gateway to some lucrative profession, but his prospects for further schooling remained limited to what Andrew could afford and would permit. Moreover, the demands on Thomas's time were increasing, for as he approached manhood and his father grew older, the burden of farm work continued to shift from weakening shoulders to those that were growing stronger. When the boy felt frustrated, which was often, Rebecca lent a sympathetic ear, but the tension between father and son continued to build toward a climax.

Early in 1830, Andrew offered to buy seventeen year-old Thomas the neighboring farm, which was owned by Peter Hill. Andrew would give Hill a mortgage for most of the cost and take title in his own name. Thomas would work the land for five years and pay off the mortgage. His father would then give him title to the farm, and he would become self-supporting at twenty-two. But in this proposal, so generous at first glance, lay an ill-concealed trap: If Thomas acquiesced, he would remain soil-bound during the very years when he dreamed of completing his education. Though nagged by recurrent misgivings, he decided to accept his father's offer, if only because it represented the path of least resistance.

But as the deal was about to be finalized, he found himself swept by waves of mounting panic. To illustrate his dilemma, let us imagine a cartoon in which young Thomas is being torn apart in a tug-of-war: Uncle Thomas Mellon and the ghost of Benjamin Franklin are tugging on one of his arms, Andrew is pulling on the other, and Rebecca is wringing her hands in agony as she watches.

Because the crisis that followed is the most memorable episode in Thomas Mellon's memoirs, the master raconteur should relate it himself:

So the day was fixed for Peter [Hill] and my father to go to Greensburg to have the papers drawn and the bargain closed. They started about seven o'clock in the morning, and I went to my work as usual, cutting rail timber on the hill above our house. I remember the spot and its surroundings well, as it was the scene on that morning of an exceedingly violent mental agitation, the result of which changed the whole course of my subsequent life. I had worked for an hour or so, more vigorously perhaps than usual on account of the excitement over my fate, which was to be sealed that day at Greensburg. From where I stood I could overlook the farm that I was to own when I became of age and it was paid for; and on which, if I should marry, I was to spend my lifetime making an honest, frugal living by hard labor, but little more. The die was cast, or so nearly so as to be almost past recall. All my air castles and bright fancies of acquiring knowledge and wealth or distinction were wrecked and ruined, and to be abandoned forever. Must this be? I suddenly realized the tremendous importance of the moment. The utter collapse of all my fond young hopes thus suddenly precipitated nearly crazed me. I could stand it no longer. I put on my coat, ran down past the house, flung the axe over the fence into the yard, and without stopping made the best possible time on foot for the town. My father had taken the only available saddle horse, but my feet were light under the circumstances. It was ten rather long miles over a hilly, rough and muddy road, in March. I noticed little by the way, for time was precious. The papers might be signed before I got there. As I gained the top of the hill above the town, I could see Peter and my father standing on Welty's corner on Main street, and soon joined them, so much exhausted that it was difficult to express myself sufficiently to allay their alarm, as they supposed something awful had happened at home. All I could say was that I had come to stop it, and it must be stopped so far as I was concerned. My father seemed bewildered at such determined self-assertion. Peter seemed rather amused than displeased. They had only had their horses put up after getting into town. They had not hastened as I had done, and were consulting what lawyer they should call on to prepare the deed. There was no discussion. My long walk and sudden appearance indicated such resolution as precluded argument. My father, although disappointed, offered no rebuke or remonstrance, and I was rejoiced that I had arrived in time, feeling as if I had escaped a great impending calamity; and our good natured neighbor, the other party interested, was most jubilant of all, saying he owed me a present for getting him out of the scrape, as he had wished ever so much to rue [the] bargain but disliked to say so. After a comfortable dinner we all returned in good humor, Peter or my father walking sometimes to allow me to ride in view of my fatigue.[26]

Thomas Mellon had declared his independence, announcing to an obdurate father and an indifferent world that he would pilot his own course. He had demonstrated a sovereignty of mind and spirit and a strength that would continue to distinguish him from many of his peers and adversaries. His destiny was now set. Come what might, he would escape from the long littleness of farming. Yet, his marathon run to Greensburg may not have been the watershed event that he imagined. For even if the ensnaring farm had been bought for him, would a man of his ambition and ability have suffered being manacled to the manure fork for very long?

Two more years crawled by like paralytic centipedes, as Thomas sweated at manual jobs that yielded little in coin or satisfaction. But one of these tasks was noteworthy: his erection of an entire house and barn on the Moore farm, which Andrew had acquired in 1831, confirms that by the age of eighteen he had mastered both carpentry and masonry.[27] With these skills, he made construction an early pillar of the Mellon family fortune.

At least one of his initiatives failed: A grocery business that he and Uncle Archy Mellon had planned to initiate at New Salem was abandoned when the uncle proved too risk averse and the nephew insufficiently motivated. Between these drudgeries and intermittent bouts of farm work at Poverty Point, Thomas struggled to squeeze in as much reading as possible. He claims to have mastered trigonometry, mensuration, and surveying all without instruction.

With a copy of Ross's popular *Latin Grammar,* he now set out to conquer the classics. Dr. David Sterrett, who was renting a house from Andrew at New Salem, agreed to give Thomas Latin lessons, and his uncle Thomas contributed a copy of *Aesop's Fables* with English and Latin text in parallel columns. After the spring planting, Thomas wrested permission to attend the Tranquil Retreat Academy, at Monroeville, which was headed by the Rev. Jonathan Gill. Though this divine insisted that the end of the world would occur before the end of the year, his academy was viewed as an auspicious preparatory school for the Western University of Pennsylvania, and Thomas enrolled in it, secretly confident that the world would still exist when he graduated. In spite of intermittent distractions by Gill's pretty daughter, Jane, Thomas studied both Latin and Greek from April 16, 1832 until June 30, 1834—a total of fifty-nine weeks, or five and a half semesters, for which Dr. Gill extracted $22 in tuition and 75 cents a week for board. At the same time, Andrew Mellon continued to impose a tithe on his son for educational absences. The record shows that Thomas worked a total of twenty-five weeks, or almost half the time, on his father's new farm about a mile from the academy.[28]

His notebook records that on May 7, 1832, he commenced reading *Selectae Profanis;* on November 5, Caesar's *Gallic War;* on February 11, 1833, Ovid's *Metamorphosis;* and on April 22, Virgil's *Aeneid,* followed by Horace. Dr. Gill then introduced him to classical Greek, and he apparently mastered it sufficiently to translate selections from the New Testament. He was galloping through the classics.[29]

But the book and the plow continued to scuffle for control of his destiny. Scraps of a diary which he kept in 1834 depict him as "hoeing corn," "cradling rye," and reading Horace. On "a wet morning" we find him pondering the letters of Bishop Gilbert Burnet, perhaps in the rain. He fights his way through the tenth and eleventh odes of *Graeca Minora* while "sloughing turnips" and "working on oats." One revealing entry reads: "Sold a horse for $28, bought 3 vols classical library."[30]

Meanwhile, in another area of life Thomas was progressing at a crawl. It was during his two years at Tranquil Retreat that he took his first halting steps toward intimacy with young women. In April 1834, the twenty-one-year-old Thomas wrote confidentially to his boon companion, Richard Beatty, about girls:

> I have applyed myself verry closely to study now nearly three months without indulging in any diversion, without participating in much pleasure, that is without enjoying female company. I find this course necessary to be adopted for many considerations. It must be adopted if one wishes to make proficiency in his studies; because . . . , if the company of an amiable young woman for whome one has a particularly tender regard is frequented, it will naturally lead one to think more of her and less of his studies.
>
> This course must be adopted if we even intend gaining the lady's esteem, for it must certainly be disagreeable to a woman to have trifling of a fellow whose circumstances utterly forbid his

proceeding in the manner in which all such things should naturally proceed.

This course may be verry hard . . . but one may flatter oneself that, if they be verry temperate for a long time, they may some time taste a little spirit with[out] endangering their moral habits verry materially.[31]

Here his studies and prospects for advancement clearly hold precedence over female companionship. Ever the puritan, he views any display of sexual interest as "naturally" the prelude to a marriage proposal and in any other context as "trifling." Still, he leaves the door open just a crack for precisely that kind of mischief. And it is here, for the first time, that he reveals the ingrained dread of moral contamination that would remain one of his signature phobias.

Four months later, we find him writing to John Kuhn—"Coon," he spells it—another student with whom he had been sharing his thoughts about girls.

But the girls—the sweet creatures—I hardly know what to say about them good enough. They are all in their respective places yet . . . Miss Jane [Gill] is at home & as good looking as usual; and the old lady is still blustering about & the old Doctor [Thomas's recent headmaster] is now in town . . . , but sometimes I have been in danger. . . .

Miss Molly Beatty I saw at meeting last Sunday, & I felt her too, for as I had to sit in the same pew & by chance next [to] her, she kept punching me with her elbow, at everything she considered comical, so that I could scarcely mind the text [and] none of the sermon. . . . Elizabeth, the little black eyed miss . . . , attracted nearly all the beaus of this cuntry, last summer. . . . But, strange as it may seem, she did not give, but rather received the "dead shot," because about Christmas she secluded herself from all her beaus . . . & was delivered of a fine daughter.[32]

The offhand grammar and atrocious spelling of these effusions add to their charming unself-consciousness. They show us the adolescent Thomas, setting out to explore the unknown continent of his own sexuality. We see him here in the champagne years of his youth, when he could still laugh at his own foibles, not just moralize about them and draw weighty conclusions. Under the spell of Jane Gill, with whom he had evidently flirted, Thomas again lapses into doggerel:

The fields and groves will wear no charm for me;
These charms, so dear, will all depart with thee.
No more at silent eve or early morn
Will I thy golden locks with wreaths adorn.[33]

Too soon, he would begin to stifle such emotions. What sense of humor he had would atrophy—would peep out only rarely and then in wan, barely perceptible glints. It would recede behind the rigid, over-controlled face of the jurist and banker, the face he would present to a world he had perhaps always regarded with shades of distrust and alarm.

Thomas's early letters also reveal a conspicuous discrimination in the kind of young women he chose to befriend. Had he been hunting for sexual adventure, he could have found it in the brothels of Pittsburgh or in the haylofts with Pennsylvania German farm girls, who were famously available. But his intimate letters to Kuhn and Beatty suggest no frivolous or lowlife involvements. Instead, we find him keeping company with young women of higher social station than his own—girls from families like the Beattys, Gills, and Liggetts, and eventually the Negleys.

Accepting, at last, that Thomas was not to be deflected from the madness of a professional or business career, Andrew Mellon wearily consented to his son's entreaties for a college education. To save a dollar in fare, Thomas walked almost twenty miles to decide for himself whether to attend fashionable Jefferson College, at Canonsburg. While attending the graduation ceremony, he observed the four hundred students closely and espied in them a frivolous dilettantism which instantly repelled him.[34] "Earnest educational purpose and enthusiasm for literary pursuits appeared at a discount; and 'how *not* to do it and yet get through it' was the more popular sentiment."[35]

His next visit was to the Western University of Pennsylvania, later known as the University of Pittsburgh, with fewer than fifty students. He preferred the smaller student body and the nose-to-the-grindstone atmosphere of the campus. "The purpose of all seemed to be work and progress, and accorded better with my own spirit and disposition on the subject."[36]

There were other considerations, too. He was now twenty-one and would be entering college belatedly. His letters to Uncle Thomas Mellon, among others, reveal a mounting concern with the slow pace at which his education had progressed. In August 1834, Dr. Gill informed him that Jefferson College would soon add mathematics and modern language requirements that would delay his graduation by a further year. The Western University, Mellon wrote to Kuhn, "does not detain students for years in useless studies merely to get money [out] of them & not make them scholars after all, as Jefferson does at present."[37]

On Tuesday October 14, 1834, Andrew Mellon transported Thomas and his meager belongings to Pittsburgh in a farm wagon that was also loaded with groceries. They halted on Third Street between Smithfield and Cherry, where the Western University occupied an imposing stone building three stories high. As Thomas crossed the threshold and became a college student, it must have filled him with euphoria and near disbelief that he was actually crossing this Rubicon in his flight from farming.

In later life, Mellon had little to say about his college years, perhaps because what he learned did little to help him accumulate wealth. He leaves a thumbnail sketch of his daily routine as one of five young men who shared an apartment at the university. We learn how they formed a sumptuary club to regulate their expenses and to apportion the daily chores, like cooking and cleaning. He adverts to his impecunious con-

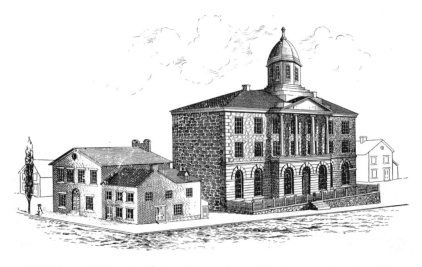

*The Western University of Pennsylvania (now the University of Pittsburgh), from which Thomas Mellon graduated and where he taught; picture dated 1833. Courtesy Heinz History Center, Pittsburgh.*

dition; he relates how he profitably operated a pay school for three months while the university was in recess and how, during another vacation, he junketed through Ohio in a predictably futile bid to peddle copies of Henry Hallam's *The View of the State of Europe during the Middle Ages.* He alludes to tedious bouts of field work on his father's new farm, a mile north of Monroeville, and thanks his mother for her continuing quiet support in his struggle for advancement.

On the subject of his curriculum, however, only tidbits of information survive. He mentions his readings in Cicero and Livy and adds that he studied French. At least one of his professors impressed him:

In Latin and Greek, mathematics and mental and moral philosophy Dr. [Robert] Bruce, the president of the college, heard our recitations. He was one of a class of men rarely met with: modest and retiring of manner, shunning notoriety, and averse to anything having the appearance of ostentation. He was highly cultured in general literature, an extensive reader, liberal minded, and a most accurate scholar in the several branches he professed. He was not only learned, but extremely critical. He had all the philosophy of Bacon and Descartes, Hume, Reid and Dugald Stewart at [his] command . . . and his lectures on mental and moral philosophy were exceedingly interesting, profitable and practical.[38]

These lectures may have helped to arouse Thomas's thirst for knowledge in the fields of social and political science, education, law, and religion, all of which he would exhaustively explore in his later reading. To some extent, he probably modeled himself on Dr. Bruce. But he gives as much credit for what he learned to his own reading in the library of the university's Tilghman Literary Society as to his courses and professors. Without arrogance or self-congratulation, he was discovering his remarkable ability to learn without instruction—to master challenging subjects simply by reading and willpower. But Thomas was not exclusively preoccupied with his studies, as the following letter, written in his junior year to a close friend, confirms:

Mr. John Duff
Dear Sir,
    . . . I am sorry to see by your letter that you have no opportunity of female society. . . . You perhaps look upon this matter very lightly; the time was when I did so too. . . . I once thought the time wasted if spent in female company. The reason was, I did not know how to derive advantage from it; and I now sincerely deplore my loss—a loss the more visible when I chanced to enter into polished company, and the more painfully felt when I see the superiority which those have over me, who have taken care to rub off the asperities of their manners by associating occasionally with polished females. It is no unimportant part of the education of a professional man at least, to make his knowledge acceptable and himself beloved. The company of the ladies, if well improved, is eminently calculated to fit one for the company of either sex. . . .

*Dr. Robert Bruce (1778–1846),*
*president of the Western University of Pennsylvania;*
*painting by John C. Darley.*

Some professions are, indeed, more independent of the good will of the women than others. This was a weighty consideration in the scale which determined my own choice. Having no natural and fiew acquired talents for pleasing the ladies, it would ill suit me to be a physician or a divine, but especially the latter. . . . One who has not obtained the graces & polish of genteel company in his youth, will not acquire it easily when grown up. . . .

As to love and matrimony . . . the best of men have their weaknesses [and] I am inclined to include this in the number. It does not comport with my theory of human happiness, at least. . . . My theory . . . may be reduced to this definition: the exercise of the mental faculties, the suppression of the passions and affections, the moral quietude of conscience. Its tendency is to cultivate our immortal part and render us happy in ourselves, independently of external objects. . . . We can look upon the honours and pursuits of the world with contempt. . . . No better illustration of this need be required than Love & Matrimony. No sooner does the lover place his affections on his mistress, than his peace of mind is blasted with a thousand anxieties. . . . You perhaps say that if we avoid the evil, we likewise forego the good. Granted. But is it not better to do without a spoonful of sugar in the bottom of a vessel, than drink a quart of vinegar in order to come at it? Do you say that my theory would tend [toward] the extinction of our species? Never fear that. There will always be fools enough to drink all the vinegar for the sake of the sugar. . . . Let knowledge be sought for her own sake, and she will soon make her votaries independent of any other source of happiness. . . .

> Yours truly
> Thos Mellon[39]

In this letter, written two years after the ones to Beatty and Kuhn, we find twenty-three-year-old Thomas weighing the ideal of marriage for the first time, and rejecting it with typical bachelor reasoning. He has also concluded that cultivation is a surer road to fulfillment than accumulation. He would reverse these priorities before long, but in later life would learn to pursue both simultaneously.

The epochal changes transforming western Pennsylvania at that time precipitated a conflict that rocked and almost wrecked the university during Thomas Mellon's attendance. In Allegheny County, rural Jeffersonian America was steadily giving ground before the advancing Industrial Revolution. Canals and turnpikes now connected Pittsburgh to the East Coast. Factories, forges, foundries, and glassworks were being built. Coal mining had begun to flourish as steam power transformed the means of production and transportation. Could the Western University of Pennsylvania continue to teach primarily Latin, Greek, and a raft of impractical studies when courses in science, engineering, and business management were what the community increasingly clamored for?

The university's president, Robert Bruce (1778–1846), was a Scottish-born Presbyterian clergyman who held a degree from the University of Edinburgh. He had made some concessions to the need for practical education in the courses he offered. Mathematics and chemistry were applicable to a variety of trades. Courses in political theory, law, modern history, and economic philosophy could serve as practical tools for a career in government. Geology and mineralogy were useful in a region of iron foundries and coal mines.

But overall, "the Bruce," as his students affectionately dubbed him, staunchly defended a preponderantly medieval curriculum at a time when the study of Caesar, Ovid, Virgil, Cicero, Lucian, Horace, and Livy, not to mention Xenophon, Demosthenes, and Homer, had come to be ridiculed by an increasing number of Pittsburghers as useless in a burgeoning industrial community.

That young Thomas Mellon, when he graduated in 1837, was immediately engaged by the university as its professor of Latin underscores how heavily he had concentrated on the classics. Looking back on his curriculum, he draws some somber conclusions.

Educational advantages depend on their relevancy to the future occupation . . . of the individual. It may be from the fact of thoroughness that Latin has always benefited me more than any other of my college studies. The Latin has been of use in its superior grammatical science and by affording a valuable insight into the derivation and original meaning of English words. The Greek and Latin classics have also been of some value historically, as affording an insight to the manners, customs, thoughts and opinions of the people, and the state of civilization in past ages. The practical branches of mathematics have also been found useful; but the Greek . . . and the higher branches of mathematics and the French . . . were entirely useless. The rapidity with which school-acquired knowledge, or indeed any other kind of knowledge fades from the mind unless frequently refreshed or recalled for practical purposes, is a factor in education not sufficiently regarded.[40]

In 1835, the university's heavy emphasis on classics, to the exclusion of utilitarian studies, triggered so much infighting among trustees, community leaders, and even state legislators that it was almost forced to close. Bruce was fired and briefly replaced by Dr. Gilbert Morgan, also a clergyman. In the perennial tug-of-war between practical and theoretical education, Morgan attempted but failed to work out an acceptable compromise. When the student body opposed him with a kind of strike, he stepped down, and Bruce was reinstated. Though Thomas Mellon supported Bruce, the defender of classical education—probably because a traditional diploma was still perceived as the gateway to most respectable professions—he would soon recognize how little this kind of learning actually counted for in a life devoted primarily to material gain.

# III

———•◆•———

## Choosing the Law,
## Shopping for a Wife,
## The Great Fire of 1845

*Beauty alone may excite love, but it does so by subsidizing the imagination to supply other good qualities; and as stern reality soon discloses the mistake, love resting on beauty alone must necessarily be short lived.*

I N HIS LENGTHY, AGONIZING SEARCH for the profession that would suit him ideally, Thomas Mellon would make no concessions to external pressure. With his draconian rejection of farming, he had taken the reins of his life in hand. Though his mother Rebecca persisted in her gentle efforts to dispose him toward the ministry, he had given only fleeting consideration to that unprofitable alternative and had long since vetoed it. "Money," he had observed in a college essay, "is to society what the element of fire is to matter, diffusing warmth and vigour through all its parts."[1] The implacable yearning to warm himself by that fire had become his guiding standard as he searched for a vocation.

As to the legal profession, I had at that time an erroneous opinion of what was necessary to success in it. I only judged from what I saw in the courts. . . . The opportunity for display and notoriety afforded the successful advocate was tempting enough; but . . . success in that line by one so nervous and diffident as I was, seemed too uncertain. I was not aware then that the money making part of the business lay in the back ground, and not in the line of speech making to any great extent; and that those growing rich in the profession were seldom seen in court.[2]

That the law is a swinging door to politics meant nothing to Thomas, for he had no political program or ambition for public office. Attracted exclusively by "the money making part of the business," he had already taken a formal step toward protecting his access to the legal profession. In Pennsylvania, admission to the bar could not be obtained until two years after the applicant had registered as a law student, and Thomas had taken that step in 1835 or '36. He had also squeezed in some courses in law during his final year at the university.

Early in 1838, he resigned his Latin professorship and began to formally train for a legal career. Judge Charles Shaler, who had returned to private practice after presiding over the Court of Common Pleas for eleven years, was now prevailed upon to accept him as a law student. Shaler treated his new apprentice with benign neglect but gave him access to the firm's extensive law library. That was all young Thomas needed.

Somewhere in Judge Shaler's chambers hung a painting that caught the apprentice's eye. It depicted an elderly lawyer seated at table between two of his clients. Grinning broadly, with fork in hand, the lawyer is about to eat a juicy oyster, while each client stares glumly at an empty half-shell lying on his plate. The clients dismally conclude:

> A pearly shell for you and me;
> The oyster is the lawyer's fee.[3]

When Thomas expressed surprise at finding such art in a law office, Judge Shaler jauntily replied that the painting made him feel less guilty when his clients experienced what it represented.

In March 1838, a minor position at the Pittsburgh courthouse became vacant. It was a junior clerkship in the prothonotary's office, and Thomas secured it through the intervention of a student he had befriended at the Tilghman Society: William Liggett, the prothonotary's son. Engaging in work and study simultaneously, he now found himself ideally positioned to master his chosen profession. For while he was reading Blackstone's legal dictionary and the other legal classics in Judge Shaler's library, he was also gaining practical experience as he wrestled with the continuous stream of litigation that passed across his desk. Of equal importance, he was rendering valuable service to litigants who would soon become his clients while also meeting and befriending the judges and attorneys who would be his peers. The senior clerk at the prothonotary's office, Thomas MacConnell, was also cramming for admission to the bar. They decided to take their oral exams, in civil and criminal law, together.

When the day arrived for Mellon and MacConnell to be examined, a board of four inquisitors was assembled in the chambers of Walter Lowrie, a future justice of the state supreme court. Also present were the attorney James Finley, whose father had been governor of Pennsylvania; Judge Thomas Baird; and another attorney, James Dunlop, who was acclaimed for his *Digest of the Laws of Pennsylvania*. They were "all able and critical lawyers," Mellon allows, "and rather jealous of each other's pretensions."[4]

MacConnell was the first to be examined, and the inquisitors expended so much energy competitively grilling him that they were at a loss as to what to demand of Mellon when his turn finally came. Judge Baird nonetheless roused himself to query "whether the consignor or the consignee should bring suit against a common carrier, in case of non-delivery of the goods."[5]

It happened that Mellon had just been listening to Baird and Finley arguing this very question before Judge Robert Grier in the district court. To rekindle their disagreement, he now deliberately parroted Judge Grier's ruling, which was to the effect that suit should be brought by the consignee.

Baird leapt to the attack and pronounced Mellon's reply erroneous. Finley shot back that it was correct. Lowrie and Dunlop now piled into the argument too. Forgotten by everyone, Mellon and Mac-Connell were able to slip out. Neither was given a hint as to his fate until the following day, when a message announced that they had both satisfied the board with respect to civil law.[6] But because their examiner in criminal law had failed to show up, they would have to return and be questioned by him.

William Irwin, the deputy attorney general for that district and a future mayor of Pittsburgh, conducted the second examination. The two candidates found Irwin stalking about in his freezing chambers, gesturing menacingly with a poker and cursing his office boy for having let the fire go out. Without inviting either student to be seated, and eyeing them both askance, he enjoined Mellon to define murder. Mellon took no chances and cited Blackstone. The inquisitor then turned on MacConnell and extracted a definition of manslaughter. Regarding both students fiercely, he ruled that anyone who could tell the difference between murder and manslaughter was fit to practice criminal law. Examination concluded.[7]

Though he chose not to open an office for several months, Mellon received his license to practice law on December 15, 1838, after less than a year of apprenticeship to Judge Shaler. The swiftness with which he had become a lawyer bears witness not only to the farcical nature of the examinations that had gained him admission to the profession but also to his native ability and relentless perseverance. The first portentous decision of his life had been to renounce farming in favor of education. The second was to become a lawyer.

At this critical juncture in his life, let us pause to take stock of Mellon's net worth; for a classic American success story cannot be chronicled without periodic, invasive examinations of purse. In early 1839 Mellon succeeded to the senior clerkship which MacConnell had vacated, and his salary rose from $20 a month to $25. That he managed to save a fraction of this cash, after paying $8 a month for board and more for additional expenses such as clothing, is a Scotch-Irish miracle. He had also managed to retain a part of his stipend as Latin professor at the university and had occasionally earned fees by copying court records. With an additional $200 from his father, he now began to speculate profitably in the discounted mortgages, small judgments, and mechanic's liens that came to his attention at the courthouse. Where a lender was clamoring for repayment ahead of schedule, Mellon would do some horse trading and offer to buy his note at a deep discount. Where a debtor had defaulted on an obligation, Mellon would weigh his own chances of being able to collect and would then perhaps offer to buy the note, again at a discount. For when it comes to collection, lawyers have an edge.

All his life Mellon would shudder at the prospect of becoming a debtor, and he never tired of repeating that aversion to debt was a family tradition.[8] But no one ever understood the accumulative power of interest better than Thomas Mellon. A relentlessly acquisitive but innately cautious man, he fell in love at first sight and forever with the formidable mathematics of compounding and was always discomfited by riskier profit-making strategies. He would fulminate against "the canker of credit" but was quick to embark on a lifelong traffic in debt obligations.[9] That he founded the Mellon family's bank is proof enough that he was comfortable as a lender.

In June 1839, he leased a small room in Pittsburgh on Fifth Street (now Fifth Avenue) at Market Alley, converted it into a law office, and hung out his shingle. The location was ideal—one block from the courthouse. His rent was $6 a month. That he spent his entire nest egg of $700 to buy a library of law books before actually going into practice suggests that he harbored few doubts about his legal ability. "Ye shall know them by their fruits," the Bible intones (Matthew 7:16), and the fruits of his early labors at the bar were revealing. As an increasing number of litigants whom he had assisted while clerking for the prothonotary brought him their legal wrangles, his schedule became steadily more crowded with appointments. As a rule, it would take a neophyte lawyer in Pittsburgh five years to accumulate $1,500 (about $35,250 in today's dollars).[10] That it took Thomas Mellon one year was yet another triumph of will over convention.

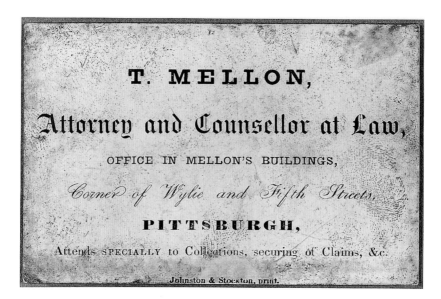

*Thomas Mellon's business card in 1840.*

Reflecting on his early years as a lawyer, Mellon later observed:

I was then at an age to possess mature judgment, . . . was of an earnest, cautious and painstaking disposition, had a good education and a rather extensive and accurate knowledge of the law, and had become favorably known to many of the business men; and what was of still more importance to litigants, I had already much experience in the methods and practice of the courts. To this I added, not eloquence so much as the faculty of persuasion on jury trials. And above all, I possessed a quality rather painful to myself but of much advantage to clients: which was that I espoused my client's cause as if my own. If I could not do this I did not engage in the case. I either believed at the outset or became convinced that my client was in the right; and under this feeling if I lost a case I felt the chagrin of being to blame for it.

He also attributes his success as a lawyer to the speed with which he could close cases and to his unconventional billing policy: "My undue moderation in charges soon led me to discover that it was often my best policy to leave the amount of the fee to the client himself. On that line most of them would hand me over much more than I would have fixed had I been insisted on to make the charge." But he adds, somewhat incongruously, "If there is any one thing more than another in which I feel that I was to blame, it is for having done too much service for too little money."[11]

To the widening stream of his legal fees, augmented by astute speculation in debt instruments, he now added a third source of accumulation: real estate. When, in 1840, he noticed that businesses were relocating to the vicinity of his office on Fifth Street, he offered to lease the ground floor of the building from his landlord, Mr. Drake, for a pittance, by offering him five years of rent in advance. Drake innocently agreed, and Mellon netted $1,000 by subleasing the space to another tenant. Discerning unrecognized value, he next bought an unfinished house on Prospect Street and resold it for a profit of $400. In 1841, he acquired his first home—a house and lot on Penn Avenue, where he lived for the next two years. By 1843 his total assets had grown to $12,000 (about $354,000 in today's dollars), and he could finally bask in the knowledge that his arduous struggle against the hated constraints of poverty had been substantially won.[12]

Thomas Mellon was now thirty years old. His years behind the plow had left him healthy, strong of limb, and disciplined in his habits. He was, moreover, strikingly handsome, with angular features that were at once bold and finely cut; a high, prominent forehead; and a distinguished profile. With his dense black hair grown long and curling slightly upward just above the shoulders, he could have passed for a well-proportioned Caribbean pirate or an English cavalier. His complexion was dark to ruddy, his brown eyes alert and inquiring under the heavy black brows that have become a family trait. He was of only medium height—five foot nine—but his abstemious eating habits would enable him to remain permanently thin in spite of the sedentary life that awaited him.[13]

Richly endowed by nature and already copiously rewarded for his early exertions, he had reached a plateau in life where we can imagine him pausing to look back with satisfaction on the rugged slope he had scaled. But, in truth, he was ill at ease. Worldly advancement had become his consuming passion, but in pursuit of it he had neglected his emotional needs. He was now learning that to stifle nature is not to obliterate it.

> With me the tender passion and love of children and domestic life was always strong—even when a boy at school I would single out some one little girl I admired above any other. After I was smitten with the ambition for a professional life, prudence compelled me to suppress any leanings in that direction: . . . When any great purpose is formed whatever would hinder it should be dispensed with, and complications of the kind would only have hindered and obstructed mine. Nevertheless throughout all my prolonged efforts the day dreams of the distant future still presented a happy home with loving wife and bright children as the ultimate consummation of my hopes: in fact I was by nature what the Germans aptly term a "family man."[14]

He had lived in boardinghouses and hotels, had roomed with four young men at the university, and had rented a room in a family home. But his itinerant lifestyle had come to irk him. After buying the house on Penn Avenue, he persuaded his parents to leave Poverty Point and live with him in Pittsburgh. Andrew Mellon stoically submitted for several months but became progressively more restless and alienated. The clop and clatter of carriages passing over cobbled streets was as foreign to him as the crowing of cocks on the dung heap was dear. Inevitably, Thomas's parents returned to Monroeville, and his new home again fell silent, except for the desultory sound of his own footsteps.

By then, the inner voices that had been whispering to him about marriage had begun to clamor for it.

The spirit of unrest would not down, and early in 1843, after my father determined to return to the country, I began for the first time to think seriously of marriage. The prospect of returning to a boarding house or a hotel was discouraging, and marriage the only alternative. Marriage at some time or other had always been in contemplation, and I had now attained to a position which would justify its consummation. I was in my thirtieth year and now was the proper age, neither too soon nor too late; with experience and settled habits not fully attainable at an earlier age, and not yet subject to the fixed tastes and crusty disposition of a bachelor, and with the possibility of a long enough life still before me to care for and train a family of children, there was no reason why I should not enter the marriage relation.[15]

That his dogged pursuit of education and aggrandizement had left him with an atrophied social life he readily admits: "I had mingled little in society, seldom even attending the theater or other places of public amusement. Reading and rest in the evenings in my own room was more agreeable."[16]

As a man of action and ideas, he could not have relished the prospect of debuting on the Pittsburgh social scene, with its mindless small talk and stuffy teas presided over by censorious dowagers. The whale hunt for a wife would also lead him into uncharted emotional waters—into the sphere of sexual intimacy that he, the puritan workaholic, had repressed and neglected. In his correspondence with John Kuhn, twenty-one-year-old Thomas had referred to certain girls as "the sweet creatures"; writing to John Duff two years later, he had acknowledged the refining effect of social contact with young females. Seven years had elapsed since the second of these letters, yet this preoccupied thirty-year-old, now contemplating the marriage market, seems uncertain as to how much he had actually learned about women. "My acquaintance with the fair sex was limited. I had been too close a student at first and was too much engaged in business afterwards to cultivate the graces popular with them. It is true I was acquainted in some few good families, two or three of them with marriageable daughters, where I had visited occasionally for rest and amusement when wearied with business cares and labors. Such visits being without serious purpose, I had always avoided pointed attentions such as would indicate affection or raise expectation."[17]

In the hunt for a spouse, as in business, he was determined to avoid risk and emphatically refused to exceed the limits of conventional ethics. "I never would trifle with female affections, nor excite groundless hopes. Honor and self respect made anything of the kind repugnant; and I always felt a contempt for those who acted otherwise to gratify selfish vanity."[18]

Whether he had ever made love must remain conjectural. An aspiring lawyer in the Pittsburgh middle class and living in nineteenth-century America, he predictably draws an iron curtain around his private life and compels the portraitist to leave a critically consequential area of the canvas blank. Though the little we know suggests that his sexual experience was scant, perhaps nil, he nonetheless set out with conspicuous self-assurance and chilly calculation to shop for a spouse. "It was an enterprise new to me," he admits, "but as I had succeeded in others more difficult, I undertook it without any apprehensions of failure."[19] He also concedes that "it was a rather more difficult task than I had expected" but then adds with bruising nonchalance, "I was impatient of spending much time upon it."[20]

He nonetheless viewed the decision which awaited him as an awesome one, and he approached it with telltale eugenic calculation: "Marriage is by all odds the most momentous event of our lives. Character, temper, disposition, taste, sentiment and inclination should all be ascertained with certainty and considered carefully. Besides this, family, ancestry, health and position should be allowed their due weight and carefully considered. I fully realized all this at the time."[21]

More to the point, he knew what kind of girl he was looking for. "Great beauty or accomplishments were not demanded. I wanted a wife for a helpmate, not for display; one who could bear up and help me in adversity should it overtake us, or share with me the satisfaction of success, as the case might be."[22] Significantly, his mother Rebecca and grandmother Elizabeth Mellon were wives of precisely this sort. Benjamin Franklin's *Autobiography* revealed that he too had landed such a spouse: "She assisted me cheerfully in my business," recalls the venerable Philadelphian, "folding and stitching pamphlets, tending shop, purchasing old linen rags for the paper-makers, etc, etc."[23]

Mellon also knew the kinds of girls he was *not* looking for: "I obtained introductions to several new lady friends, but without results. Some were too gay and frivolous or self-conceited; others too slovenly and ungainly, and others again too coarse or stupid."[24] He had turned down Sarah Liggett, a daughter of his former employer, the prothonotary, because tuberculosis appeared to run in her family. He was not breeding for defective offspring.

Late in January 1843, as his wife hunt was just beginning, Thomas was favored by a sudden stroke of luck. His longtime friend Dr. Richard Beatty asked him to serve as groomsman, or best man, at his wedding to Isabella Negley, a daughter of Jacob and Barbara Negley, whose steam-powered gristmill had so fascinated young Thomas twenty years earlier. Beatty confided to Mellon that Isabella had an unmarried sister named Sarah Jane, whom he had at first found preferable to his own fiancée but whom he had rejected, on second thought, as she was "too independent for him, had no elasticity in her composition, and did not seem to appreciate gentlemen's attentions."[25]

These are not ringing qualifications for a young woman, yet they failed to deflect Mellon from seeking a meeting with the available Negley heiress. Sarah Liggett agreed to provide the required introduction, and the two set out for East Liberty, the former Negleytown, in a horse-drawn sled.

> Soon we were in the spacious parlor of the old Negley mansion, where I found myself for the first time in the presence of her who was afterwards to become my wife. I took her in at a glance; and now, after over forty years, can well remember how she looked then, even to the fashion of her hair and every minute particular

of her dress. I see her now in the mind's eye, as she stood there in the sunlight which was struggling through the window curtains giving me a full view of her appearance—quiet, pleasant and self-possessed. I remember thinking to myself, in person she would do, if all right otherwise.[26]

This assessment was actually quite flattering, for God had fashioned Sarah Jane from the homeliest clay. An early daguerreotype taken in 1848, when she was thirty-one, shows a plain, bony woman with dark hair and severe Gothic features. But Mellon remained unflappable. "She would do, if all right otherwise," and her *other* qualifications were the ones that interested him.[27] There, in the parlor, he stood, scrutinizing Sarah Jane Negley and asking himself whether she should be "the one of destiny."

"Quiet, pleasant, and self-possessed" is how he would selectively remember her. He might have added that she was also vastly better educated than most of her peeresses. In 1825, we find her attending daily at the Edgeworth Ladies' Boarding School, in Braddock's Field, to which wealthy families sent their daughters from as far away as Cincinnati. But Edgeworth Seminary, as it came to be known, was not merely a finishing school where prissy spinsters labored to put a social polish on rough-hewn Pittsburgh maidens. Writing in 1831, during Sarah Jane's attendance, the headmistress, Mary Gould Oliver, describes the curriculum as "reading, writing, arithmetic, grammar, composition, geography, astronomy with the use of globes, natural philosophy, chemistry, history; also plain and ornamental needle work. Per annum $130. Tuition in music, $40; drawing, pencil, crayon and watercolors, $24; in oil painting, $40; French, $20."[28]

Sarah Jane Negley's schoolbooks included *History of the United States,* by the Rev. Charles Goodrich; *English Grammar,* by Samuel Kirkham; *The Eclectic Third Reader,* by William M'Guffey; *Practical Arithmetic,* by Stephen Pike; *Lectures on Botany,* by Almira Lincoln; *The Young Botanist,* by J. L. Comstock; *Modern Geography,* by J. Olney; *School Geography,* mainly by Conrad Malte-Brun, arranged by Griswold Goodrich; and *The Young Lady's Own Book,* by Key, Mielke, and Biddle. They included two other textbooks from which Thomas Mellon had also learned: *English Grammar,* by Lindley Murray, and the *Western Calculator,* by J. Stockton.[29]

Had she lived in pre-Revolutionary America, Sarah Jane would have received a vastly more rudimentary education. At best, she might have mastered reading, writing, simple arithmetic, and the basics of her religion at a church-run day school, but most likely she would have been educated at home, with her mother as the principal teacher. Sarah Jane would have been taught to cook, clean, sew, knit, make clothes, and do light farm work, such as milking a cow and feeding chickens. She would have been trained to be a wife and to raise children.

The colonial American family, exemplified by the early settlers of New England, differed radically from the family in which Sarah Jane had been reared. It was a self-sufficient unit in which two, three, or even four generations worked in different capacities to produce all the essentials of life. As a rule, the colonial family grew its own food, frequently made its own furniture, worshipped at home as well as in church, cared for its sick and elderly, and taught to younger generations the various skills that made it self-sustaining. The father was expected to direct and assist his sons to self-sufficiency. He also largely determined who would be permitted to court his daughters, for in a colonial American family marriage was not viewed as the consummation of passionate love but as a practical arrangement between two families—a contractual union that involved property, dowries, inheritances, and the like.

Thomas Mellon had been raised in a family that exhibited a number of these characteristics. Almost all the necessities of life had been grown or produced on the Mellon farm. His initial schoolroom had been in the home, where his mother had taught him the alphabet and introduced him to the Bible. His formal schooling had been deliberately minimal—the three Rs, religion, and not much more. On the farm, his father had always held decisive power. Andrew had taught his son the skills that farming required. He had also trained him in carpentry and masonry as the two labored together, building their farmhouse and barn. He had claimed the right, and had felt the obligation, to direct Thomas's course in life: to steer him into farming. When Thomas had differed with his father, his mother could do no more than gently plead for him.

Sarah Jane Negley had been raised in a family that was not only more affluent but also conspicuously more modern than the Mellons. Her father and brothers had all attained a high level of education and had entered business, the law, and other professions. No one had tried to direct them into farming. They had left home, made marriages of their choice, and raised separate families. Though the adjacent farmland still supplied food for those who remained in the Negley "mansion," the furniture, decorations, and many other necessities were purchased rather than produced at home. The family had ceased to be an inclusive unit dedicated to remaining self-sufficient by internalizing its vital functions. It had become an institution that functioned primarily as a refuge where children could be nurtured and trained for success and prepared to lead independent lives.

Whatever in the way of knowledge, poise, and sophistication was to be gained from attending the Edgeworth Ladies' Boarding School, Sarah Jane had probably absorbed. Vastly more important, she was not only an heiress but also a member of one of Pittsburgh's founding families. These were the qualifications that impressed Thomas Mellon, for whom financial freedom and respectability were tantamount. At thirty, he may have known himself well enough to understand that he would somehow achieve these overlapping goals, with or without a Negley heiress as his wife. But a union with her would gain him respectability in one stroke and would leave him free to continue accumulating wealth at a vastly higher level. Perhaps he did not ponder this shortcut to destiny in full frankness—that is, in his open thoughts—but it must at least have tinctured his subliminal judgment. When a man has innately decided on his course of action, he can rationalize or excuse it to himself in any number of ways.

Thomas studied Sarah Jane with chilly calculation, like an Arab examining the teeth of a camel. He would later confess to having felt no passion for her throughout their courtship, but with his inner voices now clamoring for a family life—with the tantalizing "plums" of wealth and respectability hanging ripe on the bough and within reach—he decided to press his suit.[30] Franklin had quipped that "an empty bag cannot stand upright."[31] Mellon had quietly decided that his own bag would always be full.

The two would sit in the Negleys' parlor and fitfully engage in small talk, but whenever Thomas attempted to become personal, Sarah Jane would deftly change the subject. "She was pleasant, cheerful and polite," he recalls, "with ready conversation on general subjects, but without affording the slightest opening towards intimacy. . . . She evinced the dexterity of a special pleader in evading all approaches to any discussion of the real business I had in hand." This began to annoy Thomas. He was also unimpressed when Sarah Jane flaunted her advanced and well-rounded education. "I was not there to take lessons in flora culture or botany, or to learn the history of birds, fishes or butterflies," he grumbles. "I did not want to spend evening after evening in admiring pictures in her album, or in having items read to me from her scrap book. But to her credit I must say that she never inflicted any music upon me."[32]

Clearly, neither of these two was smitten with the other. Sarah Jane's behavior, as Thomas describes it, suggests that they were both playing the same game—coolly eyeing each other and tallying the pros and cons of a possible union. Of the two, it took Sarah Jane longer to decide. Social considerations argued against her marrying an immigrant farmer's son. Initially, her mother and brothers must have expressed doubts about the match. But the social gap between Sarah Jane and her suitor had narrowed dramatically since the day when ten-year-old Thomas had meditated on the charmed life of Jacob Negley's children from his hillside vantage point above Negley Lane. The man whose eyes now rested on her was intelligent, articulate, exceptionally well educated, a rising star in his profession, a member of the all-conquering Scotch-Irish faction, and by every appearance a trustworthy, honorable young man. He was also rather handsome. Could a distressingly plain woman, already in her twenty-seventh year and from a family that had lost more than half of its fortune, afford to dismiss such a suitor?

As the standoff continued, Thomas became increasingly annoyed at the amount of time he had invested in this seemingly fruitless gambit. For three months, the only encouraging signal he had received from Sarah Jane was that she continued to permit his weekly visits. Was *Poor Richard's Almanac* not crammed with injunctions against time wasting? Recalling his frustration, he later devised an alternative form of courtship:

> A radical reform is needed in the art of courtship. As its object is so important, I would have it conducted in an open, candid, earnest, truthful and practical spirit. Instead of the shy, coy, evasive methods in use it should be first settled between the parties that both are candidates for matrimony; second, whether each is acceptable to the other prima facie, subject to rejection on further acquaintance; third, no love to be excited or admitted on either side until each party is fully satisfied with the nature, disposition and character of the other; and fourth, each to be bound to the other by honor and etiquette, in case the relation is declined on either side, to entertain no ill feeling in consequence, and never to divulge any information whatever obtained during such preliminary stage. The utmost candor should be observed; nothing whatever should be concealed which it would be relevant to know, and no restraint put upon inquiry. In this way each other's views could be had regarding married life and its duties, sentiments and expectations in the future, style of living and ability to support a family; as also natural tastes and appetites, and everything else of importance to be known. . . . If this plan was adopted the suitability of each to the other for such a union might with far greater certainty be ascertained beforehand, and

much misery, dissatisfaction and necessity for divorces avoided. This would be the rational course, and after it was gone through it would be time enough to begin love making.[33]

Did he believe that Benjamin Franklin would have courted a woman this way?

Skewered by the mounting suspicion that his suit was hopeless, Thomas began hunting for an alternative to Sarah Jane. In his boyhood, he had experienced "the sweet, soft sadness and tender longings of calf-love" for a girl named Mary Young.[34] The two had not laid eyes on each other since their schooldays at Poverty Point, and Thomas's lonely imagination had been steadily embroidering his memories of Mary. Under the spell of these illusions, he now rode to the farm where she was said to be living. The woman he found there was prematurely old. She wore "untidy, faded, soiled and slovenly looking garments," had "frowzy hair," and smoked a pipe. Thomas returned to Pittsburgh "a wiser but not a sadder man."[35]

"Love is but a passion like the other passions," he would conclude, "and is excited or allayed as the object of it attracts or repels: just as the other passions rise and subside. Permanent affection, like friendship, depends on esteem and regard for a worthy object. Beauty alone may excite love, but it does so by subsidizing the imagination to supply other good qualities; and as stern reality soon discloses the mistake, love resting on beauty alone must necessarily be short lived."[36]

Wearily, he resumed his pursuit of the Negley heiress. Tea, idle chitchat, and readings from her scrapbook still formed the entire program at his weekly visits, and the frequent presence of a chaperone cast an added pall over these arid occasions. What was more serious, she continued to deflect his advances toward intimacy. Did she intuit that this self-assured young lawyer was pressing his suit in arrogant expectation of receiving a speedy yes? Did he view their courtship as merely a decorous formality? Whatever the reason, she would give him no hint, pro or con, as to his prospects. It was only when he discovered that her brothers, George and Daniel, were making discreet inquiries about his habits and character that Thomas finally realized the Negleys were taking him seriously.[37]

Even then, he felt increasingly nettled by impatience and uncertainty. With his courtship now in its sixth barren month, he decided to press Sarah Jane for a "yes or no" answer.

> At the very next interview, in the dusk of evening when the clear moonlight was streaming through the curtains, we happened to be left alone for a minute or so—an unusual circumstance. Feeling that now was the time I drew my chair up closer to her than I had ever ventured before and remarked that I supposed she was aware I had not been paying attention to her so long without an object, and that I had some time ago made up my own mind and now wished to know hers, as I was satisfied if she was, to risk the future together. She neither spoke nor gave any sign. I drew her to me and took a kiss unresisted and said that would do, I was satisfied; and left her abruptly, feeling unnerved for conversation.
>
> The die was cast—I had crossed the Rubicon. And that night, as I turned the head of my trusty grey up the lane, now Negley Avenue, and passed the old quarry on the hillside, queer thoughts flitted across my mind of the time I had rested there when a boy on my first journey to the city, when I first contemplated the great meadow and mansion and imagined how proud and happy must be the family which possessed them.[38]

In a typically bruising aside, he admits that, "When I proposed, if I had been rejected I would have left neither sad nor depressed nor greatly disappointed, only annoyed at loss of time."[39] His frigid connivance in courtship may even have drawn some inspiration from the example of Franklin, who casually admits in the *Autobiography* that he dropped his suit for the hand of one woman because her family refused to pay off his debts.[40]

We are left in total darkness about the ceremony that formalized what Mellon calls "the most momentous event of our lives."[41] Where it occurred, whether in church or at home, who attended, who officiated —all this he passes over in silence. In his memoirs, we learn that "the transaction," as he revealingly calls his marriage, "was consummated on the 22d of August, 1843," which was about five weeks after the fateful kiss. With devastating indifference, he adds, "The details of the wedding are uninteresting; all such ceremonies are pretty much alike."[42] If you've seen one, you've seen 'em all.

Some insights can be gained from the details of Isabella Negley's wedding to Dr. Richard Beatty five months earlier. It was probably quite similar to that of her sister, Sarah Jane—"an old-fashioned wedding at the house of the bride's mother with an infare the next day," recalls Mellon, who attended. It is likely that the infare involved a day of food and celebration at the home of the groom and his parents.[43] Both weddings were almost certainly performed by the Rev. William B. McIlvaine, then pastor of East Liberty Presbyterian Church, which Sarah Jane's and Isabella's parents had founded.

John Glogger's oil portrait of Thomas Mellon, signed and dated in 1860, provides a forceful and memorable image of Mellon at this time. The painting is based on a lost photograph, of which only two copy prints survive. To portray the struggling young lawyer of an earlier day, Glogger effectively turns the clock back ten or fifteen years by blackening Thomas's hair and eliminating the other traces of age. More important, he retains the steady, penetrating gaze and redoubtable integrity that resonate from the photograph.

Two days after their marriage, the couple embarked on a wedding tour, as honeymoons were then called. They journeyed by stagecoach to Niagara Falls, descended the Erie Canal on a barge, and were among the very first people to travel from Albany to Boston by train. In New York City, they stayed at the fashionable Astor House hotel and came uptown to walk around the Croton Reservoir, which was situated where the principal New York Public Library now stands. After a

*Painting of Thomas Mellon as a young lawyer, by John Glogger.*
*Courtesy Thomas Mellon Schmidt.*

*An 1848 daguerreotype of Sarah Jane Negley Mellon (1817–1909).*

week in Philadelphia with Uncle Thomas Mellon, the couple set out for Pittsburgh by rail, river, and canal.

When their ferryboat almost plummeted over a dam on the Juniata River, Thomas made a discovery: "In this crisis I first noticed my wife's entire command of her feelings in the suppression of every sign of fear or alarm."[44] As her personality came into sharper focus, Thomas would also discover that his wife was far more generous than he, at least in her benefactions to charitable causes and in support of the Negleys' spiritual fief, East Liberty Presbyterian Church. But most important, she would prove to be the unspoiled, quietly resourceful squaw that he had beaten the bush to find, "a good cook and not in the least averse to work."[45] Sarah Jane's extensive education did not cause her to recoil from playing an overwhelmingly domestic role.

For the first two months of their marriage, the Mellons lived in East Liberty with the bride's widowed mother, Mrs. Jacob Negley. Thomas had evidently disposed of the house he had bought on Penn Avenue two years earlier, for in December 1843 we find him renting both office and living space in a dwelling on Fifth Street, conveniently near the courthouse. By April, the couple had returned to Mrs. Negley's home in the country, and it was there that their first child, Thomas Alexander Mellon, was born, on June 26, 1844.

Less than a year later, when Pittsburgh was ravaged by the Great Fire of 1845, history found in Thomas Mellon an honest, keenly observant, and articulate eyewitness to the only natural disaster that ever threatened to destroy the entire city:

> That catastrophe was of historical interest. It occurred on the 10th of April, a clear but rather windy day; and I was busy between watching my cases on the trial list in court and super-intending the building of a dwelling at the corner of Wylie and Fifth avenues close by the Courthouse. Soon after twelve o'clock the fire bells commenced ringing, but I paid no attention to them for an hour or two until people in an excited condition began hurrying up and down the street declaring the town was

on fire. I then went to a position in the Courthouse from which I could see the lower part of the city, and found the fire was becoming really serious and might eventually reach the boarding house of Miss Jane McLain on Third, between Wood and Smithfield, where we had been boarding during the rough winter weather. I thought it safer to remove our furniture from there to the finished part of the new building. My wife and child were on a visit at the time to our friends in the country. I ordered the carts which I had at work to the boarding house; and so rapid was the progress of the fire that it had already spread all over the district between Ferry and Wood streets, and was crossing Wood street before we had the carts loaded.

As I came up Third to Smithfield people were running in all directions wild with excitement, and cinders and burning shingles were falling everywhere, setting fire to everything combustible. I saw people on Smithfield street actually throwing china and crockery ware out of the upper windows, and carrying beds and bedding down stairs. I unloaded the goods at our new house on the hill, where they were perfectly safe, as there was no other building in the neighborhood except the Courthouse. It was brick yards on one side and open lots on the other all around. I then went upon the roof of the Courthouse, from which the sight was grand and appalling. It was about four o'clock, and the fire had progressed from Ferry street consuming everything between Fourth street and the [Monongahela] river, and was now in its utmost fury approaching Smithfield, surging like a vast flood, devouring dwellings, warehouses and churches, and our great old stone university building with all its contents. In a few minutes it approached the Monongahela House; the flames soon shot into the sky from the entire area of the building, and directly the wooden covered Monongahela bridge was on fire, one span speedily falling into the river after another, like a straw rope on fire, until in about twenty minutes the fire reached the South Side and the structure disappeared. The wind was high

*The Great Pittsburgh Fire of 1845.*
*From* Pittsburgh: The Story of an American City, *by Stefan Lorant.*

and its direction up the river, and the fire swept the entire district between Fourth street and the river, on through what was called Pipetown, as far as there was anything combustible to burn. The whole district, comprising about a quarter part of the then city, was soon reduced to a mass of smoldering coals and ruined walls. . . . The entire destruction was completed by five o'clock.

. . . I remember when on the Courthouse viewing the scene of disaster and contemplating the vast amount of wealth destroyed, that I regarded it at the time as a great calamity to the city and likely to produce a depression in business and hard times; but the result proved I was mistaken in this. Instead of depression it gave an impetus to every kind of business, especially everything in the building line. Mechanics of all kinds flocked in from other places, and all obtained ready employment at better wages than formerly; and new life and increased value was infused into real estate, and rents were higher for several years.[46]

Fire or no fire, Pittsburgh was too tough to die and too necessary to be abandoned. It would be rebuilt on the run, and, as a builder of low-income housing, Thomas Mellon would profit from the upswing in business.

As it turned out, the flames spared his boardinghouse and, more important, the office and home that he had been building at 6 Wylie Street, near Fifth. The family occupied this complex in October 1845, and it was there that my great-grandfather, James Ross Mellon, was born on January 14, 1846, a few months before the death of his namesake, Senator James Ross. Next to arrive was James's sister Emma, born in the Wylie Street home on December 26, 1847.

It may have been at this time that Thomas and Sarah Jane lapsed into the homely, affectionate custom of calling each other "Ma" and "Pa." Looking back on forty years of marriage to Ma, Pa would recall:

Her distant and independent attitude, so well maintained during our preliminary acquaintance, had made me sometimes fear a cold and unsympathetic disposition; but I found her nature quite the contrary, her feelings warm and abiding, but undemonstrative.

I have somewhere seen a division of marriages into two sorts: the one by spontaneity of love beforehand, leaving judgment and discretion to approve or disapprove afterwards; and the other requiring the approval of judgment and discretion in the first place, leaving love to follow.... My marriage was undoubtedly of the latter sort.... There was no love-making and little or no love beforehand ... nothing but a good opinion of worthy qualities, and esteem and respect.... Married as we were however, without any appreciable excitement of the tender passion on my part, I did not continue so, but as the goodness of her heart and mind developed more and more to my comprehension, love did take root and grow, and that steadily to ripe maturity.[47]

# IV

---

## The Taub, Winebiddle, and Negley Fortunes, or *What* Thomas Mellon Married

B ECAUSE AMERICANS TEND TO DEFINE themselves by their accomplishments, they view with near embarrassment the wealth that accrues to them by birth or marriage. Historians would eventually recognize Thomas Mellon as one of the memorable self-made men of the nineteenth century, a leading financier and entrepreneur of his day. That said, a full accounting cannot overlook that he was also a "wife-made" man. He knew that his union with respectable, wealthy Sarah Jane Negley was likely to have a salubrious effect on his destiny. But he was also aware that her possessions and related social position had accrued to her fortuitously by gift and inheritance from her Negley and Winebiddle forebears and ultimately from her great-grandfather, Casper Taub.

Just as the massive oak grows from a tiny acorn, a historic fortune must have its trivial beginning. The acorn from which the Mellon fortune has grown was planted almost 250 years ago. Here it is:

Fort Pitt, November 12, 1762

This is to certify that I have permitted Caspard Taub to clear a plantation at the Four Mile Spring on the old road going to Ligonier, in order to raise provisions for this garrison, and corn for the King's horses, and the conditions of the said grant are that the said Caspard Taub shall pay every year to the command-ing officer at this post for the King's use one third of all the Produces of the said Plantation, horses and cattle excepted, under penalty of forfeiting his improvement to the Crown. Given under my hand as above.

H. Bouquet, Col.
[Commanding officer at Fort Pitt][1]

The farmer Casper Taub must have been one of the earliest German immigrants to settle in western Pennsylvania. The will that he signed on February 19, 1771, is lost, but we know that his daughter, Elizabeth, came to possess the 303 acres granted by Colonel Bouquet, as well as an adjoining 259 acres acquired by her father. Though she would never progress beyond signing her name with an X, Elizabeth Taub was already the eventual heiress to 562 acres in the future Shadyside neigh-borhood of Pittsburgh when she became the teenage bride of Conrad Winebiddle.

Born at Bernzabern, in the German states, on March 11, 1741, Wine-biddle appears to have been of middle-class background and comfort-ably well off.[2] Tradition maintains that he sold the family tannery when his father died, and he immigrated via Connecticut to the Forks of the Ohio, where a small number of hardy German pioneers were attempting to settle. Around 1770, he was operating a tannery in Pitt Township and purveying horses, cattle, and leather goods, including saddles and bridles, to the British Army and other customers.[3]

After the Revolution, he accumulated farms, invested in Pittsburgh building lots on Water, Market, Ferry, and Front streets (all purchased from the Penn family), and built a second tannery on his principal farm—suggestively named "Good Liquor"—which was situated in present-day Lawrenceville, where the Allegheny Arsenal now stands.

His marriage to Elizabeth Taub was fruitful: in 1778 she bore him a daughter, Barbara, who would become Jacob Negley's wife and eventually Thomas Mellon's mother-in-law. Surprisingly, Winebiddle was a slave owner—the only one among the ancestors of the Mellons of Pittsburgh. The will that he signed on September 3, 1795, eight days before his death, confirms him as the statutory possessor of six Negroes. An assistant tanner named Jacob and his wife, Nell, were bequeathed to Winebiddle's widow, who advertised them for sale a month later.[4] Their child, Poll, was willed to the decedent's seventeen-year-old daughter Barbara, who mercifully offered her for sale with her parents, not individually.[5] A second slave couple and their child were also sold as one family.[6] Because the ownership of human beings was being phased out in Pennsylvania, only those born before 1780 would remain slaves unto death. Those born subsequently would become free at the age of twenty-eight.

Conrad Winebiddle's principal bequests to his widow and their children included four houses in Pittsburgh, a tannery, two hundred fruit trees, and three large farms, totaling more than 680 acres. But his other heirlooms tell us more about how he lived: "I also give to my beloved wife Elizabeth, her choice of two of my cows, also a horse, also her bed and furniture, . . . my desk and clock, . . . six pewter plates and six spoons, . . . a duch oven and a ten plate stove, and her tea equipage and a copper kittle, . . . also my negro boy Jacob and my negro girl Nell, also . . . the money that she has gathered by her own industry, amounting to £40 or £50."[7]

By her marriage to Jacob Negley, in June 1795, Conrad Winebiddle's daughter, Barbara, allied herself with a family that is unique in the annals of western Pennsylvania. The Negley (originally Nägeli) family was of Swiss origin but had lived in the vicinity of Frankfurt and Karlsruhe, Germany, for some two hundred years. Though his father, Johann, died on the transatlantic voyage in 1739 and was buried at sea, five-year-old Alexander Negley, his mother Elizabeth, and siblings journeyed to Pennsylvania and began to farm in Bucks County. Drawn by the promise of cheap land, religious freedom, and civil liberties, a steady stream of German Protestant farmers had been settling in Pennsylvania since the founding of William Penn's Commonwealth. These newcomers included "church Germans" of the Lutheran and

(Calvinist) Reformed persuasions as well as adherents to the pacifist sects: Mennonites, Anabaptists, Moravians, Dunkers, Schwenkfelders, and Amish.[8]

As Reformed Germans, the Negleys were not averse to soldiering. Alexander was twenty-four when he served in General John Forbes's campaign to drive the French from Fort Duquesne, which stood on the future site of Pittsburgh.[9] During the Revolution, he farmed near present-day New Florence, in Westmoreland County, and served on the rebel side in Captain Samuel Moorehead's company of rangers.[10] Early in 1778, Seneca and Wyandot Indians invaded Westmoreland County and began burning the settler cabins.[11] Whether they viewed the newcomers as squatting on Indian land or were simply responding to the British offer of a bounty for rebel scalps is not certain.[12] In any case, the Negleys were forced to abandon their homestead. Alexander and his twelve-year-old son, Jacob, traded shots with three Indians in an all-day firefight while Mrs. Negley, who was pregnant, fled with her younger children to Fort Ligonier in a wagon. The historian C. Hale Sipe records the family's harrowing escape in *Fort Ligonier and Its Times*.[13]

Alexander Negley decided to resettle in a more hospitable neighborhood. He acquired 273 acres near the Allegheny River, northeast of Fort Pitt, built a red brick house where the reservoir in Highland Park is now located, and cleared a farm that he named "Fertile Bottom."

Since his disembarkation at Philadelphia, Negley had moved relentlessly westward, following the frontier, always searching to improve his lot by acquiring larger amounts of inexpensive arable land. In this and in his willingness to fight the French, the Indians, and finally the British, he resembled the venturesome, combative Scotch-Irish settlers more than his own immigrant faction, the Germans, who normally settled in segregated communities, put down permanent roots, and were reluctant, if not entirely unwilling, to take up arms. Like Alexander Negley, the Scotch-Irish gave overwhelming support to the rebel cause in the Revolutionary War, and thousands of them fought fiercely for American independence. But Negley's fellow German settlers were more divided in their loyalty. Church Germans normally supported the rebels, though not always sufficiently to engage in the fighting, and a large minority remained loyal to Britain. The pacifist German sects refused to fight on either side.[14]

In June 1795, Alexander Negley's son, Jacob, made his fortuitous marriage to Conrad Winebiddle's daughter, Barbara, and gained control of her fortune. Four years later, Jacob Negley acquired an additional 443 acres in what would become the East End of Pittsburgh, and the combined Negley holdings swelled to 1,500 acres, all situated only an hour and a half's ride to the east of town.[15]

The Taub, Winebiddle, and Negley immigrants measured their wealth in arable land, which they amassed exclusively for the purpose of farming. But year by year, as Pittsburgh expanded eastward, the original military grant to Casper Taub, as well as the later Winebiddle and Negley acquisitions, gifts, and bequests, came to include much of suburban East Liberty and adjacent parts of the East End. A generous portion of this landed wealth eventually devolved on Sarah Jane Negley and was gratefully absorbed by her husband, Thomas Mellon.

The early Mellon fortune took shape in a way that will be familiar to anyone conversant with real estate. We see it repeated in any number of European ski resorts, where two or three families who once owned large farms at the edge of town have become land rich, build condominiums, own the most lucrative local businesses, monopolize the municipal offices, and attempt to form mini-dynasties by encouraging their children to intermarry.

Like the proprietary Penn family, Jacob Negley foresaw that the population of Pittsburgh would expand eastward, turning farmland and woodland into valuable suburbs, and like them he was determined to vigorously exploit that eventuality by becoming what we today would call a developer. But his development plan differed substantially from that of the Penns, for it was not merely a subdivision of land into saleable lots but an integrated, comprehensive effort to establish a community.

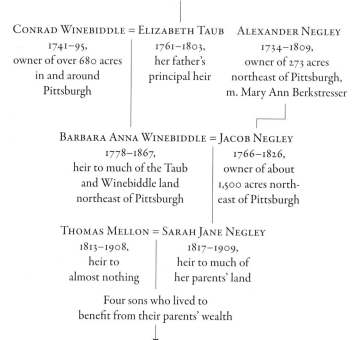

*Growth of the Initial Mellon Fortune through
Gifts, Inheritance, and Marriage*

CASPER TAUB
Will dated February 19, 1771;
received 303 acres, in 1762, by grant from Col. Henry Bouquet,
British commandant of Fort Pitt,
and acquired an additional 259 acres by other means

| CONRAD WINEBIDDLE = ELIZABETH TAUB | | ALEXANDER NEGLEY |
|---|---|---|
| 1741–95, | 1761–1803, | 1734–1809, |
| owner of over 680 acres | her father's | owner of 273 acres |
| in and around | principal heir | northeast of Pittsburgh, |
| Pittsburgh | | m. Mary Ann Berkstresser |

BARBARA ANNA WINEBIDDLE = JACOB NEGLEY
1778–1867,     1766–1826,
heir to much of the Taub     owner of about
and Winebiddle land     1,500 acres north-
northeast of Pittsburgh     east of Pittsburgh

THOMAS MELLON = SARAH JANE NEGLEY
1813–1908,     1817–1909,
heir to     heir to much of
almost nothing     her parents' land

Four sons who lived to
benefit from their parents' wealth

In 1808 Jacob built an L-shaped, two-story, yellow brick house that fronted on the west side of Negley Lane (now North Negley Avenue), just south of its intersection with Country Road (now Stanton Avenue). To highlight his adherence to Freemasonry, he incised a prominent Masonic star on the eastern extension of the house. Though none of his relatives are known to have been Masons, Jacob apparently belonged to the first Masonic lodge west of the Alleghenies, the one founded at Pittsburgh in 1785. He also cut slats in the walls for riflemen to shoot through. This seemed a sensible precaution, for though the Indians had been catapulted from western Pennsylvania some fifteen years earlier, they might return; and he had, after all, come within a hair's breadth of losing his scalp to them at the impressionable age of twelve. With porches on several sides, the house had grand proportions by the standards of that day, and it soon became known as the Negley mansion.

Jacob Negley continued to buy parcels of oak and hickory woodland northeast of Pittsburgh, clear them, and plant them with crops and fruit trees. He had a passion for scientific agriculture, on which he was exceptionally well read; he delighted in horticultural experiments and became about as near to an agronomist as could then be found in western Pennsylvania. Employing his other skills as a civil engineer and surveyor, he laid out a fledgling community named Negleytown at the junction of Frankstown Road and Penn Avenue. It would later come to be known as East Liberty.[16]

He opened a general store and also acquired the familiar roadhouse known as the Black Horse Tavern. So that bread might never be in short supply during the dry summer months, when water-powered mills ceased to function, he engaged the inventor Cadwallader Evans to design for him the first steam-powered gristmill west of the Alleghenies. This was the mill that ten-year-old Thomas Mellon had marveled at. It had been built in 1816 for the mind-boggling sum of about $30,000, and it quickly took pride of place among the industrial novelties that were beginning to appear.[17]

Though raised in the German Reformed Church, Jacob Negley had long since converted to Presbyterianism. As both denominations were founded on Calvin's theology, the change was not so radical. More important, in western Pennsylvania, where social life and business connections depended so heavily on religious affiliation, the creed of Jacob's German ancestors had become a millstone. Other Negleys would also convert to the faith of secular advantage. In Pittsburgh, what was good for business seldom displeased God.

At Negleytown in 1819, Jacob and Barbara Negley donated one and a half acres and built a church that measured forty-four feet on a side. They paid for part of the construction themselves and accepted a note

*The Negley mansion, built by Jacob Negley in 1808.*

from their Scotch-Irish neighbors for the rest.[18] Services were infrequent until 1828, when the congregation was formally organized as East Liberty Presbyterian Church. As was typical, given the Presbyterian emphasis on elementary education, this house of prayer also served as a schoolhouse.[19]

The Negleys' unpretentious brick church came to stand on part of the original land grant to Jacob's wife's grandfather, Casper Taub. Five successive churches would be raised on this site:[20] more than a century later, the Negleys' grandson, Richard Beatty Mellon, would donate the present East Liberty Presbyterian Church, an imposing Gothic cathedral designed by Ralph Adams Cram.

For several years, the development of Negleytown progressed auspiciously. To improve his connections with Pittsburgh, Jacob widened the main access route, Penn Avenue, to one hundred feet where it traversed his own land. He understood the bearing of transportation on land values: he was a director of the Pittsburgh & Greensburg Turnpike Company and had obtained its charter. For credit he could rely on the Farmers' and Mechanics' Bank, of which he was also a director.

Jacob Negley's development was the Mellon family's first vertically and horizontally integrated business. Decades later, his grandsons, Andrew, Richard, James, and Tom Mellon, would operate integrated building businesses, in which they or their father, Thomas Mellon, owned not only the construction sites but also a yard that supplied lumber, two small private banks to make construction loans and purchase mortgages, and the mines that would supply coal to heat the newly built houses. Still later Jacob Negley's great-grandson William Larimer Mellon would build the Gulf Oil Corporation as an integrated business, with exploration, extraction, piping, refining, shipping, and marketing all under the aegis of a single company. The founding of neatly integrated businesses would become a recurring strategy in the expansion of the Mellon fortune.

But for all his vision and initiative, Jacob Negley would reap only a harvest of dry leaves. To finance Negleytown, he had borrowed heavily against his real estate and had left himself vulnerable to precisely the kind of economic contraction that occurred in 1819. The Panic of that year, which almost swept Andrew Mellon's mortgaged farm away, left Negley's development hopelessly encumbered with debt. He struggled on courageously for seven more years but died a ruined man, his property under court administration and the sheriff's notice nailed to his door.

All that saved Jacob's widow, Barbara, and her children from poverty was the timely intervention of a wise and magnanimous family friend. James Ross, who had represented Pennsylvania in the U.S. Senate from 1794 to 1803 and had served as Jacob Negley's lawyer, took pity on the beleaguered family and offered legal advice and strong financial support. Whenever the payment of some particular debt required the sheriff to auction off a parcel of Negley land, Ross would

*U.S. Senator James Ross (1762–1847).*

purchase the property and then permit Mrs. Negley and her children to continue farming on it. He charged no fee for these saving interventions or for his professional advice.

When normal economic conditions at last returned, he sold only enough of the former Negley land to recoup his own investment plus 6 percent yearly interest and gave the family title to all remaining property. For his extraordinary generosity, James Ross won such gratitude from the Negley family that Sarah Jane and Thomas Mellon named one of their sons James Ross Mellon.[21] And that is how I also came to bear the name of Senator Ross, the white knight of the Negleys.

Thomas Mellon would write that Ross's power to address juries in "clear and simple words" would never be surpassed. He also admired him for his prodigious workload and for the "large fortune" he accumulated from only "modest fees" and from "investing and reinvesting his earnings with great care and attention."[22] Ross's ascent from powerless anonymity through ascending levels of the law and through profitable investments to wealth, establishment, and renown was conspicuously similar to the trajectory that Thomas Mellon would follow.

The Negley family emerged from a decade of dashed hopes and deflated real estate prices with about five hundred acres of prime real estate, most of it cleared and arable. In 1837, Ross divided the property into eight shares, one for each of Jacob Negley's children or their survivors. According to Thomas Mellon, Sarah Jane Negley received about $50,000 worth of land (equivalent to about $1.13 million today).[23] The Negleys also managed to keep their "mansion."

# V

Home Life on Negley Lane,
Raising the Mellon Boys

*The gift I would desire is your confidence,—to trust all your secrets to me;
to keep nothing back; to confide in me all your troubles and desires and
all your hopes, fears and plans; to consult freely with me about everything
without fear or backwardness; making me your most intimate friend—
never deceiving; always relying on me for sympathy and advice for what
you do wrong as well as for what you do right.*

IN HIS MEMOIRS, THOMAS MELLON gives the reader some glimpses
of himself as a young lawyer and briefly describes the professional side
of his life. But he hastens to add that his private life was vastly more
important: "All through those busy years of professional and judicial
labors my heart was in my home; it was there I was happy, and there my
feelings centered. When married and settled, the outlines of my destiny
were fixed and nothing more to project regarding them: it was now only
left to carry out the programme, to work and await developments."[1]

The "programme" was to raise a family, make money, and establish
a congenial home. As the clamor of children dispelled the silence of
his bachelor years, Thomas persisted with undiminished vigor in the
quest for which his native talents and immutable character had so
admirably suited him: the safe, steady, satisfying, delicious accumulation of wealth.

By marrying Sarah Jane, Mellon had multiplied his net worth severalfold, and though he persisted in all of his former business activities, he now conducted them on a grander scale. His incessant speculation in debt instruments was henceforth entrusted to professional brokers. And whereas his early real estate deals had amounted to little more than buying, improving, and reselling individual properties, he now became a contractor and landlord.[2]

With housing in short supply and rents holding at high levels in consequence of the 1845 fire, Mellon the lawyer made time for a parallel profession. In 1846, he erected eighteen small dwellings that he rented out at 10 percent of cost and eventually sold at a profit.[3] He would continue to build, buy, rent out, and sell single-family houses and would eventually give each of his sons a start in the building and real estate businesses. James Ross Mellon would accumulate most of his fortune as a developer of real estate and purveyor of construction supplies, especially lumber. Trading in debt instruments, speculation in land, legal fees, and of course acquisition of wealthy through marriage had all become pillars of the nascent Mellon fortune. Construction, development, and landlording now began to contribute as well.

That these activities are related to the ownership of land highlights a salient truth about Thomas Mellon: He had grown up in a personal, intimate backwater of rural Pennsylvania, where farmers hailed each other across the fences and dwelt within riding distance of small villages peopled by storekeepers and craftsmen who lived as friends and neighbors. Simple, open, and abundant, preindustrial America would remain his homeland of the heart. He would retreat only gradually and with trepidation from the Jeffersonian view that land is the only dependable form of wealth—the tangible, safe investment.

To the end of his days, land would hold no terrors for him: land, blanketed with crops or underlaid with coal; land, on which to build row houses crammed wall to wall; land, immovably, defiantly situated in the path of progress, which would therefore have to appreciate; land, which at worst muddles through.

The Industrial Revolution was meanwhile transforming Pittsburgh's rural character with a vengeance. Where the Allegheny and Monongahela rivers join to form the Ohio, smokestacks were sprouting like venomous mushrooms. Mills, factories, forges, and steamboats now blackened the air with coal smoke and yellowed the water with toxins. The damage inflicted by industry arrived early in the city that would become the world's steel factory by 1890. Already in 1829, a visitor to Pittsburgh noted that "after traveling for two weeks through white, clean cheerful-looking villages and towns, to come all at once upon dirty streets and dark, filthy looking houses stretching away in rows continuously ahead and enveloped in an atmosphere of smoke and soot which blackened everything in sight, was not a pleasant transition."[4]

In *Devastation and Renewal*, Joel Tarr leaves a graphic pen portrait of Pittsburgh at midcentury:

> Commercial activity focused on the busy Monongahela wharf, a mudflat stretching down to the river, while urban development spread across the point of land formed by the convergence of the Allegheny and Monongahela Rivers. Organized by a gridiron street plan and the centering of trade around the wharf, the city featured artisan shops, inns and taverns, small offices, and residences, which were crammed densely into the confined space. Only church spires and steamboat stacks broke the uniformly low skyline of two- and three-story brick and frame buildings. Small industries occupied the riverfronts around the edges of the settlement core. More rapid economic and population growth after 1830, especially after the opening of the terminal basins of the Pennsylvania Main Line Canal, pushed new manufacturing firms up both the Allegheny and Monongahela floodplains and across these rivers.[5]

About fifteen thousand people were living within two miles of the Monongahela wharf.

The galloping rot of industrialization intruded with increasing malignancy on the life of Thomas Mellon and his family, living in the inner city. He soon began to notice how much happier and more refreshed Sarah Jane appeared to be whenever she returned from visiting her mother in East Liberty. He also understood that his three young children needed an outdoor play area. These considerations argued persuasively for his living in the country, even if it required him to commute to his office on Wylie Street.[6]

East Liberty, which encompassed the former Negleytown, was still reassuringly rural in 1850—a suburb where people breathed air that had not just passed through a furnace, enjoyed privacy from their neighbors, grew vegetables, kept flower gardens, and felt sheltered from the increasing filth and clamor of Pittsburgh. Yes, Thomas Mellon had heaved his axe over the fence, but he knew the healthy aspects of farm life. To raise his family on fresh fruit, fresh vegetables, and meat from his own yard was an ideal he had learned on the farm; although he had necessarily deviated from it, he had never abandoned it. Farming has its advantages, especially if someone else can be hired to do the donkey work, and he could now afford a gardener. He also wanted an orchard: experimenting with raising the finest, healthiest fruit trees became a lifelong a passion. A strong case could be made for relocating to East Liberty, and in May 1848 Mellon moved his family into a cottage that belonged to Mrs. Negley and was situated on the west side of Negley Lane. Whatever misgivings he may have had about living across the street from his mother-in-law were quickly dispelled:

My motherinlaw combined the qualities of a wise, affectionate and self-sacrificing mother with first-class business ability and judgment, without in the least impairing the refined manner of the lady. Her business management of their [the Negleys'] extensive property was admirable; and she was not only a worker, but a reader and thinker . . . a kind mother possessed of superior qualities and sound, practical good sense—one whose ruling passion was the welfare of her children. . . . And what is unusual between the motherinlaw and soninlaw, her society was always agreeable, and from the time that I entered the family, in 1843, till the day of her death at my house, in 1867, not the slightest unpleasantness or misunderstanding ever occurred between us.[7]

At the cottage the Mellon children entered and left the world in quick succession. The family's life was darkened when three-year-old Emma died of congenital heart disease on December 3, 1850, but the shadows lightened when Rebecca was born on January 26, 1851. Darkness returned with her death from dysentery on August 8, 1852, but again gave way to light with the birth of Selwyn on February 11, 1853. As Thomas recalled: "The fondest of my early dreams were now becoming a reality as fortune smiled and children were born, and their young minds and affections began to open like buds in early spring time. Infancy however, beyond the natural affection it excites, was never very attractive to me. It is only after the child begins to look about it and wonder at what it sees, and ask those curious questions which philosophy cannot answer, and to give its own fresh views and opinions on subjects which puzzle older heads, that it becomes intensely interesting."[8]

Thomas enjoyed his years at the Negley cottage, "a delightful home nestled in the midst of a plot of shrubbery and fruit trees."[9] But deep down, he knew only one option would satisfy him. "I was of a disposition which could only be contented in a home absolutely my own," he insists, and in 1850 he began to build the dream nest that would embody his domestic longings.[10] The building site was on a gradual slope that shelved from Negley Lane on the east, upward to the base of rocky, wooded Black Horse Hill. The new Mellon home was built beside the Negley cottage on a gift of land from Sarah Jane's mother. It was a large white, two-story house, with green shutters, and a gabled roof punctured by several brick chimneys. Although not deliberately oversized, it had a substantial, proprietary appearance; but Mellon aptly describes it as "modest in style, without any ostentation in architectural adornments; planned for comfort and convenience, but harmonious to the eye and in conformity with the fundamental principles of good taste."[11] Built as a pre-Victorian clapboard house, it was bricked over well before 1900.

His recollections of life and decor at the Negley "mansion" probably influenced him, for the home he had found there during his courtship was similar to the one he would create: "Neither too coarse nor too fine: country life and reality blended with the refinements of wealth and education."[12] What he specifically wanted to avoid was an appearance that resonated with "the spirit of shoddyocracy common among those grown suddenly rich."[13]

From the vestibule, a visitor turning to the right would enter a small sitting room where family members could linger and chat with friends or relatives. On the opposite side of the vestibule was the parlor, which was almost never used and lay shuttered in sepulchral darkness. Straight ahead from the front door lay a staircase that led to the second-floor bedrooms and a hallway, with the dining room on the right and the library or study on the left. Paneled in dark wood, the study generated a gloom that Thomas Mellon must have found congenial, for it was to this sanctum that he increasingly retreated. There he would sit by the fireplace in the simple country rocker that had belonged to his mother and read, converse with visitors, or simply think.

We do not know how the Mellons initially decorated their new home. The decor evolved over time, as the family became wealthier, their tastes changed, and fashions supplanted one another. By 1880, a somber formality prevailed on the ground floor. Here the rooms were of generous size, with high ceilings, ponderous drapes, and thick carpets. Much of the furniture was bulky, somber, and Victorian. Scotch-Irish severity expunged the joy of life. A photograph taken in the much-frequented study reveals a print of two Scottish grouse hanging over the fireplace—mute testimony that all through the house, wall space was inexpensively filled with nondescript lithographs and engravings. Art received an indifferent welcome in this nest. If Andrew W. Mellon became a lover of old master paintings, it had nothing to do with growing up here.

*The house Thomas Mellon built in 1851 on Negley Lane,*
*later 401 North Negley Avenue.*

On the second floor, wallpapered bedrooms with plain country furniture, wooden floors, and occasional throw rugs fostered an atmosphere that was snugly labyrinthine.[14] The house had fireplaces upstairs and down that burned either wood or coal. Visitors who stumbled into the kitchen unawares were dumbfounded by its Homeric proportions and by the gargantuan brick stove. At first there was only one bathtub, a huge metal contraption which, according to William Larimer Mellon, "looked like it was made for the Loch Ness Monster."[15] Farm customs die hard, and Thomas Mellon frequently ate in his kitchen. It was there, and not in the ceremonious dining room, that he celebrated his sixtieth birthday.[16]

Six generations of the Mellon family would occupy the home on Negley Lane (later 401 North Negley Avenue) until it was demolished in 1955. William Larimer Mellon, who was born there in 1868, recalls his birthplace:

When I first knew my grandfather's house, every kind of activity associated with a farm, including the slaughtering and dressing of hogs, was regularly carried on there. Yet it was not really a farm but a country house. Already, before my time, they had started burning kerosene instead of whale oil in the parlor lamps; and the candle molds had been relegated from the kitchen to the cellar. They still used kitchen grease, not for candles but to make soap.

My grandmother [Sarah Jane] ran the home. But, since she likewise had duties to her church and to charity, she kept control of the household through old Mrs. Cox, who was called house-keeper. . . . There were a number of servant girls at my grand-father's house because there was a vast amount of household work at that time of little or no plumbing. The staff, which Mrs. Cox headed, included old Harriet, who was a kind of principal maid, supervising the chamberwork of lesser maids.

My grandfather had a passionate interest in horticulture. . . . A concern for all the processes of Nature, of life, was burning inces-santly in his strong mind. Experimenting with trees and bushes excited him and he was forever planning for and further develop-ing the productiveness of the 25 or 30 acres of the home place.[17]

Thomas Mellon's home remained the nerve center of Mellon family life until his death in 1908. During the 1850s and '60s, the four family feast days—Thanksgiving, Christmas, New Year's Day, and the all-important double birthday of Thomas and Sarah Jane, both born on February 3—were unfailingly celebrated there. Later, Tom and James, who had built houses next door and across the street, hosted the Christmas and Thanksgiving feasts.

When Thomas and Sarah Jane Mellon set up housekeeping on Neg-ley Lane in 1851, decisions had to be made about the education of five-year-old James and seven-year-old Tom. There were public schools in East Liberty by then, but the father saw them as infested with "too many of that misgoverned or neglected class of children, outcasts as it were from the parental and moral influences of a happy home, whose parents govern them in a manner calculated to produce defiance and disregard. Frequently coarse and low by nature, this class of schoolboy rejoices in vulgarity, disobedience, and contempt for study. Such associates are injurious to those of gentle and higher nature."[18]

No doubt. But, in Thomas Mellon's case, the fear of moral contamination cut far deeper. It proceeded from a puritanical phobia that also extended into other areas of life. He feared infective depravity in the U.S. Army, which he vehemently discouraged his sons from joining, when the Civil War broke out. He perceived it in democracy itself: hence the foreboding that always suffuses his meditations on popular government. At heart, he feared the "common people" themselves. He was a nineteenth-century Ulsterman—quite an extreme one, in fact—and the mere contemplation of democracy conjured up nightmares of the "wild Catholic natives" running amok along the Strule and screeching for Protestant blood.[19] In Ireland's fractured social landscape, were *they* not the majority, the feared and hated commons from whom popular government must always emanate? Was democracy not somehow analogous to government of the Catholics, by the Catholics, and for the Catholics? Far from perceiving any collective wisdom in the "common people," he was unalterably determined to protect himself and his family from what he perceived as their contagious lack of character.

There were also private schools, "pay schools," in East Liberty, and he permitted his sons to attend some of them, but never for very long. He feared that where teachers were dependent on parental goodwill, few of them would use enough force to bring the most disruptive students to heel. Haunted, as ever, by the specter of invasive dissolution, he resorted to drastic measures, built a little schoolhouse on the grounds beside his home and devised what he believed to be the ideal curriculum. James and Tom attended this school together; his younger sons Andrew and Selwyn would do so later. A number of well-behaved children from the neighborhood were also permitted to attend. A teacher, Mr. Taylor, was hired, but Thomas Mellon supervised the instruction himself.[20]

> The studies were such as would be most necessary and useful in the subsequent business of life; and the method was to train the pupil in the best way calculated to produce thoroughness in whatever was studied. In arithmetic, for instance, I required the pupil to depend on the rules which had gone before for the solution of what was presently to be resolved. . . . I would not have the teacher to assist otherwise than by referring to and requiring him to repeat and explain the preceding rules, thus leading the mind of the pupil up to a solution of the difficulty; never to permit him to proceed a single step without a thorough understanding and mastery of what had gone before.[21]

James, who kept a diary when he was eleven and twelve, writes of attending classes in his father's backyard schoolhouse, of reading the Bible, doing his homework, attending nighttime classes in astronomy, blacking Pa's shoes, and struggling fitfully to master Ma's ancestral tongue, German. But he also alludes to regular bouts of farm work: hauling sand, hoeing potatoes, hammering in his father's smithy, and feeding the chickens.[22]

That the Mellon brothers who survived to maturity would all become businessmen leaves little doubt as to the line of work their father groomed them for. He acknowledges, however, that some young men lack the particular talents for business and insists that everyone must patiently search for the occupation that nature has predisposed him to follow. "He must rise or fall, or flounder about till he finds his proper place. . . . The great misfortune to thousands is, they never find out what they are good for, or not till after great sacrifice of time and energy."[23]

His Franklinian horror of time wasting opposed him to teaching a prospective business student anything that would soon fade from memory for lack of use, such as the classics or special sciences.[24]

Granted, but what formal education *does* a student of business require? That Thomas Mellon terminated the schooling of his five sons while they were yet teenagers and instead thrust them directly into fledgling enterprises confirms that he regarded formal education as of minimal importance for business success. Of the Mellon boys, only Richard obtained a college degree, by graduating from the Western University of Pennsylvania. In 1876, Andrew would have graduated from the same institution but decided, or was persuaded, to drop out; James was withdrawn from college by his father; Tom and George were never enrolled. Instead, with a loan from Pa, eighteen-year-old Tom opened a nursery and landscaping business. At nineteen James leased the Oceola Coal Works from his father and then teamed up with Tom in a real estate, lumber, and building-supply business that they named Mellon Brothers. Similarly, Andrew, Richard, and George were put to work, starting in their teens, in construction firms that their father established for them but continued to partially own. His eldest grandson, William L. Mellon, was withdrawn from school at seventeen and installed as a shipping clerk in the family's lumberyard, his schooling and adolescence terminated. Their stories confirm that Thomas Mellon deliberately truncated the carefree teenage period in the lives of his sons not merely to teach them business skills and accustom them to heavy responsibilities during their formative years but, more subtly, to prevent them from developing their pubescent desires into distractions that might have led them astray from the business of life, which was, after all, *business.*

"Make no intimate, confidential friends till you know the private, moral character," he wrote in 1863 to seventeen-year-old James, who, with other unruly students at Jefferson College, had torn up the boardwalk and rolled a fire engine over an embankment on Halloween night. "Make no friends, that is companions of theater-going, party-going, or young men who talk of the pleasure of company and the like; not that such things are so bad in themselves as the influences and connections and temptations they bring about. Remember you are yet very inexperienced and remember particularly [Robert] Burns's advice to a young man [see *Epistle to a Young Friend*]. I think you committed it to memory. . . . What I most fear [is] placing you among strangers with so little experience."[25]

After two months, James received a follow-up letter in which his father summarized: "You have no idea now, but you will have in after life, of the vast importance in all respects to a man's happiness and prosperity to have a pure, moral character free from vice and bad habits of all kinds and to be truthful, honest and honorable in all respects."[26] To which he might have added "like me."

In a third letter, the father's puritanism runs completely amok:

Pittsburgh, January 27, 1864

Dear James:

. . . My anxiety is chiefly in regard to the company you keep. . . . Some of your companions may be weak, foolish men of good intentions but wrong notions, and they are frequently the most agreeable companions and always the most dangerous. I am not afraid of you willfully and knowingly contracting bad habits, such as drinking, smoking or loafing about stores and gallanting girls or running to parties and visiting around among young people, but unless you are careful, you get led into some of them. Indeed, I have never warned you enough against female company keeping. I know nothing which so unfits a young man for manly serious studies and business, and it is worse than useless. No man but a fool will think of marrying till he is over twenty-five years of age and in proper situation to keep a family, and for any other use in the way of company, female society is injurious. It is mostly excused on the plea of refining the manners, but this is all bosh. I have never yet seen a young man who kept up the practice that it did not make a fop or trifler of himself. . . . It is all proper to treat female company when necessarily thrown into it with proper manly politeness, but what character is more odious to males or females than a ladies' man. Both sexes despise him and no wonder. He is necessarily a trifler and intruder. What business has he hanging around girls that he can't or has no intention of marrying—perhaps exciting vain expectations on their part only to be disappointed, which is dishonorable. . . .

Another bad habit which I suppose you have shunned since making a fool of yourself and being talked about for it while at [Jefferson College in] Canonsburg is writing letters to girls. This is even worse than keeping company with them occasionally, because it is more serious and is a great injury to the girl. Who wants a wife that has been writing love letters to every fellow, and all such letters are love letters, disguise them as you will. . . . No one who has not an actual, sensible intention of marrying can write such letters honestly and read them a month afterwards and not see that he was either a fool or a deceiver.

I have not warned you sufficiently against this habit because you are so young as not to be in danger of falling into it; but now that you are among strangers, it is different, and especially when a boy has little to do, he is in the more danger. If a boy is busy, he is not likely to run about much. . . .

Your father,

Thos. Mellon[27]

Thomas Mellon was straining to limit James's social life so narrowly that one has to wonder how the boy avoided becoming a hermit or a complete libertine. And because such moral instruction was not available in schools, the father strove to indoctrinate his sons at home, in frequent, earnest conversations between parent and child. Speaking of James and Tom, he recalls:

I secured free admission to their confidence from the first, and participated in all their plans; and [more significantly!] in return secured their willing co-operation in my purposes for their benefit. . . . It was with the deepest interest and pleasure that in evenings at home, and in our Sunday walks and talks in the fields and woodlands, I would explore and forecast from the views and sentiments expressed in their free and joyous utterances the manner of men they were to become. . . . It was my care to learn their bent and inclination in order to lead it in the right direction. In this way before they were sixteen years of age I had fully discovered what pursuits or calling they were fitted for. . . . I soon discovered they were out and out business men.[28]

Which is precisely what he wanted to discover. Manual occupations were not encouraged. When young Tom and James expressed a passing fancy for becoming blacksmiths, Pa was crafty enough not to say no. He merely shifted their activities away from the village smithy to one in his own backyard, and left the boys to sweat and hammer there, with blackened faces, until they had had enough.[29]

In his memoirs, he persuades himself that he had encouraged his sons to patiently search for the vocations that their individual talents and personalities had best suited them for. But in reality, he had tirelessly schemed to narrow their range of occupational choices to the most profitable and respectable forms of business. If one of his sons had opted for a career in the arts, the ministry, the military, teaching, writing, farming, politics, philanthropy, or any low-salaried pursuit, Thomas would have viewed that son as a failure and himself as a failed parent.

Just as a kennel owner breeds for certain characteristics in puppies, so Thomas Mellon, ever the fierce eugenicist, was breeding sons who would be predisposed and properly trained to become businessmen. And because the father understood that to narrowly direct the destinies of his sons would require him to win and retain their confidence, he asked eighteen-year-old Tom and sixteen-year-old James for the ultimate Christmas present—something they had already given him but which a parent cannot ask for too often.

Christmas Evening, Dec. 25, 1862.

Thomas and James.

My dear Sons:

There is a Christmas gift which I would prize more than all things, but I am afraid to ask you for it lest you should be unwilling to give it or should promise and afterwards fail to perform.

The gift I would desire is your confidence,—to trust all your secrets to me; to keep nothing back; to confide in me all your troubles and desires and all your hopes, fears and plans; to consult freely with me about everything without fear or backwardness; making me your most intimate friend—never deceiving; always relying on me for sympathy and advice for what you do wrong as well as for what you do right.

This idea is well expressed by a poet who had the true feelings of a good and kind father. He wrote as follows:

"Oh, Children—happy word of peace—my jewels and my gold,
My truest friends till now, and still my truest friends when old;
I will be everything to you, your playmate and your guide,
Your Mentor and Telemachus forever at your side;
I will be everything to you, your sympathizing friend,
To teach, and help, and lead, and bless, and comfort and defend;
Come to me and tell me all, and you shall find me true,
A brother in adversity to fight it out for you!
Your sins or follies, griefs or cares, or young affections thrall;
Fear not for I am one with you and I have felt them all.
I will be tender, just and kind, unwilling to reprove;
I will do all to bless you all, by wisdom and by love."

You are now approaching to manhood—the time when all boys are in greatest danger, and by having your free and full confidence, I would be able to help and encourage, or to save you from temptations and perhaps deliver you sometimes from evil.

Don't give me this pledge, however, till you think over the matter well. Deliberate on it whether if you promise you will be able to keep your promise in good faith; it would be better not to promise than to promise and not live up to it. To promise and then deceive me, or hold back everything except what I should ask you about, or to keep back things you supposed might displease me would hurt me far more than if now you should refuse to give the pledge. I don't ask it at all if you don't feel able to perform it with free heart and good will; and at any rate I don't ask it for more than one year, when you will be free to renew the promise or not as you please.

Your father.[30]

As to the role of coercion in child rearing:

I had a high opinion of the strict exercise of parental authority. I had heard so much about the necessity of coercion and chastisement in the proper training of children, when necessary for their future good, and my desire was so strong to bring them up in the right way that at the outset I was in danger of overdoing the business in that line; but before long I found out my mistake, and that parental government must be tempered to suit the nature of the child. With wise, confiding and gentle natures severity is injurious. A child keenly perceives and resents injustice, and this resentment destroys parental influence for good. There are many no doubt whose evil desires or wayward proclivities must be subdued, and who require to be governed by a strong hand, and on whom kindness is ineffectual. It is one of the most delicate and important duties of the parent to determine, and firmly but kindly pursue the course best adapted to the disposition.[31]

What lends such modernity to the foregoing ruminations is that Mellon understood, more than a century ago, how parental efforts at child rearing are limited by the immutable genetic factors that are now known to determine the broad outlines of every individual personality. "The foundation for good or evil is laid in the child's nature," Mellon wrote. "If that is low, gross and sensual, with appetites or passions of any kind disproportionately strong, or the intellect weak and stupid, very little modification or improvement can be produced by either training or example. The want of wise parental influence and training may destroy what would otherwise become a good and useful character; but the best training never can supply the want of natural qualities and good disposition."[32]

Mellon saw the triumph of good genes in his sons' future: "The fact is, each individual is a mosaic work of his ancestry. His character and qualities are made up of shreds of this one and patches of that, among his progenitors. The sciences of biology and psychology are but in their infancy, and yet they disclose wonders in this direction. . . . It is discovered beyond question that both physical and moral qualities and characteristics run in the blood and are transmitted for many generations."[33]

The Romans had their gods of the hearth. The Mellons had Benjamin Franklin. In Thomas Mellon's home, the influence of the wise and frugal Philadelphian settled on everyone like a fine dust. William L. Mellon, who was reared in the Mellon home at 401 Negley, had this to say:

My grandfather revered Benjamin Franklin above all men and Franklin's name frequently was on his lips. . . . On my twenty-first birthday, Grandfather's gift to me was a copy of the "Autobiography of Benjamin Franklin." So that statue [of Franklin] in the [Mellon] bank today may be regarded as an image representing an influence that guided us. . . . Franklin became a sort of genie of the Mellon family. I cannot exaggerate this influence. Andrew W. Mellon, to the end of his life, often charted himself through strange situations with a compass needle that was no more than a question to himself: "What would Father do?" The Judge would have done, by ingrained habit and the structure of his character, pretty much what his revered Franklin would have done.[34]

As we have seen, the method by which Thomas Mellon launched his sons and elder grandsons into business amounted to total immersion at a startlingly early age. It was a strategy that relied on the premature, and therefore flattering, delegation of adult responsibility to mere teenagers, and he describes how it accelerated their natural transition to manhood:

As a general rule parents, especially such as are in easy circumstances or engaged in extensive enterprises, hold their children at too great a distance from them. They underrate their capacity for comprehension and judgment, and do not admit them close enough in their confidence. The boy readily perceives and sympathizes with his father in his cares and troubles and plans and projects. This feeling must be encouraged by kindness and confidence, to make him feel that he is regarded as of sufficient importance to be relied on. Under this treatment he seldom fails to appreciate the regard shown for him, or to fulfill the parents' hopes. His pride and self esteem sustain him in the line of duty; and he can be influenced and confirmed in the way of well doing better by this than by any other method that I have ever observed. Make your child a partner in your joys and sorrows, your hopes and fears; impart your plans and purposes. . . . You will be surprised to find out how much a five or ten year old boy can understand of the ways of men, and how readily he will enter into your views. Your feelings will attach him, and you will be gratified at the strength of character and good resolution you will inspire in him by such treatment. It produces a bond of affection between you that is not easily broken, and affords you an opportunity of insight into your child's nature which is not otherwise attainable. I experienced the benefit of such training myself, and applied it in raising my own family with the most satisfactory results.[35]

Typically, Thomas Mellon would establish one or two of his teenage sons in an enterprise that he himself still partially or fully owned. He would loan them the capital to get started and would give them full power to make business decisions. He would follow their progress with intense interest but always from a discreet distance. While unfailingly generous with advice, he was determined not to cross the nebulous line between counsel and interference. To meddle would have been counterproductive.

On one point he remained inflexible: his sons were to make their loan payments to him in full and precisely on schedule. There would be no extensions. The uncommon strictness with which his mother-in-law, Mrs. Negley, insisted on timely repayment of any loans made to her own children had at first struck him as severe. But he had come to share her conviction that family members succumb more readily than outsiders to becoming deadbeats. The ease with which familial affection can be manipulated to prevent collection does pose a temptation.[36]

"In most families," recalls William L. Mellon, "the imposition of such responsibility on a boy would be regarded as unthinkable, but in the Mellon family this was precisely the way boys were developed."[37] He also observed: "Each of the Mellon boys in turn was helped to get some kind of special opportunity. However, instead of making it easy for his sons in the beginning, Judge Mellon's way was to demand of them stiffer terms than he would have asked of any others with whom he entered into a business relationship."[38]

Mellon might have left the rearing of a daughter to his wife, if either of their daughters had lived, but the sons were clearly his to educate. Likewise, he routinely made business decisions affecting his wife's personal fortune, which at first was greater than his own. Sarah Jane's time was absorbed by the supervisory functions of an established

Pittsburgh wife: watching over the household and kitchen, giving family meals, overseeing the care of babies, and participating in charitable activities, especially those of East Liberty Presbyterian Church. She was also a good cook and an accomplished baker.

In his work *Domestic Revolutions, A Social History of American Family Life,* Steven Mintz describes the modern or "democratic" family that began to supplant the colonial family after the Revolutionary War, and with continuing modifications, is still common today. "The democratic family," he writes, "was characterized by a form of marriage that emphasized companionship and mutual affection, by a more intense concern on the part of parents with the proper upbringing of children, and by a new division of sex roles, according to which the husband was to be the family's breadwinner and the wife was to specialize in child rearing and home making. Mutual affection and a sense of duty provided the basis for the democratic family's existence."[39] The family that Thomas Mellon and Sarah Jane Negley raised fitted this paradigm quite closely.

In their marriage, the husband's personality is preserved in *Thomas Mellon and His Times,* in his correspondence, and in the public record. By contrast, the portrait of Sarah Jane, who receives surprisingly short shrift in the postmarital chapters of her husband's memoir, has faded but remains discoverable. From the surviving scraps of evidence it is possible to bring her into sharper focus.

"Ma" was a stolid woman of Germanic background, unpretentious, friendly and generous, covertly sentimental, usually undemonstrative but given to occasional snippets of hearty humor. She held herself under firm control, was unflappable and formidably efficient, sometimes quite stubborn, but strictly conscientious. She had studied botany in school and shared with her husband a lifelong interest in horticulture. But notwithstanding her advanced education, Sarah Jane did not ache with intellectual curiosity as her husband did; instead she took quiet satisfaction in the discharge of her domestic and communal functions. She lacked the Judge's brilliance but was not hobbled by his frequent pessimism, distrust, and doubt. Exuberance, which is not a puritan gift, eluded both husband and wife, but their marriage appears to have been firmly grounded on similar values and tastes—a union in which differences of character were complementary rather than frictional.[40]

"I can remember the quality of their voices," recalled William.

> My grandfather's voice was a very moderate voice. His tendency was to speak low. . . . He was very gentle, but when he would get aroused he had all kinds of fire in him. . . . My grandmother, her voice was a little stronger . . . a little bit sharper. . . . She had a little blue in her eyes. . . . When I knew her, her hair was gray. It had been dark.
>
> She was an unusually kind person but a very energetic woman. Very energetic. She ran the house. She had some servants, but she was the main engineer by a long shot . . . was a tremendous worker . . . walked fast . . . one of those people who put up apple butter and everything else, all the same day . . . just a regular worker. She was very friendly always, and would bake cake for you or anything of that kind.[41]

Thomas and Sarah Jane had eight children. Emma and Rebecca were the only daughters, and both died in early childhood. Known as Tom or "T.A.," the eldest son, Thomas Alexander, would die of cancer in 1899 at the age of fifty-four. Of the three brothers that survived to old age, the eldest was James Ross (1846–1934), named for the venerable U.S. senator. In 1853, Selwyn became the first of four sons to be born in the Mellon home on Negley Lane. He died there of diphtheria nine years later. The sixth child was Andrew William, 1855–1937, the prodigious "A.W.," named for his paternal grandfather and for his granduncle, William Mellon, who had died young. Known as "Dick" or "R.B.," Richard Beatty (1858–1933) was named for the doctor who had led Thomas Mellon to the woman he would marry. The youngest was George Negley, named for his maternal uncle. Born in 1860, he would die at the age of twenty-seven, after years of illness.

Death paid frequent visits to the family. Between 1850 and 1899, Thomas Mellon would suffer the loss of his parents, his mother-in-law, his only brother, all three of his sisters, and five of his eight children. His father, Andrew, died at the age of seventy-one:

His health began to fail early in 1856. . . . For nearly six months before the end he was unable to work from sheer debility; his appetite was impaired and sleep rendered difficult. He did not complain of pain or suffering, but only excessive weakness and fatigue. . . . And towards the last, whilst yet able to walk about, he often earnestly expressed a wish for death, and rest in the grave. . . . His mind was perfectly clear up to the last moment. . . . To him death's approach had no terrors; in fact, in the many death-bed scenes I have witnessed I have never seen it otherwise. Nature does her work quietly and peacefully, and leaves the mind to amuse itself with its ordinary thoughts and purposes until the torpor of death closes the scene.[42]

As for his mother, Rebecca: "The immediate cause of her death was an asthmatic affection, which grew upon her in her last years and pre-cipitated what debility of age was preparing; and when the end came, with seeming unconsciousness she quietly dropped into her final sleep in my arms, on the 9th day of May, 1868, at the age of seventy-nine years."[43]

But the most heartrending of these departures was that of young Selwyn, probably his father's favorite, who died horribly of diphtheria at the age of nine. Though heavily retouched, the only known photograph of him shows a child of cherubic appearance, fat-cheeked and with golden curls. On September 24, 1862, a devastated Thomas Mellon managed to write in his memorandum book, "DAY OF SORROW. At half past ten o'clock this evening one of our loved ones, Selwyn, passed away in the morning of life. It is hard, but it may be, after all, the merciful hand of a kind providence, to shield him from the heat and burden of midday and the penalties of age. But, O God, thy will be done. The parting is hard, very hard."[44]

His piercing sorrow and funereal reflections whenever a death occurred in the immediate family are moving affirmations of his claim to being a family man. Similarly, the painstaking care that he devoted to the rearing of his many children and the subsequent high regard that all of them came to have for him speak volumes about his commitment to, and gift for, fatherhood. Though the puritanical, rectitudinarian figure of Judge Mellon will continue to predominate by virtue of its conspicuousness, still, in a balanced view of the man, his austere public image must always be softened by the surprising affection and sensitivity of Mellon the father.

*Immediate Family of Thomas and Sarah Jane Mellon*

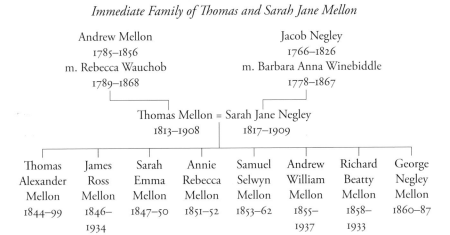

| Andrew Mellon | Jacob Negley |
|---|---|
| 1785–1856 | 1766–1826 |
| m. Rebecca Wauchob | m. Barbara Anna Winebiddle |
| 1789–1868 | 1778–1867 |

Thomas Mellon = Sarah Jane Negley
1813–1908          1817–1909

| Thomas Alexander Mellon 1844–99 | James Ross Mellon 1846–1934 | Sarah Emma Mellon 1847–50 | Annie Rebecca Mellon 1851–52 | Samuel Selwyn Mellon 1853–62 | Andrew William Mellon 1855–1937 | Richard Beatty Mellon 1858–1933 | George Negley Mellon 1860–87 |

# VI

Years of the Law,
First Encounter with James B. Corey,
The Lee Case, Clash with Colonel Black,
Entering the Coal Business,
Judge Thomas Mellon

*No one but a gentleman can be a good lawyer, and not then unless nature has fitted him for it. Natural qualities show themselves in this more than in any other profession, because it calls into activity before the public all the qualities and faculties of mind and heart, whilst other professions leave much of them undeveloped. . . . The lawyer's profession embraces the whole field of human nature and the entire scope of human knowledge. He must be intimate with the objects and feelings which actuate the busy world in every department of life.*

Throughout the 1850s, as his proliferating family and business obligations made ever-weightier demands on him, Thomas Mellon persisted energetically in the practice of law. He worked from sunup to sundown. Before the advent of commuter trains in 1855, he rose at 5:00 a.m., set off for Pittsburgh on horseback around 6:00, and returned home fully twelve hours later. "Early to bed and early to rise." By the 1860s he was taking the train to Pittsburgh from East Liberty Station or traveling on horse-drawn streetcars.

The coal dealer James B. Corey, in his memoirs, preserves an interesting vignette of the forty-four-year-old lawyer after eighteen years of practice. As the Panic of 1857 was working its economic havoc, Corey entered Mellon's law office, on Wylie at Fifth, to pay off three notes, two of which were overdue.

I reached Mr. Mellon's office at 8:00 A.M. and found a line of clients reaching into the third room, awaiting their turn. Framed on the wall was this peremptory notice:

1st.　　Your business at once.

2nd.　　The truth, the whole truth
　　　　and nothing but the truth.

3rd.　　Attention, and go.

I reached his desk at 12:30. His wife, who had been waiting, sprang to her feet and said, "I guess it is my turn now." Mr. Mellon said, "What do you want?" She said, "I want twenty dollars," and handing it to her he turned his eyes on me. "Is your name Mr. Mortgage Bond Tom Mellon?" I asked. He said, "My name is Thomas Mellon." And I said, "Mr. Mellon, you have three notes of Peterson & Corey, one four weeks overdue, one two weeks overdue and one has yet two weeks to run. I want to pay them off." On his taking the notes from a file of papers in his desk, I handed him the money and asked him how much interest was due. He replied, "I will not charge you anything for overdue interest; you coal men have had a hard time to pull through. You sit down there until I get through and I want to ask you about the state of things." After quickly getting through with his other clients he turned around and after asking me all about our trip and the conditions in the Southern market, he said, "If you see a chance to make anything, and need help, come and see me and I may be able to assist you." When I went home and showed Uncle Moses I had paid [off] the notes, he asked me how much Mr. Mellon had charged me for overdue interest. I told him he had not charged me anything. Uncle said, "The damned old coon, he

*Thomas Mellon's lifelong friend, James B. Corey (1832–1915).*

would have made me pay him not less than twenty-five dollars." But I told him he was the nicest man I had ever met, and that he told me if I saw a chance to make anything to come back and he would assist me.[1]

This appears to have been Mellon's first meeting with Corey. If so, it proved portentous. Two years later, the two men would form the first of their numerous partnerships to exploit coal properties. More important, they would remain friends for life.

Mellon's tally of victories in court, his moderate fees and swiftness in settling cases, continued to attract a stream of clients. But what probably did most to advance him at the bar was his capacity for espousing a client's cause as his own. The memorable Lee case affords a striking example of his stubbornness when defending a client's interest. This precedent-setting lawsuit involved a wealthy farmer named William Lee, his daughter-in-law, and his son, Ralph.[2] Because William owned a large, well-appointed farm, and Ralph, who had a wife and children to support, owned only a small farm, the two collaborated and worked out a deal: William would give Ralph his large farm in exchange for the small farm, and Ralph would accept the difference as his inheritance.

William took title to the small farm and immediately proceeded to sell it. Both transactions were properly recorded. Ralph and his family were permitted to occupy and work the large farm, but for unknown reasons William never relinquished title to the property. When Ralph died prematurely, he naturally left the large farm to his widow, who continued to occupy it with her children. But William became progressively estranged from his daughter-in-law and eventually sued to have her and the children evicted. He still held title to the large farm and insisted that Ralph and his family had merely been permitted to occupy and cultivate the property temporarily.

Richard Biddle, of the noted Philadelphia family, was engaged to defend the widow. Perceiving her case to be hopeless, he concluded that the only sensible strategy would be to delay her eviction as long as possible. She could meanwhile continue to work the farm.

When Biddle decided to run for Congress, he handed the Lee case over to Thomas Mellon. The latter accepted it, but with formidable misgivings, for he knew as well as anyone that undocumented real estate transactions—mere oral agreements—normally counted for nothing under Pennsylvania law. He discovered, however, that there were two exceptions: (1) where a party had physically taken possession of real estate on the strength of a mere oral agreement and had then proceeded to make extensive improvements, the value of which could not be readily determined, the said party could be permitted to remain in possession, and the oral agreement might eventually be adjudged as legally valid; (2) where two parties had exchanged pieces of property on the strength of a mere oral agreement and had then occupied the respective properties, and where one party had then sought to deny the oral agreement in order to recover the property it bartered, that same party would have to be in a position to return the property it had accepted in the original exchange. Because William had sold the small farm, he could not return it.

In court, lawyer Mellon tenaciously argued that the widow Lee's case qualified under both exceptions, and that she and her children could not be evicted. But the distinguished presiding judge, Robert Grier, who was about to take his place on the U.S. Supreme Court, emphasized in his charge to the jury that improvements on the large farm had been neither extensive nor difficult to appraise and that, although the small farm had been sold and could not be returned to the widow, she was free to sue her father-in-law for the full value of it. These "clarifications" left little doubt as to how Judge Grier expected the jurors to decide.

Mellon was privately convinced that the first exception could not be made to apply, but he continued to believe that the second might prove applicable. Moreover, he had demonstrated beyond reasonable doubt that there had indeed been an oral accord between father and son and that both had acted in compliance with it. Though no transcript of the trial survives, Mellon's principal appeal to the jury can only have been a cry from the heart for plain fairness. Where arid points of law collide head-on with common decency, should not the latter prevail? It would also have been interesting to know whether he went to tasteless extremes in attempting to fan the mawkish sympathy that a widow with young children will always evoke from jurors.

In a sensational decision, the jury threw out William Lee's apparently ironclad suit and upheld his daughter-in-law's claim to the larger farm. Judge Grier lashed back by declaring a mistrial, and the case was rescheduled for trial before another jury. Meanwhile, the widow and her children continued to occupy and cultivate the farm for another year.

In the second trial, Mellon argued precisely as he had in the first, and Judge Hopewell Hepburn, who had succeeded Grier in the dis-

*Thomas Mellon as a lawyer, circa 1860.*

trict court, charged the jurors precisely as his predecessor had done. When again they defiantly rejected the plaintiff's suit, Hepburn declared a second mistrial, and the widow harvested another crop from the farm.

The third trial was a blueprint of the first two. The lawyers Andrew Burke and Wilson McCandless presented the plaintiff's suit, and Thomas Mellon refuted it for the widow. Judge Walter Lowrie, who had succeeded Hepburn, framed his charge to the jurors so as to virtually compel their support for the plaintiff. When they again stubbornly supported the defendant, the judge wearily proclaimed a third mistrial, and the widow pocketed yet another year's income from the disputed farm.

Events now began to escalate toward a climax, for the legal community was becoming aroused. How many trials should be granted to decide this trivial case? Why had Mellon not prodded his client to compromise and settle? Was he trying to fleece the widow Lee by dragging out her lawsuit forever? Was he not demeaning the entire legal system by staging a succession of travesties in which one jury after another defied the court and handed down a decision that had every appearance of being contrary to law? These questions now hotly preoccupied the Pittsburgh bar. Finding himself at the eye of a gathering storm, Mellon decided to enlist the support of a second attorney— someone of impeccable reputation and considerable seniority. He persuaded the widow Lee to engage his old preceptor, Judge Charles Shaler.

In the fourth trial, Judge Lowrie again presided. But he now found himself face to face with Shaler, who had also been a judge and was furthermore senior to Lowrie. A composite sketch of Shaler by the historian Hax McCullough depicts him as "a theatrical public speaker with a high-pitched voice which he used skillfully to provide irony, invective, and humor." He clashed repeatedly with Judge Lowrie, for neither would tolerate needling from the other. Moreover, Lowrie had come loaded for bear: after three inconclusive trials, he was fiercely determined to end the Lee case. Mellon was equally determined to prolong it until the exhausted judge would accept a decision in favor of his client, or until the plaintiff dropped his suit. Still, it is questionable whether Lowrie would have resorted to excessive, virtually tyrannical, measures but for Shaler's merciless harassment.

When William Lee's suit had been presented, Judge Lowrie stridently insisted that because no point of law existed that could serve to confound the plaintiff's suit, counsel for the defense should not attempt to rebut it and would be prevented from doing so. Mellon was even barred from addressing the jury on the plaintiff's evidence.

Judge Lowrie's next blunder was of such magnitude that it must have left the court dizzy with disbelief: Reiterating that William Lee's suit was irrefutable, he informed the jurors that they would be denied their sacred right to decide the case and that he, Lowrie, would record a verdict in the plaintiff's favor, though no verdict had been reached or even discussed. So ended the fourth trial.

Convinced that Lowrie had now hanged himself, Mellon appealed to the Pennsylvania Supreme Court. In what amounted to a fifth trial, he won a hotly contested but resounding victory: The high court's opinion, which was read by Justice Richard Coulter, threw out Judge Lowrie's counterfeit "decision" and thunderously reaffirmed the right of every citizen to be heard in court. Indeed, the reprimand was so severe that on Lowrie's urgent pleas, and without opposition from Mellon, it was recorded in watered-down form. By then Judge Lowrie must have rued the day when he and four other examiners had granted Thomas Mellon his license to practice law.

The high court had moreover sustained Mellon's position that the plaintiff, who had sold the small farm and could not return it, had been obliged to offer it back to the widow before demanding that she relinquish the large farm. With this precedent-setting decision, Mellon contributed his mite to the evolution of Pennsylvania real estate law. Pleading her straitened circumstances, the widow Lee defaulted on all but $100 of the accumulated fees she owed to the defender who, against seemingly hopeless odds, had championed her cause as though his own in five successive trials. She retained the large farm and was still cultivating it thirty-five years later.

Mellon's bitter clash with the lawyer Samuel Black was equally revealing:[3] It was while they were both studying law at the Western University that Mellon began to perceive in Black a formidable competitor. Black was less studious than Mellon, but his insight into legal questions was admirably penetrating. When they began to practice at the bar, Black and Mellon found themselves as opponents in case after case, but they managed at first to treat one another with professional civility. An aggravating difference of personality reflected itself in their clashing courtroom styles and caused their increasing estrangement and eventual enmity. Kindhearted and generous, Black would make his case impulsively, passionately, rhetorically, and he would counter Mellon's arguments with a vehemence that began to exceed the limits of courtroom etiquette. By contrast, Mellon avoided inflammatory philippics and appealed to logic. He claims never to have composed and delivered a set speech, for that would have taken too much time, and time was money.[4] He built his cases on exhaustive research and a redoubtable command of the facts. The two also differed as to motives. Mellon practiced law primarily for remuneration; Black practiced it mainly for the fame he could win for his impassioned oratory and courtroom victories. At some point, Mellon must have suspected that Black was using the law as a stepping-stone to politics.

What Mellon dreaded was that Black would win over juries with his emotional tirades. To prevent this, he would ridicule Black for his passionate style and for the frequent absurdity of his arguments. Though he was normally quite humorless himself, humor was Mellon's most effective weapon, and he succeeded at mocking Black with enough dexterity to completely infuriate him. Their clashes in open court became increasingly violent and personal until one day Black, in a fit of mindless swagger, informed Mellon that he would subject him to physical violence the next time they met out of court. Though he lacked the burliness of Black, Mellon coolly replied that he would meet force with force. He then proceeded to arm himself with a deadly weapon, presumably a pistol.

"I . . . certainly would have killed him, had he attacked me and it became necessary," recalled Mellon. "I am aware of no duty, either legal, moral or religious, which requires one man to submit to personal violence at the hands of another. . . . Although the assault may not be likely to kill, yet the assailed party is not bound to take that risk."[5] Black appears to have reconsidered his threat of violence, for in the daily round of courtroom encounters with Mellon, he now began to act with admirable restraint. Mellon reciprocated, and their relations, though strained, became acceptably civil.

When war broke out with Mexico in 1846, Black, who had military ambitions, was elected lieutenant colonel of the 1st Pennsylvania Volunteers. As the regiment was marching to the docks to embark for Mexico, Black, who was riding with his troops, spotted Mellon standing in a doorway and watching the parade go by. He immediately rode across the street, extended his hand, and with tears in his eyes addressed this greeting to his old enemy: "Mellon, let us make it up! I may never see you again and would like we should become friends before I go." Though taken aback, Mellon appears to have accepted Black's hand, for he recalls that when the latter returned from Mexico, "we soon became faster friends than we had been bitter enemies before."[6]

Years later, when Mellon was running for his judgeship in Pittsburgh, Black, who was governor of the Nebraska Territory, encouraged him to accept the nomination and even returned from the West to campaign for him. They were close friends by then, and when Black was killed in the Civil War, Mellon reflected sorrowfully on their initial enmity: "The result of this quarrel shows we should never persist too far in fostering animosity and ill will. We can never know what is in the heart; and bitter feuds are often kept alive because the parties do not fully understand each other."[7]

Against all odds, these two had extracted mutual respect and even affection from the ashes of rage before tragedy snuffed out their friendship forever. But it was Black who had shown magnanimity, taken the initiative, and ridden across the street to offer reconciliation, while Mellon, with typical reticence, had stayed in his doorway, quietly awaiting events. At that moment, could either of them have played the part of the other?

Long after his clash with Black, Mellon once more found himself scuffling with a fellow lawyer. He was embroiled in an embarrassing collection suit that he had been forced to initiate against one of his own relatives. The opposing counsel, whom Mellon refused to name, maliciously persuaded his client to counter with a fatuous, utterly contrived equity suit that vastly increased the scope and expense of the trial. More important, he lied in court with respect to the contents of a key document that was supposedly lost but which Mellon managed to produce. Caught in his lie, the opposing counsel was humiliated. He also lost his case. But Mellon was still not satisfied and initiated disbarment proceedings against his opponent for having lied in court. Typically, the judge was reluctant to act against a fellow member of the bar unless pressed to do so by a prosecutor. He dragged his feet for a while, then approached Mellon to dissuade him from pressing his charge, but Mellon refused to back down. The offending lawyer was compelled to limp along in his practice under the cloud of a disbarment proceeding that, though never prosecuted, was also never withdrawn. Because Mellon held himself to such rigid standards in every sphere of life, he lacked compassion for people who lived by malleable principles. That said, even this quarrel might have been resolved if his opponent had taken the first step toward reconciliation, as Samuel Black had done. But again, it was Mellon's opponent who would have had to ride across the street.[8]

Looking back on his years at the bar and on the bench, Mellon offers some final conclusions about the legal profession: "No one but a gentleman can be a good lawyer, and not then unless nature has fitted him for it. . . . The medical doctor exercises his faculties of memory and observation on the kinds and qualities of medicines, and their effect on different diseases. So too the minister has his memory filled with the doctrines of his sect and texts of Scripture. . . . But the lawyer's profession embraces the whole field of human nature and the entire scope of human knowledge. He must be intimate with the objects and feelings which actuate the busy world in every department of life."[9]

> If asked by a student entering the profession what should be his chief object and best course to pursue in order to obtain remunerative business and ultimate independence, I would, after all the experience I have had in what may be regarded as a successful career of sixty years at the bar, on the bench and in the affairs of private life, say to him to devote his labor and energy to the establishment of the truth in regard to both law and facts. This is the policy of honesty and I advise it not any more on the ground of moral duty than for self-interest: because in this respect they coincide. The greatest difficulty to be overcome and which requires the highest talent of the lawyer, is to establish the facts of his case; to draw them out of the stupid or confused and often unwilling and prejudiced witnesses. . . .
>
> You may think it is a lawyer's duty, and that his ability is shown in concealing the facts and suppressing the truth against his client as well as in establishing the truth in his favor. I would say, No! Such a course is not to the lawyer's best interest in the long run. He need not volunteer to bring out facts favorable to the other side, . . . but . . . so soon as he discovers the facts or law to be against him, his best course for his own and his client's interests is to advise a settlement or compromise, or abandon the case if his client is unreasonable.[10]

Once again, Mellon reveals his signature conviction that in the legal profession, as in other spheres of life, to act with honor is the policy of rational self-interest, not merely an ethical imperative. Most lawyers would noisily affirm this view in public, but many would raucously disagree in their private thoughts. That the paths of honor and self-interest frequently coincide is suggested by the Mellon coat of arms, which bears the motto *Casis tutissima virtus*—"Virtue is the surest defense," or, loosely translated, "Honesty is the best policy."[11]

The year 1859 was crowded with memorable events. Thousands gasped in ecstatic terror as the Frenchman Blondin crossed Niagara Falls on a tightrope. Charles Darwin's *On the Origin of Species* exposed the biblical creation story as an old wives' tale and shook the natural sciences, as well as Christianity and Judaism, to their foundations. The hanging of a violent, crack-brained idealist named John Brown hastened America's plunge into civil war. And, at Titusville, Pennsylvania, Edwin Drake sank the world's first oil well, giving birth to an industry that would profoundly affect the Mellon family's future.

The year 1859 was also a watershed for Thomas Mellon, for it was then that he formed the first of his numerous business partnerships to buy and exploit coal properties at Sandy Creek and elsewhere around Pittsburgh. Writing to his son James, he names coal as "the most important article in productive manufactures," alludes to the coal business as "one of the best," and insists that "it is highly respectable."[12] He would be involved in coal mining for thirty years and would make it a pillar of the Mellon fortune. His recurring strategy was to accept a veteran collier as his partner—a man who would superintend the mining operations on a daily basis and would also hunt for new properties. James B. Corey, whose family name was already synonymous with Pittsburgh coal, headed one such partnership, for it also included George Bowman, a civil engineer and coal operator who was married to Mellon's sister, Elizabeth. As Corey and Mellon continued to invest together in various collieries, such as the Waverly Coal and Coke Company, their affinity for the coal business, and their friendship, became unshakable.

But the drains on Thomas Mellon's time increased as his business activities expanded. With five young sons at home, his domestic responsibilities, though pleasurable, were also more time-consuming. In his law practice, he had always concentrated more on profitable civil suits than on unrewarding criminal cases, but tedious litigation nonetheless took up most of his time. It was in this latter field that he decided to cut back, for his business involvements had become more profitable, and his family responsibilities more compelling, than his law practice.

He had attempted to lighten his workload by taking on law partners, but they had proved as useful as cannonballs chained to his feet. The first had been William B. Negley, a nephew of Sarah Jane's. Their partnership endured for seven years but ended in 1856 when Negley resigned to open a law firm with his brother-in-law. Mellon's next partner was a failed lawyer and former schoolteacher named Nathaniel Nelson, whom he had known since boyhood. A capable accountant, Nelson proved to be useful in keeping the books, and his superlative penmanship suited him admirably for drafting legal documents. That he asked for so little remuneration also endeared him to the senior partner. But his legal knowledge was so woefully deficient and his performance in court so ineffectual that only menial duties could be entrusted to him. Mellon's third and final partner, R. P. Flenniken, came with an exalted opinion of himself, perhaps because he had served as the U.S. minister to Denmark. He alienated so many clients by his tactlessness that he almost shipwrecked the firm. Again disillusioned, Mellon arrived at some bleak conclusions: "Where there are partners in a law firm each client looks to some one of the firm as his particular adviser, and relies on him to manage and conduct his case; and I found it impossible to transfer clients who relied on me to my partners, without losing them altogether. Indeed, as a general rule there is no benefit in law partnerships. . . . The attorney who has sufficient ability to attract clients can accomplish as much by competent clerks as by partners."[13]

By 1859, Mellon had begun to wonder whether the time had not come to close his law practice. A fortuitous way of doing so presented itself in April, when a trio of eminent barristers—the renowned criminal lawyer Thomas Marshall, his partner Stephen Geyer, and their friend Alexander Watson—called at Mellon's office with an unusual offer. Judge William B. McClure, who had presided with legendary ferocity over the Court of Common Pleas since 1850, was snowed under with cases and had been granted the assistance of an associate law judge. Would Thomas Mellon be willing to run as a Republican for this newly created judgeship? Typically, public spirit played no part as he pondered the offer:

> I regarded the proposition rather in the light of a practical joke. I had never entertained the slightest desire for office of any kind, or given a thought to seeking popularity, or indeed taken a share in party politics, and accordingly scouted the idea. But they returned again and again to persuade me of its advisability. I was overwhelmed and oppressed with business at the time, and in a mood to get rid of my law business and last law partners together if I could; and they finally persuaded me that this was the way to do it. . . . I knew nothing about party maneuvering and election-eering, but they proposed that if I consented they would attend to all the electioneering that might be required. Nothing was needed but a nomination, they said, and they professed to be able to procure that; and I was aware that no other three men in the city or county possessed more political influence in the republican party at that time. These assurances and consider-ations inclined me to accept. . . . I had never failed in anything on which I had set my mind so far, and why might I not succeed in this also?[14]

Granted, but why had three of the most eminent Pittsburgh lawyers approached Thomas Mellon to run for the new judgeship when they could have drafted any number of other candidates with superior political skills? He chooses not to confront this question, but there were those who knew the answer.

In the fall of 1852, six-year-old James Mellon and some of his Negley relatives had gathered with an enthusiastic crowd on a bridge in East Liberty to watch and cheer as the first train from the East rumbled into Pittsburgh over the Pennsylvania Railroad.[15] Five years later, the

Ohio & Pennsylvania had linked Pittsburgh to Chicago, and feeder lines from these railroads had fanned out in several directions through Allegheny County. Everyone had foreseen the benefits of linking Pittsburgh to the eastern and midwestern cities by rail, but the pitfalls and expense of doing so had been minimized or overlooked.

To induce the railroads to extend their lines to Pittsburgh, which now encompassed a population of fifty thousand, both the city and county had been compelled to offer financial incentives. They had floated bonds that paid 6 percent and matured in thirty years, and they had issued these bonds to the railroads, theoretically to buy rights-of-way and to defray construction costs. A fraudulent traffic in the bonds had quickly arisen. Many had been sold by the railroads to their own directors and other favored investors at giveaway discounts.[16] Without first procuring a right-of-way through Virginia, the nascent Pittsburgh & Steubenville Railroad had accepted bonds guaranteed by the city of Pittsburgh and by Allegheny County to finance the construction of a line to Wheeling and Steubenville. When Virginia denied right-of-way, the rails could not be laid, and the company began to founder in debt. But the bondholders were still entitled to their interest payments and eventually to the return of their principal. Related forms of payola had also become conspicuous: judges, editors, politicians, and even preachers were junketing all over America on free railroad passes.[17] Corruption and folly on so grand a scale had never been seen before in western Pennsylvania.

When the Allegheny County commissioners doubled the real estate tax in May 1857 to pay interest on the county's railroad bonds, there were raucous meetings of outraged property owners, and cries were heard for the repudiation of debt. Thomas Mellon helped to organize these meetings and frequently addressed them. He demanded that railroad companies be investigated and personally made invasive inquiries into their activities.[18] His fear and hatred of both fraud and taxation were irrepressible, and where the two were interwoven, he saw red. The bitter meditations on fraudulent municipal debt that he would later record in his memoir were largely inspired by the 1857–59 uproar over railroad bonds:

> I have often been struck in the course of my life by the readiness and ease with which the rankest injustice can be clothed with the invulnerable robe of legislative and judicial authority. . . . In our day this is most frequently consummated in the creation of public debts both state and municipal, legalized under the pretext of public wants, but in reality for private gain. Corrupt rings, by manipulating elections and the members of legislative bodies after election, obtain the legalization of their schemes, always on some plausible pretext or other but with the certainty of plundering the industrial classes in the end. No matter how iniquitous or unjust such bonds and subsidies may be in their origin, the taxpayers are always held liable by the courts for their payment. . . .
>
> Credit and the power to borrow money is the bane of cities and other municipal bodies of our day. . . . There should be no power to contract debts on the public credit, except that resting in the general [federal] government, to be exercised for war purposes alone.[19]

By 1859, Pittsburgh and the encompassing county of Allegheny had gone bankrupt attempting to service $26 million in railroad bonds. Court cases were piling up as enraged bondholders sued for unpaid interest. A strident tax revolt broke out. Republicans vied with Democrats in clamoring for the repudiation of public debt. Judges found themselves under grueling pressure to permit the two city councils and the county commissioners to default, rather than ordering them to meet their debt payments by raising property taxes.[20]

On February 16, a tumultuous antitax convention assembled in historic Lafayette Hall. It included two hundred delegates from Pittsburgh and the surrounding townships, reinforced by a multitude of demonstrators attending unofficially. Pure democracy prevailed as local politicians were hustled in, rudely interrogated, and hustled out. The agitated delegates were ordered to sit down, because many of them were standing on the chairs. Thomas Mellon, Major General James S. Negley, and Dr. Richard Beatty represented Collins Township. Mellon's brother-in-law George Bowman represented Versailles. Stephen Geyer and Alexander Watson, two of the lawyers who would draft Mellon for his judgeship, were also delegates.[21] Moreover, Mellon and Geyer were appointed to a six-man committee that quickly drafted nine fighting resolutions, all of which were thunderously approved by voice vote. The first two are noteworthy:

> Resolved, that we are utterly and irreconcilably opposed to any tax to pay the principal or interest on municipal bonds, given in payment of railroad subscriptions. . . .
>
> Resolved, 2. That while we wish at all times to treat with respect and deference the judgments of our courts, yet we believe there are occasions when resistance to the decrees of courts is the right and duty of the citizen and is necessary for the preservation of our liberties and the security of our property.[22]

That Thomas Mellon's sympathies lay with the defaulters was something he had gratuitously trumpeted about, and it was mainly for this reason that Marshall, Geyer, and Watson now drafted him to run for the newly created judgeship. He would later give studied expression to the radical views on debt repudiation that he had formed during this period and which had lent such muscle to his bid for the bench:

> The fact of repudiation is held up as a term of reproach, and the government and people of the repudiating community are stigmatized as dishonest, when in truth and in fact there is in many such cases no more injustice or dishonesty in their repudiation than would be in the repudiation of a forged note or check. . . . If

the industrial classes shall become wiser, and better organized in their own interests, the repudiation of iniquitous municipal debts will become respectable, and be oftener resorted to, until this trade of public plunderers is broken up.... It is a wrong principle to allow irresponsible politicians, mostly without any property interests of their own, to mortgage at will the private property of the citizens. It must bring about ultimate disaster.[23]

He would continue to expect this "disaster." In 1864, he wailed in a letter to James, "I feel very gloomy and melancholy this evening, and look forward to the probability of the time coming around when my home will not be in Allegheny County. Tax after tax is levied, and one batch of bonds issued after another for illegitimate purposes to such an extent that our property must be confiscated in the end."[24] That the dreaded confiscation did not occur failed to deter him from gloomy prognostications. Mellon argued that excessive taxation of property holders always burdens the poorest classes with higher rents and higher prices.[25]

Though his obsessive dread of taxation must be partially imputed to congenital pessimism and to his yearning for the freedom, safety, and dignity that accompany wealth, he traces this phobia to conditions in the land that his parents had abandoned:

Times were bad then in Ireland.... The protracted wars in which England had been engaged had rendered taxation oppressive. Every method was resorted to, to raise revenue. Every hearth and window and head of livestock, and every business transaction was separately and oppressively taxed; and after paying the rent and taxes, little was left to the farmer.

The hardships experienced by my grandfather's family and my own parents, from oppressive taxation, became so thoroughly ingrained in my nature, when a child, that I have always felt a strong opposition to it, and to all measures rendering an increase of taxes necessary. It was the universal complaint which drove our people from our homes, and swelled the flood of emigration to America, at that time.[26]

As a Republican candidate, Mellon's first hurdle was to satisfy the doubtful voters that he was actually a Republican. His reputation for stalwart individualism and nonconformist political views had evidently cast doubt on the strength of his party affiliation. To counter the impression that he was a cranky independent, Mellon extracted the following endorsement from eight Republican leaders:

May 16th 1859.

Thomas Mellon, Esq.
Dear Sir,

In reply to your request to furnish a statement of our knowledge of your political principles, we can say,

That we have known you intimately for upwards of twenty years, and your *politics* were invariably that of the old line *Whig* party whilst that party existed—and of the *Republican* party afterwards until the present time.

You were not, it is true, a rigid party man or noisy politician, but we always found your feelings and influence on the *Republican* side, and the only deviation we ever knew you to make from the party ticket was last fall and the fall before, when you opposed certain candidates on it, on the ground that you did not believe them to be sufficiently Anti-Tax—but at the same time you openly avowed your Republican principles and adherence to the Republican party.

| | |
|---|---|
| Thos. Marshall | And. McMaster (Ald.) |
| Thomas MacConnell | Thos. A. Rowley (Clerk of Court) |
| T. J. Bigham | H. S. Fleming (Ex-Mayor) |
| Geo. R. Riddle | N. Patterson (Recorder)[27] |

Armed with this endorsement, Mellon wrote to a Republican leader in Wilkins Township about the malicious rumors that his opponents were circulating:

May 18, 1859.

Mr. Emanuel Stotler

I send you herewith a copy of the statement furnished me by some of the main men of the party to confute the stories they were puling out against me on your side. I have every prospect now of being nominated. They had circulated all manner of lies against me. Out on your side, that I was a democrat—out north of [the] river where I was not so well known, that I was a *Catholic,* and in Allegheny [City] that I was a Rail Road Director. These lies, as the people are beginning to inquire about me, are all going home to roost and doing my appointment more harm than myself. I want you as a friend to get half a dozen or so to go to the Primary Meeting, take your wagon and arrange it so they will know you are going to carry Plum [Township]. I hope to carry this Township yet. You will find I have warm friends who will be there.

Yours,

Thomas Mellon[28]

In Mellon's case, the primary presented a more formidable challenge than the election, for two popular and qualified Republican lawyers, Edwin Stowe and James Kuhn, were also seeking the new judgeship, and they were favored to win in a number of townships. Whoever secured the nomination in June would almost certainly be elected in October, for Republicans heavily outnumbered Democrats.

Given his visceral distrust of ordinary folk, Mellon was fortunate in being able to conduct an almost passive campaign. He solicited the backing of key Republican leaders and influential friends but made not a single speech. His only aggressive ploy occurred when he went to the railroad station and stumbled on James Kelly, a wealthy and politically potent landowner from Wilkins Township.[29]

Mellon had known Kelly for many years and felt entitled to his political backing. He was stung to learn that Kelly had already pledged his support to Edwin Stowe. Heated words were exchanged, but Kelly remained obdurate. Lowering his demands, Mellon inquired whether he could at least ask Kelly's son for support. Kelly expressed no objection but ventured that his son counted for little politically. Mellon carefully noted this remark. He also disagreed with it. That young Kelly was a drunk who haunted the saloons and street corners was entirely consistent with Mellon's stereotype of a politician. Because an eastbound train was just then leaving the station, Mellon jumped aboard, journeyed to Wilkinsburg, and hunted up young Kelly.

Asked for his support, the son equivocated: he felt obliged to back his father's candidate, Edwin Stowe, but admitted that personally he did "not care a damn for Mr. Stowe" and pointedly added "nor very much for anyone else."[30] By then, Mellon had slipped in a jab of his own: He had hinted to young Kelly that his father regarded him as a political lightweight. As the train for Pittsburgh was about to leave, Mellon, who had still not obtained what he wanted, began walking dejectedly toward the station. He was still in earshot when Kelly yelled up the street that he would send the Wilkins delegates to support him. Mellon's initial apathy about running for office had apparently given way to a sturdy desire for victory.

He acknowledges only one ruse that contributed to his nomination. In Penn Township, a pro-Mellon organizer named David Collins lulled the opposition into complacency by promising Kuhn's managers not to contest the township. But on primary day, he sent in a line of hay wagons loaded with pro-Mellon voters, and Kuhn went down to defeat. "I was not aware of this strategic movement till after it was over," Mellon insists, "but was nevertheless gratified at its success."[31] He secured the nomination by a comfortable margin, and in the October election he trounced his Democratic rival, George Gillmore, by 7,595 votes to 4,935.[32]

Writing for the *Post,* Pittsburgh's only Democratic newspaper, the editor, James Barr, who had represented Birmingham Township at the antitax convention in February, charged that his party, in its frenzy to repudiate debt and to hold the line on taxes, had deliberately nominated a weak candidate to stand against Mellon.[33]

On Monday December 5, 1859, his commission was read aloud in the Court of Common Pleas, and after taking the oath he assumed his place on the bench as Judge Thomas Mellon. He would continue to boast that he had spent not a cent to secure his new position, apart from $150 that the Republican county chairman had assessed him for campaign expenses.

# VII

## The Storm over James's Enlistment

*In time you will come to understand and believe that a man may be patriotic without risking his own life or sacrificing his health. There are plenty of other lives less valuable or others ready to serve for the love of serving.*

O NE OF THE FEW USEFUL functions of war is that it tests people and compels them to discover and reveal themselves. Pressed by danger, they are forced to choose, without delay, between alternative courses of action and the clashing ethical principles that belie them. Such a choice was imposed on Thomas Mellon during the Civil War.

He had sent his son James to the Great Lakes region, hoping that the midwestern climate would beef up his constitution and reduce his apparently chronic susceptibility to colds, stomach sickness, and head-aches.[1] The young man had found employment as a clerk, at Finches, Lynde & Miller, a leading Milwaukee law firm, but he was not being groomed for his father's profession. "Learn the *modus operandi* of the coal business and merchandising and iron business and other important branches of manufacturing," enjoined the Judge, and hinting at possible partnership with his son, he added, "It may be useful to us hereafter."[2]

But eighteen-year-old James was not focusing entirely on his future occupation. Two years earlier, draft riots had broken out in Wisconsin when the state failed to fill its quota of troops with volunteers for the Civil War. At Port Washington, just north of Milwaukee, rioters had stormed the county courthouse, destroyed draft records, and beaten up state officials.[3] Since then, civic meetings had been held all over the state to encourage enlistments, and James had attended one of them. While America reeled from sickening accounts of General Ulysses Grant's sanguinary Wilderness Campaign, James startled his father with the following letter:

Milwaukee, Wis., May 14, 1864.

Dear Father:

I write you now in haste so this will go out in the mail. There is a company being raised now to go for one hundred days as state militia to guard prisoners, etc., which the acting army cannot take care of.

There was a large meeting held in the Chamber of Commerce last evening and money enough raised to pay the men twenty-five dollars per month and [they] will receive their regular pay from the state, but this is immaterial. I would like to go if these men are needed and we will have a very good captain, one of the lawyers of this city. It will only be for one hundred days and I think there will be no danger.

Write soon as the company will be going (if they go) on the 20th of the month so as to be back by the first of September. I don't suppose there will be any very hard service to go through and the company is made up of new beginners entirely.

Please write soon.

Jas. R. Mellon

PS. If I do not get an answer next week, I will suppose you have consented and will enlist. (I expect you to consent.)[4]

Thomas responded by telegram:

Pittsburgh, Pa., May 17, 1864.

DONT DO IT. I HAVE WRITTEN.

THOMAS MELLON[5]

The letter duly followed:

Tuesday, May 17, 1864.

Dear James:

I just this moment received yours of the 14th inst. and immediately reply that I do not give my consent. It is the duty of parents to decide for their children against what they know to be to their disadvantage however much they may wish to act to the contrary.

When mustered in these one hundred days, militia are under the absolute orders of the government to go and do whatever is directed anywhere and it is not in the danger of battle the evil lies, although that is great and bad enough, but the worst is disease and idle or vicious habits. Your constitution is not fit for soldiering. We owe nothing in the way of making up Wisconsin's quota [of troops].

It makes me sad to see this piece of folly. It comes on me unexpectedly. I thought you were attending to your studies and you are writing instead of war meetings and filling your head with soldiering. I had hoped my boy was going to make a smart, intelligent business man and was not such a goose as to be seduced from his duty by the declamations of buncombed speeches.

As to $25 a month, what signifies that? It is nothing to me. I am able and willing to pay all your expenses till you find some legitimate business that suits you, and there are thousands of poor, worthless fellows fit for soldiering, but fit for nothing else, whose duty is to go. You say if you don't get an answer this week you will take it for granted. You have no right to take it for granted until I have had time to reply and you know I would not let such an important matter pass without advising you about it.

But perhaps there is no use in advising. Perhaps it is a parent's lot to be disappointed in their hopes and expectations about their children.

Your father,

Thos. Mellon[6]

Milwaukee, May 19, 1864.

Dear Father,

I received your letter of the 17th inst. I have concluded not to go, but I am sure you need not be afraid of me ever enlisting without asking and gaining your consent, as you seem to think by your letter. I thought I would write and see what you thought about it and be prepared if I did want to go. . . .

Your son,

James R. Mellon[7]

If James imagined that he could make peace with his parents simply by caving in to them, he was dreaming. The day after his docile capitulation, a frantic letter arrived from Ma. "My dear son," she wails, "look to God and ask direction with no one-sided view of the matter and he will guide you aright." Calling him "a poor misguided boy," she ends with the cry, "Come home!"[8]

James did not come home, however, for he knew what a tongue-lashing awaited him there. Even at Milwaukee, he was not beyond the range of his father's guns. In a succession of petulant and condescending letters, the Judge admonishes his son that army life consists of "long marches in the hot sun carrying a heavy load or lying around in camp exposed to all kinds of diseases," that "no credit attaches to the services of a private soldier," that "you can learn nothing useful in the army," that "all now stay if they can and go if they must," that "those who are able to pay for substitutes do so and no discredit attaches to it," that James is suffering from "military fever," and that "only green horns enlist." Two weeks after James's thunderbolt announcement, his father concludes their correspondence on this jarring note: "In time you will come to understand and believe that a man may be patriotic without risking his own life or sacrificing his health. There are plenty of other lives less valuable or others ready to serve for the love of serving."[9]

One reason why these letters are so revealing is that the son does not disclose why he wants to enlist. By merely stating, "I would like to go," James leaves his father in the awkward position of having to take potshots at all the possible reasons why his son might be attracted to soldiering. In the polemical scattershot that he fires, the elder Mellon's signature fears, prejudices, and conceits are laid bare. But the final summation of his views on military service had to await the publication of *Thomas Mellon and His Times:*

> There is always a disproportionately large class of men fitted by nature for a service which requires so little brain work as that of the common soldier. . . . It is therefore egregious folly for men of superior talent and ability, whose services are valuable in private affairs and home duties, to go into military service as common soldiers. . . . I do not insist on this view on account of the risks of battle so much as the almost certain loss of health from fatigue, exposure, irregularity of living and change of climate and the danger of contracting idle, indolent or immoral habits. . . . There are many, it is true, who are moved by ambition and the desire for notoriety, and to such it is excusable when a high office is in their offer; but to the common soldier, or any officer lower than a general [he had to make an exception for his wife's first cousin, Major General James S. Negley], a man whose life is of much value to himself or his family should stay at home. On this account the parents and friends of young men of promise should use all their influence to guard them from the temptations brought to bear on them in times of military excitement.[10]

Though Mellon's view of military service would cause an uproar today, it was hardly extreme in 1864, when any draftee could lawfully avoid conscription by hiring a substitute for $300. Known as the "bounty system," this tunnel of flight for the comfortably well-off remained in force throughout the Civil War and enjoyed the unwavering support of President Lincoln. Every state in the residual Union was required to raise an assigned quota of troops, and where the number of volunteers was insufficient, draftees were chosen by lot to fill the quota. The historian Shelby Foote writes:

> Large numbers of men from the upper classes . . . went to the expense of hiring substitutes, usually immigrants who were brought over by companies newly formed to supply the demand, trafficking thus in flesh to an extent unknown since the stoppage of the slave trade, and who were glad of the chance to earn a nest egg, which included the money they got from the men whose substitutes they were, plus the bounty paid by that particular state to volunteers. . . . There was no stigma attached to the man who stayed out of combat, however he went about it, short of actual dodging or desertion.[11]

Whether James was ever drafted or hired a substitute is not known, but his brother Tom enlisted. Incredibly, Judge Mellon permitted Tom to volunteer in a militia regiment that was stationed on the Maryland border for several weeks in October 1862, just after the murderous fighting at Antietam. One shudders at the hurricane of opposition that young Tom must have weathered before his father acquiesced in this "folly." That the volunteers were all from Pittsburgh, from families like the Mellons, and that their colonel was "an honorable, reliable and wealthy business man of the city, William Frew," with whom the Judge was acquainted, probably proved decisive.[12] To place a stubborn son with military fantasies in a "soft" position, comfortably out of harm's way, for a short period, is after all a stratagem that influential parents have habitually resorted to. When President Lincoln's son,

Robert, expressed a touristy wish "to see something of the war before it ended," his father placed him safely in General Grant's immediate entourage.[13]

Writing to James on July 16, 1864, the Judge observed, "There is no doubt that in a general ship wreck the best way to save one's self is to keep afloat. We must move with the times and try to take advantage of circumstances."[14] Two weeks later, he gave his son a further earful about the Lincoln administration: "I am inclined strongly to believe that our government is a humbug. I fear the present administration, at any rate, has not the capacity or ability to manage this war. Their course has been one series of blunders after another since the beginning and there is no progress made except in fleecing the people."[15]

What is most remarkable about these letters is that Thomas appears not to recognize any ethical significance in a war that revolved around uncommonly clear-cut and gigantic moral issues. Did he fail to perceive the link between liberty and union that Daniel Webster had so eloquently alluded to? In his memoirs and surviving correspondence, we find nothing to suggest that he either opposed or approved of slavery. Did he view it as irrelevant? True, Thomas's brother Samuel was serving in the Confederate army, and his uncle Thomas, the mentor of his schooldays, had fallen under rebel influence. But it was almost certainly the Judge's demophobia and consequent fear of democracy that prevented him from identifying passionately with a free and united America. Leaving others to agonize over the towering ethical choices, he wails about taxes, inflation, disrupted commerce, and the snowballing national debt.

Typically, Mellon's most painful wartime experience involved the theft of several bargeloads of coal that he had shipped down the Mississippi. As always when reliving an old grudge, he leaves us an exhaustive account of what happened. In fact, he devotes more space in his memoirs to this particular misadventure than to the whole rest of the war. On learning that his coal had been stolen by Union forces at New Orleans, he stormed into Washington, D.C., personally belabored the secretary of war, Edwin Stanton, with his smoldering grievances, and sued the U.S. government for $40,000. Though Mellon got his money back, he continued to fume about the government's refusal to pay interest.[16] And coincidentally, the United States of America remained free and united.

On the day that news of General Robert E. Lee's surrender reached Pittsburgh, Judge Mellon was presiding over the Court of Common Pleas. As hysterical rejoicing erupted in the courtroom, ten-year-old Andrew W. Mellon, who was at that moment hiding under the bench, would recall that "my father pounded his gavel in an attempt to restore order. By this time, though, the lawyers had climbed up on the tables, so my father crashed the gavel down and said: 'Court's adjourned.' We left the courtroom together, but he stopped on the way to wind the clock."[17] Having never agonized over the fate of America and its ideals, Thomas could not now share in the popular relief that both had muddled through. A chilly, unbridgeable abyss would lie forever between him and the run of humankind.

Mellon's contempt for military service and deafness to the call of conventional patriotism appear to have been traditional among his Scotch-Irish ancestors, for he writes with obvious satisfaction that "our ancestors, as far as known, and all the modern branches of the family, avoided soldiering, except as a necessary duty, confining their energies to the industrial pursuits of private life; and were notable only for good habits, and paying their debts."[18]

In their eschewal of "soldiering," the early Mellons at Castletown were surprisingly atypical. In war after war, large numbers of the Scotch-Irish had fought with valor. In the New World, they had rushed to the frontier and repeatedly defeated the Indians. Thousands had fought against Britain in the American Revolution, and far greater numbers were fighting on both sides in the Civil War. But the Mellons rejected this bellicose tradition, apparently because it collided with the competing Scotch-Irish imperative to accumulate, which they regarded as paramount. In fact, Thomas Mellon comes close to recognizing no motive for human endeavor other than personal gain:

There may be a phenomenal lawyer who would practice law for the love of it, but in my forty years about the bar I did not meet with him, and have set him down to be a mythical character like the wandering jew. There may be medical doctors who would follow their profession for the mere love of the healing art and benevolence to the human race, but I have not become acquainted with them; and there are some fanatical preachers—or were some in former days (the race is now perhaps extinct)—who would preach without pay and live on faith and hope, and what they might pick up as mendicants! Such phenomenal beings are rare, but there are exceptions to all rules; the rule itself however, in all pursuits of life, is the acquisition of means to the attainment of some ultimate personal end.[19]

Clearly, the innermost circle of his concerns is not occupied by the nation, democracy, or the community, but by his immediate family. What matters most to him is not wealth for its own sake, but the safety, freedom, and respectability that wealth can confer on his children, his wife, and himself. In this, perhaps he differs from most Americans only in his refusal to parrot the conventional ethics. It is a rare man indeed who views his community as more important than his immediate family. But most people understand that serving one's country and community lends a healthy balance to life, enriches personal experience, and strengthens one's connection to a larger world. Thomas Mellon does not appear to have held this conviction either.

Though he was incapable of viewing the Civil War as an ethical conflict, Mellon remained keenly aware of the dangers and related opportunities that it presented. He invested heavily in coal properties around Pittsburgh, bought real estate piecemeal in the burgeoning suburbs, and acquired small businesses. Most of these investments would turn handsome profits during and after the war. It was also in this turbulent period that his enduring strategy of buying land along the Western railroads and around the fastest-growing cities became apparent. What was working in booming Pittsburgh would work in the booming West.

By 1864, he had become the disputed owner of a small farm and some lots that his ne'er-do-well brother Samuel had abandoned at Leavenworth, Kansas, after discovering that the titles to these properties were contested. In July of that year, he sent James from Milwaukee to inspect the holdings at Leavenworth and to take stock of the local real estate market. "Remember that every nineteen out of twenty of the people of Leavenworth are unprincipled sharpers and fleeced your Uncle Sam out of some $2000 or more in attempted speculations," the father warns. But in the next breath, he tells James to hunt for real estate bargains, offers to lend him the purchase money, and proposes to split the profits with him, net of interest.[20] Informal partnerships with his sons would become favorite devices for accumulation three years hence, when he launched James and Tom as real estate developers around Pittsburgh.

While at Leavenworth, James replied with proven diplomacy to his father's browbeating letters. His tone of filial deference is almost comic as he feigns serious attention to business and writes at length and in commendable detail about the Judge's real estate. Fending off paternal hectoring and occasional barrages had taught him how to mollify the old man. But this time he was nursing a secret that must have utterly distracted him from business and would have infuriated his father: James had fallen in love. He had arrived at Leavenworth with an introduction to his father's old friend and law client, Major General William Larimer Jr., and had become infatuated with the General's seventeen-year-old daughter, Rachel.

As James labored to pen hard-nosed letters about business while stumbling dizzily in euphoria, his father weighed the merits and demerits of Western real estate. Land had always been his preferred investment, for it appeared to present the most favorable correlation between risk and return. That it was a tangible asset did much to allay his fears, and its secondary uses, such as agriculture and occasionally mining, went further to reassure him. As he angled for additional acquisitions in the West, the Judge agonized over which cities would grow fastest and pondered whether Leavenworth would become "the emporium of Kansas." Likewise, he racked his brain over which railroads would prove most effective at spurring development, shunting in people, and sprouting new towns.

So eager was he to buy land in close proximity to the centers and conduits of population that his clear perception of danger was overcome by yearning. "These Western sharpers have their whole country checkered with imaginary cities and railroads," wrote the Judge.[21] But he would continue to acquire disparate pieces of Western land until 1890, and some of them would remain in family ownership long after his death. He would remember this period as "one in which it was easy to grow rich," when "there was a steady increase in the value of property and commodities," when "one had only to buy anything and wait, to sell at a profit."[22]

# VIII

———— •◦•◦• ————

## Closet Philosopher Mellon,
## His Infatuation with Herbert Spencer,
## Views on Religion and Education

*I believe in the evolution . . . of families. A family of particular cast and
character originates and grows to perfection and decays and dies, just as
religions, governments, nationalities and all other institutions.*

THOMAS MELLON HAD NOT BEEN LONG on the bench when
he made a delightful discovery—that judging is less time-
consuming than lawyering.[1] Since his graduation from college in 1837,
two decades of unremitting legal work, not to mention business and
family obligations, had left him little time for reading. This deprivation
had become excruciating. His tireless, searching mind had never ceased
to hunger for knowledge in the fields of history, science, education,
politics, religion, and economic theory. He had used his initial capital
—a $700 gift from his father—to buy law books and had acquired, by
marriage, the rich and varied library of Jacob Negley. Finding himself
with an unexpected dividend of leisure when his attendance at the
courthouse was not required, he now began to reread the Greek and
Latin classics and to journey through ancient and modern history. But
such reading offered him only tepid satisfaction. It was an intellectual
revolution—one that was blasting the understanding of the origins of
life on Earth—that captured his fancy during these years.

Graphed by material gain, Mellon's life had etched a steeply rising trajectory from perceived poverty to financial self-sufficiency and consequent self-respect. His arduous and protracted struggle for education and then for wealth had innately convinced him that life is a remorseless trial in which only the fit survive. Hence, when his old friend Thomas MacConnell began to send him the literature of evolution, he related to it immediately and intuitively.[2] Works by Charles Darwin (1809–84) and his contemporaries Alfred Russel Wallace and Thomas Henry Huxley now opened his eyes to the origin of species and to the consequent sea change in humanity's understanding of itself.

Charles Darwin's discovery of evolution discredited religious creation myths and left the thinking fraction of humanity stumbling in a boneyard of discredited certainties. Man, who had defined himself, with typical hubris, as a unique, immutable, divinely created being, the rightful lord over all of nature, was now exposed as a continuously evolving animal whose relationship to chimpanzees and gorillas was too close for comfort. The much-demonized agnostic Robert Green Ingersoll mischievously quipped: "How terrible this will be upon the nobility of the Old World. Think of their being forced to trace their ancestry back to the duke Orang Outang, or the princess Chimpanzee."[3] More important, the Bible would now have to be interpreted symbolically, not literally, and the natural sciences would have to be reconstituted in conformity with evolution. Judge Mellon ached with curiosity about the new theory and its explosive implications. Moreover, Darwinian evolution was exerting a definitive influence on Herbert Spencer (1820–1903), whose theories would provide Mellon with new ideas and lifelong convictions.

Spencer's gift for identifying patterns in human behavior and in the evolution of entire societies led him to become the founder of sociology. But the launching of a new science was only one step in his creation of an entire sociophilosophical system, a grand synthesis of knowledge that conformed to evolution and therefore redefined history, ethics, education, government, and even God in scientific rather than traditional terms.

Throughout his voluminous writings, Spencer adheres to an adamantly secular viewpoint. He builds an all-encompassing system of knowledge exclusively on science, not on traditional or religious dogmas. Similarly, his morality is derived from sociology, not from Judeo-Christian ethics. For God he substitutes "Force," the indefinable, ultimate phenomenon that he perceives in all of nature, including humans, and which appears to him as the sine qua non of existence—a kind of First Cause. The personal deity of Judaism, Christianity, and Islam is dismissed as an anthropomorphic fiction.

Spencer recognizes two kinds of societies. Those that are compelled to cohere by a ruler or a ruling clique he characterizes as "military." Those that have come to cohere freely, because of a deepening awareness that individuals can more effectively improve their lives by collaborating to supply each other's needs, he characterizes as "industrial."

Spencer coins the catchy expression "survival of the fittest" not as a metaphor for mindless violence but to underscore the creative nature of evolution. In an industrial society, the creative abilities of individuals undergo an ever-evolving, increasingly specialized, steadily improving adaptation to supplying human needs. Thus evolution works an inconspicuous, gradual improvement in people's lives and promises all individuals the highest possible degree of self-realization or fulfillment to which their efforts and talents entitle them.

Spencer abhors military societies because they stifle creative evolution. Governments must be restrained from unduly interfering in this process and must limit their activities to law enforcement, defense, and the administration of justice. All forms of state intervention aimed at accelerating the social and economic evolution of an industrial society, or at directing its development by fiat from above, are condemned as futile, counterproductive, and brazenly intrusive. By the same token, socialism, like militarism, is innately tyrannical and therefore incompatible with civilization.

Spencer proceeds to redefine ethics in terms of evolution rather than theology. Whatever promotes the free economic and social development of an industrial society is good. Whatever interferes with this salubrious process, such as excessive taxation, artificial subsidies, price controls, government-inflicted state planning, crime, or the violation of legitimate human rights, is ethically wrong.

However, humans play an active part in the creative evolutionary process. As thinking, ethical beings, their role is to scientifically deduce, from observed human behavior, the principles of conduct that promote evolutionary fulfillment and to accept them as rules to live by. Foremost among these principles is a secular version of the Golden Rule: that individuals are entitled to pursue fulfillment—call it happiness—in any way and to any extent that is consistent with everyone else's right to do likewise.

But Spencer warns that the long-term improvement in social and economic conditions will be interrupted by lamentable periods of backsliding, when government interferes with the healthy, natural process of social evolution. Far from envisioning a steady approach to utopia, he foresees that the evolution of laissez-faire, industrial society will reach fulfillment only after lengthy regressions into socialistic tyranny and war—an eerie prognostication, considering how much of both has come to pass.

He furthermore insists that society is not a thinking entity but only a conglomeration of thinking individuals. Because the whole is *not* more than the sum of its parts, all social and economic progress must be measured in terms of the individual's well-being. Whatever unjustly diminishes the individual is an assault on society. Moreover, it is intrinsic to the mutually complementary relationship between science and philosophy that both demand respect for the individual and call for strict limits on the role of government. This is to say that society exists for the individual, not the individual for society, and that individualism is a prerequisite of civilization.

Predictably, the newly rich of all nations stampeded to Spencer's banner and hailed him as their philosophical gladiator. But key points of his philosophy, such as respect for the individual, minimal government intervention, contempt for militarism, repudiation of socialism, minimal taxation, and the redirection of education toward problem solving, were convictions that the newly rich already held. They accorded fully with the Scotch-Irish values in which Mellon's thinking had been pickled at the hearth. Spencer's contribution was that by integrating these tenets in a systematic philosophy founded on the newly discovered principle of evolution, he empowered them with the force of natural law and consequently justified them. After a century and a half of study, debate, and analysis, Spencer's social Darwinism has suffered a loss of luster among sociologists, in part because his conclusions have so often and so flagrantly been abused in politics and history, but his influence on popular American thinking remains deep and pervasive.

Spencer particularly attracted the affluent with his view that the winning qualities that enable species to survive under stressful conditions tend to become hereditary. Not surprisingly, his social science came to be hailed as a justification for leaving the rich, who fancied themselves as natural winners, comparatively free from taxation, government interference, and legal restraints, so that they could work their economic miracles forever. Conversely, the poor were viewed as natural losers in the race of life and therefore undeserving. But this view is inconsistent with Darwin's theory, for in *The Descent of Man* he states unequivocally that moral and environmental concerns take precedence over natural selection, once humanity has progressed from a state of nature to one of civilization. In Darwin's own words: "The aid which we feel impelled to give to the helpless is mainly an incidental result of the instinct of sympathy which was originally acquired as part of the social instincts, but subsequently rendered . . . more tender and widely diffused. Nor could we check our sympathy, even at the urging of hard reason, without deterioration in the noblest part of our nature. . . . If we were intentionally to neglect the weak and the helpless, it would only be for a contingent benefit, with an overwhelming present evil."[4]

Thomas Mellon favors preferential treatment—inducements—for the proven producers, but he flatly rejects Spencer's view that talents which augur for victory in the race of life are transmissible from generation to generation. For him, the history of families is not linear but cyclical: "I believe in the evolution of families. A family of particular cast and character originates and grows to perfection and decays and dies, just as religions, governments, nationalities and all other institutions. It is a law of nature. A family of good, healthy stock, and good mental and moral qualities, rises from the common level, prospers till prosperity produces the canker of deterioration and decay, then sinks again and eventually disappears. For this reason it is much better to form relationships with rising than declining families. Where a family has enjoyed their career of wealth and prosperity for a generation or so, we may expect 'degenerate sons;' not invariably, but more frequently than otherwise."[5]

In the old Pittsburgh families he finds dismal support for this view: "The O'Haras, Robinsons, Ormsbys and Beltzhoovers were all originally hard working, careful, industrious common people, distinguished from others chiefly in having the faculties of industry, self-denial and accumulation more fully developed—the mud-sills on which fortunes were constructed which required a subsequent generation or two to scatter."[6] Moreover, "As a rule it is only the man who has passed through tribulation, and has had his energies aroused and his faculties strengthened by the necessity for great exertion, that accomplishes much in the battle of life."[7] He concludes with the thematic message of his life: "The normal condition of man is hard work, self-denial, acquisition and accumulation; and as soon as his descendants are freed from the necessity of such exertion they begin to degenerate sooner or later in both body and mind."[8]

At the age of eighty-five, he would write that if a man's "children and descendants are worthy of life in this world, the 'survival of the fittest' principle will preserve them and the wealth they inherit; will assist them greatly in promoting their purposes and growth, in the growth of respect and position. If wealth has a demoralizing or deteriorating effect on our offspring, it only shows their unfitness to live, and in that case it may be better the sooner the family or race is extinguished, which is more rapidly accomplished by the possession of wealth than by any other condition."[9]

Thomas Mellon perceived in Herbert Spencer's thought a range of implications that reach far beyond his own desire to justify a life of accumulation. For at the moment when we hear him applauding the limits Spencer places on the role of government, we also find him pondering the philosopher's effect on ethics, religion, metaphysics, and education. In the daring originality of evolutionary thinking he perceives with uneasy fascination the birth of a brave new world cut loose from traditional dogmas and definitions. He grappled with the chilling possibility that there is no personal, caring deity, and that man, with his craving for love and ideals, is after all alone and unloved in an utterly meaningless universe. Such was the specter that Darwinism raised for many Victorian thinkers and writers, among them Alfred Lord Tennyson, Thomas Hardy, A. E. Housman, and Robert Louis Stevenson.

He wistfully recalls his fascination with the recently modish philosophers Francis Bacon, René Descartes, George Berkeley, John Locke, David Hume, Thomas Reid, Dugald Stewart, and Thomas Brown, whose works he remembered from Dr. Bruce's lectures at the Western University. And he marvels at the swiftness with which these thinkers had been superseded by Darwin, Spencer, Wallace, Huxley, John Tyndall, Henry Thomas Buckle, and "Argyle" (probably George Campbell, the eighth duke of Argyll):[10]

> According to the old system [of philosophy] the mind was an entity—indeed it was nearly everything, the body being considered of little account. The one was immortal, the other but a vile worm of the dust. . . . On the other hand, according to the new system which I was now reading up [on], mind is . . . the result of bodily organism, a manifestation of chemical and electric forces, the body, the musical instrument; mental action, the music given off, which ends when the vital forces are exhausted. . . . All we

know of it is as results from mediate and immediate causes, the great First Cause of all remaining unknown and unknowable. This great First Cause, working through secondary causes in producing the phenomena of nature, governs our moral and physical being by universal and unvarying laws which it is man's chief end to learn and obey.[11]

At once thrilled and frightened to be treading on philosophical terra incognita, he now contemplates the impact of evolutionary science on traditional religion, while flirting with the daring possibility of reconciling the two:

> Nor can this philosophy, it is held, be regarded as irreligious or undevout. It claims to teach a still better religion than now exists or has gone before; to be another step in advance, as Judaism was in advance of paganism, and Christianity in advance of Judaism. The chief feature of this new religion is that it would supersede government through special providences, by government through God's unvarying law, implanted in his works of nature ... because science establishes the fact that no infraction of any moral or physical law can escape the penalty, sure and certain, which is invariably attached to it.
>
> This is a religion which regards God as a spirit, infinite and unchangeable, creating, pervading and operating all things. . . . It magnifies the Deity beyond all former conception of him. It makes him the All-seeing Eye—the Spirit Infinite, in whom we live and move and have our being; everywhere with us, discerning the innermost thoughts of our hearts; and presents him as the unknown cause of all causes.[12]

Mellon's perennial terror of ignorant, malicious humanity now takes possession of him: "This new religion, or rather philosophy of religion . . . is very rapidly permeating the mind of the general public . . . rather too rapidly, I think, for the public good." He continues:

If a personal devil and local hell is a myth, the inference of the ignorant and unthinking is that they may do as they please with impunity.... They do not realize that under the new religion the consequences of every act, good or bad, go on and on to all eternity; and that the laws of God are impressed on all his works, and apply to and govern all his creatures, animate or inanimate, as well as all thoughts and actions, moral or immoral, good or bad; that the infraction of any of these laws carries with it, in the infraction itself and its consequences, the punishment foreordained for it from all eternity. And that no one can escape the fixed effect, according to the degree of the sin or "want of conformity unto or transgression of the law of God," but must pay the penalty, either in this life or that which is to come, in the future of himself or his offspring. It does not, like the old faith, leave a loophole for the wicked to escape at the end of their evil career by turning state's evidence as it were, and obtaining a free pass to the realms of bliss. If the moral and intellectual faculties of the people could be educated to a living realization that honesty is the best policy under all circumstances, and that in the very nature of things the ways of righteousness are the only ways to happiness now or hereafter, and that the evil ways necessarily and unavoidably lead to pain and misery, they might be in a condition to be benefited by this new philosophy.[13]

How many Pittsburghers living in 1885 were capable of such ruminations?

Though Mellon's ethical conclusions are informed by Spencer, they conspicuously accord with Franklin's secular morality, which holds that right and wrong need not be defined in biblical terms but may rest on principles which have proved beneficial or detrimental to man. His own religious feelings were at least as tepid as those of his forebears. As he ponders the lengthy succession of decisions, great and small, mundane and moral, that in the aggregate amount to life, religion appears to exert only a feeble influence on his deliberations. He regards preachers as a beggarly, subservient lot and the ministry as an inferior calling that has shed its former idealism but remains useless as a vehicle for accumulation. His niggardly benefactions to East Liberty Presbyterian Church stand in jarring contrast to the regular, generous donations made by his wife and mother-in-law. Writing to James, he testily declaims, "You may put me down for fifty dollars for the church debt, but I want that to cover anything you and Thomas would give besides. I won't give fifty dollars and have you and he give besides."[14]

Mellon poses no challenge to the moral authority of Jesus but reserves the right to decide which of his teachings are authentic:

> The proposition that we should encourage wickedness and violence by extending safety and immunity to its perpetrators: as by exposing one side of the face to blows because we have been beaten on the other; or encouraging idleness and indolence by dividing all we have among the poor and consequently adding ourselves to their number; or giving away our clothing even to the coat off our back to any tramp who may ask for it, is too great an absurdity in the line of religious teaching to be imputed to Christ. . . . Sentiments repugnant to the best regulated minds, contrary to common sense and the nature which God has implanted in his creatures, as well as contrary to the interests of society, may fairly be regarded as apocrypha, and part of the old leaven of the Essenians [Essenes] which has crept into some of the manuscript copies of the Scriptures of the early church. . . . The church has from time to time eliminated many things in the Old Testament and some in the New as apocrypha; and it may be that some things still remain to be expurgated.[15]

Effortlessly, airily, he dismisses as apocryphal the definitive strictures of Jesus' ethics—precisely those that would restrain him from pursuing a life of accumulation and self-aggrandizement—by attributing them to a heretical sect of Jewish cavemen who lived along the Dead Sea.

Reading *Thomas Mellon and His Times,* one is continually impressed by his tepid adherence to conventional religion. By all indications, when he did attend church with his family, it was because in rigidly conformist Scotch-Irish Pittsburgh, token observance of the Presbyterian faith was virtually a communal imperative. As in Ireland, church affiliation was the basis of social classification, and by worshipping as a Presbyterian, he sided with the rulers, showed that he could mingle with them as an equal, could approach them for business purposes as a friend who perhaps occupied the same pew, and could expect that his children and theirs might intermarry. Respectability called for church attendance, and accumulation—for him the dominant objective of life—was crucially interwoven with respectability.

The most conspicuous effect of religion on Thomas Mellon was to reinforce his withering scorn for the native Irish and for Catholics in general. He nonetheless confesses to a measure of backhanded admiration for the church of Rome: "The Catholic system of church government is the most effective that has ever been devised for the maintenance of sacerdotal power and the procurement of money for religious purposes. . . . Admiration of the dignity and power of the Catholic priesthood is at the bottom of it."[16]

That Christianity in all its denominations may wither away completely does not appear to disturb him: "Perhaps like the other great religions which preceded it, and like Judaism which it superseded, present Christianity also will have but its time, and in the course of evolution will itself be superseded by another modified religion growing out of it to suit the progress of our race."[17]

Religion would do little or nothing to influence his behavior. The obstinate Presbyterian belief that hell is a subterranean concentration camp, staffed by cackling devils with leathery tails who herd the damned into cauldrons of scorching oil with manure forks, held no terrors for him. He had awoken from that infantile nightmare. For him it was *this* world that mattered, not the next. Cut loose from the moorings of an age of faith that was fast receding—uneasy, perhaps, but nonetheless adamant in his secularism—Mellon confirmed by word and deed that he lived in advance of his day. Though the nineteenth century encompassed all of his active life, he was already a twentieth-century man.

Because the voice of a personal god whispered to him only weakly, he was not frightened by Herbert Spencer's abstract, conceptual deity, the incomprehensible Force, the irreducible First Cause, that enlivens all of existence but cares about none of it. Here, at last, was a "god" who made no personal demands but who did provide some meaning with which to fill the black hole that lies at the center of human knowledge and consists of our unanswerable, ultimate questions about life and the universe.

One wonders whether he shared any of his radical ruminations on religion with Sarah Jane. In the interests of peace, probably not. She too was a frequent reader of religious literature, but only of the devotional kind. Her scrapbook is so cluttered with pietistic doggerel that one cannot imagine her dispassionately examining the foundations of Christian faith. Moreover, her husband rarely shared his intellectual life. He certainly excluded his children from most of it. His mode of learning was not Socratic: it required no dialogue with friends, family, a teacher, or fellow students. He was a closet thinker who learned by reading—by the interplay of his own mind with that of an author. Though a tireless searcher for truth, he searched alone.

Socrates was right: the unexamined life is not worth living. And beginning with his decade on the bench, Mellon made a point of examining life through his reading glasses. He devoured the latest, most original works on political science, economics, and sociology. Nothing—not even Karl Marx—was too controversial for him. Like Abraham Lincoln, he read for edification, not for enjoyment. Or perhaps his principal enjoyment was to feed a voracious mind. Fiction continued to bore him, and his love of poetry remained narrowly confined to Burns, whose epigrams encapsulated for him the commonsense truths of life and lent a romantic hue to his quest for wealth. If a book aroused his interest, he read it with the rigor of his legal training, as though he were establishing his grasp on the facts of a criminal case. It must have riled him when he could not understand something.

During these years of reading and reflection, he also finalized his views on education. At a glance, his protracted struggle for wealth and respectability may stand out as the principal challenge of his life. But his career was preceded by an equally desperate struggle for education, and though he won resounding victories in both of these contests, one wonders which of them loomed, for him, as the more important. In any case, he never ceased to theorize about how to educate the young.

Like Spencer, Mellon was convinced that popular government must rest on a firm basis of enlightened education. But a glance in any direction persuaded him that education was woefully defective in America and that the panorama of life was bristling with consequent perils: "I see the evils of ignorance around me everywhere," he declaims. "Wherever you see a new or absurd religion, or any sensational or false theory of society proposed, those propagating it invariably seek the lowest and most ignorant for their proselytes." In the Mormon missionaries and their converts he finds a prime example of this ignorance, and he adds that the "propagandists of nihilism, anarchy, and socialism illustrate the same truth."[18]

The first defect in American education that Mellon focuses on is the absence of compulsory schooling. Sociologists, Mellon writes, "regard the common school system supported at public expense as a socialistic measure, and indefensible on any other ground than the public policy [that] it is for the good of the state that all its citizens should be enlightened and intelligent." Yet Mellon notes that vast numbers of children do not attend school at all and are utterly neglected. "They are allowed to grow up in ignorance and vice. . . . They afford recruits for reform schools and workhouses, whence they are graduated to the penitentiary or gallows."[19]

Mellon called for mandatory public education that would promote the rule of law and favor democracy and civilization. He also believed that the prevailing school system failed by ignoring the moral faculties, which either support or undermine good citizenship and directly affect social felicity. With irony, Mellon recalls that during his years in court, "the adroitest thieves and crooks were always among the best educated inmates of the jail." Hence to develop the intellect without training the moral faculties merely "sharpens the wits for rascality."[20]

He argues for teaching schoolchildren the "first principles of ethics," by which he means a secular, consensus-based morality—logical, based on the Golden Rule, and "easily understood by the child"—a morality that would support good citizenship in a democratic context but could be taught without triggering religious contention. Tellingly, he adds that "moral training has no necessary connection with religious teachings."[21]

As though Spencer were whispering in his ear, Mellon intones that another defect in American education "is the absence of all instruction in sociology or social science. Sociology includes the science of political economy, government, and all political rights and duties—the whole philosophy of society; and yet our educational system affords no knowledge whatever of this science paramount to all others in its importance." And because "our political system assumes that every one should understand the duties of officials and the rights of citizens, and the true principles and policy of government," our schools and colleges should teach sociology.[22] He would live to see universal, compulsory education become law, and it would gratify him to know that courses in sociology are now widely available in American institutions of higher learning. But his revolutionary proposal for teaching a secular morality based on social science, rather than on religion, would meet with only gradual and mixed acceptance.

Mellon notes that the vast expansion of knowledge during his lifetime has compelled a parallel expansion in the field of education, but he insists that more knowledge could only be taught with less profundity, and he adds that academic instruction was formerly every bit as thorough. He concedes that in an ever more complicated industrial world, life is not long enough for anyone to achieve proficiency in every field of study and recommends that "the time of youth should be applied to acquiring such knowledge and training as may be best calculated to prepare each for the special vocation he intends to follow." Hence, the foremost colleges performed a useful service when they relaxed their traditional requirements in Greek and Latin to offer diplomas in a range of more useful studies. But it saddens him that a day is approaching when the elegant literature of the classics, the mastery of which was still a feather in his cap, would be cultivated only by a negligible number of specialists.[23]

He warns that "the separation between parent and child now is too great, and the power of the parent in directing the child's studies and in the choice of its teachers is too much weakened." His fear is that parents might abandon the education of their children entirely to the public school system, whereas the best policy would be for them to perform, or at least supervise, a child's instruction themselves, as he himself had done. Where parents lack the means or the qualifications to do this, he insists that a public school education should be available and mandatory.[24]

With his habitual elitism, he opposes any effort to fill the heads of average students with more than rudimentary learning. "You may cram them with history and geography and a smattering of science to some extent, but they will not have left school a year till it is all forgotten. Whilst the real student, the one in a hundred, will have progressed and would have progressed, however poor his or her educational facilities, to a fuller and more complete knowledge than any common or high school can afford."[25] He sums up: "If education was made compulsory, and sociology was thoroughly taught, we would secure an improvement in our legislation and the tone and character of our office holders, with less ignorant agitation over impracticable measures, and less encouragement to schemes of socialism and anarchism."[26]

These reflections confirm that in Thomas Mellon's hagiography, Benjamin Franklin had to make room for Herbert Spencer. But in view of their similar convictions, it is not surprising that neither one supplanted the other. If Franklin, Spencer, and Mellon could have propounded their philosophies of life to one another and held a wide-ranging discussion on economics, education, and politics, there is little that they would have disagreed on. Nonetheless, it was Franklin's statue, not Spencer's, that Mellon would place above the entrance to his bank. For it will always be more difficult to make money than to theorize about it; and, though Spencer had philosophically justified, and therefore dignified, Mellon's life of accumulation, it was Franklin who had handed him the road map to riches.

# IX

On Capital Punishment
and the Jury System;
Four Hangings; Judges McClure,
Sterrett, and Stowe

*It may seem a hard task to condemn fellow creatures to long years of con-
finement in a prison, or "to be hanged by the neck until dead"; but it is
not so hard if they clearly deserve it.*

THOMAS MELLON'S YEARS ON THE Court of Common Pleas
of Allegheny County placed him in league with three of Pittsburgh's most memorable judges and compelled him to grapple with
issues of supreme importance. The jury system which, for all its defects,
remained sacrosanct to most Americans, claimed and reclaimed his
attention, and a succession of notorious murder cases compelled him
to ponder the ancient judicial right to extinguish life. As he picked his
way through the jungle of the law, he found no shortage of fodder for
his irrepressible criticism.

When Mellon's ten-year judicial term commenced on December 5,
1859, his eccentric and controversial colleague, Judge William B.
McClure, had already presided over the Court of Common Pleas and
four other county courts for nine eventful years. The two had met in
1838 at the prothonotary's office where Mellon was clerking, and they
established an easy rapport. In their new relationship, McClure would
retain his rank as president judge of the courts. Mellon would serve as
associate law judge, but they had equal judicial powers and equal sala-

ries. Their beat would be vast, for the common pleas judges also presided over the Court of Quarter Sessions, the Orphan's Court, the Court of General Jail Delivery, and the formidable Court of Oyer and Terminer, which tried the gravest violent crimes. When judging civil suits or minor criminal cases, they would have the option of presiding either singly or jointly. But where the charge was murder, both judges would be required to occupy the bench at all times. More important, they would have to agree on the sentence.

As members of the bar, Mellon and McClure belonged to the upper crust of their profession. They were "judges learned in the law" or simply "law judges." Their subordinates, the lay judges, were not barristers but were still empowered to try minor cases and to assist the law judges, even in trials of prime importance.

McClure and Mellon were both avid readers. McClure was enamored of Shakespeare and boasted to Mellon that he could never forget an arresting passage by the Bard. He did, however, forget points of law rather easily and was in the habit of importuning Mellon to refresh his memory. Mellon, who was new to the bench, nevertheless had much to learn from a thick-skinned veteran like McClure. Thrust together, the two developed a complementary relationship and became fast friends. This was fortunate, for the authority that they jointly exercised over all of the county courts rested ponderously on mutual compatibility.

Judge Mellon embarked on his new profession by total immersion. In the Court of Common Pleas, his trial list for the three months beginning on February 6, 1860, contains ninety-four civil suits.[1] McClure lent him one of the court's two lay judges, Gabriel Adams, to help litigate these squabbles. But, in the following three-month session, which commenced on May 7, he was compelled to settle eighty-four additional lawsuits by himself.[2]

After they had occupied the bench together for several months, McClure asked Mellon what he thought of judging. Mellon replied that he felt "comfortable" in his new position but that it had been a surprise to him in one way: While as a lawyer he had frequently erred in seeing only his client's side of the argument, as a judge he could usually see both sides with surprising clarity. In full agreement, McClure likened "the position of the lawyers to that of two dogs, barking at each other furiously . . . on opposite sides of a close fence, through which neither could see the size or appearance of the other. But the judge sat in safety and indifference on top of the fence where he could see the dog on each side and quietly make up his mind in regard to the contention between them." Mellon liked this analogy.[3]

Judge McClure's hatred of criminals was so obsessive that he tended to view the accused as guilty until proven innocent. When thoroughly persuaded of a defendant's culpability, he would spike his charge to the jury with such venomous sarcasm that the jurors routinely succumbed to his direction. Mellon notes this tendency with telling lack of censure. Far from condemning his colleague's autocratic bearing and eager imposition of immoderate sentences, he is bemused by these quirky excesses and dismisses them as "a slight mental obliquity regarding criminals in general, and homicides in particular."[4]

In his ten-year term on the bench, which began in 1852, McClure had sentenced five men and two women to death—more than had been previously hanged in Allegheny County since its formation in 1788. Mellon notes with wry satisfaction that though McClure's astringency often roiled attorneys, it won him thunderous applause from the public.[5] In 1861 McClure, though virtually on his deathbed, was reelected by a landslide.

Mellon's suggestion that his judgeship had been created not merely to reduce the backlog of cases but to restrain the erratic autocracy of McClure is ironic, for the two judges appear to have collaborated without the slightest friction. "I do not remember a single unpleasant feeling between us," recalls Mellon. "We of course differed on legal points sometimes, but in regard to the conduct of criminal cases we had no difficulty at all. In ruling on points of evidence he usually deferred to me, and in regard to sentences we were always able to agree on some satisfactory mean neither too lenient nor too severe."[6] It was probably coincidental that no death sentences were handed down by the two judges after Mellon's elevation to the bench. Or perhaps would-be murderers were still paralyzed by what McClure had done to their predecessors.

That "the judge should be a terror to evil-doers" found classic expression in the opinions of these two jurists. The following excerpt from *Thomas Mellon and His Times* probably falls short of what Judge McClure would have written on the same subject:

> It may seem a hard task to condemn fellow creatures to long years of confinement in a prison, or "to be hanged by the neck until dead"; but it is not so hard if they clearly deserve it. The community or commonwealth is a family or society which has established laws and regulations for the conduct and protection of its different members, and each member is under the highest social and moral obligation to abide by and respect these laws and regulations; and when a member becomes a rebel to the community and regardless of law and order and fatally bent on mischief, he renders himself an outcast and enemy to the society to which he belongs, and assumes the consequences. If these consequences are the loss of liberty or life it is his own act: he knows the penalty and ought to be content to pay the forfeit. It is an unpleasant and painful duty for the judge to pronounce sentence of death in such cases,—a duty which devolved on me on several occasions in regard to both males and females during my term; but where it is the result of their own wicked doings, and the protection of society requires it, there need be no regrets. In fact, on the part of the unthinking multitude there is entirely too much sympathy and consideration for criminals, and too much time wasted and expense incurred by the public on their behalf; and unfortunately this unreasoning sympathy increases with the enormity of the crime. The trial should proceed speedily after the arrest in every case, and the infliction of the allotted punishment immediately after the conviction where guilt is established.[7]

Judge Mellon's concept of the "manly criminal" is equally revealing, and we will discover who inspired it:

The manly criminal whose guilt is clear can have no valid objection to a speedy infliction of the penalty of his crime. If he did not hesitate or exercise either pity or delay in depriving another fellow being of his life or property, why should he ask greater indulgence himself than he extended to his victim? It is this spirit perhaps to some extent which of late produces a growing tendency to self destruction on the part of criminals, and it is a course not to be discouraged. Criminals of this type are doubtless such as are stricken with repentance and remorse. . . . Such criminals manfully rid the world of their presence, and society of the expense and trouble of their trial and punishment. It is only the mean spirited and cowardly, for the most part, who occupy the time and attention of our courts through long trials under trumped up pleas of insanity and other excuses, and invoke public sympathy to screen them from their just deserts.[8]

As we shall see, the lack of compassion that rings so harshly in these passages is curiously at variance with the accommodating attitude Judge Mellon showed toward defendants who were on trial for their lives in his court. Out of court, he could also be a courageous defender of the innocent: When a furious crowd gathered to lynch his neighbor and in-law, Henry Menold, Mellon was challenged to show physical as well as moral courage. His son James's eyewitness account confirms that he had both:

When the Civil War broke out, there was great excitement in front of the Menold property and a great crowd of angry people. Henry Menold was a Democrat and was called a "Copperhead," and excitement arose so that the crowd had a rope to hang him, and I remember my father and Joseph R. McClintock . . . were on store boxes out in the street pleading with the people not to hang Menold. The excitement was so great and everyone I saw there who talked at all was ready to pull the rope. I never saw such a condition with vicious feelings, all because the Southern people were Democrats. After Father and Mr. McClintock had talked probably a full hour, pleading with the crowd, the excitement subsided somewhat, but Father and Mr. McClintock stayed there until the crowd had about dispersed. Menold and his family were in their brick residence and a few people trying to protect them at the gate.[9]

When Judge McClure died, James P. Sterrett was appointed in January 1862 to succeed him as president judge of the common pleas bench, and his appointment was confirmed by the required election ten months later. That Judge Mellon, who had served on the court for two years, was passed over in favor of a younger man with no judicial experience is curious. That he made no apparent effort to secure the presidency of the court for himself is equally perplexing. As usual, politics and personal connections probably played the decisive role in Sterrett's appointment. But if being superseded by a newcomer irked Mellon, it failed to diminish his assessment of Sterrett, whom he would remember as "the best jury judge I have ever known."[10]

Physically ponderous, Judge Sterrett moved and spoke with a slow deliberation that could at first be mistaken for sloth. But his penetration of human nature was swift and uncanny. He ruled with an effortless aplomb that emanated from native intelligence commingled with an air of natural superiority. His legal knowledge was encyclopedic, but he chose not to flaunt it. Pleasant, informal, unfailingly courteous, and always relaxed, he put attorneys, litigants, and especially jurors at ease instead of raising their hackles. His tact oiled the wheels of justice. Without appearing to hurry, he actually hastened every trial toward its conclusion and saved valuable time. These qualities would go far toward securing his eventual appointment as chief justice of the Pennsylvania Supreme Court.[11]

"There was nothing arbitrary or dictatorial in his manner calculated to create opposition in the jury box," Judge Mellon recalls. "He . . . would explain and re-explain to the jury, in a conversational way and mild manner, the whole nature of the case, and the character and effect of the evidence on both sides regarding it; and would do this so thoroughly that the stupidest juror could not be mistaken as to how to find."[12]

The gently coercive guidance with which Sterrett conducted his court was what Mellon came to view as the most important function of a judge.

> Whilst at the bar, I had entertained an exalted opinion of the importance of the jury, and the necessity for non-interference with its functions by the judge. . . . I commenced upon this theory, and continued to apply it for a few months, until I found it was calculated to work injustice in a large proportion of the cases tried. . . . To weigh and accord to the different parts of conflicting testimony their relative values, taking into account all the attendant circumstances, is the most difficult and important task of the legal or judicial mind, and requires a degree of training which jurors know nothing about. . . . It is from the due interposition of the trained mind of the judge in directing the untrained minds of the jurors called from the common vocations of everyday life, that the best results are obtained. . . . The judge should explain clearly to their comprehension the issue or essential points in controversy and discriminate and arrange the different parts of the testimony, and point out the relevancy and weight of the documentary evidence if any in the case, and the corroborative or detractive circumstances, and the reasons on which his instructions rest. He may even go so far as to tell the jury how on the whole the weight of evidence strikes him: indeed it is his duty in most cases to do so. . . . He may tell them how he would find if in their place so long as he does not bind them to do as he would.[13]

In March 1862, Edwin H. Stowe, one of two candidates whom Judge Mellon had defeated for the Republican judicial nomination, was first appointed, then elected to the Court of Common Pleas. His arrival completed the historic triumvirate of Mellon, Sterrett, and Stowe, which would preside over the courts of Allegheny County for more than seven years, would decide a number of memorable cases, and would send three men and one woman to the gallows.

Judge Mellon's misanthropic reflections on the jury system raise interesting questions. His barnyard dictum that "justice cannot be judicially administered by tossing the evidence to the jury as a farmer would a bundle of hay to his cattle, to be devoured indiscriminately, weeds and all," would be roundly applauded by present-day judges.[14] But, to what extent should a judge be permitted to exercise influence over jurors? Specifically, how many jurists would agree with Mellon that judges do not exceed their mandate if they confide to a jury how *they* would decide, if they were in the jury box? Furthermore, though Judge Mellon's devastating opinion of the average juror is correct, what precisely are his views on the venerable system of trial by jury, which dates back to Magna Carta and remains one of the sacred cows of Anglo-Saxon law?

> In regard to our jury system, if there is any truth in human progress, and that all systems have to be adjusted and readjusted to suit the changed conditions of society, it is high time some important changes were made in the selection of jurors, and some discrimination and restriction in the cases to which they are applicable. It is many centuries since the present jury system was adopted in England and gained abiding fame as a bulwark of popular liberty against the encroachments of the crown and persecution from government officials. But no occasion arises for the protection of the people by a jury against the government where the people have the power peaceably to make and unmake or change the government to suit themselves. If it is a govern-

ment by the people, the people need no such protection against themselves.[15]

That he calls for "important changes . . . in the selection of jurors, and some discrimination and restriction in the cases to which they are applicable," but then refuses to propose specific reforms, compels one to suspect that the "changes" he favored were radical—possibly too radical for a member of the Pittsburgh Select Council to call for publicly. However, he appears to have subsequently detailed a number of his proposed reforms, because the *Biographical Review,* published in 1897, states that Judge Mellon "would abolish the trial by a jury of several offenses, would limit the number of jurors in the trial of others to three, five, or seven, according to the degree of the offense, and he would select all jurors from members of the bar, in the manner of choosing arbitrators under our compulsory arbitration laws."[16]

Mellon's insistence that people living under a genuinely democratic government do not need jury protection suggests that, at least in America, he might not have objected to replacing the system of trial by jury. We are free to wonder how he would have responded to the suggestion that far fewer miscarriages of justice would occur if trial by jury were abolished in favor of trial by either two or three judges who could convict only by unanimous agreement and whose decisions would be subject to review, on appeal, by judges from a different community, who would be free from the pressure of local passions. In private, he might well have favored such a change.

Mellon's final year on the bench, 1869, saw the repeal of the venerable English common-law rule of evidence. This rule had excluded interested parties, such as relatives, from testifying in court; the right to take the stand was now extended to everyone. Judge Mellon charges that the principal result of this misbegotten reform was to swamp the courts with frivolous and deceitful litigation. With equal vehemence, he argues for abolishing the oath administered to witnesses. Honest folk, he insists, will tell the truth, whether or not they are sworn, but liars who take the oath will gain credibility with the jury.[17]

We come now to Judge Mellon's record in pronouncing the sentence of death. That he calls it "a duty which devolved on me on several occasions in regard to both males and females during my term" virtually compels us to ask, who were the people he sent to the gallows? What were their crimes? How did the triumvirate of judges, all equal in authority, decide between life and death? Inexplicably, Judge Mellon gives us no answers. Moreover, the surviving evidence that bears on these questions is amazingly fragmentary and amounts to little more than the press coverage accorded to a small number of sensational trials.

Three men and one woman were executed in Allegheny County during Judge Mellon's judicial term.[18] They were Benjamin Marschall, August Frecke, Martha Grinder, and Lewis Lane. All were tried in the Court of Oyer and Terminer. Because murder was a rare crime in Allegheny County, this particular court held no regular sessions and kept no permanent staff. It was convened when necessary, with the Common Pleas judges presiding. Under the 1862 regulations, in a trial for homicide, at least two of the three law judges were required to occupy the bench whenever the court was in session, and all three could preside together. It was customary for the actual conduct of such a trial to be informally relegated to a particular judge; however, the required second judge—and the third judge, if present—could always interrupt and take a hand in the proceedings. Most important, all three law judges of Allegheny County had to agree before sentence of death could be pronounced.

Mellon's first capital case was, in the event, inconclusive. In July 1862, Thomas B. Keenan and seven raucous companions clambered aboard a horse-drawn streetcar in East Liberty and headed for nearby Lawrenceville. Some of them were drunk, and it was not long before blasts of unparliamentary language rent the air. Because there were women and children aboard, the conductor, John Obey, asked the young ruffians to be civil. They responded with a volley of abuse, and Obey ordered them out of the car. Tempers escalated, and a brawl erupted. Keenan emerged with blood pouring from his nose;

*Judge Thomas Mellon, circa 1860.*

Obey suffered a stab wound in the back and another in the lower abdomen.[19]

Engulfed in bedlam, car no. 7 jolted to a halt. Keenan and his fellow hoodlums jumped off and took to their heels, but a furious crowd of witnesses in hot pursuit brought them immediately to bay. Obey, who could still walk despite his wounds, pointed dramatically at Keenan and uttered the damning words, "That is the man who cut me." Keenan managed to groan, "Oh God." That night, John Obey died of internal bleeding.[20]

Caught in a groundswell of popular fury, the judges and prosecutors found themselves under heavy pressure to hang Keenan. Because second-degree murder, or aggravated homicide, was not a capital offense, they decided to charge him with first-degree, or premeditated, murder, for which the customary sentence was death by hanging. District Attorney Jacob Miller took the position that Keenan had acted as a deliberate aggressor, because Obey, unarmed and outnumbered eight to one, could not have presented a serious threat to him. The prosecution also insisted that Keenan had acted with deliberation when he hid his knife under a seat cushion before fleeing the streetcar.

But was this truly a first-degree murder? Couldn't a stronger case have been made for murder in the second degree? Wasn't Keenan merely a drunken young brawler who in the heat of conflict had stabbed a man whom he had no logical motive to kill and had never seen before—a man who later happened to die of his wounds?

Under Pennsylvania law, in a trial for homicide, the jury was frequently empowered to convict for either first- or second-degree murder. However, the judges were required to charge the jury, and in Keenan's case they ruled out a conviction for second-degree murder. This left the jurors with a horrific choice: they could acquit Keenan and run the gauntlet of public outrage, or they could convict him of first-degree murder and send him to the gallows. They decided to convict.

Clearly, Judge Mellon and his colleagues wielded their most formidable weapon when they charged a jury. In sentencing they frequently had little latitude, and if a conviction for first-degree murder was not reversed on appeal, they had no choice at all. If the defendant claimed that he had not received justice, he could appeal to the court that had convicted him, then to the Pennsylvania Supreme Court on a writ of error, and finally to the governor. If these appeals failed, the carpenters were waiting with their scaffold and the sheriff with his rope.

Fortunately for Keenan, he had engaged the two most brilliant criminal lawyers in Allegheny County, Thomas Marshall and Marshall Swartzwelder. Before Judges Mellon, Sterrett, and Stowe, Swartzwelder protested that Keenan should have been charged only with second-degree murder, that his drunkenness had not been sufficiently considered, and that the court's blatantly coercive and restrictive charge had fatally prejudiced his case. The counsel for the defense demanded a new trial.

On February 28, 1863, the court responded to Keenan's appeal. Affirming the collective role of the judges, Sterrett ruled that "a careful revision of the testimony and charge of the Court since, by Judges Mellon and Stowe, as well as myself, satisfied us all that the verdict should not be disturbed."[21] With Keenan standing in the dock, Judge Sterrett now came to the point: "The sentence of the law is that you, Thomas B. Keenan . . . be taken hence to the jail of the county of Allegheny . . . and thence to the place of execution, and there be hanged by the neck until you be dead; and may God in his infinite goodness have mercy on your soul."[22]

But those who now eagerly awaited the hanging of Keenan were counting their chickens prematurely. His name does not appear on the list of executed persons in *Scaffold and Chair*, compiled by Negley Teeters of Temple University and sponsored by the Pennsylvania Prison Society. His lawyers, Marshall and Swartzwelder, had announced that they would appeal to the Pennsylvania Supreme Court on a writ of error, but the high court either rejected their appeal or refused to consider it, for in December 1865 Keenan was still awaiting execution. That Governor Andrew Curtin had left the death warrant lying around unsigned for almost three years suggests that he had deep misgivings about hanging Keenan and may finally have pardoned him.[23] But there are other possibilities: Did Keenan eventually commit suicide or die in prison of natural causes? Did he break jail and escape to South America? His saga still ends with a question mark.

If Keenan's killing of Obey was arguably unpremeditated and to some extent accidental, the next murder case that came before Judge Mellon left no such doubts. At daybreak on August 24, 1865, Mayor James Lowry of Pittsburgh was informed that there had been a particularly gruesome murder on Boyd's Hill, near the Monongahela River. Rushing to the scene, he was shown the remains of a young man whose skull had been smashed and whose body was lacerated with knife wounds. His pockets were empty, even his shoes had been stolen, and no one had any idea who he was.[24]

The "Boyd's Hill murder," as it came to be known, baffled detectives for almost a month. Their first break came with the arrest of Benjamin Marschall in connection with a minor robbery. Marschall was a working-class German immigrant, a jack-of-all-trades and master of none, whose command of English was rudimentary. The police ran-sacked the boardinghouse where he lived and discovered a cache of stolen goods as well as some bloodstained articles of clothing.[25]

Four days later, they arrested a second German immigrant, August Frecke, who had been identified as a crony of Marschall's. Frecke spoke no English at all. His landlady deposed that he and Marschall had come to her boardinghouse with blood spots on their shirts and had conferred there only hours after the Boyd's Hill murder. It was discovered that the two had roomed together and worked at the same brickyard.[26]

Mayor Lowry now came to Marschall's cell and informed him that he was suspected of a crime beside which burglary paled into in-significance. Anxiety began to weigh on the prisoner. "I could not look anybody in the face," he recalled, "and when I would go to write, my hand would shake."[27] After three days, he broke down and decided to tell all.

Both Marschall and Frecke were brought to Mayor Lowry's office. Before numerous witnesses, the mayor informed Marschall that he was under no obligation to incriminate himself. The prisoner nonetheless made an oral confession in German, which was then translated, written out in English, and presented to him for his signature. By signing it he confessed to the "Boyd's Hill murder" and named Frecke as his accomplice. The latter vehemently denied Marschall's allegations and stubbornly trumpeted his complete innocence.[28]

Though the prisoners admitted to having been friends, their testimony agreed on little else. According to Marschall, Frecke had persuaded him that crime was more profitable than work. To test this durable hypothesis, they had journeyed to New York, where opportunities for theft were supposed to be better, but a week in Manhattan disabused them of their illusions. On the way back to Pittsburgh, they befriended a third German immigrant named Henry Foerster and persuaded him to accompany them. Foerster wore fancy clothes, had a gold watch, and appeared to spend money quite freely. As the train rattled along, Frecke drew Marschall aside and talked him into a scheme that provided for their companion and his belongings to go in different directions.[29]

Arriving at Pittsburgh, the conspirators volunteered to find Foerster a boardinghouse and kindly offered to help carry his luggage. They led him to Boyd's Hill and were passing down an unlighted lane when Frecke sprang into action. He plunged a knife into Foerster and shoved him toward Marschall, who hauled off and stove in his face with an iron bar. Frecke now dragged Foerster out of the road by one foot, stabbed him repeatedly, and cut his throat from ear to ear. Spattered with blood, the killers stripped their victim of his valuables and took flight. They spent the rest of that night hunting for clean clothes and trying to hide their loot. This, in a nutshell, was Marschall's confession. Frecke told a radically different story and admitted to no wrongdoing.[30]

In early October, the doomsday Court of Oyer and Terminer was convened to pass judgment on these intruders from Germany: first Marschall, and then Frecke immediately afterward. In both trials, Judges Mellon and Sterrett presided jointly. The prisoners stood accused of first-degree murder.

Clutching at straws, the defense attorneys protested that Mayor Lowry had acted improperly in obtaining Marschall's confession; that the prisoner's poor command of English had worked against him; that he had obviously been lured, maneuvered, or stampeded into confessing; that he could only have offered to confess on the clear understanding that for incriminating Frecke he would be granted leniency; that his confession, as it stood, was a one-way ticket to the gallows that no sane person would have signed; and that his initial oral confession must therefore have been very different from the written one.[31]

These objections cut no ice with Judges Mellon and Sterrett or with the jury. Marschall had made no move to withdraw his confession, and the admissions it contained were supported by persuasive material evidence. For one thing, each defendant had been caught with some of the victim's belongings in his possession. The judges decided to let Marschall's confession stand, and he was convicted of first-degree murder.[32]

The case against Frecke was more problematic, for it now rested heavily on the testimony of a convicted killer. Moreover, Frecke offered his own version of events: He insisted that on leaving the train, he had not accompanied Marschall and Foerster to Boyd's Hill and had not witnessed, much less participated in, the murder. If Marschall had implicated him, it was because the two had fallen out during their trip to New York. However, Frecke was unable to adduce any evidence or testimony in favor of his story, and Marschall's confession, as it related to Frecke, was supported by both. Notably, two witnesses had testified to Frecke's having left a trunk in their keeping, which detectives had later seized and traced to the victim. Far from casting doubt on Marschall's confession, the independent testimony and evidence supported it.[33]

The jurors deliberated for forty minutes. When they convicted Frecke of first-degree murder, he left the courtroom hollering in German, "I am as innocent as our Lord Jesus Christ on the cross!"[34]

The judges found themselves with no choice as to Frecke's fate. From a strict legal viewpoint, Marschall's case may have been similarly unambiguous, but ethically it was more troubling: having confessed to the crime and implicated Frecke, Marschall was arguably entitled to a measure of leniency. However, the jury had conspicuously failed to recommend mercy after hearing his confession. Also, he had made no effort to plea-bargain, for he viewed himself as a doomed man who deserved to die and said he wanted to die.[35] Here was the "manly criminal" whom Mellon would describe in his memoirs but would not name.

Perhaps to give the appearance of deliberation, the judges delayed until November before sentencing the Boyd's Hill murderers. But by then, public attention had shifted to a serial killer whose bloodcurdling callousness was unprecedented in local history.

Martha Grinder, who lived on Gray's Alley in Allegheny City, was a married thirty-four-year-old mother who gave every appearance of being generous, considerate, and neighborly. She made a practice of sending soup, home-cooked meals, and desserts to newlywed Mary Caroline Caruthers, who lived next door. That these niceties began to have a curiously repellent flavor and sometimes left the recipient retching, vomiting, and feeling as though her intestines were on fire failed to ring any warning bells in Mrs. Caruthers's credulous head. The painful death of Martha Grinder's own daughter from a mysterious digestive disorder had also attracted nothing more than condolences.[36]

One day, Mrs. Grinder invited another neighbor, Jane Smith, over for a cup of coffee. Miss Smith would later testify to a packed courtroom that the coffee tasted like copper pennies and that she soon became deathly sick. On another occasion, Miss Smith's family shared a bowl of veal soup that the thoughtful Mrs. Grinder had sent over. They too became violently ill, and young Harry Smith, Jane's brother, died. When the remaining soup was thrown outside, their dog attempted to eat it and went into convulsions. Meanwhile, an increasing number of people on Gray's Alley were suffering from inexplicable bellyaches.[37]

Mrs. Caruthers's condition continued to worsen. When she became bedridden, her kindly neighbor would come over and offer her refreshments. On August 1, 1865, after days of torment, Mary Caroline

Caruthers died. Beside her deathbed stood Martha Grinder, looking deeply concerned.[38]

The day came—too late, alas—when Mrs. Caruthers's widowed husband, James, caught himself thinking the unthinkable. With increasing frequency, he focused on the satanic possibility that had eluded his naive wife. At last, overwhelmed by suspicion, he unburdened himself to Mayor Lowry and the police. A number of doctors who had attended the victims and were nursing their own doubts also broke silence.[39]

After spending almost a month underground, the body of Mrs. Caruthers was exhumed and subjected to a rigorous autopsy. The pathologist, Professor Otto Wuth, discovered that her stomach was saturated with arsenic and antimony. A house servant named Anna Sullivan now came forward and alleged that Mrs. Grinder had sent her to procure these very poisons from two local druggists. Prosecutors would later break their heads to find a logical motive for Mrs. Grinder's crimes, but all they could point to at her trial were some used clothing and inexpensive household articles, including a molasses pitcher and a chamber pot, that she had taken from Mrs. Caruthers's home after murdering her.[40]

Though Martha Grinder was discovered to have killed at least six people—including her own brother-in-law, a friend named Jennie Buchanan, a Mrs. Hall, and the three victims already adverted to—prosecutors charged her with only one murder, that of Mary Caroline Caruthers. Her plea of not guilty triggered the most sensational trial that Pittsburghers had ever been treated to. It opened in the Court of Oyer and Terminer on October 23, 1865, and ran for six days. The sessions attracted such a crowd of raucous voyeurs that Sheriff Stewart had difficulty wedging Mrs. Grinder into the courtroom. A succession of witnesses who had unwittingly sampled the dishes on her lethal menu now came forward to describe their vile symptoms. That the dog which had survived a taste of her infamous veal soup was trotted into court would be remembered as a lapidary tidbit of Americana.[41]

Women attended these spectacles in large numbers. A number of Pittsburgh wives even brought their knitting to court, like the companions of Madame Defarge who gathered around the guillotine in Dickens's *A Tale of Two Cities*.[42]

It is not know how many sessions of *The Commonwealth versus Martha Grinder* Judge Mellon attended, but the newspapers report him occupying the bench with Judges Sterrett and Stowe when concluding arguments were heard and the jury was charged. That Pittsburgh's peerless criminal lawyer, Thomas Marshall, would address the jury on Mrs. Grinder's behalf was something that Judge Mellon and everyone else could look forward to.[43]

Unalterably opposed to capital punishment, Thomas Marshall had defended more killers than any other lawyer in the county. He was a shrewd and tenacious counselor, but the warmth and conviction with which he pleaded were even more compelling. As Mellon listened to Marshall bravely fighting the impossible fight, not so much to save a particular life as to defend an ideal, it may have occurred to him how radically he differed from this curiously magnanimous advocate whose "most famous cases were fought without hope or thought of reward" and who believed that "the poor and helpless had a better claim on his services than the rich and powerful."[44] Yet it was Thomas Marshall who had taken the lead in drafting Thomas Mellon to run for his judgeship.

The charge that the judges had agreed on was now read to the jurors, and it effectively plugged every loophole through which the murderess might escape. Flanked by Mellon and Stowe, Judge Sterrett spoke for the court:

> This case is one of unusual importance in all its bearings and requires the most careful consideration. Whatever may be our opinions they are not to be considered. The law is only to be regarded, and on the legislators rests the responsibility. The jury must receive the law from the court, weigh well the testimony and decide as the law requires.

There is a distinction between circumstantial and direct evidence. In direct evidence, the testimony is of persons who can testify to positive knowledge. In circumstantial evidence, reasonable deductions are drawn from circumstances. Circumstantial evidence must be admitted; otherwise the best interests of society would be set at naught. One of the rules governing circumstantial evidence is that every circumstance on which the case depends must be proved as carefully as if it was the only one to be adduced. Again, all the facts proved must be consistent with each other. Again, facts and circumstances together should be conclusive, leading to the reasonable belief that the accused is the guilty one. If the case admits that any other may be the guilty party, the case fails.

. . . The evidence of the Commonwealth has been confined to facts to-day to show the administration of poison by the accused. . . . A chemical analysis of the remains has proved beyond a doubt that poison had been administered. . . . Then the next question arises: Was the poison administered by the defendant? The questions natural to ask are: Had the accused poison? Had she opportunity of administering it? Had she a motive for doing so? The fact of her having the poison in her possession is proven beyond a doubt. As to the opportunity, the testimony proves conclusively that she had ample opportunities. The proof of the motive adduced by the Commonwealth must be taken for what it is worth. There is no necessity that the motive be proved.

The question of guilt is to be decided by a consideration of all the testimony. If there is a reasonable question in the minds of the jury as to the administration of poison by the prisoner, the verdict will be "not guilty." If there is no such doubt, the verdict must be of murder in the first degree.

Also, reasonable doubt is not a mere possible doubt; it is that state of the case which leaves the mind of the juror so uncertain that he cannot say that he has an abiding belief in the guilt of the accused: it is such a doubt as . . . would cause a man of common sense to pause seriously.

If it should be decided by the jury that the prisoner committed the act but was governed by an uncontrollably insane motive, the prisoner cannot be held guilty. [However] every person is held to be sane until proved insane. Crime is not evidence of insanity. If it were, the more atrocious the crime the more safe the criminal from punishment. The proof of insanity is on the party alleging it. There was none offered by the defense.

In this case there can be no distinction of degree. Either the prisoner is guilty of murder in the first degree, or not guilty. If not guilty, it may be either in a general manner, or from insanity.[45]

On her sixth and final day in court, Mrs. Grinder was convicted of first-degree murder by a jury that had deliberated for one evening. Its verdict was received by Judges Mellon, Sterrett, and Stowe, presiding together.

With a backlog of first-degree murderers awaiting their sentences, the three law judges now conferred to determine the fate of Benjamin Marschall, August Frecke, and Martha Grinder. This could not have taken them very long.

On November 25, the court opened punctually at 9:00 a.m. Whether Mellon or Stowe were present we do not know, but Judge Sterrett definitely occupied the bench and was determined to rid himself of the odious chore that confronted him. Finding the courtroom almost empty and a mood of apathy prevailing, he suddenly ordered Benjamin Marschall hauled into the dock, and after subjecting him to a damning recapitulation of his crime, announced the sentence of the court: death by hanging. Next came August Frecke. Sentenced to death and hustled from the courtroom bellowing his innocence. Now it was Martha Grinder's turn. Sobbing lies and denials, she swayed as though about to faint and subjected her meager audience to a lamentable display of bad theater. But all it gained her was an appointment with the hangman. Having cleaned house with one mighty sweep, Sterrett recessed the court and everyone went to lunch.[46] They had plenty to talk about.

On January 12, 1866, as the two condemned men stood side by side on a makeshift scaffold in the Pittsburgh jail yard, Frecke turned to Marschall and demanded, "For the last time, will you confess that I am innocent!" Marschall replied, "I have nothing more to confess."[47] He got the last word. There is no reason to believe that Thomas Mellon ever witnessed a hanging. If he had attended this one, he would have witnessed the spectacle of August Frecke strangling for thirteen minutes, until his face became purple and pink foam oozed from his mouth and nostrils. The judges should perhaps have been made to witness their handiwork.

Precisely a week later, after hundreds of would-be spectators had drawn lots for the pleasure of watching her swing, Martha Grinder also suffered society's cleansing revenge. The "Lucrezia Borgia of Pittsburgh," as the press had dubbed her, was hanged on the same scaffold on which Marschall and Frecke had passed to eternity. In her final days she is known to have distracted herself with lengthy deliberations about how she would dress for the hangman, and the curious fixed smile that she stubbornly maintained on the scaffold lent further support to the widespread belief that her slide into madness had been continuous. Under the spell of her spiritual adviser, the Rev. Charles Holmes, she had found refuge in religion and had even confessed in writing to the murders of Jennie Buchanan and Mary Caroline Caruthers.[48] The grizzly details of her case had already been published in a pamphlet that was being hawked to the public for 25 cents.

We can only surmise how the personalities of the three judges coalesced when they made decisions. President Judge Sterrett appears to have been the court's dominant personality. Like Stowe, he was a professional jurist whose personal advancement would depend on politics. By contrast, Judge Mellon was an independently wealthy businessman who had been drafted to the bench for his fierce stand against railroad bonds; who, when drafted, had initially regarded the call as a practical joke, and who almost certainly failed to radiate much enthusiasm for judging. Moreover, he had maintained a wide bridge to the business world and had probably given the impression that he would retreat across it at the end of his judicial term. Mellon's colleagues may have had good reason to view him as a wealthy interloper and a probable lame duck.

For all of the bruising opinions he expressed, Judge Mellon could be surprisingly accommodating to defendants. The Sims case illustrates this. On March 7, 1864, a drunken twenty-year-old named James Sims stabbed and mortally wounded seventeen-year-old Howard Hamilton during a brawl. Whether Sims had committed first- or second-degree murder was left for the jury to decide. According to the *Daily Pittsburgh Gazette,*

> Judge Mellon delivered the charge of the Court, and in passing upon the question of drunkenness laid down the law to be as follows: that, under the humane provisions of the Act of 1794, making degrees of murder, the question of drunkenness was all-important, and must be considered by the jury—involving, as it did, the ability of the defendant to perpetrate "willful, deliberate and premeditated" murder, without the existence of all of which elements it ceases to be murder in the first degree. Hence drunkenness, as affecting the mental status of the defendant, was in point of fact the only question to be considered by the jury.[49]

Here, Mellon's charge to the jury is balanced, dispassionate, and devoid of coercion. The jury convicted Sims of only second-degree murder and spared his life.

In the 1866 trial of James Laughran for the fatal stabbing of George Myers during a quarrel, the defense attorney, John Kirkpatrick, petitioned Judge Mellon to include in his charge to the jury six points that would augur favorably for the defendant. Mellon included most of them. The jury convicted Laughran of manslaughter and recommended him to the mercy of the court.[50] After spending a few months in jail, he was sentenced to an additional thirty days and released.

That same year, Mellon also conducted the trial of Charles Stein for the murder of David Roberts. Stein was a saloon keeper who had fallen to quarreling with one of his customers—Roberts—over whether a cigar had been paid for. Fighting broke out among the drunken clientele, and Stein blew Roberts's brains out with a revolver.

At Stein's trial, Judge Mellon went out of his way to assist the defense by permitting twelve-year-old Andrew Stein to testify in his father's behalf, though the boy could not be sworn as a witness. More important, he acquiesced in five of the six points that the defense attorney, Marshall Swartzwelder, requested him to include in his charge to the jury. Mellon's clarification of the sixth point is reminiscent of the legal position he had taken in his personal clash with Samuel Black twenty years earlier: "If a man's property or family is attacked, . . . he is not bound to leave it or them defenseless and make his own escape if he can. He may defend them, and even take life in their defense. . . . But to excuse him under such circumstances, the danger to his life or property must be imminent and immediate, . . . and no other available or reasonably probable means of averting the danger appear to be at hand, except by killing the assailant."[51]

So charged, the jury deliberated for three hours and found Stein guilty of second-degree murder. This verdict spared his life. But the defining circumstances of the crime had been woefully inauspicious for Stein, and Judge Mellon could easily have attempted to steer the jury toward a conviction for first-degree murder.

The surviving evidence suggests that in his conduct of trials for murder, Mellon, though an unapologetic advocate of the death penalty, frequently showed leniency toward the defendant when he could just as easily have favored harshness. His bark appears to have been worse than his bite.

In May 1868, a number of agitated Pittsburghers reported that a black woman had died under mysterious and disturbing circumstances.

They spoke of the horrible torment she had suffered for more than a day, of her screaming in agony, and of her repeated cries for a doctor, all of which went unanswered. They spoke of trying to help her and of finding her door locked from the outside. And they had plenty to say about her husband, Lewis Lane.[52]

Lane was a black man who claimed to have been born of free parents in Virginia and appeared to be between fifty and sixty years old. He eked out his living as a wandering barber in the black neighborhoods of Pittsburgh and had somehow managed to rent a single room in the cellar of No. 211 Wylie Street. When he and his wife, Henrietta, were alone together, they fought like tomcats. At night, the neighbors were shaken awake by blasts of obscenity and the crash of objects hitting the walls.[53]

One day, the Lanes had lunch in their subterranean apartment with a neighbor named Gracie Allen. She would later testify that Henrietta had been cheerful and healthy in the morning, but that while at table she began to complain of a burning sensation in her stomach. By late afternoon, she was vomiting, purging, and groaning. Those who offered their assistance were berated as intruders by her husband and driven away. Instead of getting a doctor, he crossly insisted on treating Henrietta himself and muttered about going to the drugstore. He eventually clapped a padlock on the door behind which his wife lay dying and was heard to shout at no one in particular, "I'll keep all you damned niggers out!"[54]

When Henrietta died and her neighbors had voiced their suspicions to the coroner, an alderman ordered Lewis Lane's arrest. As he was being led to his cell, an attentive officer saw him toss a glass vial into one of the prison fireplaces. A sample of the contents was scraped up and sent to be analyzed. It proved to be arsenic. Pathologists discovered a vast quantity of this poison in the dead woman's stomach. And detectives, rummaging through the Lanes' apartment, found a carpetbag that contained not only arsenic but an array of other poisons—enough, in all, to kill ten people.[55] If Lewis Lane's profession was cutting hair, his hobby was the chemistry of death.

The suspect's lurid past was now swiftly coming into focus. It turned out that Henrietta had been his sixth wife. The first four had disappeared inexplicably. A fifth wife—the only survivor—would testify to Lane's resourcefulness: how first he had tried to poison her; how, when that failed, he had waited till she lay sick in bed, locked her door and then set the house on fire; and how she had saved herself by jumping from a second-story window in her nightgown. For these chemical and pyrotechnical experiments Lane had served six years in prison.[56]

By 1867, he was back on the street and had married Henrietta, but marital bliss continued to elude him. Within a year, he was heard screaming death threats at his new wife and her bastard child: "I'll burn you both up!"[57]

Lewis Lane was tried in June 1868 before Judges Sterrett and Stowe. The jurors deliberated for all of fifteen minutes before finding this "coloredman" guilty of first-degree murder, and that included the ten minutes they spent retiring to their chamber and returning. But whoever composed the charge that Judge Stowe had read to the jury must have erred too far on the side of coercion. The defense attorney, Haines, protested to the Pennsylvania Supreme Court that the jurors had been browbeaten, and, to widespread anger and disbelief, Lane's conviction was reversed.[58]

His second trial took place in January 1869, with Judges Mellon and Stowe presiding. That Sterrett recused himself from the bench suggests that he may have viewed the high court's reversal of Lane's initial conviction as a personal rebuke. It also hints that he may have authored the excessively restrictive charge that Judge Stowe had read to the jury.

When Lane was again convicted, Mellon and Stowe found themselves with no choice but to impose the ultimate penalty. Lewis Lane was hanged in the jail yard of the old Pittsburgh courthouse on April 29, 1869. To the disappointment of many, he ascended the scaffold jauntily, almost running up the steps. He had dished out death to his wives in heaping portions, but he could take it when he had to. The prolonged and impassioned efforts of his spiritual adviser, Father Kerr, had convinced him that he would plunge through the floorboards directly into heaven. To those who attended him at the last he spoke these words: "Oh yes, I am happy. I am going home and don't dread the pain of death; that is nothing. Hope to meet you gent'men above the skies. Goodbye."[59]

Lane met his Maker rakishly attired—broadcloth dinner jacket, cashmere pants, white dress shirt with stiff collar, brightly polished black slippers, and silken vest. Was he going to a fancy dress ball? He appears to have died painlessly: The inquest revealed that his neck had been cleanly broken, and the attending physician confirmed that his heart had fluttered for only about a minute. Sheriff Cluley could congratulate himself on a perfect hanging.[60]

But in Judge Mellon's decade on the bench, capital cases were rare exceptions in a river of routine litigation. On a typical day, such as February 4, 1867, Judges Mellon, Sterrett, and Stowe heard evidence in the case of a coal barge that had sunk in the Allegheny River after colliding with a tugboat. They also received the lawyer John Bailey's motion for the retrial of a civil suit, issued five summons in divorce cases, appointed an auditor to examine the dockets of court officers, admitted one Wilfred Breed to the bar, and sentenced James Laughran to an additional month in jail for manslaughter.[61] Judge Mellon's own trial list for January 30, 1868, includes fourteen civil suits. In one of these a husband was claiming damages from another man for having defamed his wife's character. Mellon awarded him $5.[62]

In the Court of Quarter Sessions, on January 30, 1869, Judges Mellon and Stowe ordered J. F. Roup to pay his abandoned wife $4 a week and fined Frank Gallagher $50 plus court costs for violating the livery stable laws. James White and three other miscreants were each slapped with a $20 fine plus court costs for "malicious mischief." A wife who was suing her husband for support learned that he had obtained a divorce from her in Indiana. The sentencing of Jeremiah Hawley and others for felonious assault and battery was postponed, and one William Happham was committed to a lunatic asylum.[63]

The daily grind of litigation was enlivened by moments of sardonic humor. On one occasion a young lawyer named Josiah Cohen arrived to present his first petition in the Court of Common Pleas and found Judge Mellon on the bench: typically, he was absorbed in writing. Mellon eventually raised his eyes and asked: "What did you say that petition is for?"

"For a charter, Your Honor, a charter for a Jewish burial ground."

"A place to bury Jews?"

"Yes, Sir."

"With pleasure," ruled the Judge, "with pleasure." More than fifty years later, Cohen, by then a judge himself, would recall this exchange, fortunately with Olympian humor, in an address to the Historical Society of Western Pennsylvania.[64]

As Mellon's judicial term was drawing to a close, he received from his colleagues an honor rarely conferred on common pleas judges, or even on justices of the Pennsylvania Supreme Court:

Pittsburgh, November 25th, 1869.

To the Honorable Thomas Mellon:

Dear Sir:

We, the undersigned members of the Pittsburgh Bar, moved by feelings of cordial friendship and high regard for you as a man and as a judge, express our sincere regret that you are about to retire from the bench of the Court of Common Pleas of this county. And now, at the end of your term of office, and in view of your long and faithful public service, we desire explicitly to declare our appreciation of the patient industry, conspicuous integrity, eminent ability and distinguished success which characterized the performance of the difficult and important duties of your official position.

In order that we may have an opportunity to express our feelings in a social and friendly manner, we invite you to meet us and partake of an entertainment at such time as you may be pleased to designate.

Hoping that this intimation of our wishes may meet your approbation, we are,

Respectfully and truly, yours, &c.[65]

The above invitation—call it a salute—is signed by ninety-three members of the Pittsburgh bar.[66] To see this regiment of old friends and colleagues paying their final tributes—passing, as it were, in review before him—afforded a round of thunderous applause as the curtain was falling on a chapter of Thomas Mellon's life.

He accepted their invitation and was treated to a banquet at Pittsburgh's plushest hotel, Monongahela House, where Britain's King Edward VII, then Prince of Wales, had stayed during his visit to the city in 1860. Judge Mellon would remember this occasion as "one of the most agreeable festivities of my life, constituting one of those bright spots by the way which afford pleasant memories to revert to."[67]

Banker and Businessman,
His Larimer and Caldwell In-laws,
The Founding of Mellon Brothers
and of T. Mellon & Sons,
Loans to Henry Clay Frick

*I have never seen a horse race or boat race, or played a game of cards in my life, or incurred any extra hazardous risks—never speculating in property of any kind without I saw a sure thing in it.*

THE AMERICAN CIVIL WAR WAS unprecedented in the scope and modernity of its devastation. The musket was supplanted by the rifle, the cannonball by the explosive shell. Wooden warships were scrapped in favor of ironclads. Wind power gave way to steam, wagons to rail transportation, battlefield combat to trench warfare. The earliest machine guns and submarines were tested. Swept by disease and starvation, the teeming prisoner-of-war camps offered grisly harbingers of later concentration camps.

In 1862, Pennsylvania was narrowly spared from a Confederate invasion by the Union victory at Antietam, and the following year, with a second rebel offensive looming, the city of Pittsburgh sealed off its vulnerable eastern approach with a line of trenches that extended along Black Horse Hill, directly behind the Mellon home. For Pittsburghers, it was a time of foreboding. Without alluding to the moral principles at issue in the conflict or to the horrific casualties suffered by Pennsylvania regiments, Thomas Mellon poured out his habitual pessimism in gloomy letters about the war's effect on business and taxation, while outside in the orchard, eight-year-old Andrew manfully guarded his father's beloved fruit trees with an empty shotgun.[1]

Thomas Mellon would have viewed the war in a more favorable light had he foreseen the dizzying escalation of business activity that it would promote. By 1863, Pittsburgh's four hundred factories were producing innumerable rifles, artillery, ammunition, and military uniforms, not to mention steam engines, locomotives, freight cars, and hundreds of miles of rail.

This frenzy of manufacturing did not end with the war in 1865. It gathered momentum and continued for eight additional years. With more than thirty rolling mills in operation, Pittsburgh was producing half of the nation's iron. Forty-six foundries and fifty-eight oil refineries were operating in the metropolitan area, and the city's numerous glassworks were turning out a third of America's window glass. As the Industrial Revolution swept America, Pittsburgh found itself awash in new money, and most of it settled on a very few. Wages remained low as wave after wave of immigrants, lugging their meager chattels in tow sacks and carpetbags, piled in from Ireland, Britain, and Eastern Europe.

With its burgeoning suburbs and satellite communities, greater Pittsburgh continued to grow exponentially. In 1823, ten-year-old Thomas Mellon had viewed with amazement the sleepy river town of seven thousand inhabitants; by 1870, it boasted a population of about a hundred and fifty thousand. Now linked to the world by steamship and cable, by rail and telegraph, Pittsburgh businessmen were selling their products globally. A thickening forest of smokestacks encircled the Forks of the Ohio, and giant coal barges plied the three rivers. Steam whistles shrieked like harpies.

"The smoke permeated and penetrated everything," recalled Andrew Carnegie. "If you washed face and hands, they were as dirty as ever in an hour."[2] Inexorably, the poisoned landscape of rampant industrialization so nightmarishly depicted by Aaron Gorson's brush was taking shape. Though Pittsburgh was generating more wealth than any American city, it had become "hell with the lid off."[3]

Thomas Mellon caught this wave of compounding riches and rode it to fruition: His coal mines flourished in response to ravenous demand from the city's mills, forges, and furnaces.[4] A swelling population that hungered for affordable housing inflated the value of his real estate. And, predictably, the swiftly compounding return from these investments was steadily disenchanting him with the practice of law. That he would soon put his grown sons, Tom and James, to work selling land, coal, and building materials confirms that he had come to see brighter prospects on the construction site, and even in the lumberyard, than at the courthouse. One "qualification indispensable to success in the legal profession is first class business talent;" he wrote, "but . . . first class business talent can mostly be utilized to better advantage in other pursuits. . . . It is in view of this fact that I have never encouraged one of my own sons to enter the legal profession. . . . Attention to other people's business is a waste of time when we have profitable business of our own to attend to."[5]

Mellon's faithful genie, Benjamin Franklin, did not have to emerge from the gas lamp to persuade him that he had wasted years adjudicating the complaints of others, while lesser men had been making greater fortunes than his: "After the [Civil] war was fully under way, . . . an impulse was given to dealings in real estate and coal and other property. . . . Business became so active that such opportunities for making money had never before existed in all my former experience; and for some two years before the end of my term, although the judicial office was entirely to my taste, I discovered that . . . my salary afforded no adequate compensation for the loss sustained by declining passing opportunities for making money."[6]

Mellon had long ago concluded that "the acquisition of wealth is really . . . a badge of merit and ability."[7] But did the heap of his wealth correctly reflect the merit and ability that supported so much of his self-esteem? The dignity and respectability of the bench appealed to him, but it was by no means the only position with these qualities. For making money there were better rocks to fish from, and beginning in 1867, he increasingly directed his attention toward business and away from the law.

Looking back on the postbellum era, he would recall, "I had two bright boys just out of school, the idols of my heart, merging on manhood, and with fine business capacities, whom I was eager to launch on this flood tide of business prosperity, and to pilot them in the channel for some part of their way."[8] The two "bright boys" were James and Tom.

As I have noted, eighteen-year-old James had early fallen in love with seventeen-year-old Rachel Larimer after meeting her on a business trip to Leavenworth, Kansas, in 1864. He had rushed back to Pittsburgh and had asked his startled father for permission to marry. That James had no job and no home of his own and was still a minor utterly failed to deter him.

The Judge, of course, withheld his consent but was wise enough not to say no outright. In the long wait that followed, we can imagine him sizing up Rachel with frigid detachment, as he had Sarah Jane. That Rachel's parents were Scotch-Irish Presbyterians, originally from Turtle Creek, just east of Pittsburgh, must have counted in her favor. Equally important, her father, Major General William Larimer Jr. had long been one of Mellon's law clients as well as his "friend and confidential adviser." Her wealthy maternal grandfather, John McMasters, had also been a Mellon client, and her uncle had been the groomsman at Thomas Mellon's wedding. That Rachel's aunt was married to the ironmaster B. F. Jones put the final shine on her credentials. Socially, the girl's papers were in order.[9]

Rachel Larimer's father had once been a wealthy promoter and entrepreneur. He had opened a bank, founded a Conestoga wagon service that hauled freight between Pittsburgh and Philadelphia, and organized the Youghiogheny Slack Water System. When the railroads came, he had founded the Westmoreland Coal Company at Larimer Station and served as first president of the Pittsburgh and Connellsville Railroad. He had invested in California gold mines and overland transportation companies.[10] His magnanimity and commanding oratorical skill had gained him political influence and won him the friendship of Sam Houston and Horace Greeley. Governor William Bigler had awarded him the rank of major general in the Pennsylvania state troops, though he had never fired a shot in anger. He was a born promoter whose vision could inspire men to follow, and in the grand scope of his dreams he was a prototypical American.

But the general's luck had run out. In 1854, an economic downturn had caught him unawares and financially overextended. Forced into bankruptcy, he had entrusted his muddled affairs in the East to Thomas Mellon and had settled with his seven sons and two daughters first at Omaha, Nebraska, where he helped to found the local Republican Party, and then, in 1858, at Leavenworth, Kansas.[11]

Determined to make a fresh start on the frontier, General Larimer had led a wagon train of prospectors across the Great Plains to Colorado in the gold rush of 1858, and had effectively chosen the site for the city of Denver by building the first permanent structure—a log cabin—where the city now stands.[12] But the boom there was short-lived: the many who had rushed in for gold with such overweening confidence had slipped away in dejection on learning that the metal was thinly scattered and could not be mined economically. By 1861 Larimer was back at Leavenworth, attempting to farm, speculate in land, and run a store. When the Civil War broke out, the general raised a company of volunteers that he was permitted to command with the humble rank of captain in the Union Army.[13]

As the Judge pondered James's intended marriage, age remained the controlling obstacle. Was his son not still a "hobble-de-hoy, neither a man nor a boy?" Had he outgrown "the vealy stage of existence?" Was he not suffering from a lingering attack of "calf love?" Two years would have to elapse before the dubious father could be persuaded that James's affection for Rachel was more than a transient attraction made fonder by absence and distance. Meanwhile, he cleverly used the waiting period to kindle his son's ambition. Reminding him that a married man must be self-supporting, he leased the Oceola Coal

*James and Rachel Mellon in 1867.*

Works to James in 1865. With marriage to Rachel as the carrot, no stick was necessary: James learned his new profession on the run, and soon more than one hundred coal workers found themselves taking orders from a teenager.[14]

A year later, the Judge informed his persistently ardent son that if after one more year he and Rachel were still of a mind to marry, they would have his consent. Nothing changed between them, or ever would, and their wedding took place at Leavenworth on June 3, 1867. For the next seven years, James and Rachel lived in an annex at the Judge's home on Negley Avenue, and it was there that their first child, William Larimer Mellon, my grandfather, would soon join the family.

In 1864, failing health had compelled Sarah Jane's mother, Mrs. Jacob Negley, now eighty-six, to accept an invitation to live with the Mellon family at 401 Negley, across the street from her own home. It was there that she spent her three remaining years, patiently waiting for the curtain to fall on a life that had begun during the American Revolution and outlasted the Civil War. By 1867, eight of her twelve children had predeceased her. She could remember seventeen American presidents, from George Washington to Andrew Johnson, had seen Indians paddling canoes on the Allegheny River in her youth, and had even owned a slave. But while musing on the immense panorama of history that lay behind her, she was also pondering the future of her valuable real estate, in the East End of Pittsburgh.

The impending demise of his mother-in-law coincided auspiciously with Thomas Mellon's decision to expand the family's business activities. In the widening torrent of Pittsburghers fleeing from the squalid inner city to the eastern suburbs, he had spotted an opportunity for vast enrichment. His plan was to form a partnership between his elder sons, James and Tom, for the purposes of dividing suburban land into building lots. He anticipated an upsurge of construction in the eastern suburbs and decided that the incipient partnership—Mellon Brothers—would also be a purveyor of coal, lumber, and other building materials.

*An 1860s daguerreotype of Mrs. Jacob Negley, born Barbara Anna Winebiddle (1780–1867), Thomas Mellon's mother-in-law.*

The Judge's own experience with partnerships had not proved entirely satisfactory. Of his law partners, Nathaniel Nelson and R. P. Flenniken had been stumbling incompetents, and William B. Negley had precipitously quit the firm. Of his coal partners, his brother-in-law George Bowman, James B. Corey, Benjamin Patterson, and David Shaw had all proved their worth, but Felix C. Negley had revealed himself as a daring and resourceful swindler. Still, Mellon clung to the partnership principle and would continue to put his sons to work, in various combinations, for another twenty years.

The prospects for Mellon Brothers appeared auspicious: Tom had disposed of his nursery business profitably, and James had sold the Oceola Coal Works for his father, netting $5,000, though coal was slumping.[15] Each of the boys had shown judgment and perseverance, and as they were also inseparable friends who differed in age by only two years, there was good reason to believe that they would fare better as partners than individually. And so, with the fond hope of establishing them in business, the proud and expectant father now launched Tom and James on the flood tide of postbellum prosperity, determined "to pilot them in the channel for some part of their way" and prayerfully hoping that they would float.

In East Liberty, directly north of the Pennsylvania Railroad tracks and east of Station Street, lay an orchard that the Judge had bought for its potential as industrial property. Tom and James rented a parcel of this land from their father, cleared it, and built two warehouses for storing construction materials and coal. One warehouse also contained their office and a hardware store. With the railroad in their backyard, the brothers built a siding for offloading coal from their father's mines and for freighting in lumber from Michigan.[16] Such was the ramshackle headquarters of Mellon Brothers.

On February 15, 1867, Tom recorded a plan for subdividing McFarland's Grove, an extensive property bounded by Oak, Walnut, East Liberty, and Main streets, into 133 lots or building sites. If the Judge did not already own this land, he almost certainly advanced his sons the money to buy it.[17] The lots, which varied in size from irregular quadrilaterals of 20 or 30 by 100 feet to a rectangular parcel that measured 50 by 242 feet, appear to have been sold vacant.[18]

A week later, on February 23, Mrs. Negley, by then near death, willed the bulk of her valuable real estate on both sides of Penn Avenue, to her daughter, Sarah Jane Mellon, and other descendants. That she acted on the advice of her executors, Thomas Mellon and George

*Thomas Mellon's son Thomas ("Tom") Alexander Mellon
(1844–99), circa 1885.*

*James Ross Mellon, circa 1868.*

Negley, is evident, because the plan for dividing and selling her property, which they rushed to implement as soon as she was dead, is specifically provided for in her will.[19]

Mrs. Negley breathed her last on May 10, 1867, at the age of eighty-nine. In the tower of East Liberty Presbyterian Church, which she and her husband had founded almost fifty years earlier, the mighty 2,760-pound bell, which was the last of her many benefactions, let its mournful tolling be heard for the first time.[20] Her property was hastily divided, and on August 19, 146 additional building sites were offered for sale by her grandsons, Tom and James Mellon.[21]

Typically, the Judge lent his sons the money to initiate their joint endeavor, but he insisted on prompt and full repayment. Sometimes he also cut himself in for a share of the profit.[22] Viewing himself as their unofficial senior partner, he was more than generous with advice: His sons lived with him at 401 Negley, and they were expected to keep him fully informed about their business. Tom and James would buy property, divide it, and build several houses as display models. They would then sell building sites for as little as $400, though many were priced at $600 and some at $1,000. They offered attractive terms: the buyer would make a small deposit and pay the balance in monthly installments of $15 to $30 over a term of six years.[23] In 1868, James and Tom were placed in charge of the little Savings and Deposit Bank of East Liberty, or "East End Bank," a joint stock company that the Judge had organized with several other investors and which his sons managed from their lumberyard. One of its functions was to provide credit for the family's real estate operations.

When they sold a building site, Tom and James would help the buyer to find a contractor, usually just a carpenter. They would furnish the lumber, shingles, plaster, moldings, mantels, grates, and other building materials. These goods and the lot itself could be acquired on one contract linked to a purchase-money mortgage. After the house was occupied, Mellon Brothers would furnish the coal for heating.[24] Soon long rows of narrow two-story wooden dwellings, crammed wall to wall, were springing up in Homewood, East Liberty, and Shadyside as the municipal authorities approved successive Mellon development plans. James called these homes "my $100 bills."[25]

As developers, James and Tom revealed the Mellon family's signature tendency to create fully integrated businesses. Banking and the sale of real estate, coal, lumber, hardware, and other building supplies served complementary purposes in their enterprise, and all were controlled, or wholly owned, by the family.

Between 1867 and 1892, Tom and James built hundreds of row houses for working-class families in the eastern suburbs of Pittsburgh. They netted $50,000 each in their first year as partners.[26] In one spectacular deal, their father lent them $25,000 to buy sixteen acres in the suburb of Homewood. They divided the land and eventually netted $150,000.[27] But theirs was a rough-and-tumble business. Adolescents and grown men who worked in the yard at Mellon Brothers risked their lives for a dollar a day. James's thirteen-year-old son, William, fell from a woodpile, plunged twenty-five feet into a coal bin, and was almost killed.[28] Tom's teenage son, Edward, recalled how a towering pile of boards tipped over and literally "flattened" and killed a laborer.[29]

As his judicial term was ending, Thomas Mellon decided to found his own private bank. It would prove to be a watershed decision and one for which there was sound logic. Pittsburgh was capturing a heaping portion of America's runaway industrial boom, and opportunities for lending abounded as vibrantly growing businesses clamored for credit. Mellon was well positioned to exploit these opportunities. With his judgeship and recently amassed wealth, he had become a prominent Pittsburgher with whom business leaders wanted to be associated. He had been made a director of the Farmers' Deposit National Bank; he had also helped found the People's Savings Bank in 1866 and had briefly served as its first president.[30] He was a major stockholder in the Savings and Deposit Bank of East Liberty, which he had organized. Most important, he had been trafficking in debt obligations for thirty years. In the jungle of usury, he was on familiar terrain.

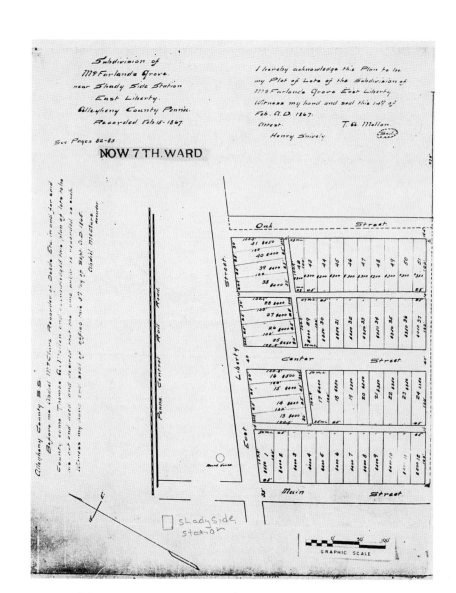

*Subdivision of a property in East Liberty by Mellon Brothers in 1867.*

Allegheny County S.S.

Before me Recorder of Deeds Etc. in and for said County personally appeared T. A. Mellon and acknowledged the foregoing plan of lots to be his act and deed and desired the same to be recorded as such.

Given under my hand and seal of office this 14th day of Feb. A.D. 1867.

Henry Snively

He was also uniquely conversant with a particular lending instrument —the DSB or *debitum sine brevi,* known as "debt without a writ."[31] Because it required a judgment on mortgages and a judgment note on personal security loans, the DSB empowered an alderman, court officer, or simply a lawyer to confess judgment and seize a debtor's property without fuss or trial. That the mortgage books of Allegheny County were becoming ever more cluttered with Thomas Mellon's DSB loans is not surprising. Already in 1840, his business card describes him as a lawyer specialized in collection cases. And though he would claim to have been habitually too lenient in pressing for repayment when he himself was the lender, his nickname "Mortgage Bond Tom" suggests that he could also be hard.[32]

Judge Mellon had thoroughly enjoyed the nimbus of respectability that had enveloped him while on the bench, and if he now became a banker it would envelop him still. For bankers stand at the epicenter of economic activity. They wield the power of life or death over nascent businesses, construction projects, and people's homes—in a word, over their dreams. Like the judge, the banker is a sacerdotal figure. Moreover, anyone who requests backing for a fledgling enterprise is likely to discover that the banker can demand an equity position before agreeing to wave the magic wand and give life to the project. This is how Thomas Mellon's sons, Andrew and Richard, would acquire a giant stake in the Aluminum Company of America and other leading enterprises.

Of equal importance is the banker's power to take over mismanaged businesses, reorganize them, make them profitable, and, above all, claim ownership of them. This is how Colonel James Guffey's floundering oil company would become the Mellon-controlled Gulf Oil Corporation. To create, to liquidate, or better yet to confiscate and rejuvenate whole enterprises is frequently within a banker's power, and it begs a certain deference that the banker normally does nothing to discourage.

Time had not diminished Thomas Mellon's haughty self-confidence when faced with a new challenge. He had leapfrogged over every obstacle to establish himself in the law, landed an heiress in the contest of marriage, secured financial freedom in an unfree world, and won the dignity of a judgeship. The challenge of opening a private bank held no terrors for him. In a day when government regulation of lending hardly existed, all he would need to open a private bank was an iron safe, a ledger book, and a pile of stationery.

"There is nothing in banking but what you ought to be able to learn in a week or two," he had written to James. "As to bank books, keeping [them] is the simplest of all kinds. I know very well I could commence and manage a bank . . . tomorrow and carry it on without any assistance as to bookkeeping or anything else, except a boy who knew the difference between a counterfeit and genuine paper."[33]

In December 1869, the recently retired Judge opened his private bank at 145 Smithfield Street. He organized it with $10,000 of initial deposits and called it T. Mellon & Sons, but he was the sole owner. His minuscule establishment occupied the ground floor of a two-story frame building—a mere rented storefront. The entire business fitted comfortably into a single room twenty feet wide and sixty feet deep.[34] It consisted of a counter, a safe, an iron stove, and some rude furniture.[35] The wood-paneled finery and spacious conference rooms of an established banking house found their opposites in this coarse little lair.

For the first few weeks, James managed the fledgling bank for his father, who had gone to Louisiana on business. The first regular employee was an inexperienced cashier named Samuel McClurken, but he was soon joined by a messenger, Walter Mitchell, who would serve in various capacities for sixty years until his death, as a vice president of the Mellon National Bank, in 1930.

The social credentials of these early employees were quietly accepted as prerequisites for working at T. Mellon & Sons. Among the officers, tellers, clerks, and cashiers, the preponderance of Scotch-Irish Presbyterian males lent a stolid, colorless uniformity, a quietly resolute philistinism, to the bank's daily life until well into the twentieth century. And it went without saying that when a position became vacant, blacks, Jews, women, and Catholics were under no pressure to apply.

*The first banking offices of T. Mellon & Sons at 145 Smithfield Street, circa 1869.*
*From* One Hundred Years of Banking *by C. Hax McCullough, Jr.*

In old Pittsburgh, the exclusion of these groups from banking and all other profitable pursuits was unwritten but broadly enforced.

The whole interior of this miniature bank could be taken in at a glance. Off to one side stood a varnished oak desk at which the fifty-seven-year-old jurist turned banker took his place on returning from the South. He occupied this station neatly attired in a black frock coat, stiff upturned collar, and charcoal bow tie. He had worn these vestments on the bench and would continue to wear them, oblivious to every turn in fashion, for the rest of his long life. Always punctiliously polite, he would rise to meet customers at the door and show them in.[36] Two rows of large plain lettering painted across the front of his diminutive establishment proclaimed the existence of

T. MELLON & SONS
PRIVATE BANKERS[37]

Despite the implications of the name, his sons were not co-owners, and he had no intention of leaving the bank to all of them equally. He would never give a business to any son who had not first expressed an eagerness to manage it and had proved himself capable of doing so. Having established Tom and James in their real estate and building supplies partnership, he would continue to own and manage T. Mellon & Sons himself, anticipating that it would eventually be passed over to Andrew, Richard, or George, who were still only fourteen, eleven, and nine.[38]

Within a year, his storefront bank outgrew the cramped little roost in which it had been born. It now required space for private rooms, for officers and additional tellers. The Judge was also tired of paying rent.[39] He wanted a proper bank building of his own and decided to build one.

On Smithfield Street, in the next block, lay a vacant lot that measured 36 by 120 feet. He bought it for $30,000, and in 1871, for an additional $28,000, he erected the tall, narrow edifice that would house the Mellon family's banking business for thirty years.[40]

Tightly wedged into a line of other buildings, the new bank stood at 512–514 Smithfield Street. It featured a cluttered neoclassical facade made of cast iron painted to simulate concrete, and it rose from the cobblestoned street to a height of four stories.[41] In Pittsburgh, where outmoded architectural styles were experiencing an aesthetically dubious revival, the new building could not have raised many eyebrows. What did attract attention was the work of art that Mellon had placed squarely over the main entrance. It was a cast-iron likeness of the patron saint of accumulation making his initial entry into Philadelphia,

*The second bank building of T. Mellon & Sons
at 512–514 Smithfield Street, erected in 1871.*

penniless, unknown, and lugging the bag of buns that he alludes to in his memoirs—Benjamin Franklin.

Customers who entered the banking lobby would turn either right or left, depending on their business. On one side lay a long counter where tellers attended to the bank's retail transactions—deposits, withdrawals, and the like.[42] Against the wall stood a bulky safe, which initially had to be wrapped around with steel cable and padlocked at closing time. This job was one of Andrew Mellon's earliest obligations at the bank that he would effectively control for sixty years.[43] The two main-floor offices, which fronted on Smithfield Street, were first used as conference rooms where customers could receive private attention. One of these later became Andrew Mellon's office.

The other side of the banking lobby was reserved for Judge Mellon's personal business affairs. Here his investments in coal and real estate were supervised and his taxes paid. Here the nagging minutiae of lending were attended to, his loans and mortgages monitored, interest and rents collected, and deadbeats threatened with foreclosure.[44]

Behind the main lobby, toward the rear of the building, was a comfortably furnished room with a desk, chairs for visitors, and a generous stock of books. Here the Judge could read and write with minimal interruption, confer with important customers, and receive old friends who came by to chat. Here he could keep an eye on business and yet luxuriate in the seclusion he craved. The journalist Harvey O'Connor penned a memorable vignette of Thomas Mellon ensconced in his "banking parlor":

> Business associates dropped in at 512 Smithfield Street to recall old times and discuss the decadence of the present. To them was revealed a philosophic spirit, a dry, crackling wit, an acrid point of view. To young men in search of financial backing he was grave, courteous, even fatherly, if they reminded him of the poor Thomas of the 1820's. To the populace he remained a cold, impenetrable figure, hardly human. It was remarked by those who knew him only casually that his stern features had never been seen to relax into a smile; indeed the lines appeared so hard that a smile would have cracked the face to bits.[45]

With the bank's employees he avoided familiarity. Arriving at work, he would walk through the lobby in utter detachment, his gaze fixed straight ahead like a blind man's. Passing officers and tellers without a word, he would make for the banking parlor and close the door behind him.[46] At noon he would suddenly reappear, retrace his steps through the lobby, pass between the heavy iron doors, and walk to a nearby hotel or restaurant for his solitary, parsimonious lunch. Similarly, even after sixty years, his son Andrew would enter and leave the bank with seldom a nod, much less a "Good morning," to people who had shared the workplace with him for decades.[47]

The new bank building on Smithfield Street would undergo repeated onslaughts of internal restructuring and shelter a variety of occupants. On the first floor was T. Mellon & Sons, but two upper floors were for many years leased out to the Union Insurance Company, which Andrew Mellon had acquired.[48] Somewhere upstairs was an auditorium that could be rented for concerts, lectures, or religious gatherings. In the 1890s, William L. Mellon's oil exploration, leasing, and pipeline business would occupy the second and third floors.[49] In one of the two cellar apartments was a restaurant-saloon, in the other a barber shop where the Judge got his haircut.

An early advertisement in the *Pittsburgh Commercial Gazette*[50] emphasizes the bank's full range of retail services:

### T. MELLON & SONS' BANK
512 & 514 Smithfield Street
Pittsburgh, Pa.

Transacts a General Banking Business

Accounts Solicited

Issues Circular Letters of Credit for
Use of Travelers, and Commercial Credits

IN STERLING

Available in all parts of the world;

also, issues Credits

IN DOLLARS

For Use in This City, Canada, Mexico, West
Indies, South & Central America.

While the new bank building was still under construction, a deceptively frail-looking young man, slight of build and only twenty-one years old, dropped into Thomas Mellon's office. His name was Henry Clay Frick, and he had come to borrow money. Though Frick's principal genius would prove to be his managerial skill, he saw that a fortune was waiting to be made in the emerging coke industry. Coke, which fueled the revolutionary Bessemer process for making steel, was the residue that remained after a quantity of soft coal had been baked for three days in conical beehive-shaped ovens, sometimes called "flaming igloos." By borrowing on his inheritance and admitting partners, Frick had become the substantial owner and sole manager of a new coke company. Fifty of the beehive ovens would be required to begin production, and he had come to T. Mellon & Sons for a loan of $10,000 to build them.[51]

So there sat Thomas Mellon, the wily, seasoned lender, running his eye over young Frick to size him up for a loan. That the prospective borrower was scarcely more than a boy, and that he had been trained as an accountant and had only just begun to manage a number of yet-unprofitable coke properties, argued vehemently against lending him anything. On the other hand, it could not have taken a veteran collier like Mellon very long to perceive that Frick, though lacking in practical experience, had amassed an impressive fund of knowledge about the overlapping coal and coke industries. He must also have projected some of the qualities that would always distinguish him: discernment, persuasiveness, daunting self-assurance, and the drive of a freight train.

Andrew Mellon would later recall his father's initial impression of Frick: "That young man has great promise," the Judge had allowed. "He is very careful in making statements, always exact and wholly reliable. He is also able, energetic, industrious, resourceful, self-confident, somewhat impetuous and inclined to be daring on his own account, but so cautious in his dealings with others disposed to take chances that I doubt if he would make a successful banker. If he continues along his own line as he has begun, he will go far unless he over-reaches. That is his only danger."[52]

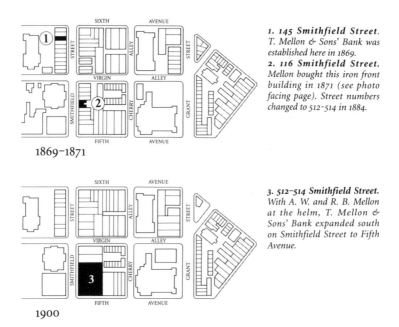

1. **145 Smithfield Street.** *T. Mellon & Sons' Bank was established here in 1869.*
2. **116 Smithfield Street.** *Mellon bought this iron front building in 1871 (see photo facing page). Street numbers changed to 512-514 in 1884.*

**1869-1871**

3. **512-514 Smithfield Street.** *With A. W. and R. B. Mellon at the helm, T. Mellon & Sons' Bank expanded south on Smithfield Street to Fifth Avenue.*

**1900**

*Street maps showing first and second Mellon bank buildings.*
*Courtesy University of Pittsburgh Press; maps by Christopher H. Marston.*

Family connections figured into Mellon's decision, too. Frick was a grandson of Abraham Overholt, the wealthy distiller whose beloved rye whiskey had petrified so many Scotch-Irish livers. Moreover, if Frick's biographer, George Harvey, is correct, Thomas Mellon's father, Andrew, had been a friend of Overholt's, and the distiller's daughter, Elizabeth, who became Frick's mother, had known Thomas Mellon when they were children.[53]

That the banker probably saw something of his former self in the bright young hustler who stood before him may have proved decisive. At any rate, he decided to gamble on Frick and in the spring of 1871 lent him $10,000 for six months at 6 percent, secured by 123 acres of undeveloped coal land at Broadford, in Westmoreland County. By late April, Frick had fifteen coke ovens built and blazing. By July all fifty were in operation, and he was back at T. Mellon & Sons asking for an additional loan to build fifty more.[54] But this time the banker

*Henry Clay Frick in 1870, at age twenty-one.*
*Courtesy West Overton Museums Archives.*

hesitated. When an officer who reviewed Frick's application advised against a second loan, Mellon sent his veteran coal partner and friend, James B. Corey, to report on Frick's operations at Broadford and, more subtly, on the man himself.

Corey was astonished to find Frick living in a miner's shack, littered with "prints and sketches."[55] That artistic impulses had broken out like cancer in the young man caused the philistine Corey to hesitate but failed to undermine his approval of "the young man with the cast iron nerve."[56] His report to Mellon was generally favorable: "Give him the money. . . . Lands good, ovens well built; manager [Frick] on job all day, keeps books evenings . . . knows his business down to the ground." Still, Corey felt constrained to add, "May be a little too enthusiastic about pictures, but not enough to hurt."[57]

Mellon approved the second loan, and up went fifty more coke ovens. He admitted that "the loans being made to Mr. Frick were larger than Mr. Frick's material resources justified," but added—as it turned out with thundering understatement—that Frick "was of a character to succeed."[58]

To highlight the main point in Frick's initial encounter with Thomas Mellon, let us return to the moment when he applied for his first loan at T. Mellon & Sons. It was a scene that would be reenacted many times in the Mellon family's history. A conspicuously intelligent and motivated young man was applying for a loan with which to found a business. Mellon had three choices. He could refuse to lend; he could lend, with repayment of the loan as his sole objective; or he could lend and angle for partial ownership of the new business. In Frick's case, he chose the second alternative—to lend, on the calculated gamble that Frick would be able and willing to repay. When Frick did repay, Mellon could claim that his judgment had been vindicated. But he could have profited far more handsomely if he had secured an equity position in Frick's enterprise. Perhaps he attempted to do so, and Frick refused. Or maybe he decided to forgo partial ownership because he was already overinvested in coal. We do not know everything that transpired between these two. But, in all likelihood, Mellon acted with characteristic wariness and decided that simple repayment of

Frick's loans would suffice. His son Andrew, who had an incomparable eye for detecting opportunities in the continuous stream of lackluster proposals that flow across a banker's desk, would have striven for an equity position in Frick's partnership.

There lies a categorical difference between Thomas and Andrew Mellon. The Judge had been raised to farming, and its influence weighed heavily on him: Though determined to become wealthy, he would remain a cautious, steady, safe accumulator—a farmer of money—who believed in compounding, not in advancing by risky brilliant strokes, and who hated even the semblance of gambling. "I have never seen a horse race or boat race, or played a game of cards in my life," he would crow, at the age of seventy-two, "or incurred any extra hazardous risks— never speculating in property of any kind without I saw a sure thing in it."[59] In 1864, writing to the eighteen-year-old son who was speculating in commodities, he wails, "James, remember always the risks. I have seen so many enterprising, energetic and smart men in my past life get wealthy and again lose it all in speculation that I am confirmed in my opinion that a man never ought to risk much. I have always speculated in real estate or something that I knew had intrinsic value in it equal to my investment and that if I could not sell at a profit, I could hold till a more profitable opportunity."[60]

Thomas Mellon had listened patiently to his father's contemptuous diatribes against every pursuit except farming; he had heard him berate lawyers as scoundrels and businessmen as thieves. But Thomas had rejected his father's impassioned warnings, heaved his axe over the fence, and abandoned farming to become first a lawyer, then a businessman and banker. But paternal admonition had never ceased to whisper, and at the crucial junctures, when a phenomenal opportunity lay within reach, the voice of caution would overrule his yearning. As a Mellon who had seen the fragility of good fortune from Ulster to Pittsburgh, he could not repress the fear that after decades of laborious accumulation, he might yet lose the hard-won fortune that had given dignity to his life, and that his father, whose wisdom he had so firmly rejected, might be laughing in his grave.

Long after the Judge's death, Andrew Mellon, when pondering a weighty decision, would think aloud, "What would Father have done?" Conversely, he was fond of sentencing ill-conceived business proposals to death with the terminal remark, "Father would not have done that."[61] But, in truth, he lunged for opportunities that Father would never have touched, among them Gulf Oil, Alcoa, Carborundum, Koppers, McClintic-Marshall, New York Shipbuilding, and Standard Steel Car. Born to wealth and comfort, he did not flinch, as his father did, at the mere thought of risk. When an extraordinary opportunity appeared, he would spot it immediately, tackle it on the run, and cling to it. With unfailing vision, dogged initiative, and prodigious managerial skill, he heaped up one of history's staggering fortunes, whereas his father became merely affluent. On a list of the wealthiest Pittsburghers compiled in 1886, Thomas Mellon, with an estimated $1,500,000, is tied with five other contenders for thirteenth place.[62] By contrast, Andrew Mellon's fortune would grow to approximately $350,000,000 at its peak in the late 1920s.[63] With Henry Ford and John D. Rockefeller, he was one of the three wealthiest Americans of that day.

The five-year period ending in 1872 reveals a startling expansion, in both scope and variety, of Thomas's business endeavors. He continued to extract and purvey coal, typically in league with professional partners who managed his mines and distributed the product. With James and Tom as "hearty and reliable coadjutors," he had founded a highly profitable real estate and development business that also purveyed lumber and construction materials, and he envisioned— correctly, as it turned out—that his sons would continue "to execute with judgment, prudence and alacrity whatever I should plan."[64] In 1872 he had made his initial foray into mass transit by acquiring and refurbishing the bankrupt Pittsburgh, Oakland & East Liberty Passenger Railway, a horse-drawn streetcar line on which he had frequently ridden to work. He also owned an iron foundry, a machine works, and various assets that he had foreclosed on.[65] But most important, he was now the sole proprietor of a financial institution that would ride out catastrophic depressions and bump over every obstacle to become the Mellon National Bank and eventually the BNY Mellon Corporation. With T. Mellon & Sons, he had unwittingly founded his family's flagship enterprise and had laid the cornerstone of its fortune.

A warm glow of satisfaction must have seeped through the chilly Judge as he surveyed the growing jumble of his possessions. It must also have delighted him that in James and Tom he had found the driven, resourceful, and tamely malleable apprentices he had wanted as sons and business partners. Also, two joyous events had recently brightened his family life: On June 1, 1868, James and Rachel had presented him with his first grandchild, William Larimer Mellon, who would play a distinguished role in the family's history. Equally important, the Judge's eldest son, Tom, had married Mary Caldwell.

Mary had gone to school in Leavenworth with Rachel Larimer. As daughters of two Pennsylvania families that had moved to the frontier, the girls had been friends since childhood. Mary was the daughter of Captain James Caldwell, who had raised and commanded a company of Pennsylvania volunteers in the Mexican War. On the final day of combat, September 13, 1847, Captain Caldwell had been mortally wounded in fierce fighting at the Belén Gate during the storming of Mexico City. He had died there six days later, one of the last American soldiers to leave his bones in the halls of Montezuma.[66] Mary, then six years old, had been raised by her elder brother, Alexander Caldwell, who would eventually represent Kansas in the U.S. Senate. On a business trip to Leavenworth, twenty-five-year-old Tom Mellon was introduced to Mary by James's wife, Rachel. "The latter's good opinion of her had its influence," conceded the Judge. "In family and character also she was every way acceptable."[67] With the main obstacle to their union thus removed, Tom and Mary were joined, on March 10, 1870, in what would be a long and happy marriage. The couple built their home at 337 Negley, directly beside that of the Judge.

Like General William Larimer, Senator Alexander Caldwell was an ambitious entrepreneur with related political involvements. During the Civil War, his wagon works at Leavenworth had built thousands of "prairie schooners" to supply the Western forts. He had served as president of the First National Bank of Leavenworth, organized the Kansas Central Railroad, and served as president of the Missouri Pacific, which he had extended to Leavenworth. His obligatory resignation from the U.S. Senate for alleged corruption would not impair his standing with the Mellon family nor his credit at T. Mellon & Sons. "Alexander Caldwell is still one of the leading men of Leavenworth, with whom we have had close business relations," the Judge would recall in 1885.[68] The same year, we find Caldwell in debt to T. Mellon & Sons for $125,000, which he had probably applied to his real estate acquisitions in Idaho (where a town still bears his name). Thomas and Andrew Mellon would invest in the Idaho and Oregon Land Improvement Company, which Caldwell had founded in 1882, and his influence definitely persuaded them to make some of their real estate investments in Colorado, Wisconsin, North Dakota, and Idaho —states where the Mellon name would come to be "sprinkled all over the title records."[69]

General Larimer also played a part in persuading the risk-averse Judge Mellon to invest on the unfamiliar American frontier, where opportunity beckoned brightly but lawlessness and economic gyrations augured caution. Already in 1855, General Larimer had planned a town where the Platte River joins the Missouri and was encouraging his friend Thomas to invest in the project.[70] But it was not until the 1860s that Mellon began to buy property along the Western railroads and around population centers like Leavenworth. He pursued this strategy on a grander scale during the 1870s and invested in the Dakota land bubble of the '80s; his frontier investments concluded with his ill-fated transportation scheme at Kansas City in the '90s. Some of these speculations would leave him with stinging losses, as we will see. But he was a farmer by birth, and land would remain his security blanket— irrationally, perhaps, but unalterably.

# XI

—◆·◆·◆—

## The Panic of 1873, His Finest Hour

*It was a bitter pill for me however to acknowledge present inability to pay
every demand upon me. . . . Neither myself nor any of my ancestors so far
as I knew had ever been in that condition before. . . . [It] gave me more
vexation and mortification than all the other adverse circumstances of
my business life put together.*

B Y 1873, BUSINESSES WERE FLOURISHING from coast to coast
as the postbellum boom rolled on. In Pittsburgh's vibrant economy,
anonymous men were appearing whose names would soon become
household words: Henry J. Heinz had founded the food-processing
concern that would introduce his celebrated "57 Varieties," and George
Westinghouse was manufacturing the air brakes that would bring him
fame and fortune. B. F. Jones's American Iron Works and Fort Pitt
Foundry were "puddling" record amounts of cast iron, and Andrew
Carnegie was reintroducing the revolutionary Bessemer process for
milling steel. Thomas Mellon and his sons persisted in selling hundreds
of building lots and finished houses, but they were also purveying
record amounts of coal and lumber. While Henry Clay Frick struggled
to establish himself in the coke business, T. Mellon & Sons, which had
bankrolled his endeavor, netted a profit of almost $20,000 in its first
three years of operation. The ranks of the newly rich continued to

swell, and in 1872, they founded the Duquesne Club as their watering hole. While the vast majority of Pittsburghers toiled in obscurity, if not in destitution, the city's flourishing businessmen coasted along on a wave of prosperity. But the wave was about to break.

There are buildings in Rome that still bear, on their outer walls, the high water marks of the Tiber during one or another of its catastrophic floods. Similarly, the cross-section of a tree trunk is marked by the growth rings that follow the stresses of each successive winter. And those who find their primary satisfaction in amassing and retaining wealth will be similarly scarred by the economic cataclysms through which they must pass. For them, the periodic recessions, panics, corrections, and depressions that see the net worth of their possessions, and therefore of their lives, ebb away are periods of torment. Thomas Mellon was to live through six of these debacles, the panics of 1819, '37, '57, '73, '93, and 1907. Because crises are moments of truth, it is illuminating to follow him through the severest crisis of his life.

As a small boy, he had almost lost his home in the all-encompassing economic collapse of 1819; now, at the age of sixty, he would suffer through a still more fearsome catastrophe. It began in May 1873, when panic swept the financial centers of Austria and Germany. America was spared until September, when the Northern Pacific Railroad failed and precipitated the collapse of Jay Cooke's precarious banking empire. Thomas Mellon would never forget the mortal anxiety and scorching humiliation he suffered that year:

On the 16th of September, 1873, while seated at my desk, Mr. Whitney, our notary public, on his customary call at three o'clock, looked in and inquired if I had heard the news of Jay Cooke's failure. I replied, no. . . . This news did not disturb me, indeed it scarce attracted my attention, as we had no business relations with Cooke or his railroad projects. . . . The same evening however I had occasion to attend a party where many of the bankers and leading business men of the city were present, and found they regarded it seriously on account of the sudden panic it had produced in the Eastern cities. The next morning the cry of the newsboys everywhere on the streets was "All about the panic." . . . Instead of calming down and affairs assuming their usual course, the apprehension and excitement spread everywhere, and became more and more intensified every day by successive failures all over the country, until by the 1st of October we were in the midst of the most disastrous and extensive panic and collapse since that of 1819.[1]

Pittsburgh banks began to fail almost immediately, because many of them held their reserves in the New York lending institutions that had been hard hit by Cooke's insolvency. A second round of bank failures followed in November, as business activity ground to a halt and demand for coal, iron, glass, and oil nosedived. The Pennsylvania Railroad began to lay off trainmen, and before long thousands of miners, factory workers, and other wage earners were being dismissed or forced to accept devastating pay cuts. In Pittsburgh and its satellite communities, twenty thousand men and women—a third of the labor force—found themselves unemployed by year's end. Evictions, foreclosures, and sheriff's sales became a part of daily life as landlords struggled to collect rent and people fell behind on their mortgage and loan payments. The grim spectacle of breadlines became ordinary, and the Mellon wives opened a soup kitchen for the indigent at the family lumberyard in East Liberty.[2]

Recalling the debt crisis that locked up credit and vaporized the overconfidence that had preceded it, Mellon would come to write:

Dealings and business transactions had been carried on so generally on credit that everybody was largely both debtor and creditor, and now that clearings could no longer be made by an exchange of mutual obligations, a dead lock and general collapse was the result. . . . The demon of credit had destroyed confidence, and suddenly called a halt in the mad career of speculation. . . . Nobody wanted property at any price, because it could not be applied in payment of debts, or held without shrinkage of value and loss. Property of all kinds remained, but it was set afloat in search of its true owners, who could only be discovered through the tedious process of judicial sales in the bankrupt[cy] and other courts.[3]

As depositors drained their accounts, the fear that the banks would fail became a self-fulfilling prophecy. T. Mellon & Sons had been awash in cash only days before Cooke's failure, but Judge Mellon had made a large cash investment in Pennsylvania Railroad bonds "so well endorsed as to be considered gilt edged." The result was that only $60,000 remained on reserve to cover $600,000 of deposits at the two Mellon banks. The Judge recalls that his customers were not aware of the shortfall and that "no one entertained the slightest apprehension regarding our solvency as I was always looked on as impregnable. They were still making their usual deposits from day to day, but in rapidly diminishing amounts owing to their own diminished receipts. And the checks and drafts on us grew rapidly in excess of deposits, and our cash balance at the close of each day showed a steady decline."[4]

That he had reduced the bank's cash reserve to a level that neither prudence nor precedent could justify is the only error he admits to, but it amounted to an astonishing lapse of judgment for such a disciplined and risk-averse banker. If there was rumbling under the earth just then, it was Benjamin Franklin rolling over.

The Judge's plight also illustrates that in 1873 private banks, like T. Mellon & Sons, were not yet safe repositories for wealth. National banks enjoyed the enviable right to issue currency notes and were therefore backed by the U.S. government. But in return, they were required to hold minimal reserves and to limit their lending. Similar restrictions applied to the state banks, for they too were government supported. But private banks existed in a virtual state of nature. Wholly unregulated, they were free to lend as much as they liked, on little or no collateral, and were not required to hold minimum reserves. Their long-term survival depended entirely on the wisdom and self-discipline of management. In a booming economy, private banks would typically succumb to greed and litter the record books with poorly secured loans. When the cyclical economy then swung from boom to bust, these flimsy lending institutions would topple like bowling pins. And because the private banks frequently deposited their assets with the state and national banks, their massive failure would place the entire banking system at risk and send shock waves through the whole economy.

Faced with mounting obligations and dwindling reserves, the Mellons went on a drive for cash. The Judge called in overdue loans. Tom and James sent out runners to collect on overdue notes for lot sales and building materials. Their success was only partial, but the funds they scraped together helped the family to bump along through the worst of the crisis.[5]

Franklin had said it: "We must all hang together, or assuredly we shall all hang separately."[6] That these early Mellons were fighting shoulder to shoulder with such discipline, tenacity, and mutual affection for their rapidly dwindling share of the American Dream was a tribute to the qualities that Thomas Mellon had implanted in his family. But it was also a wrenching spectacle:

It became painfully clear that we could not sustain the heavy drain if affairs did not take a sudden turn for the better. But instead of any change for the better it grew constantly worse.... The securities we held, though perfectly sound, could not be converted into money at any sacrifice; and being absolutely certain that we could pay the depositors every dollar in a very short time, I did not feel called on to make any exceedingly great or extraordinary sacrifice to meet the unreasonable demands of such as I knew did not need their money and were only acting under the impulse of fear and alarm.

It was a bitter pill for me however to acknowledge present inability to pay every demand upon me. Neither myself nor any of my ancestors so far as I knew had ever been in that condition before. In fact it was rather our habit to pay cash and not contract debts at all.[7]

The Judge's dilemma must have caused him to reflect bitterly on the irony of his plight. That a man who had garnered so much of his wealth by ensnaring others in debt now found himself similarly ensnared amounted to an agonizing cosmic joke. To default would not only cause him hardship and subject him to mortifying humiliation; it would discredit the moral basis of his life and the work ethics he had always accepted on faith: that "the natural principles of human affairs invariably result in rewarding each according to his merits," that "name and fame are incidental to well doing," and that "well doing" must lead to doing well.[8] More than once he must have vainly pleaded for the saving advice of Franklin, his friend behind phenomena, but Heaven remained silent.

The end was approaching and already in sight. The extremely disagreeable announcement must be made, which I knew would cause a very great sensation, as we were supposed safe if there was safety in a bank anywhere. After all our exertions, the cash balance for both banks fell to nearly twelve thousand dollars. . . . I considered it better to keep this much on hand, to meet any necessitous cases of depositors likely to suffer for want of their funds; and at the close of banking hours on the 15th day of October, 1873, I directed the officers to stop payment the next day to all except special cases, but not to close the doors of either bank.* I thought it more satisfactory to customers to keep them open, and continue the officers in their places to explain the situation to those interested. And this did have a good effect in preventing alarm; we had no run nor excitement at either place; and . . .

*On the matter of dates, the Judge's memory fails him. He stopped payment at the Savings and Deposit Bank of East Liberty on November 11 and at T. Mellon & Sons on November 12.

whilst we met many anxious faces, there was not an unkind word or disagreeable reflection made by any one. On the contrary we were met mostly with manifestations of surprise and sympathy. . . . And after all I found the situation not nearly so unpleasant as I had feared, although the contemplation of a suspension, and having actually to succumb at last to a condition which I had never anticipated as possible, gave me more vexation and mortification than all the other adverse circumstances of my business life put together.[9]

Throughout the crisis, Mellon daily confronted the draconian choice between inviting disgrace by defaulting on his obligations in order to save what remained of the family fortune, or defending his reputation by meeting every obligation until no money remained. Drawn and quartered between wealth and respectability, he waffled and agonized and miraculously emerged clinging to both. In less than three weeks, he was again able to make payment on all checks and to fund every withdrawal.[10] Like a battle-scarred, tempest-tossed warship, with her sails in tatters, her masts broken, and bilges awash, T. Mellon & Sons was, incredibly, still afloat. The father and his sons had kept their heads, collaborated wisely, and muddled through.

The victory was a somewhat Pyrrhic one, however. The Judge's belief in banking had been severely shaken, and he proceeded to liquidate the Savings and Deposit Bank of East Liberty, though it had returned a steady 12 percent throughout its five-year existence and had met every obligation to its depositors.[11] Should he also liquidate T. Mellon & Sons? What future could he reasonably expect for his badly savaged, four-year-old private bank? Was it not banking, with its damnable, ensnaring obligations, that had just caused him the worst public humiliation of his life? Wouldn't he and his sons have been better positioned to ride out the Panic and its devastating aftermath if they had left usury well alone? Should he remain a banker?

Twelve years after the Panic, he would reminisce: "I was disgusted with banking and had it under consideration whether or not to wind up the business altogether. . . . It was some considerable time before I fully made up my mind to continue. . . . Finally, in view of the fact that an office with a couple of clerks was necessary for the transaction of my private affairs, and but little more expense would be required for a banking business in connection with it, and having a very excellent vault and banking room in the city, I decided to continue the business."[12]

T. Mellon & Sons was one of only two private banks in Pittsburgh that survived the Panic. What also survived was banker Mellon's primary stock in trade—his reputation. Now in the third century of its history, the bank that Thomas Mellon refused to scuttle has been reconstituted five times and is currently known as the BNY Mellon Corporation.

When T. Mellon & Sons resumed normal operations in December 1873, what the family could not foresee was that it had only begun to run a gauntlet of perils. Jay Cooke's failure in September had triggered a sudden and precipitous plunge in stock and bond prices. Cash had all but vanished, and twenty-seven Pittsburgh banks had suspended payment or succumbed to bankruptcy.[13] But real estate had declined more gradually and would not bottom out until the depression itself did so in 1877. This was fortunate, because from 1874 to 1876 the Judge and his sons could sell land as a last resort when they needed cash. That James and Rachel were able to junket across Europe to Egypt and Palestine in 1875, after building a large house at 400 Negley Avenue, confirms that the Mellons still had ample reserves at their disposal. That the Judge was able to build a railroad from Latrobe to Ligonier in 1877, precisely when real estate was bumping its bottom, confirms that at no point did the Panic and subsequent depression so impoverish or demoralize the Mellons that they could not launch a significant venture.

The gravest threat to the Mellon interests had been the insolvency of their debtors. Contracts for lumber and building materials had not been honored, and the Judge's deposits at two banks had disappeared, along with the banks themselves. He and his sons had also accepted mortgages for hundreds of building sites in the East End. But they wisely offered the mortgagors that defaulted easier terms for repayment, and among the properties that they were compelled to foreclose on were many that they managed to hold until land values recovered.[14]

While real estate gradually slumped toward its nadir in 1877, T. Mellon & Sons rose from the ashes in a sluggish but steady recovery. Though the beleaguered bank netted only $14,000 from 1876 to 1880, the demand for credit remained robust, as sagacious entrepreneurs hunted for deflated real estate or bankrupt businesses that could be revitalized. In 1876, Henry C. Frick obtained a credit line of $100,000 at T. Mellon & Sons and began to acquire insolvent collieries. The Mellons bought residential and commercial property at sheriff's sales, and Andrew Carnegie, who had seen the future and believed it would work, erected his gargantuan steelworks at Braddock. As the harshest depression since 1819 bottomed out, an increasing number of astute and disciplined businessmen focused on opportunity instead of disaster. Their reward would be to prosper in an economy brutally purged of the weak by natural selection. America was witnessing an economic example of Herbert Spencer's "survival of the fittest" that Thomas Mellon and his sons would never forget.

The diversification of their investments also contributed significantly to the Mellons' financial survival in 1873 and in the subsequent years of depression. If the profits of T. Mellon & Sons were graphed for the period beginning in September 1873 and ending in mid-1877, the graph would plunge precipitously in the first two months but would then rise steadily. Similarly graphed, the value of Mellon real estate between 1873 and 1877 would form a gradually descending trajectory, and coal properties would decline even more gradually, bottoming out in 1879, when the volume of coal shipped on the Monongahela had dropped 36 percent from its 1873 peak. That banking and real estate fared inversely as the post-Panic depression progressed meant that the Mellons were continuously sustained by at least one pillar of their fortune.

By 1879, deposits at T. Mellon & Sons had swollen to $1,000,000, and for this resurgence Andrew could take much of the credit. In 1874, the Judge had given his nineteen-year-old son a desk at T. Mellon & Sons and was training him for banking. That we was in virtual control of the bank's day-to-day operations in 1876 leaves no doubt that he had won his father's confidence and was playing a key role in the bank's steady recovery.

Sixty years after the Panic of 1873, Andrew and Richard Mellon, who as teenagers had stood by their father and brothers in that memorable and instructive catastrophe, found themselves engulfed by the Great Depression. As lending institutions defaulted and panic-stricken withdrawers rushed the Mellon banks, seventy-eight-year-old Andrew, who had seen all of this before, calmly managed the crisis by telephone from London, where he was serving as ambassador to Great Britain. He called for calm and directed the family's two principal banking houses, Mellon National and Union Trust, both of which remained financially sound, to support the weaker banks that they controlled under the umbrella organization known as Mellbank.

On March 4, 1933, as President Franklin D. Roosevelt was taking the oath of office, dozens of financial institutions had already closed their doors, many of them forever, and more were failing by the hour. At banks that remained open, the harassed tellers faced lines of with-drawers that extended out of doors and down the street. Prophets of doom crowed that the whole American banking system was collapsing and that Bolshevism would now come to power. Though Governor Gifford Pinchot had proclaimed a bank holiday in Pennsylvania, Mellon-owned savings and lending institutions opened their doors, punctual to the minute. At the Mellon-controlled Union Trust Company, President Henry McEldowney, who was not known for subtlety, sent an unambiguous message to customers. He placed a large, trans-parent enclosure, like a cage, in the banking lobby and filled it to the brim with wads of currency. Every overwrought withdrawer who came to snatch his savings away from one of the tellers could see for himself that there was more where that came from.[15]

At Mellon National Bank, an actual count revealed that more than ten thousand customers swarmed into the main lobby between 9:00

a.m. and 12:15 p.m. They found a staff of tellers and officers calmly conducting business as usual. They also found seventy-five-year-old Richard Mellon, then in his final year of life, moving from one knot of agitated withdrawers to the next, assuring them that all the Mellon banks would unquestionably honor their obligations. By noon, the customers had regained their composure, and many had gone home.[16]

From the Panic of 1873 and its bitter aftermath, Andrew Mellon had learned at his father's side that a depression engenders its own recovery. When the prices of formerly inflated assets and commodities can fall no farther, the depression bottoms out, and recovery follows as the concluding phase of an agonizing but natural corrective cycle. Whether the most painful phase of this cycle could be mitigated by government intervention was a question that Andrew Mellon had to answer during the early Depression years, when he was secretary of the treasury. Looking back on the Panic of 1873, which had been permitted to run its course, Mellon, who was not a Keynesian, appears to have decided that most kinds of intervention would be ineffectual, perhaps even counterproductive—that economic collapses were necessary for the purgation of excesses and would occasionally have to be endured, like outbreaks of flu. Hence the oft-repeated charge that he took no vigorous action to prevent or later to remedy the unprecedented depression of the 1930s. To what extent President Roosevelt's publicized spending programs contributed to jump-starting the economy, or "priming the pump," as he called it, will continue to be debated by economists and historians. But it is difficult to imagine that his modest New Deal initiatives did much to mitigate a multinational disaster of such magnitude. By all appearances, FDR took office just as the Great Depression reached its nadir. That left him free to claim credit for the subsequent recovery—which, in fairness, he did help to hasten by the vibrant hope that he aroused in the American people at one of the blackest moments in their history.

The six-year depression that began in 1873 transiently disrupted the careers of Judge Mellon and his sons but failed to alter their lives. The year 1880 found Andrew still living at 401 Negley and working at the bank with his father. Teenage Richard also continued to live at home and worked as a messenger, debt collector, and roving factotum for T. Mellon & Sons.

The Mellon lumberyard in East Liberty had not been sold. When real estate began to recover, James and Tom returned to work at the yard and, with their father's continued backing, resumed the sale of building sites, coal, wood, and other construction supplies, all in the name of a revived Mellon Brothers. By 1883, dozens of row houses were again rising in the eastern neighborhoods of Pittsburgh as one Mellon development plan after another was approved and implemented. On May 1, 1884, the Judge observed with satisfaction that the family's net worth had resurged to $2,500,000 and that the Mellons "were again doing nearly as well in all branches of our business as before the panic."

In 1871, Sarah Jane had given Tom a plot of land at 337 Negley Avenue, next to the Mellon home. She later gave James a plot directly across the street, at 400 Negley, and by 1874 both brothers had built the unsightly Victorian mansions in which they would live happily ever after. If the Judge viewed these dwellings as pretentious, he muted his disapproval in deference to what they symbolized. It delighted him that James and Tom were now "occupying elegant homes beside me— the fruits of their industry and ability—and conducting profitable business wisely and well."[17]

As in Ireland and later at Latrobe, so now, on Negley Avenue, a third Mellon enclave (this one all on former Negley land) had formed around the original family home. Christmas dinner at Tom and Mary Mellon's became a tradition, and the Thanksgiving feast would be hosted year after year by James and Rachel. But the Judge and Sarah Jane continued to officiate at New Year's celebrations and on their double birthday, February 3, until the end of their days.

In 1875, the Mellon homes were staffed by a minimal number of servants. The household of James, Rachel, and seven-year-old William L. Mellon included a cook, a maid, and a coachman.[18] That same year, a cook-factotum, a maid, a coachman, and a gardener were the only live-in servants at the Judge's home, where Andrew, Richard, and George were also still living.[19]

James and his father soon linked their homes with the first crude telephone in Pittsburgh. It consisted of two tin cans joined by a length of wire that spanned Negley Avenue.[20] Those who used this contraption sounded like rats squeaking at opposite ends of a drainpipe. By 1880, T. Mellon & Sons and the Mellon Brothers partnership had Bell telephones, but the Judge remained unlisted and may still have been squeaking advice to his sons through the tin can.

# XII

───•◦•───

## The ABCD Lawsuits

*You must bear in mind that your fellow men for the most part have in them a taint of insanity, or mental or moral obliquity, and you may as well regard them accordingly. . . . In a community of crooks, cranks, imbeciles, and weaklings of all degrees, the stream of human affairs cannot be expected to flow smoothly.*

DURING AND AFTER THE Panic of 1873, as Thomas Mellon struggled for financial survival, his life was further aggravated by four personal lawsuits. He reflects on these cases in a fascinating chapter of *Thomas Mellon and His Times* titled "Vexatious Litigation," but he refuses to name his opponents and refers to them merely as A, B, C, and D. Despite insisting that his memoirs were "not written for the public," he admits that "a stray copy might fall into hands where such facts might cause pain if names were given and parties known."[1] That he published two editions from which all mention of these cases was omitted suggests that he may also have harbored doubts about his fairness in reporting and commenting on them. Then too, by naming his opponents, he might have exposed himself to further litigation. The late Paul Mellon was intrigued by these lawsuits because they reveal so much about his grandfather, the Judge.[2]

A's case amounted to an amazingly unsophisticated swindle that nonetheless succeeded.[3] While Thomas Mellon was lunching at Reineman's restaurant on Smithfield Street, A, whom he describes as "a little fellow whom I had seen about the Courthouse as a factotum or runner for an attorney of rather questionable character," approached his table and asked whether he would be willing to sell a particular five-acre lot in the suburb of Braddock's Field.[4] Mellon replied that he would sell the lot for $5,000. A then disappeared, but he soon returned and announced that he would buy the property himself. His terms, however, were laughable: an infinitesimal deposit, followed by annual payments for five years. When Mellon spurned the offer, A disappeared again, but quickly returned with a prospective "buyer." Once more the proposed terms for payment were ludicrous. But when Mellon again refused to sell, A sprang his trap and claimed a commission for having found someone willing to buy the property. No written brokerage agreement had ever been concluded, but A, with his "buyer" bearing false witness, was able to persuade the court that a verbal agreement had been concluded and that he was entitled to a commission.

While admitting to neither guilt nor error, Mellon decided that from then on he would discuss potentially binding real estate transactions only in the presence of a witness. He also concluded that where a crooked lawyer can be found to hatch such a plot and where a perpetrator and a false witness are willing to carry it out by committing perjury, virtually anyone can be defrauded with impunity.

What cries out for explanation is how Mellon, an eminent former judge of the very court that was hearing his case, could have been worsted by "a little fellow" whom he had seen about the courthouse and "an attorney of rather questionable character."

B's case proved infinitely more menacing and more revealing.[5] By all appearances, B was honest, intelligent, and enterprising—a seemingly unstoppable young entrepreneur of the kind that Mellon himself had once been and could still identify with. He further ingratiated himself by always affecting a respectful, filial attitude toward Mellon, who was twelve years older. That B had left his family's coal firm under nebulous circumstances was something Mellon knew but failed to inquire about. That he had been expelled from it by his own relatives, and with good reason, was something Mellon would learn too late.

In September 1859, just before his election to the bench, Mellon formed a partnership with B "for the trade and business of mining, running, and selling coal." B would contribute the Baldwin and Cheney Coal Works, which he had just bought, and would then attempt to locate, purchase, and manage additional coal properties. Mellon would pay for these acquisitions and would also give B an initial yearly salary of $600. They would share the profits in whatever proportion each had contributed to the partnership.

While this arrangement worked tolerably well at first, B soon revealed that he could act with suicidal lack of judgment. In a steeply rising market, he obligated the partnership to furnish huge quantities of coal to two major customers at a fixed price for five years. When the price of coal doubled, B employed unethical devices to wiggle out of the ruinous agreements he had made. By furnishing an unacceptably low grade of coal and deliberately missing delivery dates, he eventually harassed one of the two buyers into voluntarily renouncing his contract, but presumably not without damage to the partnership's reputation. Rumors that B was a crook were by then flying in all directions, and lawsuits arising from his malleable business ethics were being passed along to Mellon for litigation. But having not yet experienced his partner's treachery personally, he continued to trust him and did not even bother to audit their joint accounts.

In 1862, with America beset by civil war, B got "the military fever," as Mellon calls it, and formed a company of volunteer cavalry. His anticipated absence from Pittsburgh compelled them to dissolve their partnership and settle accounts. When B returned from the service not long afterward, however, they quickly reentered into various kinds of business relationships. B rented a coalfield from Mellon, mined out far more coal than he admitted to, and even slithered out of his rent payments by offsetting them with fictitious repair bills that Mellon was liable for. All the while, there were paper trails that would have revealed B's innumerable skullduggeries, but Mellon neglected to follow them.

It was the Panic of 1873 that led to B's undoing. Property values, which began to decline that year, did not recover until 1880, and Mellon, who had lent B a large sum of money, found himself holding debt instruments that were no longer wholly secured. When in 1876 he sued for a lien on B's personal property, B initially agreed not to contest the suit; but when it came up in court, he promptly changed course.

B now insisted that their partnership had never actually been dissolved—that he, having no knowledge of the law and acting blindly on Mellon's professional advice, had agreed to a merely *provisional* dissolution, because Mellon had insisted that B's absence in the army required it. He charged Mellon with having repeatedly assured him that the dissolution was entirely technical and that their partnership was for practical purposes still valid. B now filed a countersuit in which he claimed to be the half owner of all Mellon's coal holdings and accrued profits since 1859. He furthermore claimed that Mellon was responsible for half of the debts that B had piled up over the same period. If his suit had prevailed in court, not only would B's debts have been wiped out, but Mellon would have owed him about $150,000.

What saved Mellon was his routinely thorough documentation. Armed with meticulous records of his dealings with B, he persuaded the court that, after their partnership had been legally dissolved in July 1864, he and B had dealt with one another as independent individuals, not as partners. B lost his suit.

In *The Mellon Family,* Burton Hersh incorrectly identifies B as Mellon's intermittent coal partner, James B. Corey, and the University of Pittsburgh Press uncritically repeats this error in its 1994 reprint of *Thomas Mellon and His Times.*[6] This is grossly unfair to Corey, of whom Thomas Mellon would write in later life, "I have no friend outside of my own family whom I regard so highly as you, always sincere and true."[7] Any examination of court records would have instantly revealed that B was Felix Casper Negley, a first cousin of Sarah Jane Mellon.[8]

C's case involves a fraud of more limited scope.[9] C was a failed lawyer who had married a wealthy woman and was dividing her land into building sites and selling them. His policy was to charge a down payment for each lot, accept a purchase-money mortgage for the rest, and then sell the mortgage at a discount. His banker, Judge Thomas Mellon, bought these mortgages regularly, though on several occasions he had caught C making false representations to him about debt instruments.

Mellon admits that where he regarded a particular mortgagor as uncommonly reputable, he would sometimes fail to probe his credit-worthiness with sufficient rigor. Such was the case when C sold him two purchase-money mortgages, one given by the municipal treasurer of Pittsburgh, the other by a wealthy, respectable merchant. When these borrowers defaulted on their payments, an investigation revealed that both mortgages had been fraudulently drawn up.

C had given out deeds for two building sites—one to the municipal treasurer, Christopher (later "Boss") Magee, and another to the afore-mentioned wealthy merchant; but with their connivance, he had falsified the deeds to reflect a higher sale price and consequent greater underlying value than existed in either property. He had then drawn up two inordinately large mortgages for them to give him as payment for the two properties, and he had sold these mortgages to Thomas Mellon. To protect themselves, C's accomplices had extracted from him indemnity bonds that obligated him to reimburse them for the mortgage payments and to hold them blameless in case their scam was discovered.

When C failed to supply his cronies with money for the mortgage payments, they both defaulted. The customary inquiry was made, and Mellon determined that C and his accomplices were guilty of criminal conspiracy. That he could probably have sent them to jail gave him some welcome leverage in dealing with them. He now sued for, and obtained, liens on the personal property of both mortgagors, and though they had the brass to present C's indemnity bonds as a defense, the court ruled against them. This effectively secured the wealthy merchant's mortgage, for he owned sufficient personal property. But the smidgen of property that Magee owned was already mortgaged and could not be attached. Similarly overloaded with debt, C himself now teetered on the brink of bankruptcy. But Mellon discovered that he owned a farm in Washington County that still had some equity in it, and he demanded that C give him an indemnity mortgage on the farm to protect him against possible loss on the fraudulent mortgage that was still inadequately secured. Faced with criminal prosecution, C had no choice but to agree. He showed cunning, however, in persuading Mellon to lend him a few hundred dollars on the farm and to include in the mortgage agreement a provision that Mellon *could* lend him more, if he chose to.

When Magee continued to default on his payments, Mellon resorted to his indemnity mortgage, foreclosed on C's farm, and then bought it himself in a sheriff's sale. This stripped C of all income, for his law practice had never amounted to a hill of beans, and he had frittered away most of his wife's fortune while leaving the remainder encumbered by a mountain of debt. Desperate, reckless, and drunk, he now concocted a crude but daring scam.

In a sensational damage suit, he charged that Mellon had broken an unwritten agreement to advance him $25,000 on his farm; that only a few hundred dollars had been advanced, and that Mellon's failure to lend more had prevented him from constructing buildings on his property, forced him to renege on his debts, and, through foreclosures and sheriff's sales, brought ruin to his real estate development business. Though the loan agreement contained absolutely no provision for a $25,000 advance and made any lending beyond what the agreement provided for contingent on Mellon's approval, C doggedly insisted that there had been an oral understanding, only a fraction of which had been honored and which had mistakenly been omitted from the written agreement. In one stroke, he blamed all of his misfortunes on Mellon and demanded $500,000 in damages. The case gave C a tailor-made excuse for continuing to default on his innumerable debts; and the sheer magnitude of his claim enveloped him in a nimbus of celebrity, which he reveled in as long as it lasted.

Again, what saved Mellon was his habitually careful documentation, for the paperwork clearly revealed that C had repeatedly omitted, misrepresented, or deliberately falsified vital information in his mortgage transactions. The case boiled down to one question: Had Mellon orally obligated himself to loan C $25,000? And, as the court could not resolve this question by accepting the word of an unmasked hoaxer and lawbreaker in disregard of impeccable documentary evidence to the contrary, it was compelled to support Mellon against his opponent. Writing confidentially to his son, Richard, the Judge identifies C as one Michael O'Hara Jr.[10]

Mellon found the last case, that of D, especially painful because it involved an old friend who in 1839 had been his first law client.[11] D was a stonemason who had gradually branched out into real estate and construction. When payment for his work was not forthcoming, he would engage Mellon to file claims or property liens in his behalf. And when payment was long overdue, he would borrow small amounts from Mellon to make ends meet.

In an effort to expand his business, D eventually bought four vacant lots on Wylie Street and began to improve them. His need for capital increased sharply, and so did his borrowings. By 1853, he owed Mellon $2,000—more than he could expect to repay without damaging his business.

Lawyer and client put their heads together and agreed to the following deal: D would give Mellon a mortgage for $4,000, secured by his Wylie Street lots; Mellon would relieve him of $2,000 in debt and give him six lots on Webster and Roberts streets, appraised at $2,000 altogether. D would be free to improve and eventually sell the six lots, hopefully at a profit, and would then pay off his mortgage. To avoid a conflict of interests, Mellon, who was still D's creditor, resigned as his attorney.

The years passed, and D's predicament steadily worsened. The reckless abandon with which he managed his business was now accompanied by a slide into drunkenness, and his income, which had dwindled to a trickle, went straight down his throat. But Mellon continued to support him with additional loans and always lent a sympathetic ear when he dropped by at the office to pour out his personal problems and ask for paternal advice. D had a wife and children by then and had built them a home on the Wylie Street property, but house and land were both encumbered by his mortgage and by other loans from Mellon.

In 1857, a judgment for $11,000 was entered against D after a delinquent tax collector, for whom he had posted bond, jumped bail. With all hope gone that D would ever be able to pay his debts, Mellon now foreclosed on the Wylie Street property and bought it himself in a sheriff's sale. Out of sympathy for D and his family, he allowed them to continue living in the house for only a nominal rent, but even that was not paid. The day came when all that stood between D's family and the gutter was $10 a month advanced to them by Mellon.

The outbreak of civil war gave a sharp lift to property values in Pittsburgh, and by 1863 the house and four lots on Wylie Street had appreciated sufficiently to offset most of the losses which Mellon had sustained in unpaid rent and bad loans to D. He now sold three of the lots at a good profit, but kept the fourth lot where the house was situated. D was informed that he could continue living there if he and his wife signed a declaration confirming that they were renting tenants with no claim on the property and that none of it was held in trust for them. They signed in January 1864.

Six years later, D came to Thomas Mellon for a loan to reestablish himself in business. He claimed to have seen the folly of his ways, insisted that he had forsworn the bottle, and could actually point to some money he had made on disparate masonry jobs. The leopard had changed his spots. If Mellon, who was his oldest and most generous benefactor, would, as a final act of largesse, make him one last loan, he would soon be self-sufficient and could even pay rent. He asked for $200. Mellon lent him $250.

*Thomas Mellon in 1882; photograph by Frederick Gutekunst.*

Nine more years elapsed. By 1879, D had not paid a penny of rent for twenty-one years. His business had withered away completely, and he was a full-blown alcoholic. At this late date, Mellon finally applied for an order to evict D, his wife, and their children, who were grown but still in the home. He expected no contest to his petition, but at the hearing, which was conducted before an alderman, D appeared with a lawyer and filed a spirited countersuit.

He insisted that Mellon had bought the land and house in 1858 under the terms of a secret oral trust agreement, and that he had bought and was holding the property for D but had consistently refused to deed it over to him. Mellon, of course, presented a mountain of countervailing documentary evidence and quickly obtained from the alderman an order for the D family's eviction. But with a shyster lawyer whispering in his ear, D was able to delay their departure for two additional years.

When a jury threw out D's challenge to the alderman's ruling, he and his family were finally evicted, and Mellon repossessed the property. But that was still not the end, for D now brought an equity suit charging once again that Mellon had bought the property for him in trust as part of a secret agreement; that rising property values had long ago repaid Mellon for all of D's debts, and that D was now, at long last, entitled to clear ownership of the house and lot. When his leaky, foundering case was again rejected, he towed it into the Pennsylvania Supreme Court, where it was at last sunk with finality. Thus the saga of D, which had begun with his early defaults in the 1850s, did not end until 1881. An examination of court records and Pittsburgh directories has revealed that D was without doubt one Thomas Scott.[12]

Mellon's discussion of these cases is a revealing exercise in self-criticism and introspection. The Judge's bedside bible, Benjamin Franklin's *Autobiography,* includes a similar effort in which Franklin describes a number of critical missteps—"errata," he calls them—that cost him dearly. In some of these errors, he admits to ethical lassitude as well as folly. Mellon confesses to no moral culpability, only lapses of judgment, but he concedes that the lapses were grave.

His friends and even his cashier had warned him against allying himself with the reputed schemer B. Moreover, he had witnessed B's unscrupulousness in dealing with others. Yet he had resumed business relations with B on the latter's return from military service and had continued to trust him so blindly that, until the final treachery, he had not even bothered to audit their accounts. Likewise, he had doggedly persisted in his business relationship with C, though he had caught the latter making "false representations" about debt instruments. And he had carried the drunken deadbeat D along with loan after loan instead of evicting him and seizing his assets.

"I never was a very good judge of private character," he concedes.[13] But that was hardly the whole story, for many a rascal had failed to hoodwink Thomas Mellon. The con men who succeeded in doing so for long periods had two characteristics in common: they made a favorable first impression by appearing to be earnest, motivated, disciplined men, at once honorable and intelligent, men who reminded him of the young hustler he himself had once been. They also sensed that the way to gain his friendship was to affect a respectful, filial attitude. Those who pretended to regard him as he regarded Benjamin Franklin were the ones who found the breach in his otherwise formidable defenses.

But even this blind spot does not fully account for the enigma of an otherwise wary man's enduring vulnerability to scoundrels of a particular stripe. For the cases of B, C, and D did not occur simultaneously. C unmasked himself in 1873, B in 1876, and D not until 1879; but there is nothing in Mellon's handling of B's case that suggests he had learned anything from the treachery of C. And his utter surprise on being snakebitten by D confirms that he had learned little or nothing from the two previous betrayals.

In all likelihood his selective blindness was that of an honorable man who has difficulty perceiving in others the forms of corruption that are alien to his own nature. Conversely, he was quick to recognize the qualities of honesty, sound judgment, and perseverance in others because they formed the bulwark of his own self-esteem. Perceiving these qualities in Frick, he had loaned him money on insufficient collateral. But he had also lent to rogues like B, C, and D, whose obvious rascality had escaped him. It may also be true that Thomas Mellon, an introvert and loner who mingled only awkwardly with people, clung rather blindly to the handful of friends he made. For friendship is a weak form of love; and in love most people learn nothing but are condemned to keep repeating their errors.

Noting that the thoroughness of his paperwork was all that saved him in the cases of B, C, and D, he stresses the need for complete documentation of all business transactions and frequent settlements with debtors and partners. But he admits that an ounce of prevention would have been vastly more effective. His advice to his descendants: "It is the best policy to avoid low, tricky, dishonest and trifling people as much as possible in your dealings. You will always deal more safely and profitably with the better class." With overtones of Lord Chesterfield, he adds, "In short, I would advise you to keep the best company you can get into, in your business life as well as in social life."[14] He would have agreed with Heraclitus, Novalis, and Thomas Hardy that "character is fate":

> These cases will also show the impolicy of helping men who cannot help themselves, of trying to keep them on their feet contrary to the law of their natural gravity. You may carry such men along for a time in the vain hope of holding them up, but they are sure to sink to their proper level whenever let go; and whenever you have to abandon them and try to save yourself, it matters not how much you have done in the past, you will certainly gain their lasting ill will for discontinuing your support. It has been one of my failings to sympathize with and extend assistance to lame ducks of this kind. . . . I could see very well how easily I could succeed myself if in their place, and would make the mis-

take of supposing success by them equally easy. . . . In such cases you must not take the man's own plausible theory of what he can accomplish, or how he can accomplish it. You must look at what he has accomplished already, and determine your line of dealing with him accordingly.[15]

In these troublesome cases, he finds much to buttress his bleak view of human nature, and he charges the businessman with responsibility for recognizing and protecting himself against a diversity of mental defectives:

Apart from the "real hardened wicked" class, you must bear in mind that your fellow men for the most part have in them a taint of insanity, or mental or moral obliquity, and you may as well regard them accordingly. You will meet with the harmless imbecile, rendered so by nature or bad habits. . . . Then you have the smart, cunning idiot to contend with, who is always overreaching himself by his own shrewdness . . . engaging in questionable enterprises and trying to draw others in with him. Then you have the hair brained, visionary speculator. . . . He is himself utterly impecunious, but always full of plausible schemes with millions in them, and ready to take you in on the ground floor. . . .

I speak of these classes as idiotic, or tainted with mental or emotional insanity. . . . All who do not pursue the right course are so affected. . . . But the right way is exceedingly narrow and difficult, judging from the small number who succeed in following it. . . . A well balanced mind, properly regulated passions and emotions, and sound judgment are rare qualities in the same person. . . .

In a community of crooks, cranks, imbeciles, and weaklings of all degrees, the stream of human affairs cannot be expected to flow smoothly. . . . Whenever you find yourself worsted in a bargain, deceived or disappointed by some one in the fulfillment of his obligations, or when you become involved in litigation, do not waste your time in fault finding. . . . Rather blame yourself. Inquire into your own past course in the matter: how you allowed yourself to be imposed on, why you were off your guard, what sources of information you neglected; what facts appear now which you could have known beforehand by a proper degree of vigilance, and which, if known, would have saved you the loss or trouble in question. Trace what elements of your own conduct contributed to or made possible the difficulty or mistake.[16]

Prolonged applause.

# XIII

—◆—

## Early Life of Andrew W. Mellon,
## His Friendship with Henry Clay Frick

*[Andrew Mellon's] dominant characteristic, even as he moved from late
adolescence to early adulthood, was an almost oxymoronic amalgam of
shy yet self-confident self-sufficiency.*

> *David Cannadine,* Mellon: An American Life

BRILLIANT, DRIVEN, AND ENIGMATIC, Andrew was at once
the best known and least knowable of the Mellons. His education
began at the little private schoolhouse that his father had built in the
yard on Negley Lane to impose the kind of instruction he believed in
so fervently and to protect his children from harmful influences and
distractions. In this chapel of learning, first Tom and James, then
Andrew and Selwyn, were taught to read, write, and cipher by a single
teacher whom the Judge appointed. But when nine-year-old Selwyn,
the favorite of both his parents, died of diphtheria in 1862, the schoolhouse was closed forever.[1]

Diphtheria, the gruesome killer of children, had become a near epi-
demic in Pittsburgh. Wild theories ricocheted among terrified parents
as to what caused the disease, for germs had not yet been discovered.
Under this threat, Thomas and Sarah Jane Mellon may have felt relieved
that some of their remaining children had been dispersed to distant
locations: The Civil War was in progress, and Tom had been serving

*Selwyn Mellon (1853–62).*

safely in a company of volunteer infantry on the Maryland border. James had just entered Jefferson College at Canonsburg, the apparently frivolous institution to which his father had disdained to apply. Richard and George, who were four and two, would have to remain at home, but seven-year-old Andrew was sent to live with his aunt, Elinor Mellon Stotler, and her children at McKeesport. He attended school there for a couple of years; this proved to be one of only two brief interludes, prior to his marriage at the age of forty-five, during which he was not living at home with his parents.[2]

In 1864, we find him attending the grade school on Grant Street at Strawberry in Pittsburgh.[3] His father would drop him off there en route to the law courts and pick him up after work. For several years, the two commuted between home and the city, sometimes on horseback when the weather permitted, otherwise on the horse-drawn streetcars or by train from East Liberty Station.[4] Judge Mellon enjoyed his son's company and would sometimes take him along to the courthouse. It amused Andrew to hide under the bench unobserved and listen to his father's authoritative voice and the gavel tapping directly overhead.[5] "There was . . . daily communion between father and son," recalls William L. Mellon.[6]

More important, Thomas was drawing closer to Andrew than to any of his other children. Selwyn's death had wrought a subliminal change in him that was beginning to affect his style of parenting. "Every stern and reproving word the father had uttered to his older boys, and especially the lost one," recalls William, "he now tried to redeem by gentle words spoken to little Andy."[7]

Thomas had lost two daughters and now also his favorite son. In old age he would lament, "Time has brought me consolation in all other deaths but this: for Selwyn I cannot be comforted. . . . For his manly qualities he was a favorite with us all. Vigorous and healthy, thus cut down in the early morning of life!" Haunted by his memories, the father blamed himself with tragic vehemence. "The recollection of every little unkindness I subjected him to affects me with remorse. When I review in memory his short life in sickness and in health, I discover nothing to justify the slightest harshness of treatment. His earnest and beseeching look of entreaty rejecting the medicine I was trying to force on him from time to time in the vain hope of saving his life, still accuses me of cruelty."[8]

Was a just providence punishing him for what he now perceived as the overbearing severity with which he had raised his elder children? Sickened with guilt, he clutched for a second chance. He would raise his next son, who happened to be Andrew, the way he now believed that Tom, James, and above all Selwyn should have been raised—with more freedom and less hectoring. Andrew was quick to sense and to accommodate his father's transformation. Their relationship underwent an extraordinary metamorphosis. Andrew became the new Selwyn—his father's second chance, and soon also his father's favorite.

The Judge had firmly decided to rear not only Andrew but Richard and George with greater leniency. Of the three he would come to write:

> I was not as strict with them as I had been with their older brothers. Whatever might be the case with other children it was evident that severity was not the better course with mine. They would any of them listen cheerfully to reason and conform to its dictates. Kind treatment and enlightenment was all which was needed to lead them in the right direction; and the death of our dear Selwyn had softened me so much toward those who remained that a harsh word or action to any of them went against the grain. The education of these three was provided for mostly at home.[9]

Little had changed, however, in the father's ambition for his sons and in the program for training them to accumulate. In 1864, James writes that nine-year-old "Andy has a load of potatoes and apples for marketing tomorrow." He was also selling bundles of hay for the passing horses on Negley Lane, and there was a durable family legend that his mother occasionally had to buy back vegetables that Andy had uprooted and sold from her garden. His falcon's eye for opportunity was beginning to open, and the humble first fruits of a business career that would span seventy-three years and would leave its mark on America had begun to ripen.

That said, there appeared to be nothing extraordinary about young Andy. His biographer, Burton Hendrick, who composed a sketch of the boy from disparate scraps of information, depicts him as an "unplayful" child, "remote, a light-haired, blue-eyed boy, slight of figure and quiet, unassertive, even shrinking in manners . . . a rather uninteresting child."[10]

Two years later, the Judge placed eleven-year-old Andrew in a day school that prepared students for admission to the Western University. This was the second time he had overruled his doubts about the usefulness of higher education. In September 1862, he had placed James at fashionable Jefferson College, some twenty miles from Pittsburgh. But memories of his own unfavorable impression of Jefferson must have been stoked to a boil when he learned that James had celebrated Halloween by falling in with a boisterous mob of students who had torn up the boardwalk at Canonsburg and rolled a fire engine over an embankment.[11] James had been allowed to pursue his studies till the end of the school year, but his persistently poor health and capacity for boyish mischief had persuaded his father to withdraw him from college in 1863 and send him to work in the Great Lakes region, where the climate was rumored to be healthier and the environment less conducive to conduct unbecoming.

Thomas Mellon would send Andrew to college, but his apprehensions remained. According to his grandson William L. Mellon, the Judge "had figured out that these rich men's sons from all over the country were there [in college], and a pretty good percentage of them weren't worth a damn, and these fellows . . . would come home and not amount to anything, no matter Caesar Augustus or anything else they had in their minds."[12]

Thomas Mellon's preponderantly classical education had helped him to access the legal profession, but it had proved useless in business.

More important, he had successfully launched James and Tom in their real estate partnership, the former with only a year of college training and the latter with none at all. And though a case could be made for higher education in the disciplines that related directly to business, he was vastly more preoccupied with maintaining a strong presence in the lives of his children while they were still impressionable and at high risk from harmful distractions. It was at home more than in any school that the prevailing influences cried in unison for worldly success and conspired to promote acquisition as the be-all and end-all of life. It was at home that the Mellon boys had been drilled to earn pocket money by selling farm produce and doing odd jobs for their parents. It was at home that the conversation always returned to strategies for solving commercial problems and accumulating wealth. At meals, the younger brothers, Andrew, Richard, and George, were continually reminded that James and Tom were succeeding admirably in business. The air was heavy with the imperative to acquire.

As a teenager, Thomas Mellon had been clumsily dragooned into farming by his opinionated, inflexible father, but he had rebelled. Andrew Mellon was now being firmly drafted into business, but by a vastly more subtle and persuasive parent; and, like his elder brothers, he would tamely acquiesce. Of the Mellon boys, it was Andrew who would prove the most amenable to paternal direction. But he also revealed a tendency toward independence. As a teenager, he would slip away in the evenings to play poker and, we assume, smoke and drink with a number of other teenagers at the home of a neighbor named Pennock Hart. Andrew would smoke cigars, drink moderately, and remain an avid poker player for the rest of his life—all activities that his opinionated father did not approve of.

In 1869, he entered the Western University of Pennsylvania, but he was enrolled as a day student and continued to live with his parents and brothers. In the thirty years since Thomas Mellon's attendance, the university had achieved a more even balance between classical and practical studies. Without diminishing the availability of Latin and Greek, history, philosophy, literature, and modern languages,

Chancellor George Woods now offered courses in chemistry, physics, civil engineering, mathematics, political theory, military science, and economics.[13]

According to family lore, Andrew would have graduated from the university in 1873 but for the fact that he was mortified at having to make the required dissertation and dropped out just before earning his degree. But the documentary evidence argues for a different scenario.

Andrew was only fourteen when his name appeared in the university records. We read there that in the fall of 1869, he studied algebra, arithmetic, elementary physics, and German. His courses for 1870–71 included Latin, physics, bookkeeping, algebra, penmanship, grammar, and rhetoric, but he appears to have skipped the entire last quarter of the academic year. In 1871–72, we find him enrolled in the collegiate "special course" and studying physics, rhetoric, essays, mental and moral sciences, German, and mathematics. His grades averaged out to somewhat better than a gentleman's C—satisfactory but not outstanding.[14] As a day student living at home, he continued to avoid the social and intellectual life of the university.

A number of Andrew's college essays have survived. They are tepid effusions compared with the trenchant equivalents that his father had authored at a comparable age, but they attest to paternal influence and suggest the direction of his development.[15]

Andrew quotes "Early to bed, early to rise" from a copy of Franklin's *Autobiography* that the Judge must have pressed on him. He concurs with his father's conviction that a classical education is of little use to the prospective businessman. He underscores the crucial function of railroads in the economy and notes with satisfaction the superabundance of coal in Pennsylvania. In an essay on philosophy, he rejects the view that life is ultimately mysterious and adheres to the belief that all "mysteries" will be explained.[16]

Having read some history, he rankles at Oliver Cromwell's rudeness and slovenly attire but admires his pertinacity. Queen Elizabeth I gets high marks for managing her affairs astutely. Daniel Webster is envied for having overcome his awkwardness as a public speaker—something

Andrew would never manage to do. Young Mellon insists that women could master a number of professions currently monopolized by men, and he looks forward to the day when they will be admitted to colleges. Finally, his conviction that art galleries have a civilizing effect on society may have faintly foreshadowed the colossus that he would erect in Washington, D.C.[17]

Not all of the views expressed in these essays would have pleased the Judge, but some of them clearly reflect his influence, and together they offer a rough sketch of the man Andrew was becoming. As a teenager, he was already disciplined, focused, inclined to good manners, and conservatively inclined—determined to conform rather than rebel, but clearly intrigued by the future. More important, he was a preponderantly secular, unspiritual youngster, already preoccupied with business and tamely reconciled to the acquisitive role for which his father was grooming him.[18]

The university records corroborate the view that Andrew was to graduate in the class of 1873 and that he almost did so. But because he is not recorded as having taken a single course in the twelve preceding months, it appears that his attendance in both the preparatory and collegiate departments of the university was sporadic and that he never registered for the four-year degree.[19]

Andrew's failure to graduate could not have caused his father much grief. In fact, his father may well have withdrawn him from the university. What mattered to the Judge was that his sons would graduate from the Mellon home, which functioned as an informal but intensely demanding business school. Their father's passionate preoccupation with education was lifelong, but he would continue to view academic honors—mere degrees—with contemptuous indifference.[20]

What he did view as essential was that each son should be situated in the profession for which his talents ideally suited him and in which he felt correctly placed. In Mellon Brothers the Judge had created such an occupation for James and Tom. He was determined to do as much for his younger sons.

In 1870, when Andrew was still a student, his father would bring him to the bank as a part-time employee on Saturdays and during vacations. Two years later, when he left the university, he was quickly presented with a challenge. The Chestnut Street Theater in Philadelphia had fallen behind on its mortgage payments to T. Mellon & Sons, and the Judge was becoming alarmed. He had drilled his son in the basics of banking: monitoring loans and mortgages, bookkeeping, foreclosures, and sheriff's sales. But did the seventeen-year-old have enough business sense and pertinacity to solve a particular problem? To find out, the Judge sent his son alone to Philadelphia with authority to act on the bank's behalf.

While staying at the home of his Mellon cousins, Andrew asserted his right to take over the theater, placed it under better management, and then attended performances for a month to satisfy himself that all would be well. According to an old family quip, he was so preoccupied with counting the audience that he couldn't remember the play.[21]

Next his father sent him to Baltimore to buy two tracts of land—eighty acres in all—that lay along the turnpike to Washington, D.C. Most of the property would later be divided and profitably sold, but a certain sliver that was too narrow to build on would be retained because of its roadside location. This apparently useless strip was eventually sold to one of the street railways for a hefty profit.[22]

About this time, the Judge decided to launch Andrew as a real estate developer and purveyor of building supplies. He founded for him a development firm similar to Mellon Brothers and interrupted the schooling of fourteen-year-old Richard so that he could join his brother as an assistant and junior partner. Thus began the embryonic collaboration from which Andrew's historic partnership with Richard would grow.

Once again, the father helped his sons get started. He sited their business at Mansfield (now Carnegie), Pennsylvania, which was distant enough from Pittsburgh to avoid competition with James and Tom. He loaned his sons money to buy land for a lumberyard and helped them acquire additional acreage to divide and sell. These purchases left the teenagers in hock to their father for $40,000.[23]

Andrew and Richard struggled along for eighteen months and managed to accumulate $3,000 between them. But the Panic of 1873 swiftly confronted Andrew with his first critical decision—whether to persist in his new venture or to extricate himself and Richard with minimal loss. He decided on the latter course, and his judgment was sustained by events. The ensuing depression proved far longer, deeper and more excruciating than the Judge had foreseen, and it confirmed that his son's unseasoned judgment had been sounder than his own. A farmer who had just sold Andrew twenty-five acres was persuaded to take his property back, and, when the lumberyard of a competitor was swept by fire, Andrew eagerly leased him his own yard for ten years. A "masterly stroke," crowed the Judge, with contemptuous lack of pity for the luckless competitor, who was subsequently forced to pay a hefty rent for six unprofitable years.[24] Only the fit were meant to survive.

In 1874, nineteen-year-old Andrew returned to his desk at T. Mellon & Sons. With his father's help, he would set out to conquer the high ground of banking—to "exercise his judgment in making bargains, buying notes or securities or the like, as a general business man or president or manager of a bank," as the Judge put it.[25] By 1875, he was receiving $75 a month in salary and 20 percent of the bank's income as an incentive.[26] A year later, he was directing its daily operations with a power of attorney—testimony to the swiftness with which he was mastering his new profession.[27] Reassured by Andrew's proven ability, the Judge increasingly retired to his sanctum behind the banking lobby.

Once again, father and son found themselves commuting between 401 Negley and Pittsburgh, only now they ate all of their meals together, spent five days a week working in adjoining offices, and read together in the gloomy library at 401 Negley in the evenings. It is delightful to imagine these two as they became inseparable—as the torch passed imperceptibly from the founder to his brilliant son. And one has to wonder just when it dawned on the teacher that he himself had sired the incomparable student.

Though each of the Judge's sons exhibited a distinctive personality, Andrew differed categorically from the others. His brothers were amiable, open, and fun-loving. They made friends effortlessly, their lifelong marriages would be mutually enriching, and their children would remember them as capable, affectionate fathers. Andrew, by contrast, had a fortress mentality. Ill at ease in company, he formed human relationships only rarely and fitfully. Little emerged from him; almost everything had to be reabsorbed. He would become a prodigy in business and finance, but emotionally and socially he limped through life. Until the age of forty-five, he lived compatibly with his parents. His childhood home would remain his refuge. But from what?

In 1876, the Judge confirmed Henry Clay Frick as a preferred customer of T. Mellon & Sons by granting him a credit line of $100,000.[28] By then, Frick had probably already met Andrew Mellon at the bank, where Judge Mellon is said to have introduced them. In Frick, Andrew at last found a true friend.

Henry Clay Frick and Andrew W. Mellon were not self-made men. They came from well-off families and had been raised in comfort. Neither flinched at the prospect of risk, perhaps because neither had known poverty. Thomas Mellon recoiled from any form of gambling, but he averted his gaze when Andrew went to play poker with Clay, as Frick was called.

Clay was six years older than Andrew. He was also much better read. During a weekend at Broad Ford, Andrew found his friend engrossed in volumes of Thomas Addison and Thomas Babington Macaulay, and Lord Chesterfield's letters to his son.[29] Perhaps it was then that young Mellon recognized how narrowly the Judge had focused his education. While developing a new industry, the "Coke Baron," as Clay would soon be known, was also developing himself. He had learned about clothes while working in a haberdashery and had come to stickle on appearances, especially his own. William L.

Mellon, who knew him well, recalls that "Frick appeared in public only when he was dressed as if the minute in which you saw him was the most important occasion of his life."[30] But the art dealer René Gimpel was quick to perceive a second personality lurking behind the dapper facade that Frick presented to the world: "His features are so regular, his face so pleasant, that he seems benevolent, but at certain moments you see and comprehend that you were mistaken, that his head is there, placed on that body, for his triumph and your defeat."[31]

In jarring contrast to the self-conscious and retiring Andrew, Clay was poised and authoritative. He lacked warmth but mixed easily with people and diffused an aura of saturnine toughness seamlessly intermingled with gentility. His influence on Andrew Mellon was deep and multifaceted. Early in their friendship, he caused the reticent Andrew to step out into Pittsburgh society, something that the Judge must not have liked. In 1880, the two embarked on a grand tour of Europe; and again, in 1896, '97, and '98, they perused the art museums, private collections, and dealerships of the Old World. They sojourned in England, and Clay's Anglophilia grew on Andrew. That they came to patronize the same London tailor caused a startling improvement in Andrew's suits. In 1900, Andrew would marry Nora McMullen, an Englishwoman to whom Clay had introduced him,[32] and in later life he would serve as American ambassador to Great Britain.

When Andrew Mellon wanted company, which was not often, he tended to mingle with humorous extroverts like his brother Richard or quietly self-assured leaders like Clay Frick. Men of pronounced character afforded him relief from the narrow confines of his sandstone personality. Similarly, he enjoyed the flamboyant showmanship of "Diamond Jim" Brady; the unctuous flattery of the world's premier art dealer, Lord Duveen; the posturing of the oil prospector James Guffey, who dressed like Buffalo Bill; and sometimes even the buffooneries of his wife's lover, a failed British actor named Alfred Curphey.[33] That complementary personalities attract goes far toward explaining the lifelong friendship that gelled so firmly between Andrew and Clay.

But Clay was the leader: Andrew would write to "Dear Mr. Frick," and the older man would reply, "Dear Andy."

They both became driven collectors of art but differed in the depth and amperage of their aesthetic sensitivities. Frick's love of art was ingrained, for it dated from his impecunious youth: at that time he could ill afford to collect the works of any recognized painter, but James B. Corey had found him living in a shack littered with prints and sketches.[34] By contrast, Mellon revealed no appreciable interest in art before the age of forty. It was Frick who aroused in him a passion for acquiring masterpieces and possibly also a genuine love of art. At the least, Frick introduced Mellon to the leading dealers and showed him how to buy. As the century was ending, Mellon began to collect—first timidly, then ravenously. The rest is history.

The Mellon family benefited handsomely from its long association with the Coke Baron. In 1886, Frick and Andrew Mellon formed the Fidelity Title and Trust Company, which would metamorphose into the Union Trust Company. In 1899, they jointly invested with William Donner to found the Union Steel Company, which was quickly sold for a phenomenal profit, and in 1902 Frick became a major shareholder and director of the Mellon National Bank, as T. Mellon & Sons came to be named. But what particularly endeared him to established Pittsburghers and to the Mellons was his draconian repression of the Homestead Strike of 1892, an event that I will return to.

Andrew Mellon remains a paradox. No environmental influence that we know of can account for the obsessive self-absorption and incapacity for human relationships that distinguished him from his sociable, entirely normal brothers. That his peace of mind depended more on the absence of people than on their presence is curious and disturbing. A business associate would recall that "Andy never had an intimate. Not even to his brothers did he open the soul within. Had he 'got religion' he would not have told it to God."[35] An early acquaintance would remember him as "solitary but not melancholy; seclusive but not moody; achieving but never boasting; shrinking but not fearful;

silent but never stupid; removed but not eccentric; rivaling but not envious."[36] "His dominant characteristic," notes his biographer David Cannadine, "even as he moved from late adolescence to early adulthood, was an almost oxymoronic amalgam of shy yet self-confident self-sufficiency."[37]

It is likely that Andrew's definitive introspection and solipsism were not acquired but genetically based traits. His son, Paul Mellon, had this to say: "When I think about Grandfather's [Thomas Mellon's] cold and cerebral attitude toward his marriage, it does not seem impossible to me that my father inherited a similar coolness or calculating attitude not only toward marriage but also in his relationships with other people, men and women, and later not only with his wife but with his children."[38]

Andrew may have inherited his father's "cold and cerebral" disposition, but the two also differed conspicuously. If the Judge's character was flawed, it did not prevent him from forming a number of lasting friendships, making an enduring marriage, functioning as a caring and effective parent, or imparting to posterity, in an epic autobiography, his life's accumulated wisdom. Andrew met none of these challenges. Yet it was probably from the mortar of their shared deficiencies as much as from their common strengths that the Judge cemented a more durable bond with Andrew than with his other children. Though father and son did not march to the same drumbeat, they marched with a similar limp.

Such was the silent, inscrutable sphinx, the fledgling financial prodigy, emotional cripple, and bundle of contradictions who now carried the mace with an ever steadier hand at T. Mellon & Sons.

# XIV

$\cdot\!\!\bullet\!\!\cdot$

## The Mellons Build a Railroad, Leadership of the Family Passes to Andrew

*Men in any condition of life will act better if treated as gentlemen; and this was the theory we acted on. . . . It was admitted by all who saw the progress made that my sons had the faculty of obtaining good men and good work without noise or bluster. . . . The progress was such that at the end of sixty days from the commencement the first train entered Ligonier.*

AFTER PLUNGING PERILOUSLY IN the Panic of 1873, deposits at T. Mellon & Sons swelled back to $600,000 within twelve months. But Pittsburgh real estate continued its gradual slide, as did the price of coal, and boom conditions in any sector of the economy were slow in returning.

The four years following the Panic witnessed a substantial decline in the aggregate Mellon fortune, but the Judge was still able to pick an occasional plum from the investment schemes that were touted to him. One of these entailed the construction of a small railroad from Latrobe, southeast of Pittsburgh, into the Alleghenies and through Loyalhanna Gorge, to the village of Ligonier.

Bent on opening the Ligonier Valley to commerce, a number of wealthy individuals formed a syndicate in 1877 to build the proposed railway. When its members came to T. Mellon & Sons for financing, the offer they made reflected their desperation.[1] William L. Mellon, who at the age of nine would play a bit part in building this railroad, recalls what happened:

> These men from Ligonier had come to my grandfather, Judge Mellon, who was prominent, widely respected and well-to-do. They had offered him four-fifths of the capital stock of $100,000, a bonus of $10,000, to be raised by subscription among the people of the valley, and a mortgage on the railroad for whatever it might cost him to complete and equip it, this mortgage to be paid off out of the net earnings. But Grandfather saw quite plainly that unless there were "net earnings" he would never get his money back.
>
> Now Grandfather had a will with more metal in it than is the common heritage of humankind. When it came to investments that jaw of his did not relax any more than the doors of a locked iron safe until his mind had explored every possibility of losing some of his money. He almost never made mistakes when he was paying out money and was habitually careful because he had been brought up in a school where everything was hard. . . . On top of this ingrained quality of his character he had developed a superb judgment. No amount of talking or "selling" influenced him. He made up his own mind deliberately, soundly. In consequence, he rarely failed to make money out of his investments.
>
> So, while my grandfather found the railroad offer tempting, he was less strongly tempted than were his sons, who were eager for the excitement and glamour of such a venture in that thrilling era of railroad building. They urged it upon Grandfather.[2]

Those who did most of the urging were Tom and Richard. In their eagerness to become railroad men, they envisioned an array of rosy prospects for the little line. But their father viewed it as he did every investment proposal—with the eyes of a lynx. He knew that the amount of commercial and passenger traffic between Ligonier and Latrobe, the junction with the Pennsylvania Railroad, would be meager. But the men who had approached him knew this too, and they had sweetened their proposal with such generous terms that he could not lose much money, even if everything went wrong—especially as he had beaten the syndicate down to settling for a narrow-gauge railway, which would cost less to build.

"I am sure now," continues William, "that a considerable measure of my grandfather's satisfaction in the business was that it suited and advanced his plan for educating his sons. . . . It appears to me that the Ligonier Valley Railroad was something my grandfather entered into largely because of his fourth son, Richard B. Mellon, who was 19 in 1877, the year the railroad was built. Nevertheless, about every member of the Mellon family pitched in."[3]

Early in September 1877, Judge Mellon journeyed to Greensburg and gave formal approval for the project. He placed Tom, an experienced builder, in overall charge of construction and gave him young Richard as an assistant. James, who had been Tom's business partner for a decade, was to furnish the rails, ties, spikes, and other materials. Typically, Andrew chose a sedentary role: he would serve as secretary of the new line and would look after its paperwork from his desk at T. Mellon & Sons. The Judge had even given his nine-year-old grandson William a job—to count the wagons and pedestrians that passed through Loyalhanna Gorge and to make a note of any goods and produce they were carrying. So began the only business venture on which Thomas Mellon's whole immediate family would work as a team.

After Tom had personally resurveyed the rail line to guard against legal entanglements, he and Richard formed their labor gangs and appointed foremen. The going wage for railroad work was 90 cents a day, but the Mellons offered a dollar. Equally important, Tom placed a barrel of beer on the line every morning, at some distance from the railhead, and told his workmen that as soon as they laid rails up to the barrel, they could have what was in it. With these inducements, and when a number of idlers and malcontents had been sacked, the men went to work with a will and built the railroad in two months.

As he watched his sons and the gangs of laborers laying rails, Judge Mellon pondered one of history's little ironies: "Coincidences sustain the adage that 'history repeats itself.' The visit to my sons on this occasion produced a serious though interesting train of reflection as I looked across the valley at the old turnpike road. There was the spot where, sixty years ago, . . . I met with my two uncles, then about my sons' age and engaged in precisely the same kind of work as they are now; and my grandfather visiting his sons then for the same purpose as I am visiting mine now. In those sixty years what a web of varied experiences!"[4]

To which he might have added that the rude country road on which he had found his uncles laboring in 1818, when he and his parents arrived from Ireland, followed the old military wagon track that his sons' maternal ancestor, Alexander Negley, had marched over in 1758, when General Forbes reconquered western Pennsylvania from the French and Indians.[5]

On December 1, 1877, the first train chugged out of Latrobe heading for Ligonier. The only passenger car, which Sarah Jane had decorated, was crowded with three generations of Mellons, headed by the Judge. All of his sons were aboard, Tom and James with their wives. Seventy years later, William L. Mellon, by then the last surviving passenger of the first train to Ligonier, still recalled the effusive pleasure of his teenage uncle Richard, who wore a cap which announced his officious role: "Conductor."[6] If the engineer, Sam French, had wrecked that train, all the Mellons could have perished, and many things might have been different. As it turned out, they arrived at Ligonier to a boisterous welcome from the crowd of villagers who had gathered to marvel at the hissing, snorting, rattling contraption that stood before them.[7]

When the first train whistle shrieked in Ligonier Valley, it signaled not only the arrival of the Mellons; it heralded the advent of modern times. For the valley was now linked by rail to Pittsburgh and beyond. Farm produce could be swiftly delivered to market. A lively trade in lumber sprang up. From the encircling hardwood forests came thousands of railroad ties, bark for tanneries, and the pit posts that held up mine shafts all over western Pennsylvania. The Judge extended a feeder rail line to the coal-mining area several miles beyond Ligonier. Innumerable granite blocks, hacked from a mountainside quarry above Loyalhanna Gorge by the firm of Booth & Flinn, were soon being freighted out as paving stones for the streets of Pittsburgh.*

While Tom was installed as its first president, Richard managed the railroad from day to day. He remained at Ligonier, sold tickets, dispatched freight, operated the telegraph, and served as conductor and sometimes even as engineer. He was almost a one-man railroad. If the freight rate had to be raised, it was affable, persuasive Richard who went out to placate the angry locals. In 1878, he persuaded his father to lease four hundred acres on Loyalhanna Creek from the Darlington family. It was there that Richard built Idlewild Park as a site for religious camp meetings and as a weekend picnic ground for Pittsburghers.

By 1890, an increasing number of wealthy businessmen were building retreats in the Ligonier Valley. With deer, bear, and grouse in the woods, trout in the streams, and pheasants in the cornfields, there was much to indulge a Scotch-Irishman's predatory instincts. Richard Mellon adored hunting, fishing, and riding in the valley, and he remained a familiar figure there for fifty-five years. He acquired thousands of wooded acres, built an uncommonly comfortable log cabin, and named his conjoined property Rolling Rock Farms. This was the hideaway to which he escaped with rod and gun, bottle and cigar, whenever he could create a hiatus in his business obligations. The most sociable of Judge Mellon's sons, he seldom came to the valley alone but brought his friends, family, business associates, and hangers-on to hunt, fish, and ride with him. It was to house this stream of eager guests as much as to create an arena for his beloved outdoor sports that he eventually built the Rolling Rock Club. Richard is gratefully remembered for

*The Flinn of this partnership was William "Boss" Flinn, the Republican Party leader of Allegheny County.

having relinquished control of the club to its members. All that he reserved for himself was the right to pay for most of its upkeep year after year. Of the numerous benefactions that his descendants have bestowed on the valley, an unusual one is the reconstruction of old Fort Ligonier, where Alexander and Jacob Negley had found refuge from the pursuing Indians in 1778.

As a rule, the immigrants who settled America were determined to make good in their adopted country. But, more subtly, all of them came here secretly fantasizing about what they would do if they *did* make good. For many tenant farmers from Ulster, the secret fantasy was to live like their former Anglo-Irish landlords, whom they still covertly envied and admired. Descendants of the Scotch-Irish who flooded into western Pennsylvania are still determined Anglophiles. Like their former landlords, they hunt, fish, ride, and play golf. By contrast, the native Irish, who flooded into many parts of America, were generally Anglo*phobes*. They despised their former landlords and trampled on all things Anglo.

Ironically, the deep fissures that fracture Irish society along religious lines were immediately imposed by the Presbyterian Scotch-Irish immigrants in western Pennsylvania. There they established themselves as the rulers, and they achieved a measure of hegemony that has proved amazingly durable. The Anglicans, known in America as Episcopalians, came to be tolerated as respected outsiders. The Catholics, relegated to their usual position, wound up having to build their own country clubs.

James and Rachel Mellon also established themselves in the Ligonier Valley. Around 1900, they bought contiguous parcels of woodland on Ross Mountain, northeast of Ligonier, until they owned more than 1,100 acres. Some of this land had belonged to Robert Morris, a signer of the Declaration of Independence for Pennsylvania, and the historian C. Hale Sipe determined that the homestead from which Alexander Negley and his family were driven by the Indians stood on these very acres.

In 1900, James and Rachel chose a spectacular site on their new property and built a zany imitation medieval castle that could have passed for the birthplace of Dracula. Situated on a promontory from which the mountainside shelves steeply down to farmland hundreds of feet below, the castle boasted a row of rusty cannons, a dog cemetery, and an elaborately landscaped maze of flower gardens. Rachelwood, as the estate came to be named, is still Mellon-owned but is currently leased to the Pennsylvania Game Commission as a wildlife experimentation facility.

Eight generations of Mellons and their Negley ancestors have dwelt, farmed, hunted, ridden, fished, and worked in the Ligonier Valley. In fact, the Rolling Rock Club has become the fourth Mellon enclave, after Lower Castletown, Latrobe, and Negley Avenue.

In the seventy-five years that it operated, the Ligonier Valley Railroad hauled 30 million tons of lumber, 24 million tons of coal and coke, 9.5 million passengers, and 5 million tons of quarried stone, most of it for the firm of Boss William Flinn. It was nonetheless one of Thomas Mellon's least remunerative ventures. Its profits, which peaked during World War I, never amounted to more than a trickle, and when the old wagon route from Latrobe was paved over as far as Ligonier, rail transportation became even less profitable.

The construction of the Ligonier Valley Railroad marked the end of an era in the Mellon family's power structure. Thomas Mellon had recognized that the projected railroad could yield only meager returns, but believing his capital to be safe, and knowing that only a modest investment would be required, he permitted his sons to build the little railroad as a lesson in venture capitalism. Because Andrew Mellon would have turned his back on any venture that lacked the potential for immense profit, it is clear that in late 1877, the Judge was still effectively, as well as formally, directing the family's business affairs.

By 1880, however, twenty-five-year-old Andrew was on his way to assuming leadership of the family. That fall, the Judge's nephew, William A. Mellon, settled into 401 Negley for what was to be a two-year stay. He would eventually write to Andrew Mellon's biographer Burton Hendrick: "In this last batch of notes, I have come to the subject of the family's deference to Andy. This deference had a turbine power, concealed but mighty in its bearing of cause and effect, in Mellon history."[8]

He observed: "The important solvent factor of deference [to Andy] existed finely without words. . . . Andy did not demand it, nor did his father declare it. All the others caught and breathed its atmosphere. . . . About the house, he never claimed or ordered, never complained or suggested. . . . He never found fault with anything his father said or did."[9] Elsewhere, William noted: "The father cringed to that one son in every mental projection. 'What would Andy think? What would Andy wish? How would Andy have it?' ruled his every answer to requests—ruled his doing or not doing anything."[10]

Thomas, who had always asked, "What would Benjamin Franklin have done?" was now asking, "What would Andy do?" And, in later life, Andrew, who had come to respect his father's wisdom, would return the compliment by asking aloud, often in the presence of others, "What would Father have done?"

Of life at 401 Negley between 1880 and 1882, William recalls, "The old home was kept quiet, close and blinded, under Aunt's [Sarah Jane's] influence, which Uncle always respected. The sitting room, off the dining room, was for the family; and the parlor with its square piano was kept in its sacred darkness. . . . When Aunt's relatives came, they had the sitting room. When Uncle's callers came—Andrew Carnegie, Frick with Andy [Mellon], and old neighbors, old-timers— they found him with me, the inseparable, in the library."[11] William describes the Judge's reception of these callers: "In appearance, as a figure, to all folks and citizens, Judge Mellon truly suggested a mark of chilliness; but with friends he was well met, if we add that they passed on before the welcome became worn. He was not good at loitering, after interest lagged."[12]

On family relationships, William writes:

On his private affairs we never precipitated inquiries. Even his wife and sons never did so. . . . Any of us shuddered when a kindly stranger or intrepid neighbor crossed the personal barrier with a solicitous inquiry on his health, wealth or any other invasions of his holy ground. . . . This wall around him was undeclared but was sacred, even in his family. No one but entire strangers ever blundered against it; and strangers soon sensed the forbidden ground.

. . . The wedded union of Thomas and Sarah was exemplary in its sense and practice of loyalty and duty, in the perfect, old-fashioned way; but . . . it was not a case of tender love and sentiment. . . . They roomed and slept together and never were separated . . . [but] they were not lovers, nor even company for each other, just good domestic partners.

There was a taken-for-granted loyalty, mutuality and sympathy between all members of the family, but there was no emotional sentiment. . . . The father held at heart, all his life, a concern for his wife and sons, affectionately and truly, in everything that involved their health, happiness and success. This concern was not nervous nor on sharp edge, as all went well always. He had a tender heart, and his grief at the death of his eldest and youngest is memorable. His wife was tender-hearted and capable of full sympathy, but not of grievous suffering. She was motherly and dutiful, but more stoical. It was the way of the Negleys.

The disposition of the members toward the father, while passive and taking for granted everything concerning him, was empty of provision and regard for his personal delights, his comforts, his literary indulgence, and for his success in his legal battles and his civic enterprises as a member of the City Council. . . . He haggled along with his reading and writing mostly by himself, with his bad eyesight. Aunt and the boys read [to him] a little, as they came and, restlessly, went. His wife took note of his routine. His shirts were handy in the drawer, and his other things were in regular place. He dressed and undressed himself, put on his collar and tie. . . . In every way, he was as an uncle or as a father's cousin, paying his board and going daily about some affairs of his own.[13]

What William noticed but failed to comprehend is that the Mellons were held together by a kind of undemonstrative affection that recoiled from overt expression—an affection that the members silently treasured but could not have voiced without embarrassment. Speaking of the Mellons he had known, John Bowman, a chancellor of the University of Pittsburgh, observed that they were covertly sentimental but held themselves "under Scotch control." Bowman adds, "A Scotchman never tells his wife he loves her. He knows it and she knows it, but they don't *talk* about it."[14] Call it Scotch-Irish love.

# XV

## The Judge's Clashes with Organized Labor: The "Great Uprising" of 1877, Prosecution of David Jones, Slander Suit against the *National Labor Tribune*

*Such is the primary school of aggressive socialism; a constant clamor of wrongs suffered and rights denied, but never a word about reciprocal duties to be performed. The workingman is taught to consider his status as a worker fixed and permanent, and not a transition state of working up and out to independence. That would be desertion to the camp of the enemy.*

THE PANIC OF 1873 AND SUBSEQUENT depression did little to restrain the torrent of immigrants seeking work that had been flowing into Pittsburgh and its industrial satellite communities for twenty-five years. Conspicuous among the recent arrivals were thousands of Catholic Irish fugitives from the potato famine. Other sizable contingents streamed in from the Welsh and English coalfields and from Eastern Europe. Those who found work in the mines and steel mills of western Pennsylvania earned better pay than comparable workers abroad, but they were normally required to toil twelve hours a day, seven days a week, and under such hazardous conditions that many died before the age of forty. In some neighborhoods, the pretentious mansions of the newly rich stood within walking distance of crowded hovels where working-class families subsisted in grinding squalor. Most of the immigrants embraced democracy, but some believed that a day was approaching when toilers like themselves would somehow become collective owners. A few looked to violence for their deliverance and became revolutionary socialists or anarchists. The question that confronted and confounded America was how its new industrial wealth should be divided among capitalists, managers, and workers. Every interest group answered this question in its own favor.

Those who owned or managed the mines and factories around Pittsburgh were as a rule of Scotch-Irish or Pennsylvania German origin; so were most of the judges and other elected officials. Families like the Fricks and Mellons, who were descended from these early waves of immigration, formed an insecure ruling class that viewed the new industrial work force warily, even with alarm. Their fears were amply realized in the "Great Uprising" or "Roundhouse Riot" of 1877.

The Pennsylvania Railroad had come to be resented, perhaps hated, by most Pittsburghers. It had fixed a stranglehold on the local economy and wielded its autocratic power over commerce with sneering disregard for every interest save its own; and in the 1850s it had saddled Pittsburgh and Allegheny County with crushing taxation to service its ethically controversial bonds.

By 1877, the fearsome depression that the Panic had triggered four years earlier was finally approaching its nadir. But no one knew where the actual bottom would occur, and businesses kept cutting expenses to offset declining income. When the Pennsylvania Railroad doubled the length of its trains, halved the size of their crews, and cut the wages of its Pittsburgh work force, the irate trainmen went on strike and unwittingly ignited a social explosion of unprecedented violence and magnitude. With large numbers of miners and other workmen collaborating, the rail strike spread from coast to coast on a groundswell of indignation and paralyzed the whole U.S. economy for the first time.

On July 21, a National Guard contingent from Philadelphia, which had been sent to reopen the rail line, was met at Pittsburgh's Union Station by a defiant crowd of strikers and demonstrators. Taunted with insults and pelted with rocks, the harassed soldiers opened fire indiscriminately, shot twenty people dead, and wounded many more. Among the dead were women, children, and other presumed by-standers. Outraged citizens piled into the streets. A heterogeneous multitude of rioting demonstrators, vandals, and thieves, in which the striking train workers counted for little, descended on the Pennsyl-vania Railroad yards and torched 1383 freight cars, 104 locomotives, 66 passenger cars, and 39 buildings, including the station. A railroad roundhouse in which the hard-pressed troops found overnight refuge may have been all that saved them from being slaughtered. The follow-ing day, they killed more demonstrators and beat a chaotic retreat from the city through crowds screaming for their blood.

The restraints of civilization broke down for forty-eight hours, and Pittsburgh succumbed to its first and only bacchanal of looting. Gun shops, groceries, and liquor stores were robbed; vigilantes armed with shotguns and hunting rifles guarded the banks; and a Vigilance Com-mittee headed by Thomas Mellon's in-law, Major General James S. Negley, struggled vainly to restore order. At last, on July 23, the barba-rism subsided, leaving Pittsburgh shattered, shaken, and nervously subdued.

Many established Pittsburghers had at first sympathized with the strike. Businessmen, property owners, managers, judges, and politi-cians, though distrustful of organized labor, had, on the whole, quietly applauded the union men for their spirited challenge to the almighty railroad. What they could not have foreseen was the draconian repres-sion by military force, not to mention the arson, vandalism, and cyni-cal looting that followed.

To Thomas Mellon, the bloody mayhem of July can only have fore-shadowed the socialist revolution that he feared was imminent. These events lent gratuitous confirmation to his misanthropic conviction that ordinary humans are "crooks, cranks, imbeciles, and weaklings . . . who have in them a taint of insanity." Refusing to discriminate between the strikers and the mob of vandals, looters, and hoodlums that had absorbed and swept them along, he would continue to fulminate against

*Aftermath of the Great Railroad Strike or Uprising of 1877:*
*vandalized Pennsylvania Railroad yards at Pittsburgh.*
From Pittsburgh: The Story of an American City, *by Stefan Lorant.*

the "vicious classes," which he viewed as inimical to private property and therefore to civilization.[1]

For years, the Judge had freighted his coal and lumber over the Pennsylvania Railroad, which counted among its former directors his early benefactor and uncle, Thomas Mellon. But, though inimical to the uprising, he cannot have harbored much affection for the railroad, either. Twenty years earlier, he had raucously campaigned for the repudiation of its arguably fraudulent bonds. After the uprising, while others bewailed the loss of twenty-five Pittsburghers shot dead in the streets, Mellon raged against the bond issue that was voted to reimburse damaged businesses for $2,772,349, of which $1,600,000 was earmarked for the railroad.[2]

Mellon's inflammatory warning that "this country has lately served as an asylum for the spendthrifts, the desperados, and other criminal classes of the Old World" was a tasteless exaggeration.[3] But no one could deny that organized labor had demonstrated its power to trigger a sequence of events that could lead to earth-scorching violence and death. In the parlors of influential Pittsburghers, it came to be accepted that the recently arrived industrial workers, many of them Catholics, were flocking into labor unions and could form a potentially dangerous underclass that might have to be forcibly restrained.

A "communistic dance of death and destruction" was the *Pittsburgh Commercial Gazette*'s hysterical description of the uprising.[4] The New York *Independent,* a religious publication, broke into stridently unchristian language: "Bring on then the troops—the armed police—in overwhelming numbers. Bring out the Gatling [machine] guns. Let there be no fooling with blank cartridges. But let the mob know, everywhere, that for it to stand one moment after it has been ordered by proper authorities to disperse, will be to be shot down in its tracks. ... A little of the vigor of the first Napoleon is the thing we now need."[5]

In their uphill pursuit of happiness, in their fury and their frustration, the miners and industrial workers had sought improved conditions in three venues: politics, the courts, and unions. In politics, they quickly found themselves bedeviled by an unsympathetic state legislature, elected mainly from the rural, nonindustrial counties. In the courts they were confounded by judges who routinely favored the rights of property owners. Lacking other alternatives, the work force began to organize itself into unions.

Shortly after the Great Uprising, a Welsh-born immigrant named David Jones began to stand out as a labor organizer in Allegheny County. Jones appears to have slipped into his new role fortuitously:

after working his way through Mount Union College in Ohio, he had settled at Homestead, near Pittsburgh, and become a teacher at the Blackburn School, where his pupils were mainly miners' children. He had worked in the mines himself, could relate to miners, and had an easy grasp of their problems. When scattered strikes swept the collieries around Homestead in 1878, Jones exhibited his fraternal support for the strikers by camping with them and sharing their hardships. They doubled his teaching salary, invited him to join Local 860 of the Knights of Labor, and chose him as their "checkweighman." Mine wages were geared to the amount of coal that the miners cut, and Jones's job was to monitor the weighing of coal.[6]

Significantly, checkweighman Jones was also studying law. For the time being, union organization presented an interesting challenge. But the next chapter of his life would be different. Jones was ambitious and had no intention of choking on coal dust forever.

In 1879 he led the miners of the Monongahela Valley in a strike that won them a wage hike of 40 percent. Finding himself a hero, he seized the opportunity to form a Miners' Association. He was elected its general secretary and began recruiting throughout the Monongahela coal fields.[7] The following year, he learned that the Waverly Coal & Coke Company, which operated mines at Smithton, in Westmoreland County, was loading low-priced coal into one of the Walton family's barges on the Monongahela. Waverly was a colliery of moderate size that employed three hundred hands, paid $70,000 a year in wages, and mined 2.5 million bushels of coal per year. The company had decided to fill a contract that threatened to drop the cost of coal transported by river from 3.5 cents to 2.5 cents per bushel. This was expected to have a ripple effect in the coal market, especially with respect to the crucial price of coal transported by rail. Because wages were geared to the coal price, Jones had reason to be alarmed. He assembled the Waverly miners, engaged a six-piece brass band to stir their martial fervor, and exhorted them to strike.[8] He was now on a collision course with Thomas Mellon.

Fate had dealt David Jones a number of winning cards, among them intelligence and initiative. He had parlayed these gifts into a superior education, had learned to speak forcefully in public, and could now rely on the loyalty of a multitudinous following. Supremely self-confident, he was inclined to be impatient, would not suffer the interference of fools, and tended to run his union autocratically. "There was neither vice president, secretary, treasurer nor executive committee to advise or suggest," recalls the labor chronicler Andrew Roy. Jones "was as much of an autocrat as the Czar of Russia."[9] But to Thomas Mellon, Jones was merely one more labor demagogue attempting to promote himself on the backs of his gullible partisans.

With strident rhetoric and blasts of martial music from his band, Jones prevailed on the union miners at Waverly Coal to lay down their picks and walk off the job. Some of the nonunion men apparently walked off too, for a number of them would later testify that Jones had browbeaten them to do so. That every miner was obligated by contract to give sixty days' notice before quitting was a nagging detail that their leader advised them to disregard.[10]

On November 18, 1880, as he was boarding a train at West Newton, Jones was arrested and packed off to jail. Fifteen other members of the Miners' Association were also placed behind bars. When his bail had been fixed at $1,000, Jones managed to borrow the money and quickly walked free. But he now knew that the charges against him were serious: criminal conspiracy to fix the price of labor, hindering miners from accepting work, and exhorting them to break their contract. He had also learned that his accuser was the legal counsel and substantial owner of Waverly Coal—Thomas Mellon.[11]

Ironically, Jones and Mellon had more in common than either of them would have cared to admit. Both had come to America as impecunious immigrants. Both were intelligent and imperiously aware of it. Both had set their sights on scaling the rugged slope of society to attain comfort and respectability. Both had struggled fiercely for education and supported themselves through college as part-time teachers. Both had decided to become lawyers: Jones was studying law with a future mayor of Pittsburgh, the reformer George W. Guthrie.[12]

If Mellon and Jones had met under different circumstances, they might even have become friends. One can imagine the sixty-seven-year-old judge handing the twenty-seven-year-old law student a copy of Franklin's autobiography and giving him avuncular pointers on how to work his way "up and out"—how "well doing" leads to doing well. But Mellon was a mine owner, Jones headed the miners' union, and they lived in the nineteenth century.

That a labor leader could be charged with criminal conspiracy for having urged his union to strike for higher wages may appear outrageous today, but it was common in 1880. Written deep into Pennsylvania law was the archaic axiom that labor is "a vendible commodity," like beans or potatoes, and that any concerted action aimed at forcing wages higher is an actionable conspiracy to fix prices. The state legislature, called the General Assembly, had enacted a statute in 1872 that protected the right to strike, but it had left standing a previous law against hindering anyone from accepting employment. Strikers who attempted, by threat or humiliation, to hinder nonunion workers, or scabs, from taking their vacant jobs thus infringed on the freedom of others and were breaking the law. When in 1876 a subsequent statute had attempted to define the lawful means that strikers could employ to further their objectives, the courts had countered by broadening the definition of "hindering" until it more or less criminalized effectual collective bargaining.

Jones's predicament was unenviable: he needed a lawyer, but his pockets were as empty as the coffers of his union. To be convicted of conspiracy could land him in prison for months or even years. He was preparing to shed his role as a labor organizer, was studying for his bar exams, and may already have been planning the political career that would see him elected a burgess of Homestead and later a member of the General Assembly.[13] A lengthy jail sentence would have blasted his plan to shimmy up into the middle class.

The principal newspaper that rushed to Jones's defense and gave front-page coverage to his upcoming trial was the *National Labor Tribune*. A vocal and articulate workers' weekly, the *Tribune* was arguably the most influential prolabor publication in America. Its editor, Thomas Armstrong, insisted that Waverly Coal and Thomas Mellon were the true "conspirators," because by prosecuting Jones they were attempting to undermine the rights of workers and their leaders to speak freely, to assemble peaceably, to organize, and to quit work if they so desired.[14] He also complained bitterly that the state's antediluvian conspiracy law was being prejudicially invoked against labor and routinely disregarded as it applied to business. "When the Lamp Chimney Manufacturers' Association combined to shut the men off from four weeks' wages," fumed Armstrong, "nobody alleged a conspiracy. There are indeed few acts of association, whether of capital or labor, that are not conspiracy if tested through the 'Waverly law screen.'" Alluding to the role of Jones, he insisted that an association of workmen had just as much right to hire a business manager as a company did.[15]

With his trial now fast approaching, Jones placed an urgent appeal in the *Tribune* for contributions to his legal defense fund. It was aimed at the miners, and he was none too confident about their response: "You have passed your resolutions, poured out warmly sympathetic words, and made your handsome promises; now we will test your sincerity. Should you give only one-third of the amount necessary for the defense, we shall not be disappointed, as this has been the rule among the miners. It is usual with them to see their servants and officers getting into trouble in their cause, and then cruelly letting them get out themselves as best they can." He concluded with a call to arms: "This case is of equal interest to all wage workers and union men everywhere. . . . Although this is the miners' case, yet the rights involved and imperiled are every workingman's rights, and your fellow toilers will severely censure and not forgive you, should you not contribute ample means to have the defense—really the defense of Labor—ably and successfully managed."[16]

Jones's appeal triggered a shower of $2 and $3 contributions from miners and other union workers all over Pennsylvania.[17] Money even trickled in from out of state. That so many Americans had been persuaded to focus on the venerable freedoms that would be at risk in the forthcoming contest was largely the work of Armstrong and his paper.

David Jones was tried by the Court of Quarter Sessions at Greensburg in February 1881. The prosecution charged that he had masterminded and precipitated a conspiracy to artificially elevate the price of labor, that he had counseled the miners to break their contract and had alternately browbeaten and bribed them to strike, and that by insult and intimidation he had hindered nonunion men from filling the resulting vacancies. Thomas Mellon, who had brought these charges, must have been following events closely, because for him the stakes were almost as high as they were for Jones. A victory by Waverly Coal would reinforce the state's mile-wide definitions of conspiracy and hindering, with the result that effectual collective bargaining would remain a marginally criminal activity. A victory by Jones would have the effect of narrowing these all-important definitions and would emphatically reconfirm the rights of free speech and freedom to assemble, but it might imperil a nonunion worker's right to accept employment from any employer.

Each side had marshaled and trained up a team of witnesses. In support of Mellon's charges, the Waverly superintendent, Lewis, testified that the men had gone on strike mainly out of fear, by which he meant that work had been progressing normally until Jones arrived and began stirring up trouble.[18] A number of workers apparently corroborated this assertion.[19] Others testified that Jones had alternately attempted to threaten and bribe them; that, resorting to carrot and stick, he had warned them to quit working, otherwise "bands of music would be brought in and the half of Pennsylvania, if necessary," but that if a strike were launched, "large sums of money could be had."[20] Nonunion men apparently complained of having been smeared as "scabs" and "blacklegs."[21]

Miners who testified for the defense said that Jones had acted merely as an adviser, that the union men had made their own decisions, and that their leader had neither compelled them to strike nor hindered anyone from taking a vacant job. Some even insisted that they had only laid down their picks in protest after hearing of their leader's arrest.[22] We are free to suspect that a number of witnesses testified according to whom they feared more—their employer, who appeared to be heartless and intransigent, or their autocratic union boss.

No transcript of Jones's testimony appears to have survived, but its coverage in the *National Labor Tribune* and other papers preserves a number of his responses and discloses his line of defense. He evidently scoffed at Mellon's allegations of hindering and vehemently denied that the strike amounted to a price-fixing conspiracy. American workers had every right to quit their jobs, and he as a union leader had felt obliged to advise them to do so. His remark that "bands of music would be brought in and the half of Pennsylvania, if necessary" had not been intended as a threat but merely as a figure of speech, and it had been understood that way by the miners. His comment that "large sums of money could be had" should not have been understood as a proffered bribe but rather as a harmless reference to the generous financial support that striking miners could count on from their fellow workmen all over the state. He denied having bribed, intimidated, humiliated, or otherwise hindered miners from working; he had merely pleaded with them to quit voluntarily. Neither had he attempted to bar nonunion men from filling vacancies at Waverly; he had merely tried to *dissuade* them with moral arguments. "Coaxed" is the word he used.[23]

With respect to the statute of 1876, which protected "lawful" strike activities, Jones must have wondered how a labor leader could "lawfully" discharge his responsibilities, if even "moral persuasion" could be construed as either hindering or conspiracy.[24] He must also have emphasized the lofty issues that were at stake in his trial: freedom of speech, freedom to assemble peaceably, the legitimate pursuit of happiness, labor's presumed right to strike in some organized effective manner, and the proper definitions of hindering and of criminal conspiracy to fix prices. He could also have claimed—justifiably—that his record as a labor leader contained no appeals for violence and showed him to have been a frequent advocate of arbitration.[25]

Judge James A. Hunter, who conducted the trial, was of Scotch-Irish ancestry, but a Democrat and, like Jones, a former schoolteacher. As the trial progressed, both sides eyed him uneasily, for neither could be certain how he would wield his crucial influence. The charge he delivered to the jury unleashed a storm. Citing the centuries-old English common law, which Pennsylvania still adhered to, he explained that "combinations of workmen to raise the price of wages . . . are indictable. . . . Each may insist on raising his wages, but if several meet for the same purpose it is illegal and the parties may be indicted for conspiracy." On the other hand, he quoted from the Pennsylvania statute of 1872, which held that

> it shall be lawful for any laborer or laborers . . . acting as individuals or as the members of any club, society or association, to refuse to work or labor for any person or persons, whenever in his, her or their opinion the wages paid are insufficient, and the treatment of such laborer . . . by his, her or their employer is brutal or offensive, or the continued labor by such laborer . . . would be contrary to the rules, regulations or by-laws of any club, society or organization to which he, she or they might belong. . . . Provided, That nothing herein contained shall prevent the prosecution and punishment, under existing laws, of any person or persons who shall, in any way, hinder persons who desire to labor for their employers from doing so, or other persons from being employed as laborers.[26]

After reviewing the testimony, Judge Hunter posed a number of pivotal questions: Did Jones's actions truly amount to a conspiracy aimed at fixing the price of labor? Had he attempted to hinder anyone from working or from accepting employment at Waverly Coal?[27]

Because the witnesses flagrantly contradicted each other on these related points, the jurors would have to decide which way the evidence tilted. Their definition of hindering would be crucial. In a democracy, bona fide persuasion can never be prohibited, and hindering, in the strict sense, can never be permitted. But at what point does persuasion become so intense that it amounts to hindering? Is mere rudeness a form of hindering? Were union miners hindering their nonunion colleagues if they berated them as "scabs" and "blacklegs"? Could anyone be certain these words had even been spoken? If they had, could Jones be held responsible? However the jurors defined hindering, their definition would be arbitrary.

Another bone of contention was whether the miners had broken their contract. Arguably they had, for the document required them to give sixty days' notice before striking. However, it also provided for a penalty if they struck without sufficient notice, which suggested that compliance with the agreement was optional.[28]

Confounded by a welter of contradictory testimony, wandering in a maze of ambiguities, beset by questions that could only be answered arbitrarily, the jury faced its unenviable task. "You will take the case," concluded Judge Hunter, "and render such a verdict from the whole of the evidence as will meet with the approval of your consciences."[29]

So charged, the jury found David Jones guilty of having hindered Waverly miners from working and of having criminally conspired to fix the price of labor. He appealed to the Pennsylvania Supreme Court, but it refused even to consider his plea. At first Thomas Mellon and the Pittsburgh establishment must have been drunk with pleasure. By reaffirming the prevailing inclusive definitions of conspiracy and hindering, the court had conceded Mellon's principal point. But, simultaneously, the *National Labor Tribune* was swamped with indignant letters from aggrieved supporters of labor. A woman railed, "Judge Hunter's charge to the jury at Greensburg seemed to be an exhibition of natural ignorance and narrow-mindedness unequaled by any I ever read. . . . This charge, worthy of a jury of 200 years ago, or a thousand, is not worth the trouble of criticism by points—the same being partial from beginning to end, claiming more knowledge of common law than of common sense."[30]

But those who had lusted for the court to vent its indignation by slapping Jones with a heavy sentence must have been sorely disappointed. Judge Hunter fined the union leader $100 plus the cost of his own prosecution but sent him to jail for only one night.[31] Thus the court soured Mellon's victory by signaling its sympathy for labor. In fact, Jones's only meaningful punishment was that he apparently contracted smallpox in jail.[32]

Mellon now turned his guns on the *National Labor Tribune* for its doggedly one-sided coverage of the Jones case. Had its editor, Armstrong, not depicted Waverly Coal as a greedy, ruthless, insensitive enterprise merely because it refused to pay higher wages than the market would bear? Had he published a single word of censure when Jones had brazenly "advised" the miners to break their contract with Waverly and to strike without giving notice? Did the *Tribune* secretly condone reckless disregard of contractual agreements? Was its obsessive call for redefining the conspiracy and hindering laws merely a prelude to demanding their abolition? Mellon believed he knew the answers to these questions. He was fed up with the paper's infuriating bias and had even come to doubt its commitment to the rule of law. Armstrong's practice of publishing openly subversive extracts from out-of-town newspapers had so alarmed Mellon that he recorded one such item in his memoirs, from the *Ohio Valley Boycotter:*

> Unionism must be enforced. When a class of men is forced by the encroachments of capital to form a trade society for the prosecution of their standard of comfort, the authority to sustain it must be made absolute. No one, nor any one of the minority, has the right to secede and combine with other influences to lower the standard, and if the right to secede is admitted, our combinations are useless.[33]

To this unabashed tidbit of tyranny Mellon opposes his own view of the lawful, legitimate role that a labor union is entitled to play:

Labor organization is not in itself wrong; true social science justifies it for all legitimate purposes. But combinations of employees to procure higher wages than the market rates, by resort to coercion through the means of sudden and concerted strikes, and hindering and preventing others from taking their places with a view to suspend the work of their employer until he is compelled to accede to their terms: this compulsory element of the strike is neither just nor legitimate, and is contrary to the first principles of civil liberty. They have a right, one and all, to quit their employment when dissatisfied, but they transgress the rule of social order whenever they undertake to coerce their employer and other workingmen by compulsory methods. They forget that this is a free country, and that every man is the owner of his own labor, and has the right to dispose of it as he pleases; and that every operator has the right to manage his own business without let or hindrance from others, so long as he does not transgress the law.[34]

On the last day of 1881, Thomas Mellon, James B. Corey, and other Waverly partners filed a $70,000 lawsuit for conspiracy and libel against the *National Labor Tribune* and against General Secretary David Jones of the Miners' Association. "It makes us feel rich to be sued for so much money," quipped editor Armstrong, whistling in the dark, "but we fancy there will have to be an unprecedented inflation of the currency before the complainant pockets the cash."[35]

Though Waverly's profits had taken a hit from the strike and its name had been blackened by the *Tribune*'s one-sided coverage of Jones's trial, actual damages to the company could not have amounted to $70,000. Mellon and his fellow plaintiffs might howl like underdogs, but in fact they were on the offensive. With the right judge, they might lay more lashes on Jones, who, in their view, had received only a slap on the wrist. But what particularly caused them to salivate was the prospect of bankrupting and silencing the *Tribune*. In both endeavors they failed. Though Mellon showed his usual pertinacity by appealing the lawsuit to higher authority, it was rejected conclusively by the Pennsylvania Supreme Court in 1883.

Mellon's philosophical position was not devised as a legal stratagem. He had extrapolated it from personal experience, filtered it through the distorting lenses of his prejudices, and fortified it by years of reading and pondering. In the two subchapters of his memoirs that deal with the abiding tug-of-war between labor and capital, he cites or quotes from the works of Adam Smith, David Ricardo, Jean-Jacques Rousseau, John Stuart Mill, Karl Marx, Ferdinand Lassalle, Mikhail Bakunin, François Babeuf, John Rae, Robert Owen, Henry George, Émile de Laveleye, Charles Fourier, George Rapp, John Noyes, Étienne Cabet, Richard Ely, Jacques Pierre Brissot (de Warville), Johann Rodbertus, Edward Atkinson, Francis Walker, William Weeden, Vida Scudder, Claude Bastiat, Wilhelm von Humboldt, Peter Kropotkin, and of course Herbert Spencer.[36] Thomas Mellon was probably as well-read, and as opinionated, on the subject of economic theory as anyone in Pittsburgh.

For decades he had meditated uneasily about labor and its frictional relationship to capital. He had tested various conclusions against the wisdom of his own experience and, above all, against the strong undercurrent of self-interest that underlay so much of his reasoning. He had followed the twisting paths of logic charted by thinkers with guiding fixations contrary to his own, and he had stopped short when he perceived where these paths were leading. With few exceptions, his Spencerian mindset steered him back to a comfortable line of reasoning.

Labor, in Mellon's view, is a commodity like any other, and its price floats up or down, according to supply and demand. If savage hordes from Eastern Europe were streaming into western Pennsylvania and looking for work in the mines, mills, and factories, wages would inevitably drift lower. Any attempt to manipulate the labor market, even for humanitarian purposes, was an utterly futile violation of natural law and would inevitably be avenged as the free market ruthlessly reasserted itself. William Penn's Pennsylvania, a beacon of religious and political tolerance and openness, was now Spencer's jungle, where only the fittest survived. Such manipulations belong to the battle plan of socialism, which in turn is a tyranny of the mediocre aimed at punishing winners and rewarding losers.

As Mellon read and pondered in the seclusion of his library, an opposing view of labor and capital was relentlessly asserting itself on the national stage. In the bustling workaday world that encircled the Mellon home but did not penetrate its walls, the steady development of Judeo-Christian values was advancing the view that human beings are entitled not merely to life, liberty, and the pursuit of happiness but also to food, shelter, elementary education, safety in the workplace, and a smidgen of free time between bouts of toil. In the Jones and *Tribune* cases, this view of entitlement wrestles with the harsh free-market philosophy of Mellon and Spencer. That labor's appeal, in these cases, was to human decency as much as to points of law was potently expressed by Armstrong of the *Tribune* when he condemned Pennsylvania's conspiracy and hindering statutes as "the direct outgrowth of a miserable selfishness which regards a dollar as of greater moment than human flesh and blood; of perverted minds that have come to consider the teachings of Christ as very good theory for Sunday reading, but not intended for practice in the real affairs of this life."[37] To which Mellon might have replied that a business is expected to make money; the teachings of Christ are about giving it away. Another unresolved conflict that stirs in these cases revolved around the nature of property. If the right to private ownership cannot be viewed as absolute in an industrial society, to what extent must it be subordinated to communal needs?

Where the Judge errs completely is in viewing violent, revolutionary socialism—"rabid" socialism, to use his expression—as the emerging ideology of American workers. Wherever he looks in the labor movement, he espies the apostles of revolutionary socialism spreading their venomous message. He ascribes its prevalence to "a demoralized condition of public sentiment, which may require blood to purify."[38]

The working class is always extolled as the sole producer, but wrongfully disinherited owner of both capital and wealth. Capitalists and employers are ever represented as foes and oppressors of the workingmen, and an irrepressible conflict as existing between employers and employees. The whole end and aim of labor agitation of late would seem to be to create discontent in the minds of the working classes and animosity against their employers. They are taught to expect a millennium only when, by universal organization under competent leaders they shall be able, peaceably by legislation or by force if necessary, to overthrow the present wage system, and compel an equal division of capital and profits among themselves: thus emancipating labor from what they represent to be a condition of bondage equal to, if not worse than slavery itself.

Such is the primary school of aggressive socialism; a constant clamor of wrongs suffered and rights denied, but never a word about reciprocal duties to be performed. The workingman is taught to consider his status as a worker fixed and permanent, and not a transition state of working up and out to independence. That would be desertion to the camp of the enemy.[39]

This particular kind of "desertion" is precisely what David Jones was being accused of. His consuming ambition, imperious style, and clear determination to make the law his ladder to middle-class propriety marked him in the eyes of many as an opportunist whose objective was not to fight for the workers but to leave them far behind and far below. An uncommonly articulate miner named John Bonner cited Jones in the *Tribune* for his "lucrative love of loquacity."[40] And its editor, Armstrong, warned Terence Powderly, leader of the Knights of Labor, that Jones "is very ambitious but is learning. He is an indiscreet talker so far as saying 'I,' Big 'I' at that. . . . If he does not do right, . . . sit down on him."[41] Armstrong's misgivings proved oracular: once admitted to the bar, Jones sundered his connections to labor, quickly succeeded in his law practice, made a grand tour of Europe with his wife, and wrote a travel log.[42] During the bitter and sanguinary Homestead Strike of 1892, as volleys of gunfire rent the air, Jones was not to be seen on the barricades. He had found his roost in the Pennsylvania House of Representatives, the lower chamber of the General Assembly. Like Andrew Carnegie, also a genteel progressive, Jones had concluded that absence of body was better than presence of mind.

Mellon continues:

> The workingman . . . is never advised to persevere in well doing, or to save a portion of his earnings that he may become his own employer, and finally an employer of others. Nothing is ever proposed to better his condition, but labor organization and warfare against capital and employers; and the prevention of competition among workingmen themselves by limiting the hours and amount of work. By such means it is proposed to bring about a state of affairs whereby the entire product and profits of labor will be equally divided among the laborers. It seems never to occur to them that the means they propose lead directly to the enslavement rather than the emancipation of the workingman. Restrict individual effort, remove all incentive to excel his fellows or improve his condition by asserting the advantages nature may have bestowed on him in a greater capacity for work and a higher intelligence to direct it, and you reduce the best to the dead-sea level of the worst. No better method could be devised to crush out the spirit of individual liberty, and produce a nation of slaves submissive to the will of their masters.[43]

That a small percentage of penniless, undereducated immigrants should have failed to perceive the futility of attempting a socialist revolution in America is understandable. Likewise, it should not have surprised Mellon that among labor leaders, a number of minor demagogues would attempt to curry favor with their credulous adherents by proclaiming that the solution to labor's problems lay in the violent overthrow of American institutions.

Despite Mellon's erudition, he also remained blinded by irrational fear that a socialist revolution could take place in America. He persevered in this belief despite the overwhelming evidence that social and economic realities would combine forcefully to thwart any such upheaval. His own state, Pennsylvania, was overwhelmingly rural and agricultural. Private ownership was written deep into the law and formed a part of the enduring consensus. Armstrong of the *Tribune* was alluding to the intransigence of this consensus when he sneered at the "farmer law" of Westmoreland County, in his coverage of the Jones case.[44] Miners, factory workers, and mill hands amounted to only a small minority statewide and never formed a majority even in the industrial counties. Was it reasonable to expect that they could mount a credible threat to private ownership, in defiance of all the powers that be? Driven mad by frustration and helplessness, union workers might resort to violence, break the law, and steal or destroy private property. That some of them had committed such acts during the Roundhouse Riot of 1877 understandably discomfited Thomas Mellon, the more so because he lived only a short distance away. But any threat that union workers posed to the moral standard of private ownership existed only in the uninformed imaginations, and perhaps the guilty hallucinations, of the wealthy. This is easy for present-day Americans to perceive, because they look back on one hundred years of predominantly peaceful competition between labor and capital. But in Thomas Mellon's day, when the surging Industrial Revolution was towing America at full throttle in God knows what direction, the future appeared to dance with horrific possibilities.

What Mellon correctly perceived as endangered in the Jones and *Tribune* cases was the proposition that private ownership is a natural, absolute right, rather than a qualified privilege that society has the power to extend but can also modify or revoke. That during the industrial era the "right" to own property was coming to be viewed as relative rather than absolute aroused fear in those who owned property and desire in those who did not.

Mellon and his opponents revealed an identical warp in their rationale when they tended to view the Waverly clash as merely one battle in a war that could not end until one side had defeated the other. In their frenzy to demonize one another, Mellon and most of his adversaries remained blind to the truth that in a democratic industrial society, labor and capital will quarrel intermittently but must nonetheless coexist in a state of nonviolent, albeit uneasy, equilibrium. Economic realities place limits on how much each side can wrest from the other. Starving workers cannot work; and workers who succeed at extracting excessive wages destroy the competitive edge of their business. These are the limits within which labor and capital act out the ritual tug-of-war that determines where wages will temporarily settle. More important, through the agency of government and the courts, society allots to each side the legal advantages—call them "weapons"—that crucially affect this enduring contest.

In early industrial America, labor found itself struggling on a mudsill that tilted hopelessly in favor of capital. One writer who remained oblivious to this truth or dismissed it as superfluous confirmation of Spencer's principles was William B. Weeden, author of *The Social Law of Labor*. Thomas Mellon read Weeden's book carefully, underlined a number of reactionary passages, and finally inscribed the following comment in his own copy: "This writer goes to the root principles of society, and the institutions which grow out of it in its different stages.—Thos Mellon, April 5/84, $1.20."[45]

# XVI

———•·◆·•———

## A Passage to Ireland,
## "Sinking" the Island

*It certainly would be a blessing to the [native] Irish themselves, if by some social force they could be scattered over all the earth, and not a vestige of them left on their own soil. They would soon become absorbed by other races; and by intermarriage, and life under other influences, in a few generations the mixture would be an improvement of both, as is already shown in the population of the United States and elsewhere.*

FOR FORTY-SIX YEARS, THOMAS MELLON had treasured the memories of his early childhood in Ireland: of emerald meadows along the Strule, of walking on the walls of Londonderry, of the unembellished Crossroads Meeting House where he and his parents had worshipped in severe austerity, and, above all, of Camp Hill Cottage, where he had first seen daylight and had lived until his sixth year. It is unlikely that he ever relinquished the hope of someday revisiting the scenes of a childhood so rich in remembrance. But, more subtly, the prospect of determining with finality how accurately his detailed and colorful recollections of that distant time corresponded to reality had come to fascinate him. When James and Rachel Mellon embarked on a visit to Ireland in 1875, the Judge, relying wholly on childhood memories, was able to describe for them the old homestead at Lower Castletown and give them precise directions on how to find

*A square-rigged brig like the* Alexander, *the ship that carried Thomas Mellon and his parents to America in 1818.*

*The steamship* Celtic, *on which Thomas Mellon returned to Ireland in 1882. Courtesy Peabody Essex Museum, Provincetown, Mass.*

it. They located Camp Hill without difficulty and returned with photographs that proved the cottage was not only standing but, by Irish standards, habitable.

The longing to revisit his birthplace continued to nag at the Judge until in 1882, on three days' notice, he impulsively decided to embark for Ireland. He was accompanied by his youngest son, twenty-two-year-old George, who had been fighting tuberculosis and was expected to benefit from breathing sea air on the transatlantic voyages. The two sailed from New York on August 12 aboard the *Celtic,* a ship of the White Star Line, which would later launch the *Titanic.*

The voyage itself had novelties: "Twice we had the pleasure of admiring the great whale in his native element," recalls the Judge, "spouting a puff of white spray into the air at regular intervals, like the discharge of steam from a locomotive; and as often some fifteen feet or so of his back would appear on the surface like a canoe turned bottom up."[1]

Nine days out of New York, they came in sight of a stern and rock-bound coast which, in its gray severity, bore scant resemblance to the Emerald Isle of song and story but was unmistakably Ireland. As their ship dropped anchor at Queenstown (present-day Cobh), in the Cove of Cork, the sixty-nine-year-old Judge must have marveled that, whereas his immigrant voyage from Londonderry to the New World by square-rigger in 1818 had consumed a mind-boggling three months, he had now crossed the same ocean by steamship in only nine days.

"I can scarcely claim Irish nationality," he wrote three years later, taking pains to distance himself from the indigenous population, "but ... Ireland was the land of my birth, and home of my immediate ancestors, ... and apart from all ancestral connection, I know of no other country whose history is more curious and suggestive. Certainly no history presents a richer field for the sociologist to trace the effect of laws and institutions, civil and religious, on national and private character."[2]

If the Judge launches his controversial philippics against the native Irish on a pseudo-sociological note, he quickly lapses into his true voice: "Whilst Ireland existed as a separate nation, it appears jealousy, feuds and wars between the chiefs of its clans, by courtesy called kings, and savage atrocities among the people, constituted the normal condition of the country."[3] He continues:

> No other spot of its size on the earth has produced such marked variety of human character, or suffered greater vicissitudes of condition, or succeeded so long in attracting the attention of the rest of the world by its incessant strifes, atrocities, and abortive political agitations.
>
> We find in all people trained for ages in this mode of life, where the passional or emotional part of their nature receives more scope and training than the judgment or intellectual faculties, the passions and emotions acquire the ruling power and direct the actions. . . . Where hate, fear, jealousy and revenge are in constant exercise, these malevolent passions are the most developed, and predominate. We find precisely the same conditions resulting from the same causes among our North American Indian tribes, and among the tribes of interior Africa, and wherever else the savage state exists: producing a sparsity of population and a state of degradation approaching the nature of the predatory animal. These bad qualities were so long and thoroughly cultivated among the Irish, and so perfectly ingrained into their nature, that modern civilization has as yet been unable to extract the virus.[4]

Heavy laden with stereotypes and bristling with prejudices, father and son nonetheless disembarked at Queenstown, grimly determined to face the "wild Catholic natives." That George stepped ashore with a revolver concealed in his luggage testifies to what his father had taught him about the Irish. But then the father's brain had been laundered with equal thoroughness on that subject by previous generations of Mellons. We are all the victims of other people's prejudices.

Predictably, hostilities broke out between these tourists and the first Irishman they met, a porter whom they engaged to haul their luggage to the Queen's Inn with a donkey cart. As night had fallen and the streets were poorly lit, and because they now found themselves unarmed among the papists (their unlicensed revolver having been seized in customs), father and son refused to use the sidewalk for fear of being mugged. They warily proceeded down the middle of the street, following the porter and baggage. Their little procession was halted, however, when the donkey cart became stuck in a pothole, and, from then on, the Irishman, George, and the Judge had to push both cart and donkey. They were rescued by the hotel porter, but only temporarily, for he gave the donkey man his fee, but not a tip. Accordingly, when George and his father had gone to bed, the untipped donkey man could still be heard downstairs, bellyaching for money. Next morning he was back at the hotel, insisting that "gentlemen" had always tipped him and demanding to speak to "the gentleman" personally. There followed a ludicrous confrontation in which the Judge, who had foolishly gone downstairs to end this fracas, found himself protesting that he and George were not gentlemen, just ordinary Americans, while the Irishman, with palm extended, kept proclaiming their gentility. The meager coin that it cost him to escape from this muddle must have looked cheap when the Judge at last grudgingly handed it over.[5]

Thus they bumped along from one importunity to the next, committing to memory whatever confirmed their prejudices and turning a blind eye to anything that did not. When the hotel assigned them a pathetic cripple to cart their baggage to the train station, they gave him a generous gratuity, and George, who was the kindest of Judge Mellon's sons, even denounced the town for having no humane society. But typically, instead of welcoming an opportunity to help a desperately needy fellow human, they again regarded themselves as victims of a calculated fraud.

At Cork, they felt besieged by the tangle of disheveled hack drivers, self-appointed tour guides, and "Irish hoodlums" who scavenged in front of the Victoria Hotel.[6] When, on a tour of the town, their driver showed them a spring of "holy water" which had been diverted to a nearby brewery to make "holy" beer, the Judge pontificated that "utilizing ignorance and superstition to obtain wealth and fame is not confined to the Irish political agitator and the American labor agitator exclusively."[7]

When they appeared in the court at Cork to declare their "peaceable intentions" before a magistrate and obtain a license for George's revolver, what they saw there impressed Thomas Mellon as the "perfect embodiment of arrogance, ignorance, filth and viciousness"—enough, he decided, to make a Pittsburgh court look civilized. Worse yet, the place reeked of fish. "We had now *done* Cork," concludes the father with relief.[8] But, prior to making his blissful escape to Dublin, he and George visited Blarney Castle as a final, odious chore. Wherever the sight of "miserable and dirty looking women and children," living in roadside shanties, appeared to mar the idyllic landscape, it confirmed to the Judge that "by nature all is lovely / And only man is vile."[9]

He inquired about some people who appeared to be squatters and was told by the hack driver that they were tenant farmers who had been evicted for nonpayment of rent. When the driver added with emphasis that anyone who took over the lease of an evicted tenant deserved to be murdered, it dawned on the Judge that this man was not objecting "to the amount of rent, but to the payment of rent at all, or debts of any kind." This attitude found no favor with banker Mellon. Asked whether America would send over an army to drive the British out of Ireland, he retorted that in America "only the more ignorant portion of the Catholic Irish . . . took much interest in Irish politics." It alarmed him that among ordinary folk there appeared to be "massive ignorance of political possibilities and . . . a large class trained in vicious disregard of law and order, and educated to build all their hopes and expectations on the coming of an impossible event—the independence of Ireland and its restoration to the Celts."[10]

Nothing stuck in his craw like Irish emancipation. He had always stridently supported Britain's claim to the island, and not merely because British rule was all that appeared to stand between the Ulster Protestants and their vengeful slaughter by their Catholic neighbors. His obsession with maintaining the social hierarchy and his fear of the working classes inclined him to view British rule as something that had proved its worth in the long course of history. Incessant demands for the mother country's withdrawal from Ireland led him to some unvarnished conclusions: "If we look into the Irish clamor about English usurpation and oppression, we find there is nothing in it. The British government has as perfect a right to Ireland as to any other of her possessions—I might say as much so as to the soil of England itself."[11]

England's policy towards them [the Irish], it is true, has been unwise and unfortunate. But its unwisdom has been on the side of too great leniency and toleration. Government of the Irish, to be beneficial to themselves and safe to others, must be with a firm and steady hand: as one able historian expresses it, "A government strong, just and impartial, is Ireland's sovereign necessity." They have always admired and respected power; but despised weakness and vacillation. [Oliver] Cromwell (who slaughtered them by the thousands) was the only ruler who understood their nature, and governed them accordingly. Had his policy been continued, Irish agitation and Irish grievances would long since have disappeared, and the Catholic population would at present be enjoying the same peace, prosperity and contentment as the Protestant part of the population.

Their connection with England all along has been one of discontent, complaint and strife; and their condition, in the main, one of poverty and wretchedness. They have never assimilated with the rest of the population of Great Britain in spirit and feeling, and to this day manifest much of the malevolence, deceitfulness, indolence and reckless unthrift of the original savage character—good workers and industrious when compelled by necessity and led by a boss, but careless, wasteful and shiftless when not under restraint.[12]

At Blarney Castle, George and the Judge were again subjected to "Irish taxation"—this time by a woman who crept into the ruins and misrepresented herself as their tour guide. By then, even the Judge was beginning to accept such importunities with weary resignation. Under the subheading "Small Frauds," he declaims in his memoirs that "a visitor in this part of Ireland must expect imposition and importunate exactions and constant begging at every step."[13]

From Blarney, the tourists hurriedly decamped to the nearest railroad station and clambered aboard the next train for Dublin. There, the Shelbourne House hotel, with its British imperial ambiance, afforded them welcome relief from the desperation and squalor of Cork. The following morning, their convictions about the native Irish were resoundingly confirmed when, driving through Phoenix Park, they were shown the "bleeding piece of earth" where Lord Frederick Cavendish, the chief secretary for Ireland, and his colleague, Thomas Burke, had been knifed to death by Irish assassins three months earlier. That Dublin Castle reminded the Judge and his son of the Pittsburgh arsenal shows how much it must have impressed them.

Their whirlwind tour continued:

Next we visited the Old Parliament House, which used to ring with the boisterous and abortive eloquence of the historic characters of the renowned Irish Parliament, a body which at all times contained more first class demagogues of the noisy but timid type, than any other legislative body of the same size in the civilized world. And in driving away we paid our respects to the ostentatious monument to Daniel O'Connell, the prince of Irish agitators of his day, but neither the first nor the last of that line of characters of which Ireland has always had an abundant but unprofitable supply.[14]

It was now decided that George would detour to London to consult a leading British authority on tuberculosis. The Judge would journey north to his birthplace in his beloved Ulster. That father and son parted company for a few days suggests that George's condition had not worsened. Which of them got the revolver remains a mystery.

As the train rocked and swayed on its way to Omagh, Thomas Mellon's spirits began to soar. The prospect of testing his distant childhood memories against reality filled him with a preternatural excitement that even tinted his perceptions. His memoirs are suddenly colored with "richly cultivated fields and green meadows, with patches of black bog and brown heather and occasional glimpses of the sea." He sings of the river Strule, by which he was born, as being, for him, "almost as sacred as the Ganges to a disciple of Brahma," and then adds with delight that the little stream beside the rail line turned out to be the "sacred" Strule.[15] That somewhere on this train ride he would leave the devious, slothful, credulous land of Saint Patrick and enter the sober, disciplined, industrious realm of Protestant Ulster must have enhanced his euphoria.

He reached Omagh at dusk and took a room at the White Hart Hotel. Next morning, August 25, he walked over to the old jail, where he notes with ironic satisfaction that "hundreds of criminals had been hanged in the olden time when sheep thieves and like offenders suffered the death penalty more certainly than murderers do now."[16] After breakfast, he set out in a jaunting car with a driver to revisit the scenes of his first six years. Lord Mountjoy's forest, he found, had disappeared with the dynasty of the Mellons' former landlords, but the Crossroads Meeting House, where he had suffered his initial encounter with Presbyterian hellfire, was still standing and substantially unaltered, though so badly in need of repair that he thought it a "fitting place for a dance of witches."[17]

After leaving the old meeting house we crossed Cappaigh [Cappagh] bridge, where the Strule in all its gentle beauty opens on the view. . . . All along the banks of this delightful stream my ancestors had indulged in the exciting sport of landing the lively trout and vigorous salmon. Many were the exploits with fly and fishhook here, which I had heard related by my father and my uncles.* . . . I gazed on the river and its beautiful scenery with tender emotions, and could not leave it until I took a walk of several hundred yards along its grassy banks, and dipped and drank of its water with my hands.[18]

It is tantalizing to imagine the sensations that must have churned within him as he approached his birthplace: the reactions of a man who once long ago laid eyes on a precious stone of the rarest quality; who for sixty years has dreamed about that stone, and who now suddenly finds it actually before him once more; who can reach out and touch it for one incomparable moment and then never again. Such emotions come from the wilder shores of the heart and are as rare as century-old wine.

After remounting it was but a short distance till we crossed the railroad and were in sight of the place to me the dearest of all—the Camp Hill with our cottage at its foot. Here it lay before me with the river on one side and the heathery turf bog on the other. . . . A strip of fine farm land lying between this turf bog or moorland and the river is what chiefly constitutes Lower Castletown. There I found it all as I had left it so long ago, and just as I still remembered it, with no apparent change whatever. . . . We drove into the yard in front of the house unceremoniously, where I alighted and directed my driver to unhitch and feed his horse with as much confidence as if the place was my own, and evi-

*We have to suspect that these farmers used worms.

dently to the surprise of the woman of the house, who was standing in the door.

I introduced myself as having lived there over sixty years ago, and now desired to look over the old house and place; and further explained that I should be greatly obliged, besides compensating her, if she would get us something to eat, to which she cheerfully assented, proposing to send for her husband to show me around. This I declined, I needed no guide; I was at home again, and preferred to be left alone with my thoughts. My heart was full. There was no spot on the place or its surroundings which I did not remember and know where to find. . . . All were there in their places as accurately as the Camp Hill cottage itself, with the stable and the small orchard beyond the flush.[19]

As the wintry old man passionately inspected his birthplace after an absence of the best part of a lifetime, he was tapping into hidden veins of emotion that the ever-prosaic Scotch-Irish reserve for home and family, and for the resplendent scenery of his homeland. That Robert Burns's poetry is steeped in these sentiments accounts for much of its appeal to the Scotch-Irish and to Thomas Mellon. We find him awkwardly enraptured as he putters about in this forest of distant remembrance. The landscape and even the flora are painfully dear to him. Lapsing into the vernacular of his childhood, he refers to the field behind Camp Hill as a "croft" and to the riverside slope as a "brae." The grass becomes "furze," the shrubs "broom." For an ephemeral moment, the iron mask of emotional suppression cracks open, and he releases a startling effusion of feeling.

From the owner's wife, Mrs. Joseph Steele, he eventually accepted a lunch of

good wheat bread, nice fresh butter and milk, and tea, with fried ham and eggs, all as palatable to a hungry traveler as anything I had met with in the great Shelburn Hotel at Dublin. I sat down to this delectable meal in the same spot where I had sat at our meals long before. . . . And there was the great open fireplace. . . . There was the hearth where I used to stir the fire of nights to afford light to my father to read to my mother from the American Gazetteer the glowing accounts of the richness and abundance of the lands, and the liberty and freedom of the people from taxation and rents, in the United States.

When through with our luncheon I examined the bed room and the niche in the back wall, called there an outset, where my bed had been, and still containing a child's bed. . . . I then visited my grandfather's old place down the lane, passing the cottage where I used to have the desperate conflicts with the irate ganders. . . . I soon found the ruins of my grandfather's house with his initials cut in the stone which had been the lintel above the door. . . . Not one of our name, and not one of the names of those who were our immediate neighbors, is now found in Castletown. But I found elsewhere in the neighborhood one old man of our name and connection, poor and obscure; and after a pleasant interview, and gladdening his heart with a gold piece, I left him and met with his son the next day in Omagh. . . .

I had now examined all and every part of the place and its surroundings, and . . . it but remained to take a last parting view of my early home with its familiar objects, and tear myself away. It was growing late in the evening, and the scene beautiful. I took a look of last farewell at it all as we passed again over Cappaigh bridge, and out of sight forever. . . . So farewell to the home of my childhood. Adieu to the reality of its beautiful presence, but its sweet memory will remain to the last![20]

Proceeding by train to Victoria Bridge, he journeyed, again in a jaunting car, to the townland of Kinkit, where his maternal ancestors, the Wauchobs, had farmed for nearly two hundred years. He was warmly received there by cousins who appeared to be prospering and whom he had not seen since 1818, when they were all children. Before leaving, he asked his cousin, Samuel Wauchob, the perennial loaded question:

I inquired if there was any agitation . . . among the neighbors. There was, he said, but it was confined almost exclusively to the Catholics, who are not numerous in that part of the country. "Here lives one of them," he said, pointing to the straw-covered hut of a laboring man, with a goat tethered near it on the roadside. "The priest made him sell his pig last week and divide the price between the church and the Parnell Fund, although his children were badly in need of the meat." What a heavy penalty, in all ages and all conditions, is imposed on ignorance and superstition! Here was a poor laboring man with a small family, a landless Parnellite, the victim of priestcraft and demagoguery, who would sell the bread from his children's mouths to satisfy his political and religious prejudices.[21]

The role of Catholic priests in the lives of the native Irish summoned forth Mellon's withering disdain. The Irish Catholic, Mellon wrote, has

always been subject to the depredations of two kinds of parasites of society—the temporal and the spiritual—the demagogue and the priest. These two species always hold sway in proportion to the ignorance of the people, and it repays them to preserve that ignorance by which they subsist. The priest carefully supervises the literature and the schools on the pretext of protecting the true faith; the demagogue inflames their prejudices in order to blind them to the impolicy or absurdity of his schemes. Both sides unite in depredating on the poor peasant and ignorant laborer. The political parasite unites with the priest to compel the peasant to sell his pig to pay Peter's pence, and the priest unites with the politician to compel him to sell his cow as a contribution to the Land League.[22]

One source of the Judge's contempt for Irish Catholics was his view that they were incapable of thinking independently. The Presbyterians and their fellow Calvinists, the witch-burning Congregationalists, were hardly free thinkers either, but the Presbyterian ministers based their dogma on supposed rational extrapolations from Scripture. Their appeal was to logic. They cited biblical texts to support their theological positions. Their catechisms were in pseudo-Socratic question-and-answer form. They placed their reasoning on the table and virtually ordered parishioners to examine it. They demanded literacy and education because believers had to be able to read and understand the scriptural texts on which their faith rested. By contrast, the Catholic priests feared all but parochial education that made no appeal to reason. They maintained a list of forbidden books and claimed absolute authority in faith and morals by apostolic succession from Saint Peter. To Thomas Mellon, this was slavery. His self-respect rested squarely on intellectual freedom—on the inalienable right to choose his values, to chart his course through life, to read whatever interested him, and to accept or reject the conclusions of others. His individualism was sacred. Any attempt to dictate his opinions or deny the sovereignty of his judgment amounted to intellectual castration and was received like a declaration of war.

In his fiercely unapologetic individualism, he may appear to embody the attitude championed by Samuel Butler in *The Way of All Flesh*. But the comparison is forced. Mellon displays a defiant autonomy of mind in his conclusions on literature, religion, social science, education, politics, and jurisprudence, but his intellectual freedom is always held in check by a granite bulwark of Scotch-Irish prejudices.

Pressing on by rail to Londonderry, he walked, for the first time in sixty-four years, along the storied walls that had withstood the bitterly contested siege of 1689 and which remain the nonpareil monument to the Ulster fortress mentality. And there once more he gazed with worshipful approval on the mighty cannon known as Roaring Meg, which, in his view, had showered such gratifying destruction on the besieging Catholics. He paused before the statue of George Walker, the Protestant clergyman who had ably and courageously commanded the defenders of Derry during the Great Siege, and he saw in this monument of Walker, standing with one hand on his Bible and the other on his sword, "a shining example of the former force of religious opinion." On hearing a blind old bagpiper playing "Derry Walls Away," he confessed that "no music that I have ever heard could excel it in exciting the passions or putting 'life and metal in the heels' of those inclined to dance. Those old Irish and Scotch airs have their origin in the wild depths of human feeling."[23]

Those "wild depths" were precisely what he feared. Like liquor, which he also abjured, music threatened his obsessive self-control. Not surprisingly, the puritan who had expressed relief when his prospective bride did not "inflict any music" on him was repressing a yen for melody in his reputedly tone-deaf heart.

Two days later, on August 30, Mellon arrived at Glasgow on the overnight steamer from Belfast. Doubtless he had always wanted to visit Scotland, his ultimate land of origin. But specifically he longed to visit the birthplace of Robert Burns, the poet laureate eternal of the Scots, and the only poet whose works he had ever truly loved.

A short train ride brought him to Burns's home town, Ayr, and to the Queen's Arms hotel. From there, he proceeded by carriage along the very route that Burns's fictional "blethering, blustering, drunken blellum," Tam O'Shanter, had taken as he galloped away, panic-stricken and intoxicated, from the witches and warlocks of his florid imagination. Ahead lay the River Doon and Burns's tourist-trampled birthplace. Mellon tarried there to inspect the poet's cottage and was delighted to find it a near replica of Camp Hill. The generous and perceptive evaluation of Burns's poetry that appears in Mellon's travel log for that day reveals as much about the writer as it does about the poet.

I was nurtured in the moral, social and religious sentiments of the Scotch—for the Scotch and Scotch-Irish are the same in their characteristic elements; and it may be on this account I am so warm an admirer of Burns: because none but those imbued with the Scotch nature can fully appreciate the truth and beauty of his poetry. He above all others has revealed the inward springs of the Scotch disposition. Some of his expressions, it is true, regarding the sexual relations may seem indelicate to refined taste, but we must consider the time and state of society in which he wrote; and his satires on sectarian dogmas and religious characters may seem occasionally to reflect on religion itself, but no one can say they were undeserved under the circumstances. A solid substratum of truth underlies and justifies it all.

. . . What could be more beautifully descriptive of the evanescent nature of sensual pleasures than the lines beginning, "You seize the flower, its bloom is shed . . ."? Or what literary production presents such keen irony and subtle humor as is embodied in that unique tale of "Tam O'Shanter"? [24]

Mellon continues: "Then, as a picture of the rural cottager's life of his day, what could exceed his 'Cotter's Saturday Night'? Where can we find such portrayal of the true Scotch character for earnest loyalty to home and family, religion and duty—or such a picture of parental and filial affection, mingled with a due proportion of commendable family pride among the poor and lowly?"[25]

"And what other author has ever given, in such small compass, wiser and more practical worldly advice, or a sounder moral code, equal to every day wear yet good enough for holiday dress, than is found in the 'Epistle to a Young Friend?'"[26]

He concludes: "The beauty of Burns' pictures of character lies in their exact correctness; no strain, no exaggeration. Every Scotchman is well acquainted with the Tam O'Shanter type; and the cotter's humble but upright family is to be found on almost every farm; whilst Andrew, the young man, ardent but afraid to start, and anxious to learn the right way to success in the battle of life before him, is found in many Scotch households."[27]

Appropriately, there was also an Andrew in the Mellon home, where the Judge required all of his children to read and ponder "Epistle to a Young Friend," and James was assigned to memorize it in full. The following lines were ones that the Judge had strained every nerve to live by, and dearly loved, for they lent a nimbus of romance to his quest for wealth while poignantly defining the "American Dream." And when his sons recited them for him, he would frequently rise and join in:

> To catch dame Fortune's golden smile,
> Assiduous wait upon her;
> And gather gear by every wile
> That's justified by honour;
> Not for to hide it in a hedge,
> Not for a train attendant;
> But for the glorious privilege
> Of being independent.

On the day after his pilgrimage to Ayr, the Judge was back in Glasgow. With five hours to spare before departing for Edinburgh, he visited the cathedral, which is touted as the finest example of Gothic architecture in Scotland. And it was there, while walking alone beneath the soaring ceiling, along rows of fluted columns, that the flinty old Judge took one more halting step on the path of self-discovery:

I had been brought up a Presbyterian or Rationalist—because the Reformation itself was nothing but a Rationalistic movement against ritualistic formality—and I had the idea that there was nothing in the aesthetic or emotional in religion; but here I was, for the first time, convinced of my mistake. The antiquity and magnificence of the building itself was calculated to produce a feeling of awe; but whilst admiring it, a sound commenced as of distant rolling thunder, and came on swelling and increasing in volume until the whole building was filled with peals of music, the grandest and most inspiring in its effect of anything of the kind I had ever experienced, and I stood spellbound until it ceased.[28]

With cracks appearing in his puritanism, and music once more producing an echo in his leathery soul, it was perhaps time for him to return to Pittsburgh. But he hazarded a few more days abroad. The afternoon train bore him to Edinburgh; from there he continued by streetcar to Dunfermline, the birthplace of his acquaintance Andrew Carnegie. The following day, September 1, was crammed with junkets to sites associated with the life and works of Walter Scott. Unimpressed by the meager remains of Melrose Abbey, Mellon noted that "the most favorable light to view it is in Sir Walter's descriptive poetry, which relieves it of much of its rudeness."[29]

His ramble through dilapidated Melrose inspired a theory that is too obvious to deny and too outrageous to accept:

Any Pittsburgher who saw our ruined Courthouse after the fire need not go to Europe to hunt up old abbeys and castles. The chief difference between an American and European ruin is that the one remains but a few weeks until removed and replaced by a new structure; whilst the other remains undisturbed for centuries, and becomes venerable and venerated through the enchantment of age and its consequent traditions. Those of Europe are paying institutions. Streams of tourists visit them continually, and are all taxed for admission. . . . Our people are behind the Europeans in this line of thrift. We have no difficulty at home by means of our mobs and conflagrations in producing elegant ruins of great splendor on short notice; but we are too impatient to wait a few centuries for the profits to be realized from their preservation. The tradition and story to render them interesting could easily be supplied. Incidents and characters commonplace at first would magnify into importance by lapse of time. Our ruined Courthouse, for instance, would produce enough stories of schemes and mysteries, pains and troubles, of parties and criminals, to supply all attractions in that direction, if properly written up by a Walter Scott.[30]

At Abbotsford, Scott's home for many years, the astonished Pittsburgher was guided through the author's vast collection of weapons. Here were the rusty knickknacks of chivalry—swords, lances, helmets, armor suits, and battle-axes—as well as firearms from every epoch since the invention of gunpowder, and even a camp kettle that Caesar's army had left behind. Prominently displayed were innumerable gifts that the mighty and exalted had showered on Sir Walter—all eagerly accepted and lovingly squirreled away. Such was the secluded eerie where Scott had fantasized a courtly world of knights and ladies that never existed, except in his works.

The Judge's final visit that day was to Dryburgh Abbey by the River Tweed. Here was a far more extensive and interesting ruin than Melrose, and in one corner of the spacious council hall, which once had resonated with the rhythmic murmur of monastic prayers, sheltered by the final vestige of a ceiling that had long since fallen, he stood at last before the grave of Sir Walter Scott, of which he observed: "Those wild ruins in this solitary domain, with nothing of the modern world in sight or hearing to disturb the repose, afford a most appropriate resting place for what is perishable of so renowned a man."[31]

Next morning, after yet another of his lightning forays—this one to Holyrood Palace and nearby Arthur's Seat—Mellon boarded a train for London. It may have been on the subsequent rail trip that he recorded in his travel log for that day the following conclusions about Scotland and her two preeminent poets:

Scotland has an interest to me and to all human beings, as the country of men of thought and ideas energetically carried out. The Scotch and Scotch-Irish—the latter but a Scotch colony—monopolize business and wealth, and almost dominate politics and religion wherever emigration carries them. They owe this to their qualities of thrift, economy, intelligence and industry. But apart from Scotland's "canny" business qualities, she is queen of the emotional and philosophical. When or where has Scotch philosophy been excelled in the analysis of the intellectual and emotional faculties? The readers of Reid, Stewart, Brown and Hamilton can answer. The keenly discriminative quality of the Scotch mind is established in her religious catechisms, as well as her poetry and fiction. When or where have Burns and Scott been excelled in beauty, depth or variety? Burns, the man of the people, or democrat; Scott, the aristocrat, the champion of the artificial in society—each a born master. The mission of Burns to exalt the lowly by bringing the hopes and fears and joys of their hearts into respect and admiration, teaching them contentment and reliance on their own efforts and resources of enjoyment; the mission of Scott to preserve what good might be extracted from that wild admiration for rank and caste, and that disinterested spirit of chivalry which Don Quixote, the French Revolution, and modern democracy have dispelled.[32]

The Judge had whistlestopped through Catholic and Protestant Ireland, maintaining a rail-roasting pace and effortlessly blinding himself to anything that called for a reassessment of his prejudices. Did the mere crossing of a small island under full steam entitle him to make comparisons between the Scotch-Irish and their hated southern neighbors? He decided it did:

Any one who would journey from Dublin to Derry, as I did in the summer of 1882, would find in Cork and Dublin, and other towns, and in the rural districts of the south of Ireland, extreme poverty, squalor and discontent, idleness and unthrift; with every hackman or peasant a politician; and all opposed to paying rent or debts of any kind; and under the absurd belief that the people of the United States would send over an army to set them free from what they are taught to believe a state of oppression. Yet so soon as the line is crossed from the Catholic into the Protestant end of the island, a marked difference is seen: no talk of oppression or political complaint is heard. You find the people thrifty, industrious and attentive to their private pursuits, resembling the better industrial classes of Scotland and the United States. Rent in arrear is a rare exception. You find the farmers who hold their land under lease laying up more money, after keeping their families and paying rent and expenses, than the farmers on rented farms of a much larger size in our own country. So too, when you cross the channel into Scotland, you find a thrifty, prosperous and contented population, as much so as the Protestant Irish, and all under the same government, laws and conditions. What is the reason of all this difference?[33]

The "reason," of course, is that an insatiably rapacious England had reduced the native Irish to grinding serfdom after robbing them of their land; excluded them from the vaunted "liberties of the subject," tirelessly attempted to annihilate their religion, degraded them to a socially untouchable underclass, and intermittently slaughtered them by the thousands. The Scotch-Irish, on the other hand, had been solicited by Britain to settle in Ulster, where land expropriated from the indigenous Catholics had been offered to them on deliberately attractive terms and where they had been confirmed in a limited number of civil liberties, including the right to worship as Presbyterians.

As he gropes for a final answer to the Irish question, Mellon finds himself toying with a mild form of ethnic cleansing: "It certainly would be a blessing to the [native] Irish themselves, if by some social force they could be scattered over all the earth, and not a vestige of them left on their own soil. They would soon become absorbed by other races; and by intermarriage, and life under other influences, in a few generations the mixture would be an improvement of both, as is already shown in the population of the United States and elsewhere."[34]

In London, George, who felt revived after being treated by the eminent physician Sir James Bennett, was waiting for his father at Morley's Hotel in Trafalgar Square. Next morning, the two engaged a hack for the day and visited Hyde Park, London Bridge, Prince Albert's monument, the Tower of London, and other attractions. September 4 found them at Westminster Abbey, puttering about in a forest of statuary, where the graves of monarchs, prime ministers, and poets laureate were continually underfoot. Determined to see the metropolis from on high, the Judge clambered up the endless flights of winding stairs to the dome of Saint Paul's Cathedral but was disappointed by the view. Father and son then journeyed to Liverpool on an afternoon train and next day, embarked for America, via Queenstown, on *The City of Montreal*. After enduring a storm of near-hurricane force, the landlubbers escaped to terra firma at New York on September 17, 1882. Thus ended Thomas Mellon's only foreign journey—"the most interesting and pleasurable trip I have ever experienced; one of those which we like to go over again in memory, affording some of that enjoyment which makes life worth living."[35] He and George had spent fourteen full days in the Old World and nineteen full days at sea.

This chapter focuses on Thomas Mellon's contempt for the native Irish because it sheds light on his unshakable misanthropy and strident elitism. In the two-dimensional Irishman caricatured in his autobiography, we see the artist's fear and hatred alternating like the twin edges of a dagger. We are told that the stereotypical Irishman is an habitual lawbreaker and shirker of contractual obligations, such as rent or debt. He is lazy, violent, gullible, uneducated, resistant to discipline, mindlessly religious, frequently drunk, indeed almost unhousebroken. And are these not precisely the character traits that would preclude anyone from becoming wealthy? More to the point, has anyone completely expunged these menacing, slovenly traits from his own personality? Is there not an "Irishman" lurking in each of us, whom we have had to grapple with and have finally wrestled into the closet but who keeps hammering on the door to break out? Thomas Mellon is innately convinced that, in an average human being, the

"Irishman" is out of the closet. On this charge, the Judge rules that everyone is guilty until proven innocent. "What a miserable, foolish animal is ignorant humanity," he confides in a letter to James. "You will always find ignorance, superstition, folly and consequent misery closely united. . . . See how people are led by the nose. . . . The more ignorance, of course, the more ease with which they are led and the more tenacity with which they follow their leaders."[36]

In his last years, the aged Judge, who for some moments had been lost in thought, sprang suddenly to life and startled his grandson, William L. Mellon, by announcing that he had just found the answer to the Irish question: "Sink the island."[37]

# XVII

---◆·◆·◆---

## The Reluctant Politician

*I have for over forty years been combating municipal abuses without any appreciable effect. The drift has been steadily towards folly and extravagance, and those who oppose it are usually in the minority.*

IN THE POST–CIVIL WAR ERA, as corruption increasingly blighted American politics, Thomas Mellon's doubts about the future of democracy continued to deepen. While refusing to declare for an alternative form of government, he had come to view the perils and defects of the existing one through a magnifying glass while contemplating its benefits through the wrong end of a telescope. That he himself perfectly exemplified those benefits may have eluded him.

Touring the conquered South in 1870, he witnessed a session of the Louisiana state legislature and saw in it a chilling example of democracy gone awry:

We attended one or two meetings of that august assembly, the legislature of Louisiana; and it was suggestive to see a presumably dignified body comprised of stolid, stupid, rude and awkward field negroes, lolling on the seats or crunching peanuts, except when the white leaders would by sign or signal arouse them to what was going on, at the point where their votes were wanted:

these white members among them standing in with the governor and other carpet bag parasites in promoting all manner of corrupt schemes to rob the property owners and taxpayers. It was a sight depressing to the hope of popular self government; and the same danger to popular institutions still exists: now as I write, fifteen years afterward, this want of popular intelligence is the pressing evil both North and South.[1]

By 1879, the Judge had become acquainted with the Common and Select councils of Pittsburgh—where no inattentive black representatives were to be found but where an increasing number of councilmen were voting on signal from "Boss" Christopher Magee. What particularly roiled Mellon is that the two councils were assessing property owners, like himself, with heavy taxes to service and repay an increasingly burdensome load of municipal bonds, which he believed that city officials and local businessmen were profiting from. His acquaintance with this form of venality was bitter and of long standing, for it dated from the scandals over railroad bonds that had driven him into politics and onto the bench twenty years earlier. Corruption in all its forms was anathema to him: It offended his rigid puritanical morality, augured for higher taxation, and amounted to *waste,* a deadly Franklinian sin.

Typically, Mellon fumes about the kinds of political corruption that affected him directly or caused him alarm. But in the post–Civil War era, known as Reconstruction (1865–1900), the abuse of public trust was virtually all-encompassing. It was part and parcel of the prevailing political system of America.

In 1828, Andrew Jackson had won the presidency on a platform that differed radically in substance and spirit from that of previous administrations. Doubting that the incumbent bureaucrats would implement his program with maximum effect, he had emptied the government offices and filled them with men whose loyalty to him and his platform was beyond question. He had established the "spoils system."

During Reconstruction, the spoils system functioned as a reciprocal relationship between political parties and their supporters. As
surging industrial growth overwhelmed the ability of federal, state,
and municipal governments to control and direct it, a rapidly increasing portion of public works and improvements had to be allocated to
private contractors. Because public service was not a career but a tem-
porary reward for party loyalty, the ruling political party on every
level of government would fill the available offices with its supporters.
The officeholders would then dispense lucrative contracts and other
favors to party loyalists, and those who received patronage would support their benefactors. Because a ruling party could distribute many
kinds of favors, elections were fiercely contested. Party loyalists who
stood to benefit would turn out en masse to bribe and cajole the voters. In this way, rampant political corruption caused a vastly greater
percentage of Americans to vote than do so today.[2]

In public affairs, Thomas Mellon had always been guided by his
own judgment, not by party affiliation. The policies of Daniel Webster
and Henry Clay had found favor with him, hence his former support
for the Whig Party against its Democratic rivals. After the Whigs'
phlegmatic disintegration, he had allied himself with the newly
organized Republicans, and in 1859 he had been elected to the bench
under their banner. But escalating taxes linked to the unbridled
flotation of bonds during the Civil War had eroded his support for
President Lincoln's administration, just as the subsequent era of graft
had alienated him from the piratical government of the bumbling,
arguably well-intentioned President Ulysses S. Grant.

In 1872, Mellon had tested the political waters by delivering a
number of campaign speeches in support of the moderate Republican
reformer Horace Greeley, who was seeking the U.S. presidency in a
barn-cleaning effort to oust the nefarious Grant administration.
Mellon's old friend and in-law General William Larimer was vigorously
campaigning for Greeley and may have prompted the Judge to do
likewise. But America was not yet prepared to discard its foremost

living hero, and Grant's rudderless, alcoholic misrule was extended for four more years. Even when his party abandoned him in 1876, the swarm of rapacious office seekers who had ridden to power on his coattails remained entrenched at the state and municipal levels, where Republican governments still ruled.

In Pittsburgh, the old Grant men continued to suck from the public udder like fatted calves. But new Republican leaders were appearing as well. Through their surrogates in the bicameral city legislature, the former municipal treasurer, Christopher Magee, and his emerging accomplice, William Flinn, were stealthily fixing a stranglehold on local politics. Recalling "Boss" Magee and "Boss" Flinn, the journalist Lincoln Steffens poignantly observes: "Magee wanted power, Flinn wealth. Each got both these things; but Magee spent his wealth for more power, and Flinn spent his power for more wealth. Magee was the sower, Flinn the reaper. In dealing with men they came to be necessary to each other, these two. Magee attracted followers, Flinn employed them. The men Magee won Flinn compelled to obey, and those he lost Magee won back. . . . Molasses and vinegar, diplomacy and force, mind and will, they were all mated. But Magee was the genius. It was Magee who laid plans they worked out together."[3] A serious biography of this "genius" would be timely.

Magee's autocracy was inspired by the definitive models of urban machine politics—New York and Philadelphia. Among his own, the Boss could lecture about Tammany Hall like a history professor. To a friend, he crowed that the political machine he was piecing together, one man at a time, would be "as safe as a bank."[4] And it was.

Magee built his "ring" by recruiting the owners of small businesses, including grocers, saloonkeepers, and liquor dealers. Anyone who could extend credit to customers was a little banker, had influence in the wards, and could easily be molded into a politician. Magee would sound out a loquacious grocer and fund his election to one of the two city councils. Saloonkeepers were easy to recruit because they depended on their liquor licenses. Anyone who needed a piece of official paper to

*The Pittsburgh political bosses Christopher Magee (left) and William Flinn.*

ply a trade was fair game for the Boss. Those who depended on protection from the law were bled mercilessly. Houses of prostitution had to be rented from Magee's agents; otherwise the police would raid them. And the prostitutes had to buy their furniture, liquor, and finery at huge markups from businessmen who belonged to the ring.[5] Pittsburgh has been called "Hell with the lid off," but it was no better with the lid on. According to Steffens, "Boss Magee's idea was not to corrupt the city government, but to be it; not to hire votes in councils, but to own councilmen: and so, having seized control of his organization, he nominated cheap and dependent men for the Select and Common councils."[6]

Magee stooped to conquer: He was affable, diplomatic, endlessly ingratiating, a master of persuasion, rarely and reluctantly overbearing, never vindictive, extravagantly generous in forgiveness—very Irish. But his confederate, "Boss" William Flinn, the Republican leader of Allegheny County, was made of sterner stuff. Heavy-handed, dour, and rapacious—quick to reach for the whip—Flinn inspired fear, not affection. Magee and Flinn were like molasses and vinegar.

With Magee's cheerful connivance, Flinn's construction company, Booth & Flinn, was awarded lucrative contracts for public parks and buildings and enjoyed a near monopoly on the paving of roads in rapidly expanding Pittsburgh. Municipal contracts for road work were written so that only Flinn's asphalt would qualify, and his "Ligonier blocks" were specified as the only acceptable paving stones.[7]

Magee's investments in transportation and natural gas did not conflict with Flinn's. His Duquesne Traction Company became the city's foremost streetcar line. He also served as agent for the Pennsylvania Railroad, first in Allegheny County and then statewide. The Boss held numerous directorships, and his paper, the *Pittsburgh Times,* gave him a booming voice in urban affairs. Yet he wielded his decisive power from the shadows. Refusing to serve as mayor or to sit on either of the city councils, he placed the mayor on a short leash and packed the councils with loyal grocers, butchers, and bartenders—and added his brother William, who was elected to thirteen consecutive terms. All through the 1880s, Magee held no government post but controlled the municipal offices by filling them with surrogates. There was cunning in his studied refusal to rule conspicuously.

In defiance of all that unsuited Thomas Mellon for elective office— his portfolio of sacrosanct prejudices and stereotypes, his misanthropic timidity and obdurate pessimism, his doubts about democracy and ingrained contempt for government—he decided to foray into the jungle of politics. He had a pecuniary motive for doing so, as we shall see, and he might also have sustained some damage if men with interests adverse to his own had acquired power. But more important, he had gradually, grudgingly, acquiesced in Socrates' enduring argument that a wise man seeks public office to prevent lesser men from gaining it. For without doubt, and with some justification, he had always viewed himself as wiser and more capable than the run of humanity. A man of uncommon intelligence and proven ability cannot blind himself to these qualities.

The municipal charter of Pittsburgh, Steffens points out, "lodged all powers—legislative, administrative, and executive—in the councils,

Common and Select. The Mayor was a peace officer, with no responsible power. Indeed, there was no responsibility anywhere. There were no departments. Committees of councils did the work usually done by departments, and the councilmen, unsalaried and unanswerable individually, were organized into what might have become a combine, had not Magee set about establishing the one-man power there."[8]

The Common and Select councils of Pittsburgh were elected on a franchise limited to taxpaying male property owners. Because the councils wielded so much power that could be misused for personal enrichment, the political parties campaigned vigorously for council seats, and voter turnout was heavy. In 1879, Thomas Mellon ran for the Common Council, the lower chamber, from his own neighborhood, the Nineteenth Ward, and won a landslide victory. Six years had passed since the Panic of 1873, but business had still not recovered. That the Judge's wealthy East End constituents—mostly burghers of Scotch-Irish or Pennsylvania German origin—shared his frantic, lifelong determination to cut municipal spending and hold down property taxes virtually assured his election. That the Catholic Irish lived in another part of town helped too.

Elected in February, Mellon attended the opening council session on April 7. His peers were a varied crew: four shopkeepers, four lawyers, three tobacconists, three bookkeepers, three clerks, two grocers, two butchers, two brewers, two hotel keepers, a school principal, a bricklayer, a brickyard owner, a tailor, a carpenter, a druggist, a farmer, a glassblower, an iron worker, a block maker, a real estate broker, a stable owner, an insurance agent, a saloonkeeper, and a liquor dealer.[9] The Judge found refuge from these yeomen in the company of his former law partner, William B. Negley, who represented the neighboring Twentieth Ward and was Sarah Jane's first cousin. Negley had served six consecutive terms as president of the Common Council but had finally bowed out in favor of another Republican, William Thompson.

The Common and Select councils presided over a vast array of municipal services: They controlled the budget, levied property taxes, and fixed the salaries of city officials. They paved and lighted the streets, ruled on transit franchises, set traffic regulations, and were empowered to erect public buildings and create parks. They oversaw the city's water works, its gas, electricity, and sewer systems, and its police and fire departments. Between 1870 and 1890, when the population almost doubled every ten years—when Pittsburgh was approaching the zenith of its industrial preeminence and was manufacturing two-thirds of the nation's steel and half of its window glass—it fell to the city councils to direct the hectic expansion of its municipal infrastructure.[10] That this expansion would give a hefty lift to property values in the proprietary East End, where Thomas Mellon and his sons were not only major landowners but also developers, was a powerful incentive for the Judge to raise his voice in politics.

Faced with a steady stream of decisions, some of them urgent, the councillors were compelled to be flexible. If a Democrat was shopping for votes to light an alley in his ward where people were being robbed after dark, and a Republican was fighting to extend the sewer system in his own constituency, the two would cross party lines and vote for each other's measures. On both councils, deal-making was the political breath of life.

Still, party affiliation was important. About one-sixth of the councilmen were Democrats, elected mainly from the Irish Catholic wards. The rest were Republicans, but of two distinct types: Those who belonged to the "caucus," which huddled before every session to plot party strategy, were beholden to the Flinn-Magee ring. The rest, like Mellon and Negley, billed themselves as "independent" Republicans, but they would vote with the caucus or ring when it suited them.

At Mellon's first council meeting, he and Negley attempted to distance themselves from the Flinn-Magee Republicans by sponsoring a strongly worded condemnation of "ringism." Because of his long and distinguished service on the council, it was Negley who introduced the resolution; but it expressed Mellon's political viewpoint so perfectly that it seems likely they composed it together.

WHEREAS, The government of the city requires thorough integrity and active economy in each and every act of the Councils, and of each of its members, therefore,

Resolved, That in all legislation we will consider the just interest of the city only, and that the aiding and abetting of any contractor or office holder, or seeker in his interest as opposed to that of the city, shall be looked upon as "ringism." . . . We simply adopt the term for the purpose of designating the line between honest legislation and defrauding the taxpayers.

Second, We regard any future increase of the city debt as a calamity, and to be vigorously avoided except so far as may be indispensably necessary . . . , and we deem it the duty of Councils to work for . . . a fair reduction of the rate of interest.

Third, We pledge ourselves to favor and promote general and uniform laws for the city government and the assessment and collection of taxes in the most efficient and least expensive method. . . .

Fourth, The city's present and prospective financial condition demands a system of the most thorough and radical retrenchment of expenditures; and we pledge ourselves to support and promote such system by all possible means, among which should be the abolition of every office, or board, or commission, or department not absolutely indispensable to city government. . . .

Fifth, We pledge ourselves to promote no private interests at the city's expense, and to recognize no claims to office, or emoluments founded on political party service.

Sixth, We hold that the Chairman [normally the council president] should ignore all parties and should appoint his committees with reference to the ability and knowledge of the members . . . and that no committee should withhold or delay any matters submitted to it, because its party or a majority of its members are opposed to it, and want to smother it. . . .

Seventh, That we shall advocate the passage of a law making all the general offices of the city elective by the people.[11]

Here was Mellon's political credo as well as Negley's, and we can imagine them proudly affixing their names to it. Unfortunately, everyone else voted for it too, including the "ringsters" against whom it was directed.

In subsequent sessions, Mellon called for retrenchment in the city's traditionally scandal-ridden water authority. The council approved his initial proposal to cut costs by unifying the old and new waterworks, but it rejected his subsequent motion to simply slash water rents without regard to the consequences.[12] Wherever he looked he saw waste or corruption. Often he saw both. Where a penny could be shaved from the city budget, he was waiting with his axe. As he defined himself politically, his voice became familiar. It was the voice of a double-issue zealot: The two issues were to hold down property taxes, with little regard to the consequences, and to oppose machine politics. He could be hard: When the Police Committee called for passage of "an ordinance to provide for the care and maintenance of wounded, sick or poor taken to the station houses," Mellon cast the only negative vote.[13]

He was never afraid to be the sole opponent of any measure. His voting record as both a Common and a Select councilman confirms that on at least a dozen occasions he stubbornly cast the only dissenting vote. Yet he was by no means a total maverick. Of his 1,160 recorded votes, 989, or 85 percent, were cast with the majority.[14] David Koskoff's claim in *The Mellons* that "almost invariably Councilman Mellon's votes were cast with the minority" is blatantly incorrect. So is the implication that Mellon's role on the two councils was ineffectual.[15]

His record of attendance at council sessions shows him to have been neither diligent nor derelict. A resolution that he introduced at the beginning of his first term and which was overwhelmingly adopted calls for every member's record of attendance to be published. Hence we know that out of 284 Common and Select council sessions, he attended 212, or 75 percent.

On balance, he retained the respect of his peers. After three weeks on the Common Council, Mellon was elected chairman of its Committee on Surveys.[16] When he impetuously demanded "a better plan of government for the City," his colleagues concurred and President William Thompson appointed him to a special committee for rewriting the city charter.[17] A year later, President William Ford appointed him to the committees on roads and ordinances.[18]

His intermittent shadow boxing with the Flinn-Magee Republicans continued. Reelected in 1880, he opened the new session with a futile slap at the ring and its caucus:

> *Resolved,* That the permanent organization existing among certain of the members of Councils, and known as the "caucus," be enlarged to include all members of this Council without distinction of party.
>
> 2. That the expressed object and purpose of said organization be changed from "promoting the welfare of the Republican party" to promoting the welfare of the city.[19]

One can imagine the muffled wave of chuckles that must have rippled through the chamber at this ineffectual barb—the sudden rush of tongues into cheeks and the Boss's amusement when he heard that old man Mellon was again tilting at windmills. Councilman Siebert's saving motion to shelve the resolution indefinitely was accepted.[20]

In 1881, Mellon was elected to the Select Council. Looking about, he saw new faces but quickly perceived the old political fault lines. Here, again, were the grocers, butchers, and saloonkeepers, the loyal infantry of Magee's Republican ring, as well as the outnumbered Irish Catholic Democrats and the small knot of independent Republicans to which Mellon stubbornly adhered.

At the second session, he winded his familiar horn for retrenchment:

> *Resolved,* That in view of the fact that our taxation for city and county purposes is already burdensome; and that taxation for State purposes . . . is stretched to the utmost, and yet has fallen short of meeting the Government expenditures to the extent of

one million eight hundred thousand dollars, and resort to real estate [taxation] is imminent;

Therefore, it is the sense of the Council that strict economy and retrenchment should be the rule in all its legislation; and

*Resolved,* That we recommend the same course to our city delegation at Harrisburg.[21]

The foregoing was approved without resistance and forgotten without delay. Mellon then turned to his favorite punching bag: he called for consolidation and retrenchment in the city's waterworks and demanded that inessential employees be fired. By then, council president Henry Gourley had appointed him to the Committee on Water, which enabled him to keep harassing the water authority. He had also been seated on the committees for retrenchment and reform; legislation; and railroads.[22] When his peers invited eulogies for the assassinated U.S. president, James A. Garfield, Mellon seized the opportunity to fulminate that "our laws are no longer a terror to the evil doer," and that there was "a time when the public sentiment would no more have tolerated the advocacy of Communism and Nihilism, and other enemies of social order, than it would to-day tolerate the expression of disrespect to the great man whose death we are here to lament."[23]

But Mellon's rising influence in politics was about to be waylaid by two resounding defeats. In November 1881, Andrew Carnegie caused a stir by offering to Pittsburgh the first of his innumerable free libraries. He was prepared to erect the building at a cost of $250,000, provided that the city agreed to contribute at least $15,000 a year toward its maintenance.[24] On balance, Carnegie's offer was favorably received; however, the maintenance provision caused many citizens and city councillors to hesitate and some to balk completely. There was also a legal snag: under Pennsylvania law, Pittsburgh was not permitted to obligate itself for the purpose of maintaining libraries. In February 1883, a joint committee of Common and Select councillors called for the required change in state law and recommended unanimously that both councils accept Carnegie's offer provisionally.[25]

In some respects, the offer of a free library for Pittsburgh must have appealed to Mellon. He had always been an eager reader, had found much of life's reward in books, and took a lively interest in education. It must also have occurred to him that if he opposed Carnegie's offer, his friendship with the almighty industrialist might be jeopardized. On the other hand, to saddle the city with maintaining a grandiose public building in perpetuity evoked the usual visions of doom. With Pittsburgh already bumping against its statutory debt ceiling, the repeal of a state law that wisely restrained municipal squandering would surely cause budgetary incontinence. He speculated that Magee's flunkies on the two councils—his butchers, grocers, and saloonkeepers —might float bond issues to build imposing architectural monuments bearing their names and then levy back-breaking property taxes to service the bonds. Benighted landowners, like Mellon, would again be the victims. Typically, his negative imagination broke its leash. He immediately girded for battle and placed before the Select Council an alternative resolution:

> WHEREAS, The proposed Act of Assembly is of doubtful legality and policy, and even if successful in evading the constitutional limit of city debt, it would form a dangerous precedent in that direction, and
>
> WHEREAS, The maintenance of a public library of the kind by general taxation is an unwarranted stretch of the taxing power and an injustice to tenants and small property owners who are the actual taxpayers in the end, and
>
> WHEREAS, Mr. Carnegie's generous proposition is in the nature of a donation, and should be carried into effect on that line and not made the cause of taxation, and we believe there are sufficient public spirited capitalists in this city to carry it out on the same line Mr. Carnegie intended it, therefore

Resolved, That a Special Joint Committee of Councils be appointed to canvas the capitalists and business men of Pittsburgh and Allegheny for 250 subscriptions of not less than $1,000 each for the purpose contemplated by the report and Act of Assembly in question.[26]

Mellon's resolution amounted to a Carnegie library that would be maintained for the public entirely by wealthy individuals—for most people a truly "free" library. His resolution passed the Select Council by twenty-three votes to seventeen, but he offered to contribute only $2,000 toward the project himself.[27]

Carnegie, who was following these developments, must have been indignant. No one had ever offered Pittsburgh such a large or culturally beneficial donation. Yet far from prostrating itself in gratitude, the Select Council, under Mellon's influence, had responded with a counterproposal! Were the councillors using an extraneous state law to evade the negligible outlay for maintaining his munificent, civilizing benefaction? Were they covertly pressuring him to endow the library as well as build it? If he agreed to do so, it would set a devastating precedent: His libraries were to bear his name, and he had probably already decided to dot the Earth with them. If he endowed the first one, he would be expected to endow them all, and that expense would vastly reduce the number he could afford to donate. He also had a sound reason for insisting that wealthy communities, like Pittsburgh, should support their own libraries: "I am clearly of the opinion that it is only by the city maintaining its public libraries as it maintains its public schools that every citizen can be made to feel that he is a joint proprietor of them. . . . And I am equally clear that unless a community is willing to maintain public libraries at the public cost, very little good can be obtained from them."[28]

Carnegie must have reflected bitterly on Mellon's die-hard opposition. Had they not chatted amicably at the Judge's home on several occasions?[29] Had their mutual affection for Robert Burns, Herbert Spencer, Benjamin Franklin, free enterprise, and the Scottish people not cemented a kind of bond between them? Yet here was Mellon, brazenly denouncing the terms of his unconscionably generous gift. If there were any communications between these two during their tug-of-war, they have not survived. That their friendship did survive is remarkable.

Mellon's resolution passed the Select Council on February 6, 1883, and was taken up by the Common Council six days later. In the interval, Carnegie's agents must have lobbied intensely against Mellon's proposal. They must have served notice on a number of key councillors that the ironmaster was not amused by their tepid response to his proposed donation and might now withdraw it.

Carnegie desperately needed Boss Magee's support, and he must have obtained it. The two had already established a cozy rapport, which would ripen into criminal conspiracy when Magee arranged for Carnegie to acquire 144 acres of prime municipal property for about a quarter of its actual worth in his notorious acquisition of the City Poor Farm at Homestead in 1890.[30] But that plot was yet to be hatched and would not be discovered until long after the perpetrators had died.

When the Common Council convened on February 12, it scuttled Mellon's resolution by a vote of fifteen to six, with the Flinn-Magee ring opposing him.[31] His support in the upper chamber also began to erode. A week later, when Negley's law partner, David Bruce, moved that the Select Council withdraw its support for Mellon's proposal, it did so by a vote of thirty to seven. Even Negley voted with the majority.[32] Carnegie had won.

Even so, it was not until October 25, 1886, that the Select Council formally agreed to accept the Ironmaster's offer. On that day, Thomas Mellon registered his implacable opposition by casting the only dissenting vote.[33] And another year would elapse before a change in state law enabled Pittsburgh to assume responsibility for maintaining the proposed library.

Carnegie's imagination had not been idle during the years of foot dragging and obstruction by the city councils and state legislature. By 1890, he envisioned not only a free library but a cultural village with extensive facilities for art, science, and technology. The overall cost of his donation had jumped from $250,000 to $1,000,000, and the city was now being asked to pledge $40,000 a year for maintenance instead of $15,000.[34] Mellon would have scrambled to accept the Ironmaster's initial offer if he had known how it would grow.

One has to wonder how the Judge would have reacted to the proposed Carnegie Library, institute, music hall, and museums if he had known that they would contribute more to the city's cultural development than any other institutions except the University of Pittsburgh and that his family's destiny would be intertwined with them. His granddaughter, Sarah Mellon Scaife, would find in the Carnegie Museum of Art a permanent home for her superlative collection of paintings. His great-great-grandson, James Mellon Walton, would become president of the Carnegie Institute. The Mellon Institute of Industrial Research and the Carnegie Institute of Technology would be conjoined to form Carnegie-Mellon University. And the Carnegie Museum of Natural History would send William L. Mellon to the South Sea Islands; his son, Matthew, to Central America; and the author to Africa on a number of enjoyable expeditions to collect mammals, reptiles, and birds as scientific study specimens.

On the other hand, today, as Pittsburgh's businesses continue to flee the city and its people migrate to the sunshine states, when the population has dwindled to less than it numbered in Thomas Mellon's day, when the tax base is crumbling and the coffers are bare, Pittsburghers can look back wistfully on the day when a flinty old judge warned the city government about assuming burdensome and continuing financial obligations.

The other dead-end political crusade for which Mellon would be remembered was his die-hard effort to obstruct the building of Henry Hobson Richardson's gargantuan courthouse for Allegheny County. The events leading up to that confrontation were set in motion shortly after noon, on May 7, 1882.

It was a Sunday, and streams of Pittsburghers were walking home from their churches to lunch. Those who passed the venerable courthouse on Grant Street began to notice smoke oozing from its roof and dome. At 12:25, the first alarm was sounded, and within minutes engine crews from all over the city were galloping toward Grant's Hill, their bells jangling wildly. But the fire was already out of control and would have to run its course.

Shortly after two o'clock, John Chislett's 148-foot-high neoclassical dome, a landmark since 1841, began to sway. The terrified, fascinated crowd surged back to a safe distance and waited with bated breath. At last, with a sound like muffled thunder, the hulking dome came crashing down, and with it the roof from which young Thomas Mellon had watched the Fire of 1845. When the last flames had flickered out, all that remained were the massive Doric columns that fronted the portico and a ragged rectangle of ruined walls. The courtrooms where Mellon had argued the Lee case and where Judge Sterrett had read the death sentence to Martha Grinder were filled with mountains of broken masonry and charred, fallen beams.

The urgent task of building a new courthouse and jail for Allegheny County fell to the three elected county commissioners, Robert Mercer, Daniel McWilliams, and George McKee. Miraculously, all three proved to be honest and capable public servants. They studied courthouses in Albany, Chicago, Detroit, Buffalo, Washington, Philadelphia, and Indianapolis, picked the brains of government officers, and developed specifications for the kind of facility that Allegheny County needed. In 1883, they invited five leading architects to submit preliminary drawings for a new courthouse and adjoining jail. Andrew Peebles of Pittsburgh, John Ord of Philadelphia, William Boyington of Chicago, and Elijah Meyers of Detroit all agreed to compete. The only one who declined was George Post of New York, and he was promptly replaced by Henry Hobson Richardson of Boston.

In January 1884, the commissioners displayed drawings from all five architects and invited public comment. They eventually chose Richardson to build the courthouse, not for the aesthetics of his proposal but "because he seemed to have the best ideas of what we wanted and his plans have more good points about them, things we think desirable."[35]

*Henry Hobson Richardson in character.*

Henry Hobson Richardson was an affable, three-hundred-pound prodigy who sometimes carried his infatuation with medievalism to the extreme of posing in a monk's habit. That the defunct Romanesque style of cathedral architecture that so completely enthralled him had died a natural death seven centuries earlier cannot have flustered him more than transiently. He had adapted it to modern conditions and revived it to public acclaim. Pittsburgh would therefore have a "Richardson Romanesque" courthouse and a matching jail.

The commissioners now announced that they were ready to accept bids from contractors. When no firm offered to do the work for less than $2 million, tight-fisted taxpayers began to see red. On August 27, the *Pittsburgh Commercial Gazette* reported that "ex-judge Thomas Mellon has addressed a letter to the Commissioners objecting on behalf of the taxpayers to their proceeding with their work."[36]

Predictably, Mellon ranted about the magnitude and probable cost of Richardson's courthouse, but he also blasts its style:

> Good red brick would be superior to granite both in beauty and strength. . . . As to the remarkable square tower rising 150 feet or more above the roof of the Court House, it strikes me and others as like a fine building with a grain elevator erected upon it. No one could imagine until he is told, what it is for. . . . As to court rooms, rooms about forty feet square would be the right thing and best serve the purposes of justice. The general public have no necessary occasion to be there. There is no need of lobby space for loafers and hangers-on.[37]

Mellon appears to scoff at the muted but widespread belief that the law requires pompous architecture to support its dignity. While passionately committed to the rule of law, he clearly believes that the vaunted "majesty of the law" resides either in the hearts of a law-abiding people or nowhere. Likewise, he is unmoved by the argument that respect for law grows stronger where large audiences can witness the impartial administration of justice in theater-sized courtrooms. And though he would surely have balked at conducting court in a building that had sunk into laughable disrepair, he would have been perfectly content to do so in a courthouse that was merely unpretentious—of brick instead of granite. What he found lacking in Richardson's courthouse was the element of modesty, which he viewed as indispensable to good taste. Caesar Augustus had found Rome a city of brick and had left it a city of marble. Thomas Mellon would have urged him to leave it as brick and to invest the difference in a coal mine.

*The Allegheny County Courthouse, designed by Henry Hobson Richardson.*

If Mellon had harbored more than a passing interest in architecture, he might have added that the proposed courthouse was deplorably derivative in style; that its principal features had been copied from forgotten medieval architects; and that it was rescued from being a mere pastiche of archaic, misappropriated motifs only by the ingenuity with which Richardson had spliced what he had stolen. But, the same could be said about almost any distinguished public building of that day. Architects of the Gilded Age and their patrons were notoriously disinterested in originality.

Pressing ahead regardless, the county commissioners announced that they had accepted the bid of Norcross Brothers, a Massachusetts firm, to erect the monumental courthouse and jail for $2,243,024. Mellon, meanwhile, gathered his forces and prepared for legal action. On September 10, 1884, an officer appeared from the Court of Common

Pleas and served notice on each of the county commissioners that a bill of complaint had been filed against them by Judge Thomas Mellon; his perennial ally, James B. Corey; Councilman John Anderson; banker William W. Patrick; Councilman John Wilson; and eleven other plaintiffs.

Mellon and his allies charged that the courthouse had been "injudiciously and extravagantly planned"; that it was "greatly in excess of what would be required"; that its erection would entail "an expenditure burdensome and oppressive to the taxpayers"; that, with normal cost overruns, the statutory debt ceiling of Allegheny County would have to be exceeded; that the county electors had not voted to raise that ceiling as required by law; and that the county would probably have to defend itself in court to repudiate debts unlawfully contracted in its behalf.[38] The plaintiffs therefore petitioned the court for relief, as follows:

> First—By a decree enjoining the defendants from entering into the proposed contract with Norcross Bros. or [for] any sum in excess of the constitutional limit.
>
> Second—That defendants be enjoined from contracting any indebtedness beyond the sum of 2 per centum of the assessed valuation of the taxable property of the county without submitting the question of such increase to the electors thereof.
>
> Third—That defendants be enjoined and required to prepare plans and specifications for suitable buildings, but such as can be erected without imposing oppressive burdens upon the taxpayers of the county, or exceeding the constitutional limit of indebtedness.[39]

In his remarks to the press, Commissioner Robert Mercer was unapologetic. He pointed out that for the county to exceed its statutory debt ceiling, the combined courthouse, jail, and architect's fee would have to total more than $2,505,000. He quoted figures to show that the total cost would fall within that limit and insisted that the contract with Norcross Bros. and the agreement with Richardson left little room for extras.

Rebutting the charge of extravagance, he added, "When we were debating as to the cost and extent of the building, we sought the advice of several of the largest taxpayers in the county. . . . Such men as [steel magnate] B. F. Jones, of Jones & Laughlin, [steel magnate] William Metcalf, [Councilman] John Jackson of the Fourth Ward, and others agreed that a handsome building was very desirable. We also made careful inquiry of the different county officers as to the amount of space that would be needed, calculated on the increase of business during the past twenty years, and the probable needs of the county within the future."[40]

He might have elaborated on this by pointing out that Pittsburgh had almost doubled its population in the previous decade, that new immigration was continuing at the same rate, and that a proportionate increase in civil and criminal litigation had to be anticipated. "The result of these investigations," he continues, "we published in pamphlet form and sent to the newspaper offices, to members of the Chamber of Commerce, and to many large taxpayers and public spirited men. . . . The plans for the building were on exhibition for a long time in the Orphans' Court room. During that time, . . . not less than five hundred persons daily came in to see them. The plans proposed by Mr. Richardson were conceded to be the best by men who were competent to judge."[41]

That Boss Flinn's construction company failed in its bid to build the courthouse and had to be content with digging foundations for the jail is almost proof that the commissioners were honest. They also appear to have driven a favorable bargain for the county, because Flinn himself remarked that his firm could not have built the courthouse out of brick for what Norcross Bros. was charging to build it out of granite.[42]

When the Court of Common Pleas dismissed Judge Mellon's lawsuit, he appealed to the Pennsylvania Supreme Court and compelled Allegheny County to defend itself, at a cost of $2,000 in legal fees, which were billed to the "tenants and small property owners" through their taxes. Not until January 1886 did the high court dismiss his suit with finality.

Wonder of wonders, the Richardson courthouse wound up costing more or less what the commissioners had projected. In an era of public plunder by scurrilous officeholders, three competent and incorruptible men had somehow been found to pilot the mammoth project to completion. Though strenuous efforts were made to belittle them in the press, all three commissioners were reelected that fall, and to this day their work remains free from the slightest whiff of scandal. As Mellon and the opposition had feared, Allegheny County was compelled to float an $800,000 bond issue to meet construction costs, but the additional debt was offset by increased revenues from other sources. The courthouse and jail were therefore completed without any overall increase in the county debt. This outcome may not have satisfied Thomas Mellon, but it must have astonished him.

On balance, the Judge viewed himself as a failed politician, but his actual record presents him in a more favorable light. Bluntly forthright, contemptuous of machine politics, almost raucous in his insistence on austerity, he cast himself as an opponent of the ruling Flinn-Magee ring and thereby forfeited much of his influence on the two councils. Yet he remained a familiar and respected figure in public life. Though never a professional politician, he was an obsessive one. His constituents and fellow councillors knew which axes he had come to grind, and on most issues it was easy to predict how he would vote.

While introducing a stream of proposals for retrenchment, he nonetheless voted regularly to repair, improve, and extend municipal roads, sewers, and water mains not merely in his own constituency but throughout the city. Though a leading banker, he continued to call for the repudiation of "fraudulent" bond issues, as he had done for more than twenty years. His awesome consistency earned him a large measure of admiration, and to those who shared his political obsessions he was beyond reproach. The affluent, conservative suburbanites of his East End constituency chose him as their standard bearer in five consecutive elections, until he refused to continue serving. His final vote as a councillor was cast on March 28, 1887. The issue was whether funeral processions should have the right of way. He decided they should not.[43]

Mellon unambiguously recorded his views on the practice of certain professions, such as farming, soldiering, banking, business, and the law. Though he failed to express himself with equal clarity on the practice of politics, his interest in public affairs was lifelong and intense. From the numerous political opinions and observations recorded in his letters and memoirs, and from his voluminous record as a city councillor, it is easy to reconstruct the Judge's convictions with respect to politicians and their profession.

He stridently endorses the Scotch-Irish view, seconded by Herbert Spencer, that meaningful improvement in the quality of life must be affected by individuals striving to improve their lot. He scorns the native Irish for habitually turning to political demagogues and to government for what they desire. It is individuals who must work their way "up and out," from the demeaning constraints of ordinary life to the financial freedom on which human dignity depends, and they do this by making money.[44] Business is therefore a supremely dignifying occupation. Politics, whether we call it public service or demagoguery, is for those who lack the character and ability to succeed in business and must therefore enter a less demanding race for inferior rewards.

He grudgingly respects the politician who seeks power in order to defend or promote commendable principles and causes. But the career politician arouses his contempt. Anyone who seeks public office for its own sake is devoid of principle and therefore reprehensible. A politician who knowingly panders to the ignorance and prejudice of constituents or attempts to confound political rivals while secretly agreeing with them would earn the Judge's unremitting scorn.

A backward glance at his eight years in politics leaves him typically mired in gloom: "No more unsatisfactory position could be held by one of my disposition. I have for over forty years been combating municipal abuses without any appreciable effect. The drift has been steadily towards folly and extravagance, and those who oppose it are usually in the minority."[45]

Municipal abuses, folly and extravagance—Mellon's moral abhorrence of machine politics was sincere, but he applied a different standard in business. T. Mellon & Sons retained Boss Magee's mortgages and underwrote his bonds. The Mellon-owned Ligonier Valley Railroad continued to freight immense numbers of granite blocks from Boss Flinn's quarry in Loyalhanna Gap. The Judge would live to see his sons, Andrew and Richard, include Boss Flinn in their syndicate to exploit the Spindletop oil properties at Beaumont, Texas, in 1901. But, mercifully, death would blind him to the fitful, half-hearted efforts of Andrew and the Judge's grandson William to operate the Republican political machine in which Flinn, Magee, Quay, and Penrose had found their roost.

As he ponders the darkening prospects for American democracy, the Judge lapses effortlessly into his familiar Cassandra voice. "In early years I had great faith in our form of free government to preserve the blessings of individual liberty: but of late, seeing the way political power is obtained, and the character of those who obtain it, I begin to lose confidence, and feel that the form is no protection."[46] But he continues:

> Notwithstanding all this, I am not discouraged. An energetic, industrious people can bear a great deal of exaction and misrule, and at the worst there is always room for the survival of the fittest. . . .
>
> I have faith in the principle of regeneration. It works for preservation through evolution and change, and belongs to social organism of every kind, as well as to individual religious hope. Were it not for this recuperative or regenerative principle in humanity, society and the race itself would have gone to destruction long ago.[47]

That he concludes these funereal ruminations on a surprisingly hopeful note is perhaps because he suddenly remembered that anyone who loses *all* hope for democracy ceases to be an American.

# XVIII

—◆•◆—

## Andrew the Financier,
## His Father's Influence

*Insofar as my personal views are concerned, I am, as you say, primarily a
business man in my training and outlook. I may add, however, that while
I wish to see policies adopted which will make for the prosperity of business, I believe that this will also be for the general prosperity of all in a
state like Pennsylvania, where the condition of industry necessarily effects
labor and all the other elements in the community.*

*Letter from Andrew W. Mellon to James Witherow, May 12, 1926*

ONE WAY TO HIGHLIGHT THE JUDGE'S wide-ranging influence on his best-known son is to look closely at Andrew W.
Mellon in late middle age, when he had reached the stratospheric
level of finance. He was then president of the Mellon National Bank,
as T. Mellon & Sons had come to be named in 1902, and his brother
Richard, who occupied the adjoining office, was vice president. Now
known as "A.W." and "R.B.," the two had been inseparable since
childhood and would remain so. They consulted on every major
decision, and it was symbolic that their offices were separated only by a
pair of swinging doors.

Most Americans would not hear of Andrew Mellon until he took
office as secretary of the treasury in 1921, but among the nation's foremost bankers and industrialists, his name was already spoken with rev-

erence. In the steady stream of applicants who approached the Mellon Bank with business proposals, many insisted on making their presentations to Andrew Mellon himself. Of these hopefuls, some got as far as Richard, but most were directed to bank officers. The very few who finagled an audience with A.W. found the experience memorable.

Andrew Mellon made an immediate and arresting impression. Deeply incised in his long, somber face were the fine, hard lines and elegant bone structure that he had inherited from his paternal ancestors. His luxurious silver-gray hair and prim mustache were always perfectly trimmed. His delicate, finely sculpted hands and long, tapering fingers had obviously suffered no labor. Nothing about him suggested that he was the grandson of tenant farmers from Ireland. Strikingly handsome in adolescence, he assumed in middle life a nimbus of elegance and distinction that appeared to suffuse the entire man. Only at the last did his inscrutable face, which America had by then come to recognize, assume a haggard and world-weary look.

Like his father, Andrew led a sedentary life, shunning all strenuous activities. His only exercise was to take walks, yet he never gained weight. Endowed with a lanky frame, he accepted nature's invitation to dress impeccably. His expertly tailored suits reflected the understated refinement of his taste. There, as in much else, the influence of his lifelong friend Henry Clay Frick was palpable. The Judge, by contrast, had cared but little for appearances and, oblivious to fashion, had dressed in outmoded styles.

Andrew Mellon bore no resemblance to the stereotyped businessman so often portrayed in cartoons—the beefy, overbearing plutocrat who hollers at his cringing employees and hammers on the boardroom table with both fists. On the contrary, he was meticulously polite. "I wonder whether it would be convenient for you to . . ." was A.W.'s way of giving an order.[1] But his manners did not emanate from empathy or warmth. They were the evidences of unconquerable shyness. He had a fortress mentality, was emotionally self-sufficient, and probably confided his innermost thoughts to no one.[2]

Though he made it a point to discuss weighty financial decisions with his brother and partner, Richard, and with their closest associates, he appeared to trust completely in his own judgment and rarely asked for advice or invited suggestions.[3] To believe that he was not aware of his natural superiority in the sphere of business would be absurd. He was nonetheless strikingly modest, almost self-effacing, cared nothing for conventional honors, despised flattery, quailed at the limelight, and was indifferent to criticism unless it reflected on his integrity.[4]

Because his life was primarily a conversation with himself, his human relationships amounted to a sideshow. In 1900, against his father's advice, he had married twenty-one-year-old Nora McMullen, an Englishwoman less than half his age, and she had lost no time in taking a lover. He also failed as a parent. His diary does reveal an awareness of paternal responsibility, and his nephew William depicts him as an engaging father who romped with his children and even played with their toys.[5] But Paul and Ailsa Mellon would remember him as a distant and uncommunicative father—scrupulously conscientious, unfailingly generous, but one who needed solitude more than companionship.[6]

The totality of Andrew's absorption in his work was obvious. In the Judge's other sons, the urge to accumulate had been counterbalanced by a healthy array of additional interests and commitments. In Andrew, the critical balance between business and the restorative, countervailing spheres of life—such as family, friends, recreation, reading, and study—remained tragically lopsided. One has to wonder whether genetic factors had predisposed him to live such a monomaniacal life of acquisition. His father's influence had certainly encouraged it.

Like the Judge, he entered and left the bank in silence, passing officers and clerks as though they were invisible.[7] People would remember him as frequently lost in thought, but his distraction was subtly selective: in the spheres of life that engaged his formidable intellect—business and, later, art—he was shrewdly alert. There were those who resented his remoteness and mistook his innate self-absorption for

*Andrew W. Mellon, "A.W." (1855–1937), as secretary of the treasury, circa 1921.*

*Richard B. Mellon, "R.B." (1858–1933), in 1931.*
*Library of Congress.*

snobbish disregard. But like his father, he cared too little for social life to give himself airs. Neither of them could tolerate more than a few friends and close business associates. They judged others by character and talents, especially by their facility for accumulation. In that respect, they were both unswervingly egalitarian.

Andrew Mellon pondered business decisions with the same frigid calculation that his father had shown when scrutinizing and courting Sarah Jane. He plotted his course with meticulous deliberation. If time permitted, he crossed and recrossed every bridge before he came to it. Nothing that could be planned was left to chance.[8]

His mode of reasoning was distinctive. He proceeded to conclusions by extracting and relating a vast jumble of facts until they formed a mosaic of truth. An acquaintance of his, Chancellor John Gabbert Bowman of the University of Pittsburgh, thought he knew where banker Mellon had learned to reason inductively. "Andy's job was to read out loud in the evening to his father. . . . The old judge had Andy . . . read over and over out loud to him from Spencer's *First Principles*. . . . Spencer applied his first principles to the kitchen: Everything had to be worked out and analyzed, all broken down and put together again. Every process. A.W. got that into his head as a boy."[9]

In this roundabout way, Andrew came to share a smidgen of the erudition that his father had struggled to acquire and then deliberately withheld from his sons. Like the Judge, Andrew was a careful, disciplined, methodical thinker who reexamined his line of reasoning repeatedly before pronouncing it sound. Because this took time, he wholeheartedly shared his father's annoyance at being rushed. Bowman recalls this conversation:

> I went into his [Andrew Mellon's] office one day and wanted him to do something, and he wouldn't do it. I said, "You have got a slow mind."
>
> He just jumped right out of his chair. . . . He said, "How do you know I have got a slow mind? What made you say that?"

"Well," I said, "by just dealing with you, just bringing you in things and you put it off as long as you can, not because there is anything incomplete about it, but if you can dally it, you do."

He said, "How else do you know I have got a slow mind?"

I said, "I watch your face, for one thing, when I talk to you."

He got a chair over by the fireplace. He said, "Sit down here." He said, "Nobody ever told me I had a slow mind."

I said, "That don't make any difference. . . . I'm telling you that's what you've got. I don't say you haven't got a penetrating mind. It finally gets awful deep down, and you stay put on what you find, but it takes you a long time to do it. And that's what I mean by *slow*."

Finally he said, "Well, I have known this all along, but nobody else ever *told* me that!"[10]

What Bowman failed to recognize is that Mellon's mind was only "slow" by preference. His logic was fastidious, in fact somewhat vain, like his personal appearance. The prospect of error discomfited him as much as a grease spot on his immaculate shirt, and where there was nothing to be gained by rushing, he would delay an important decision. But unlike his father, he could instantly spot a passing opportunity and had the daring to lunge for it. When William Donner brought him a scheme for manufacturing nails and wire, Mellon began angling for a share of what came to be Union Steel before Donner had left the office.[11] When Alfred Hunt and Arthur Vining Davis approached him with a novel process for manufacturing aluminum, he moved with alacrity to cut himself and Richard in for a giant share of what came to be the Aluminum Company of America. His father would have focused on the risk while minimizing the opportunity. He would have procrastinated and missed his chance.

In an interview, A.W. wasted no time on preliminaries. Like his father, he was too focused on matters of importance to make small talk, and his frequent opening line, "What can I do for you?" would give the visitor an unambiguous shove. Yet there was nothing peremptory in his manner. He spoke slowly, thoughtfully, in low, considerate tones, and often with disarming awkwardness. He was sparing with words, but those that he uttered flew straight to the mark. As he searched for precisely the right expression, his mouth would occasionally hang open for several seconds, and his struggle to express himself sometimes ended in a kind of stutter.[12] When speaking in public, his diction was halting, often muffled, sometimes barely audible, and his self-consciousness could be excruciating to watch.[13] He was a paraplegic speaker but a phenomenal listener when his interest was fully engaged.

When listening to a business proposal, Mellon, a lifelong poker player, would assume an inscrutably saturnine expression. He would sit casually, with one leg slung over the other, his left elbow resting on the desktop, his patrician head leaning against his palm. From between the fingers of his right hand, the familiar rat-tailed cigar—a "needle," as he called it—would languidly trail smoke as he clutched for the truth or falsehood that lay hidden in the stream of words. He would take notes with an ordinary pencil on a plain pad of lined yellow paper. If his interest flagged, he might indulge his habit of doodling, but he refrained from vulgar expressions of boredom, like yawning or stretching. As he listened, his gaze might wander, focusing now on the ceiling, now on the wall, but his eyes made a powerful impression when he fixed them on the visitor. "Sharp blue daggers darting at you" was how a friend would remember them. After a meeting with Mellon, Chancellor Bowman recalled, "He stood there with a dominant overall rocklike quality. Austere, alone, serious—I had not seen so much of these qualities in any man before."[14] Others recalled his "dreamy," "wistful," "far-looking" gaze.[15] From the familiar portrait by Sir Oswald Birley, which would appear on the standard 3-cent U.S. postage stamp in 1955, he gazes forth with an expression of knowing appraisal, as though he were evaluating the viewer for a loan. The impression he made depended on the prejudices that each party brought to the meeting, but his was a memorable look.[16]

On rare occasions, when his excitement or annoyance became irrepressible, beads of perspiration would stand out on his chin and forehead. It was then that he sometimes sallied from behind his desk and paced the room. But ordinarily, he bore himself with steely control, just as his father had done. Those who attempted to penetrate the hard enclosure of his reserve found that they were drilling into granite.

A.W. also inherited his father's atrophied sense of humor. A bemused chuckle was as far as he could go toward laughing. Though not an accomplished raconteur like the Judge, he would sometimes relate an amusing anecdote about one or another of the businessmen he had known. When the yarn related to his father's penny-pinching ways, which it often did, he would tell it with obvious affection.[17]

In an interview, A.W. angled for the vital information that supported his decisions. As the visitor spoke, the banker would normally remain closed-lipped, concentrating like a chess master. But every so often he would draw his interlocutor out with an abrupt query like, "How do you know that?" or "What good would that do?" To the pronouncement that only one individual was qualified to manage a certain enterprise, Mellon might counter, "Why not somebody else?" By darting these challenges at the visitor with the persistence of a small child, he would probe the soundness of his reasoning.[18]

He had X-ray vision for spotting the hidden defects in a business proposal. Of the chemist who brought him a complicated invention that was beyond his technical grasp, Mellon, who knew that no one can put a patent on sunshine, at once demanded, "Can—this—thing—be—owned?" To the group that presented him with a plan for rigging the coal market, he replied, "There are five good reasons, gentlemen, why your undertaking is bound to fail." He then listed the reasons, using his fingers for emphasis.[19]

"He could see through a proposition quicker than any man I have ever known," recalled Henry Phillips, one of Mellon's accountants. "For instance, he would send for me and say, 'So-and-so wants to do such-and-such. What do you think of it?' Well, I would spend maybe a couple of days analyzing it in my own mind. And I would take my findings down to him. 'Oh,' he would say, 'that's the weak point in the whole thing.' Well, I had been two days finding that out. He knew it right off the bat."[20] One has to wonder whether Mellon actually wanted Phillips's opinion or was merely testing him.

Like his father, A.W. was woefully proficient at dissecting financial statements. Almost every petitioner came armed with sheets of figures that he would draw out at a strategic moment and place before the banker. Mellon would peruse these papers with a raptor's eye and quickly place his finger on the point of deliberate concealment. "What does *this* mean?" he would ask. And as the visitor squirmed and attempted to equivocate, the banker would follow up with a number of prying questions until every fault in the statement had been exposed.[21] When he had to reject a proposal, which was almost always, he would often fall silent and simply shake his head in compassionate despair.[22] He was never rough.

Mellon could be attracted to a business proposal for surprising reasons. An art collector since 1896, he had come to perceive similarities between an attractive painting and a well-structured corporate deal. Chancellor Bowman drew him out on this subject:

> I started one day asking him, "Did buying these pictures have any influence on your career?"
>
> He said, "Very much."
>
> "In what way?"
>
> He said, "I don't buy a picture when I first look at it. I have it hung up where I see it. And then, if the thing begins to have a meaning to me and the corners and sides and bottoms and all around mean something and it all holds together, maybe I like it. But if it doesn't hold together—if this corner down here doesn't mean anything in relation to its center—then I don't want it. Now," he said, "a business deal is just like that."[23]

But in a more fundamental way, art and business remained separate spheres of his life. However free-thinking and futuristic he may have been in business, his taste in art remained unswervingly retrospective and would continue to reflect the Judge's Scotch-Irish adherence to things that had proved their worth. While true connoisseurs were already collecting Picassos, Mellon remained indifferent to the emerging art of his day and obdurate in his preference for universally acclaimed painters. However aesthetically sensitive he may have been, his yearning to *own* art could be aroused only when the painter was a recognized master.

The perception of beauty in a work of art can kindle in the viewer a craving for ownership. But this craving is more often aroused by the sheer rarity of artistic masterpieces and by their consequent desirability as collectibles. Hence the most driven collectors of art are frequently philistines who fail to understand or appreciate what they buy. Late in life, under the lingering influence of his deceased friend, Frick, Andrew Mellon became a compulsive acquirer of old master paintings. In the tangle of his motives, pride of possession appears to have figured as heavily as perceived beauty, but he was also driven by a deeper yearning. Asked by Bowman why he collected art, Mellon replied, "Every man wants to connect his life with something that he thinks eternal."[24]

The Judge cared nothing for painting and could not have influenced his son in that sphere. They did have in common a lack of sensitivity for the other arts. Both were indifferent to music and rarely attended the theater. The Judge read intensively, but for edification, not for pleasure. Andrew, whom he had dissuaded from developing a probing philosophical mind, read material that he had brought home from the office and occasionally a business-related book.[25]

From Andrew's desk, it was only a few steps through the swinging doors to Richard's office. The swish of these doors was heard repeatedly as one brother pushed in to consult the other. As they colluded in earnest discussion of some business-related subject, the cloud of cigar smoke would swirl and thicken around them. They were a study in contrasts. While A.W.'s angular face and rail-thin figure confirmed his descent from the Judge, R.B.'s rounded features and stolid, ample frame linked him at once to the Negleys.

Richard lacked the chilly reserve and frequent mental absences that were so typical of his elder brother. He would stride into the bank, beaming and tossing off greetings, and would pause to chat or joke with the employees.[26] While Andrew sat in his office, swamped in the labyrinthine proposals that lay before him, Richard puttered around the main banking lobby checking to see that the inkwells were full, that the piles of deposit slips were in the pigeonholes, and that the wastebaskets had been emptied.[27] If the art of living requires us to continually divert ourselves from the certainty that life is short, Andrew did this by escaping into his thoughts, Richard by embroiling himself in the minutiae that lay about him.

In business, Richard's guiding ambition was to enlarge the Mellon National Bank and to improve its administration. Like his father, he had come to view the family's flagship enterprise with proprietary affection, and he enlarged it by acquiring smaller banks all over the state. He also gave the institution a friendly face by making ordinary depositors feel like valued customers. A man who kept only $100 on account could still expect that his loan application would be given precedence because he was a Mellon customer. This was largely Richard's doing.[28]

The Judge had never ceased to regard Pittsburgh as the family's revered and permanent home. His innate provincialism was further developed and magnified by Richard into a strident civic pride. "We are here to do all we can for Pittsburgh" was a frequent remark that Richard is remembered for.[29] To him, and later to his son General Richard Mellon, the Iron City was unique, and its interests should have precedence over other causes. Those who waylaid the brothers for donations to Pittsburgh charities normally fared better if they approached Richard, who would then lean on his wavering brother to make a joint contribution.[30]

"My brother and I . . ." came to be a familiar expression in boardroom discussions and public announcements. But on important occasions, it was normally Andrew who spoke. Similarly, the bank's weightiest correspondence was normally conducted by Andrew. He was the leader.

"If you want to borrow $5,000, you see Dick; if you want $50,000, you see Andy." Such was the conventional view of their relative importance.[31] What it left unsaid was that Andrew depended on his brother in several ways. He knew that Richard had precisely the qualities that he himself lacked, notably a facility for easy communication with people and a consequent insight into personalities. Also, as Bowman points out, Andrew tested his own inductive conclusions against Richard's wisdom, which was largely intuitive.

There was this basic difference between them. A.W. would take up a proposition just the way he did a picture. He wanted all the facts. He wanted to know the meanings of the corners and sides and bottom as well as the center. And he analyzed it. R.B. got a general impression of the whole thing and said, "I don't like it," or "I do like it," or "I don't care what the facts are, that fellow is no good." He got a wisdom right out of the ground. And the fellow was nearly always right.

They worked in totally different ways, and that was their strength. One of them got an impressionistic judgment; the other got an analytical one.[32]

Though the two brothers often approached a problem from radically different viewpoints, their mental paths would almost always converge. If a difference of opinion remained, Richard deferred to Andrew. That he could do this without feeling belittled was Richard's most extraordinary quality, and it served him well, because otherwise the brothers could not have collaborated.

Then too, the brilliant but emotionally repressed Andrew drew strength from the friendship of his jocular, extroverted, patently "normal" brother. Richard sensed Andrew's vulnerability and fiercely protected him. On one occasion, when Frick spoke critically of Andrew in the presence of other businessmen, Richard lunged at the Coke Baron and attempted to slug him.[33] Indeed, the boisterousness with which R.B. vented his passions, as when he heaved an inkpot at the bookkeeper Howard Johnson, must have exasperated his soft-spoken, unemotional brother, but nothing could shake their friendship.[34]

Andrew also relied on Richard to perform the family's social obligations, which frequently overlapped with its business activities. If an exclusive coterie of New York bankers invited Andrew to dinner, he would often avoid the unpleasantness of having to mingle by sending Richard to represent him. For whereas Andrew was painfully self-conscious and always awkward in company, Richard exulted in the uproar of social life. His eager humor was ever ready to spring, and his hearty laughter would rock the Duquesne Club at lunchtime. Unlike Andrew, he was a family man, an effective husband and father whose constant presence lent a supportive equilibrium to Andrew's one-dimensional, solipsistic life.

Paintings by Frederick Remington and Charles Russell came to grace Richard's walls because they rekindled memories of his years in Dakota Territory, but on the whole art meant little to him. His cultivation focused on the other spheres of life. He adored fine food, the best whiskey, and superlative Havana cigars; he loved his pedigree horses and bird dogs, custom-made fly rods, and engraved shotguns. The ultimate country squire, he lived for the Rolling Rock Club, his nonpareil happy hunting ground, where he could tramp the fields with a 12-gauge shotgun, lash the streams for trout, ride to foxhounds, and live like his grandfather's Anglo-Irish landlords.

The Judge had invested in banks, real estate, construction, coal mines, and public transportation, but he had never angled for quick paper profits and had always derided stock-market speculation as perilously futile. With rare digressions, Andrew adhered to this view. A man who asked his advice on how to get rich quick received this reply: "I have never made anything myself in speculation. My father taught me to shun it, and I must say that all my observation in business has corroborated the fact that money cannot with any degree of safety be made in that way. Investment for prospective increases in value is another thing, but that method would be too slow to accomplish what you desire."[35]

The Judge and his son believed in founding or buying into businesses and then expanding them. They were builders, not speculators, and they demanded a say in management. Neither tended to play on the sharp or low. Like Benjamin Franklin, they believed that in business the path of intelligent self-interest was always an honorable one.

Thomas Mellon was forty-two years older than Andrew, and the contrast in their business strategies owed much to the transformation of America from a primitive industrial nation to a more mature one in the interim. Father and son believed in natural resources, and each invested heavily in the staple fuel of his day—the Judge in coal, Andrew in oil. Both saw opportunities in public transportation, such as street railways. But Andrew had a futuristic eye and immediately spotted the prospects for aluminum and carborundum, for the Koppers coke oven, for steel-framed buildings, for manufacturing railroad cars and even ships from standardized steel parts. His father remained wary of inventions, partly because the future itself alarmed him.

Father and son were bankers, but the father focused on money lending, with its shopworn rewards—interest, profitable foreclosures, buying and selling mortgages. Andrew discovered in banking the superlative tool for acquiring a guiding interest in start-up companies and then transforming them into gigantic wealth-generating enterprises. He would remain a banker but would find his natural habitat in high finance, the ultimate level of banking.

The Judge had struggled up from poverty, had witnessed catastrophic depressions, and would remain stubbornly risk-averse. His son, who had been raised in comfort and plenty, pursued a more venturesome business style that sometimes alarmed his father. A visitor to the Mellon home in 1880 recalled how Andrew had congratulated himself for having collected on a poorly secured loan and how his father had then slyly remarked that it would have been better if he had lost the money; that would have taught him a lesson.[36]

The Judge's tireless calls for caution may have restrained Andrew from the impulsive missteps that so often cause an inexperienced heir to stumble fatally. But Andrew swiftly improved on his father's capacity for managing risk. His most profitable ventures—Alcoa, Carborundum, Koppers, Gulf Oil, Union Steel, New York Ship Building, McClintic-Marshall, and Standard Steel Car—would have proved too volatile for the Judge. Yet only one of these—Gulf Oil—was inordinately risky, and then only at first. The results that A.W. achieved are impressive enough when calculated in dollars. Adjusted for risk, they are phenomenal. Still, there were times when Thomas Mellon must have felt like a hen that had hatched a duckling.

John D. Rockefeller made his fortune in oil, the Duponts in chemicals, Henry Ford in automobiles, the Duke family in tobacco, Frick in coke, and the Vanderbilts in railroads. "Put all your eggs in one basket, and then watch the basket," was Carnegie's advice. By concentrating on only one single sector of the economy, these captains of industry heaped up fortunes that far surpassed that of Thomas Mellon. Where he exceeded them was in the range and flexibility of his business acumen. For the Judge had routinely demurred from seeking fortune in any particular field. He had clutched for opportunity where he perceived it, and the sheer diversity of his enterprises bears witness to the multiplicity of talents that he had fused into a single shaft of intelligence that could be focused into any sector of business. This and a rigid insistence on limiting risk were the cornerstones of his strategy for compounding wealth.

Andrew Mellon learned his father's strategy at the hearth, then vastly elaborated and refined it and applied it to build a portfolio of industries that became a model for the conglomerate firm in the twentieth century. His biographer Burton Hendrick aptly summarizes Andrew Mellon's definitive talents: "His judgment seemed unerring in regard to both ideas and men. He almost infallibly selected the one proposal that promised success and at the same time found the inevitable man."[37] To which Hendrick could have added that Andrew's unerring judgment in business matters was the only leadership quality exhibited by this curiously self-conscious and uncommunicative man.

That said, even infallible judgment would have counted for little without a corresponding drive to propel it. If that drive initially sprang from the son's affection for his father and a consequent longing to fulfill paternal expectation, it was certainly not diminished by his father's death. That business preoccupied him almost exclusively for half a century begs the question why. When a *New York Times* reporter queried, "What have you to say about being a rich man?" Mellon, who was then secretary of the treasury, stumbled trough the following reply: "Why . . . I . . . I . . . don't know what to say. I . . . I . . . suppose I am . . . what they call a rich man. . . . They tell me so. . . . I'm not particularly conscious of it. . . . I don't use money . . . for myself. . . . I don't spend much . . . on myself. . . . I have always . . . just worked . . . done what needed to be done . . . in business. . . . I didn't try to make money . . . especially. . . . I'm not interested in it . . . in money. . . . I don't care . . . but well . . . I . . . I can't think of anything to say about it."[38]

Mellon was neither cynical nor devious, and his typically inarticulate response has the ring of truth. With some elaboration, it might have read like this: "My father trained me as a banker and more generally as a businessman. I wanted to please him and tried hard to master these skills. My work became enjoyable because I was good at it. To found new companies, fuel them with money, place them under sound management, and help guide them to maturity is the thrill that I have lived for. Specifically, my task has been to spot the truly outstanding opportunities, to fully exploit them, and to surmount the obstacles as they arose. Where I have done my work well, money has never been a problem."

Recalling his uncle, Andrew, William L. Mellon emphasizes that "A.W. used banking as a constructive force just as definitely and as understandingly as the industries which he helped to create used electricity as a force, used it to make things go. Though all the adventures of Sinbad the Sailor usually ended in the enrichment of Sinbad, he never is regarded as a money-grubber because we remember the adventures rather than the riches. Yet, for some perverse reason, successful businessmen are differently regarded."[39]

As a director of more than forty companies, Andrew Mellon was expected to maximize the return from these concerns. He could never have been indifferent to profit and surely took pride in the phenomenal fortune he had made. But he must also have gloried in exercising his genius to create the mammoth corporations that would live after him and form a giant segment of America's industrial base. As with many of the world's powerful, A.W. did not focus on wealth primarily for the immediate pleasures it could yield him. He regarded it mainly as a tool for building. Whereas the Judge, lacking a comparable talent, engaged in business to accumulate wealth—not as an end in itself, but as a pass to freedom and self-respect—Andrew measured himself by what he had built.

Among the driving forces that propelled A.W., a number of additional motives stand out as likely. To some extent, business probably served him as an exhilarating form of high-stakes poker that helped to save him from lurking boredom. But without doubt, subliminal motives were also interwoven in the unflagging catalyst that powered his relentless acquisitiveness.

"The drive to acquire, in Mellon, . . . was an essential, perhaps preponderant, part of himself, which had already become a substitute for, and an escape from, close interpersonal relationships and commitments," concludes his biographer David Cannadine. "The single-minded pursuit of money is often associated with some form of stunted emotional growth, which the successful accumulation of wealth intensifies rather than allays, and this, too, could . . . be said of Andrew. And wealth-gathering permitted no rest for the acquisitive personality. Because its ceiling is limitless, the competition which helps create it is unrelenting, and the risks of loss or failure or public hostility are never fully allayed, and all these concerns certainly help explain why Mellon worked such long hours so unrelentingly."[40]

No biographer can determine with certainty what it was that powered this curiously closeted and driven man. But this much is known: only in his final years did the dual challenge of directing America's finances and of creating the National Gallery of Art at last succeed in substantially diverting him from business.

His religious sensibilities appear to have been even more withered than those of his father. He rarely attended East Liberty Presbyterian Church and had tellingly left Richard to pay for its entire construction. Writing to his estranged wife, Nora, he invokes God's blessing on her and promises to remember her in his prayers.[41] But these may have been figures of speech. His friend David Finley, who came to head the National Gallery, volunteered, "I was never certain that Mr. Mellon believed in the hereafter. . . . I think Mr. Mellon was hopeful but not particularly convinced."[42] The perception of order in nature nonetheless sent vestigial stirrings of religious wonder through him. "How strange that order is in growing things," he confided to Bowman, "and in rocks, in rivers, in waves on the sea, in the movement of stars."[43]

The Judge viewed politics as a dubious profession that attracted men of flawed character, luring potential if not actual demagogues whose ingrained weaknesses ill suited them for the more honorable, more challenging, and frequently more creative pursuit of business. But he feared politicians for their power. That decisions which vitally affected business might be made by its opponents or simply by fools was his recurring nightmare. Andrew Mellon came to view politicians in much the same light. Like his father, he was determined to exert political power in favor of business and to protect business from its perceived adversaries.

By 1920, his objectives were undergoing a natural transformation. At sixty-five, he had begun to feel his mortality and to wonder how people would remember him. Would they be distracted from his founding contributions to American industry by vulgar fascination with the heap of his wealth, which now equaled the budget of a small country? Should he not commit the dwindling remainder of his life to one or more causes that were indisputably praiseworthy?

His friend, U.S. Senator Philander Knox, was pressing him to join President-elect Warren G. Harding's incoming cabinet as secretary of the treasury, and the offer had thrown him into a quandary. Like his father, he distrusted and disliked politicians as a class. He also knew he would be woefully miscast as a public official. On the other hand, his spectacular success at imposing sound principles of finance and management on a wide variety of major businesses hinted that he might be able to do as much for America. "The Government is just a business," he would come to write, "and can and should be run on business principles."[44]

After lengthy procrastination, Mellon accepted Harding's offer to head the U.S. Treasury and did so for eleven years, under three presidents. He adroitly refinanced and vastly reduced the national debt, enacted tax legislation aimed at stimulating business, and labored like Hercules to collect war debts from the nation's former allies. He also played a guiding role in the replanning of Washington, D.C., and it may have been in the lengthy discussions with his architects, among them John Russell Pope, and while walking alone through the capital city, as was his custom, that he began to meditate on the need for a national gallery of art.[45]

As long as America prospered extravagantly under his fiscal guidance, Mellon was hailed as a prodigy. But the Great Depression, which commenced during his final term, triggered a savage reassessment of his policies. With its usual genius for hindsight, the public, which had labeled Mellon as the greatest secretary of the treasury since Alexander Hamilton, now berated him for having failed to curb the final binge of speculation that preceded the crash. That Britain, France, Germany, and the other industrial democracies were engulfed by the same economic catastrophe was conveniently overlooked by Mellon's howling critics.

Where A.W. revealed a regrettable lapse of character was in his frequent, stumbling incursions into the fetid politics of Pennsylvania. When Senator Boise Penrose died, in 1921, leaving the Republican political machine bossless and adrift, all eyes focused on Andrew Mellon, who was a member of President Harding's cabinet and one of the three wealthiest Americans. To help him keep state politics in tandem with business, he installed his unqualified and reluctant nephew, William L. Mellon, as Republican Party chairman and ineptly attempted to operate the political machine that Penrose had bequeathed to no one. In the Republican primaries of 1926, A.W. and his partisans, notably Joseph Grundy, passed out a staggering $1,804,979 to frustrate William Vare's nomination for the U.S. Senate and to promote that of the incumbent George Pepper. In Allegheny County, which was Mellon turf, Senator Pepper's campaign hired 35,350 "poll watchers" at $10 each. The New York *World* jibed that if each of these observers and his spouse had voted for Pepper, "the whole Mellon-Pepper electorate in Allegheny County was purchased."[46] That the practice of hiring poll watchers was not only lawful but widely practiced by both political parties speaks volumes about the brazenness and rascality of Pennsylvania politics. When Senator Pepper still managed to lose in the primary, A.W. and the state Republican leaders rallied behind Vare for the November election. Again, a tidal wave of Mellon money was released into the electoral process. Vare's "purchased" victory triggered such a groundswell of outrage that the U.S. Senate refused to seat him. The Republican leaders of Pennsylvania, A.W. among them, had once more demonstrated their indifference to the need for cleaner government. In an unpublished biography of Andrew Mellon, which was suppressed by his son, Paul, Burton Hendrick passes final judgment on A.W.'s political forays:

> His most glaring failing . . . was a lack of idealism in civic affairs. The darker aspects of American politics apparently never shocked him. His comments on the use of money in the Pennsylvania primaries of 1926 afford melancholy reading from this point of view. This deficiency was one which Mellon had in common with practically all business leaders of his time. Politics had always seemed to be part of the industrial struggle itself. If the life of business depended on suppressing foreign competition by a protective tariff, . . . American industrial leaders demanded, as a nat-

ural right, the privilege of selecting the legislators who framed the "schedules." In this way developed the politico-industrial alliance, with its Penroses, its Aldriches, on one side, controlling legislation and naming candidates for office, and the business chieftains on the other, providing the money contributions that made their efforts so effective. The most squalid aspect of this amalgamation of politics and business was manifest in the government of city and state, of which Pennsylvania had always served as a glaring example. Mellon unquestionably formed a part of this system. That he saw no evil in it, or at least that he closed his eyes in view of the advantages the system brought him and his business contemporaries, the record . . . made plain. In any appraisal of the man, therefore, this serious disqualification must be put upon the debit side.[47]

In a letter to James Witherow, who had inveighed against the Republican political machine in Pennsylvania, A.W. takes a position that his father and every other Mellon would have rushed to endorse: "Insofar as my personal views are concerned, I am, as you say, primarily a business man in my training and outlook. I may add, however, that while I wish to see policies adopted which will make for the prosperity of business, I believe that this will also be for the general prosperity of all in a state like Pennsylvania, where the condition of industry necessarily effects labor and all the other elements in the community."[48]

The Judge had denounced machine politics, railing against it privately and in public. His futile but die-hard opposition to the Flinn-Magee ring had won him respect in the Pittsburgh city councils, and his knock-down, drag-out collision with the venal councilmen of Kansas City, which was yet to come, would make him a local hero. By contrast, Andrew Mellon came to accept machine politics as endemic to Pennsylvania. And his bosom friend, Frick, who cultivated a symbiotic relationship with both Flinn and Magee, must have shown him how to deal with the bosses.[49] While others protested that to swamp the electoral process with campaign funds was to undermine democracy, A.W. continued to work within the prevailing political system.

Yet the father's viewpoint on political corruption and that of his son may not have differed diametrically. In the Judge's lexicon, the term *corrupt* applied mainly to ethically malleable politicians, political rings, and nefarious railroad officials. Whether he would also have opposed the lawful but grossly excessive use of money to keep politics in lockstep with business is questionable. That he crows of having spent only $150 on his campaign for the bench hints that he might have balked at any appreciable expenditure for political purposes.[50]

Thomas Mellon had drilled Andrew in the catechism of Scotch-Irish values, placed his nose on the trail to wealth, and given him a whiff of the scent. He had trained him to sober habits, made him memorize Burns's "Epistle to a Young Friend" like a bedside prayer, and subjected him to total immersion in Franklin's chiseling parsimony. He had taught him the fundamentals of real estate, construction, and conventional banking and acquainted him with a variety of other businesses. This training had given Andrew tools that he would employ with astounding effect. But to view him as merely a more sophisticated clone of the Judge would be preposterous. He came to possess his father's yen for taking profitable advantage of the world, but, unlike his father, he would change the world.

He was not an inventor but a mighty backer of other men's inventions —not an original thinker but one who recognized an original proposal at first glance, would deftly position himself to take advantage of it, and then prodigiously direct its development. The same story kept repeating itself. A brilliant young man, struggling and in distress, would solicit Mellon's backing to exploit an ingenious discovery or invention. By offering financial assistance, the banker would secure a heaping equity position for himself and his brother Richard in the resulting enterprise. Where management was ineffectual, he would impose sound principles of finance and administration. As a last resort, he would replace the manager.

This strategy, which came to be known as "the Mellon system," was essentially a more sophisticated elaboration of the Judge's plan for exploiting coal properties. Individuals with knowledge and initiative but without sufficient capital—men like Benjamin Patterson, James B. Corey, and Felix Negley—had repeatedly approached Thomas Mellon for backing, and he had taken them in as partners, provided the required financing, and then stood aside to let them manage the enterprises.

Typically, the mammoth companies that Andrew Mellon was instrumental in founding and nurturing began as private concerns, owned by a small number of long-term investors. Their stock was not traded on exchanges. Their earnings were not distributed as dividends but reinvested to accelerate growth. The white male Protestant executives who staffed these concerns were tight-lipped, single-minded epigones who espoused an unshakable loyalty to the Mellon business complex. A pall of confidentiality hung over their activities. They kept the company reports brief and unspecific. After decades of service, they were proud to call themselves "old Mellon men."

The Aluminum Company of America (Alcoa) became a prime example of the Mellon system. Founded as the Pittsburgh Reduction Company, the firm owed its existence to Charles Martin Hall, a brilliant young chemist who had invented an electrolytic process for inexpensively reducing aluminum from bauxite. In 1889, Hall's partners, Arthur Vining Davis, Captain Alfred Hunt, and George Clapp, came to T. Mellon & Sons, handed A.W. Mellon some pieces of aluminum, explained its uses, and sent him an aluminum teapot. The sight of a world-transforming opportunity did not leave Mellon paralyzed. When the visitors asked for a loan of $4,000, he lent them $25,000, began to buy shares in their business, became its banker for life, and eventually built up a massive position for himself and brother Richard in the resulting Aluminum Company of America.

In 1900, Mellon revealed his definitive gift for finding inconspicuous prodigies. Reaching far down into the ranks of banking, he drew up a man with no startling qualifications, an assistant cashier at the Pittsburgh National Bank of Commerce and the son of a house painter. His name was Henry McEldowney, and Mellon installed him as president of the Union Trust Company, which he and Frick had founded.

"H.C.," as McEldowney came to be known, proved a brilliant manager, a surefooted arbiter of risk. In the thirty-five years that he headed Union Trust, its total resources soared from $5.5 million to more than $295 million, and H.C. himself became the highest-paid bank president in America. But the haunting question remains: Just *how* did A.W. spot this potential prodigy among the tangle of anonymous yeomen who teem on the ground floor of every lending institution?

In 1895, Edward G. Acheson, a self-taught inventor who had worked with Thomas Edison, presented Andrew Mellon with a luminous "pebble" that looked like a diamond. Angling for effect, Acheson seized the little stone and slashed a deep incision in the glass paperweight that lay on Mellon's desk. The banker was transfixed. What he had just witnessed would be remembered as the scratch heard around the world. Asked where he had obtained his diamond, Acheson countered, "I made it." What he had made was carborundum, the toughest known abrasive, a substance with myriad industrial uses. A.W. extended credit to Acheson for a carborundum manufacturing enterprise when no one else would do so. The Mellon brothers bought $50,000 worth of bonds in Acheson's enterprise, began accumulating its stock, and established a dominant Mellon stake in the resulting Carborundum Company.

The Mellons were latecomers to the steel industry. In 1899, William Donner sought A.W.'s backing to found a company for manufacturing nails, wire, and steel rods for reinforced concrete. Before Donner could leave the office, Mellon invited him for dinner at the Duquesne Club to work out an agreement.[51] The result was Union Steel, in which the Mellon brothers, Donner, and Frick became joint owners. They fashioned the company into a formidable steel producer in only three years, and by 1902 U.S. Steel felt compelled to buy the new company—a possibility that Mellon and his partners must have eagerly anticipated.

For no apparent reason, the grossly inflated price tag that Mellon and Frick placed on Union Steel was accepted, and they netted over forty times their initial investment. Here was an instance where Mellon atypically lunged for a fast, ethically questionable paper profit, perhaps under Frick's influence.[52]

Mellon was quick to recognize the potential for assembling railroad cars, ocean liners, and battleships from standardized steel parts; hence his heavy backing in 1899 for Henry G. Morse's New York Shipbuilding Company and three years later for K. T. Schoen's Standard Steel Car Company and its flamboyant promoter, "Diamond" Jim Brady. Henry Ford did not begin to mass-produce automobiles on a similar assembly-line basis until 1913.

In 1900, William L. Mellon introduced two young engineers, Howard McClintic and Charles Marshall, to his uncle Andrew. They wanted backing to found a company for erecting structural steel buildings. Foreseeing the age of skyscrapers, A.W. invested heavily in the resulting McClintic-Marshall Construction Company and helped to direct its spectacular growth. A list of memorable projects the company completed includes the George Washington Bridge, Grand Central Station, and the Waldorf-Astoria Hotel in New York, as well as the Golden Gate Bridge in San Francisco, the University of Pittsburgh's Cathedral of Learning, the Kennedy family's Merchandise Mart in Chicago, the giant Tata steelworks in India, and the system of locks along the Panama Canal.

When the automobile supplanted the horse and carriage, Andrew Mellon invested in oil—an industry that would enable him to profit from the automotive revolution without risking the uncertainties of the nascent automobile manufacturing industry.

In 1900, John Galey and Colonel James Guffey approached A.W. for a loan to drill some exploratory oil wells at Beaumont, Texas. He was well acquainted with these men and knew them to be accomplished prospectors, or "wildcatters." In the early 1870s, Thomas Mellon had bankrolled Galey to drill for oil forty miles northeast of Pittsburgh, and for a short time makeshift wooden derricks bearing names like

"Mellon 1" and "Mellon 2" had pumped oil along the Clarion River. These wells quickly ran dry, but they marked the Mellon family's debut into the embryonic oil industry, which would come to form the principal prop of their fortune.[53]

Guffey, with his ten-gallon hat and bushy mustaches, was a familiar figure at T. Mellon & Sons. Andrew Mellon had invested heavily in Guffey's Trade Dollar Consolidated Mining Company, which came to exploit a vast lode of silver in Idaho. For a number of years after 1897, this company had returned more income to the Mellons than any of their other businesses. It had fueled many of their subsequent acquisitions, and Guffey had come to be held in proportionately high esteem.[54]

With a credit line of $300,000 from T. Mellon & Sons, Galey and Guffey drilled into an immense lake of oil, and their strike, which came to be known as "Spindletop," put Texas on the map as a major oil-producing state. To finance and develop this field, A.W. organized the J. M. Guffey Petroleum Company, later known as Gulf Oil.

Andrew Mellon's last major business initiative was his takeover and reorganization of the Koppers Company. Events followed a familiar pattern. Dr. Heinrich Koppers had invented a revolutionary coke oven that preserved the by-products of coal—benzene, tar, toluol, and the explosive TNT—instead of spewing them into the air as pollutants. In 1915, Koppers's manager, Henry Rust, requested Andrew Mellon's backing to fully develop and aggressively market the new oven. The Mellons invested heavily. Because World War I had broken out, the company at once expanded its sale of coal derivatives, including TNT, to the combatants. A.W. retained Henry Rust as manager, and the firm began its relentless expansion.

The size of Mellon's fortune is difficult to determine, even in round figures. His accountant, Henry Phillips, gives an estimate of $350 million for the fortune at its zenith, in 1928 (worth about $4.5 billion today).[55] By comparison, Andrew Carnegie had received $360 million for his steel company in 1901, but the intervening years of inflation make Carnegie's relative net worth substantially greater. In any event, both men died under vastly reduced circumstances. Retired from business, Carnegie poured the bulk of his fortune into building thousands of free libraries, among other charitable bequests, and Mellon, who lived on into the Great Depression, was forced to liquidate assets at distressed prices to purchase the Medician art collection that he gave to the American people in his own lifetime, and to build the National Gallery of Art to house it. However, if this art collection is viewed as A. W. Mellon's in an informal historical sense, then the fortune he left behind is today of incalculable magnitude.

When Mellon focused on art, he looked backward in time. When he focused on business, he looked forward. The skillful exploitation of inventions and discoveries preoccupied him for much of his life and accounted for most of his family's fortune. In *The Chemistry of Commerce,* Professor Robert K. Duncan, a chemist at the University of Kansas, had called for the creation of research facilities that companies could engage to solve their scientific and industrial problems. A.W. seized on this concept and gave it life. The Mellon Institute of Industrial Research, which he and Richard founded in 1914 as a memorial to their father, enshrined A.W.'s consuming belief that the future of business was linked to science. In 1967 it merged with the Carnegie Institute of Technology to form Carnegie-Mellon University.

The National Gallery of Art, which remains the largest private gift ever made to the United States, may be Andrew Mellon's pharaonic pyramid, but his principal contribution to humanity is very different. We find it in his massive, unyielding, and consistently effective application of science to the satisfaction of human needs. By mass-producing thousands of useful products at affordable cost, the giant corporations that he nurtured to maturity have improved the quality of life for hundreds of millions of people. And the military products of these corporations have proved equally significant. Recalling World War II, in which the survival of civilization had come to depend on the Allied air forces, Alcoa's chairman, Arthur Vining Davis, penned this tribute to the memory of Andrew Mellon: "Without airplanes, inadequate fighting power; without aluminum, inadequate airplanes;

without Alcoa, inadequate aluminum; without Mellon, no Alcoa."[56] Though philanthropy was not his primary motive, Andrew Mellon was, at least obliquely, a historic benefactor of humanity.

His detractors routinely point out that Mellon was born to wealth and that this diminishes his achievements. Granted, he was not self-made. But it is difficult to imagine that a man of his character and ability would have achieved much less in the race of life if his father had not been wealthy. The element of luck, which figures in every fortune, can also be overemphasized in his case, as it has been in *The Mellons* by David Koskoff. Actually, luck wrought havoc with a number of Mellon's investments. Gulf Oil, Alcoa, Carborundum, McClintic-Marshall, and New York Shipbuilding all floundered for extended periods. It was A.W.'s unshakable belief in his own judgment and his consequent salubrious influence on management that finally made these ventures spectacularly profitable.

Thomas Mellon's influence on Andrew was manifold and pervasive, but Andrew's virtuosity had more to do with their differences. The spark of his own genius was the star that he steered by. His father had never digressed from conventional strategies of accumulation, but in a long life devoted to applying them he had only amassed a few million dollars; Andrew was, at one point, more than a hundred times wealthier.

The invention of paint cannot account for Michelangelo, and no amount of paternal-hearth training can more than fractionally explain the phenomenon of Andrew Mellon. The Judge had subjected all of his sons to the same relentless indoctrination and had given them a running start in business. But there was only one A.W.

# XIX

## The Judge Writes His Memoirs,
## How to Defeat Poverty

*I cherish the hope that, should an old copy of the book happen to fall into the hands of some poor little boy among my descendants in the distant future, who, inheriting a share of my spirit and energy, may be desirous of bettering his condition, it may tend to encourage and sustain his commendable ambition.*

FOR THOMAS MELLON, THE DECADE that began in 1879 and saw him age from sixty-six to seventy-six consisted of harvest years in which his sons prospered exceedingly as businessmen, the enterprises he had founded continued to grow, and his fruitful family tree sprouted leaves. But these were also years of sorrow. The first blow fell in 1879, when his only brother, Samuel Mellon (born in 1825), died at 401 Negley during a visit to Pittsburgh.

Samuel Mellon had failed as a clerk in his brother's law office, left home at eighteen, and become an itinerant shopkeeper in Texas. He had married, fathered six children, and served in the Confederate Army. A trail of failed grocery stores and losing real estate speculations marked the course of his ineffectual passage through Texas and through life. "Two causes held him down financially," recalls the Judge. "Although never extravagant or wasteful, he was always liberal beyond his means; but the chief cause was credulity. . . . Any plausible and designing schemer who would obtain his confidence could persuade him into ruinous transactions."[1]

After witnessing Samuel's early death, the Judge poured out his grief in a memorandum rich in extravagant heartbreak, like an Irish wake. That he concluded it with an allusion to the afterlife suggests that at least one dogma of Christianity had survived his dalliance with Spencer's atheism. It is also revealing that though he was to raise Samuel's orphaned son, William A. Mellon, in his own home for two years and later employ him as a factotum, he nonetheless accepted $2,000 from Samuel's widow toward the repayment of a $3,000 loan. There was toughness in his generosity—in his love.[2]

Two months after his brother's death, he lost his brother-in-law, friend, and coal partner, George Bowman (1820–79). Next to depart was Archy Mellon (1795–1883), his lifelong friend and last surviving uncle. His sister, Elinor Mellon Stotler (1819–84), passed away in the same month as his brother-in-law and business partner, George Negley. That five of his closest relatives had passed away in only five years must have whispered to the Judge that the sand in his own hourglass was also draining and that the last major project he envisioned—to write his autobiography, as Benjamin Franklin had done—should not be delayed.

The year was 1884, and circumstances made it the ideal moment for Thomas Mellon to become a chronicler. At seventy-one, he had reason to assume that the landmark events of his life lay behind him, and that any remaining challenges would amount to hills rather than peaks. Yet his mind still held the keen edge that creative writing demands, and his zest for life, which alone can fuel a vibrant memoir, had not ebbed away. Then too, with Uncle Archy gone, he was the last surviving Mellon to have made the crossing from Ireland. The family's early history would be lost if he failed to record it.

Fortunately, he had time for a project of this magnitude. With Andrew in charge at the bank and with James and Tom ably managing Mellon Brothers, time—the remorseless measure of life, the ultimate capital, which Franklin had warned him to conserve and which he had spent a lifetime learning how to ration and utilize—was now heaped upon him. He had already jotted down "notes" and procured "materials." By visiting relatives in Ireland and Pennsylvania, he had collected a trove of genealogical data.[3] As we have seen, he had also kept a journal of his trip to Ireland, Scotland, and England, if only to let off steam. Sometime in 1884, he began to enlarge on these disparate writings and to fashion them into a continuous narrative.

In a back room at T. Mellon & Sons, the aged Judge, whose eyesight was failing and whose handwriting had become a scrawl, began to dictate the story of his life to a female stenographer. Convinced that his days were numbered, he was struggling to record what only he could pass along to the younger Mellons. He lamented that his few surviving friends were now "in the sere and yellow leaf of life," and he added that at the end of our earthly journey "we are made to see or at least feel, with the wise man, that all is vanity. And so we are prepared to step out without regret."[4] Had he known that more than twenty-two years would pass before he "stepped out," his tone might have been more cheerful.

*Thomas Mellon and His Times* opens with a preface in which the Judge states with compelling logic his reasons for putting pen to paper. "Is a knowledge of our ancestors of any use to us?" he asks rhetorically. "Is there any benefit to be derived from knowing their character and habits, and what manner of men they were of? We may have inherited no worldly possessions from them, but never can ignore the legacies of good or bad qualities they are sure to have left us by heredity. . . . Some should be cultivated, others repressed: and if we knew just how we came by them, and how they cropped out or were manifested in our predecessors, we might deal with them all the more intelligently."[5]

His absorption with cultivating "good" inherited qualities and repressing "bad" ones immediately fixes the viewpoint that he adheres to throughout the book—that of a confirmed eugenicist who writes for his living and unborn family, the defenders of Fortress Mellon, rather than for its besiegers, the mentally and morally defective public.

But the Judge is miles from being a genetic determinist. His intense preoccupation with self-mastery and education confirms that he believes the malleable element in human personality to be immense. But he gets high marks for placing due emphasis on the immutable, hereditary element, which has so often been played down or disregarded.

He views a literary portrait as vastly preferable to a graphic one, knows how such a portrait should be executed, and perceives what it could accomplish.

> How much more satisfactory would it not be if we could have a true representation of our ancestor's course through life from first to last, as in a panorama: showing his thoughts and actions, his good and bad qualities, what were his feelings on trying occasions; how he bore prosperity or adversity; what were his views on the current affairs of his day; what his motives and methods, and what he accomplished or wherein he failed; how he performed his duties as a citizen and fulfilled his domestic relations. Such a picture would bring him home to us in his working clothes, and reveal the hidden ties between his nature and our own.[6]

Making such a record strikes Mellon as a rational duty and an efficient one. "Every one who has spent a long and active life in varied pursuits must have had many experiences which rightly or wrongly he conceives would be beneficial to those coming after him. . . . It is a natural desire to give others the benefit of what we know. . . . Might it not therefore be the preferable course to put into some lasting form beforehand all we may deem worth saying, rather than leave it to the hurry and confusion of the final parting?"[7]

By branding his dearest values, convictions, and prejudices on the family as an immutable credo, he contrived to cast the longest possible shadow over his family's unfolding history. Speaking of his living and unborn posterity, he concludes that "the only excuse for what I have written is the hope that after I am gone I may continue in some degree as a mentor to them and their descendants."[8]

With obvious fondness, he adds: "I cherish the hope that, should an old copy of the book happen to fall into the hands of some poor little boy among my descendants in the distant future, who, inheriting a share of my spirit and energy, may be desirous of bettering his condition, it may tend to encourage and sustain his commendable ambition.... It may serve to impress on him the truth of that important rule of life which demands labor, conflict, perseverance and self-denial to produce a character and accomplish purposes worth striving for. And it may tend to assure him that such a course carries with it more real satisfaction and pleasure than a life of ease and self-indulgence."[9]

As we have seen, Mellon views the history of powerful American families as cyclical rather than linear: a family rises from rags to riches, reaches a peak, and then slides back to rags. What goes up must come down. But he also believes that what comes down can go back up, for he accepts the principle of regeneration, which he has witnessed in plants and which he views as the possible salvation for a faltering American democracy.[10] In the likely event that his family might one day fall from affluence, he is prepared to speed its regeneration by charting in his memoirs the path to prosperity for any ambitious descendant, as Franklin had guided him. Addressing this hypothetical descendant, he writes:

> I have for many years been rated as a millionaire, and perhaps justly so. But gratification or happiness does not increase proportionately with wealth. Beyond a competence sufficient to produce a feeling of independence and afford the ability to help one's family or a friend if in need, or the opportunity to indulge in some such harmless extravagance as this performance which I am now about finishing, wealth adds nothing to enjoyment.
>
> But if happiness does not increase proportionately with wealth, it is to be remembered that hardships and discomforts never fail

to increase proportionately with poverty, and that the lower you sink, or the lower you find yourself, the harder it will be to work up and out financially. You may take this consolation, however: if poverty is a cruel master, you will find it also a great coward, and utterly unable to withstand courage, industry and economy. Courage and hope, in poverty, are golden, and the time and place to begin the battle is just at once, and wherever you find yourself. Never wait for something better to turn up. Engage in whatever you are best fitted for, and make yourself useful to others, remembering it is not favor but self-interest you must appeal to. This course will secure patronage or employment when no other will; and once you are fairly started, all that is needed is perseverance and constant saving of some portion of your earnings or income. Saving is of vital importance, and has never been properly appreciated by any economist except Franklin.[11]

Born into "poverty," as he defines it, Mellon had battled, to pulverizing effect, against the apparent "humiliations" of his condition, and he now exalts the strengthening, fortifying effect of destitution on character. "Poverty may be a misfortune to the weaklings who are without courage or ability to overcome it, but it is a blessing to young men of ordinary force of character: it protects them from excesses, withholds unwise pleasures and indulgences, teaches the value of time and of wealth, and the necessity of well doing to better their condition. It brings out their latent energies in a manner to train them thoroughly for the active duties of life."[12]

That poverty can also inspire avarice, cruelty, lawbreaking, and ruthless manipulation he fails to comprehend or chooses to overlook. The only danger he perceives in poverty is that, having overcome it with such a flourish, his memoir might read like a succession of enviable triumphs and hobble his descendants with a delusional feeling of ancestral pride. "Family pride founded on ancestry, without good qualities in themselves to sustain it, is a sure sign of weakness and degeneracy: yet just enough such pride to produce self-respect, in connection with average good qualities, is a valuable preservative against low associations and bad habits." He concludes his preface with an impassioned plea to his present and future family: "And finally, let me entreat those of my descendants into whose hands this memento of affection may fall, to handle and preserve it with care, remembering that it is committed to them for safe-keeping not only for themselves but for their descendants likewise."[13]

The Judge had one further reason for writing his memoir: he enjoyed it. An accomplished raconteur loves to tell an intriguing story.

The unabridged text of *Thomas Mellon and His Times* spans 638 pages and encompasses about 225,000 words. That the aging narrator was able to complete this tour de force "in the hours and half hours snatched from business for a period of over a year" is astounding.[14] His work may have been speeded by the paucity of editing. He appears to have subjected most of the text to no more than one hasty brush-up, and much of it retains the rough-hewn quality of an extemporaneous manuscript, in which the lack of compactness and polish nonetheless creates an impression of ingenuous urgency. We feel that the aged narrator is rushing to deliver his message while there is yet time.

What his memoir lacks is the particular force and beauty that only a well-crafted, irreducible form can generate. Rambling and frequently repetitive, the book would have benefited from a more logical chronology, stricter editing, and abridgment by about 25 percent. As it is, it draws its force from the passionate sincerity and consistency of the self-portrait. It is a vigorous, engaging odyssey, elegantly written and suffused with the thinking of a stridently opinionated, severely judgmental, but formidably capable old man who has cultivated his mind by lifelong reading, who is substantially self-educated and financially self-made, and who has mastered his destiny by strength of character and thought deeply about life.

With candor, he unburdens himself on a wide range of controversial subjects, such as crime, excessive taxation, political corruption, creeping socialism, private versus public education, capital punishment, military service, and the dehumanizing tendencies of industrial society. Where his opinions are politically incorrect, he slams them on the table without apology, even with deliberate defiance. And, though he occasionally betrays a flash of ignorance or succumbs to spleen on a subject that triggers his volcanic prejudices, he repeatedly amazes us with the verisimilitude and unexpected ring of modernity that suffuse so much of his writing.

A telltale sense of alarm enlivens this memoir. The author views himself as besieged by a Darwinian world of "crooks, cranks, imbeciles, and weaklings," which is at best indifferent and at worst hostile, and in which both mental and physical fitness are required to survive. In the struggle of life, Scotch-Irish mentality remains his fortress against menacing or debilitating influences. With wisdom, energy, and chilly calculation, he has risen from the status of an impecunious farmer and has fought his way to human dignity and self-respect in the form of financial freedom. Wariness and pessimism harmonize with boundless vigor and a passion for life as he tells his story.

We are treated to evocative pen portraits of prosperous farmers, lawyers, and businessmen, but the success stories are interspersed with vignettes of habitual losers, like his brother Samuel. Thomas Mellon has learned that character is fate, and he extols the qualities that have piloted him to success, notably discipline, self-reliance, learning, initiative, perseverance, and plain honesty.

Infatuated with eugenics and firmly convinced that mental and physical traits are hereditary, he combs the Mellon and Negley ancestries for instances of congenital disease, insanity, weak character, and bad habits. He finds his relatives and in-laws to be overwhelmingly "of good stock"—healthy and long-lived, thrifty, industrious, law-abiding folk who traditionally abhorred debt and avoided the "folly" of military service.

Utterly without hubris, he subjects the upward trajectory of his life to a candid examination. He has ended his servitude to the soil, landed an heiress in the contest of marriage, and fashioned his sons in his image. He has been elected to a judgeship as well as to the city councils and is a self-made millionaire. On the minus side, he admits to having almost lost his private bank through an inexcusable lapse of judgment in 1873, and he painfully acknowledges that his blindness to the wickedness and folly of certain business associates resulted in protracted, costly, and almost ruinous litigation. These were giant missteps, but because he learned from them, they were not suffered in vain but formed a part of his education and therefore of his rising path through life.

The proximity of tragedy quietly informs his narrative. Philosophically, but with sorrow, he dwells on the tragedies of life that no amount of wisdom, calculation, or magnanimity can avert. Three of his children proved unfit to survive (at the time of writing; he was spared the knowledge that two more would predecease him). The narrative has a tone of premonitory dread, in part because he wrote in a day when life expectancy was only forty and when infant mortality would strike an average family at least once—but also because of his innate pessimism.

In the panorama of American life as it has evolved since his youth, he finds plenty to complain about. The superabundance of new wealth has corrupted politics and created "artificial wants."[15] Saving has given way to squander. Murder, larceny, vandalism, insanity, and suicide are all on the rise. With free immigration, America has become a sanctuary for Old World scoundrels. The prison population is ballooning. Family ties have weakened. Children rejoice in vulgarity, insolence, and sloth. Education is more comprehensive but less thorough. The cost of living has doubled. The working man, who once had a personal relationship with his employer, is now swallowed up in the anonymity of his union and finds himself at the mercy of self-serving labor leaders and political demagogues. But what alarms Mellon most of all is the creeping spread of socialism: "The desire of him who has nothing, to share with him who has; the desire of the idler, the worthless and good for nothing, to place himself on a footing of equality with the careful, the industrious and thrifty."[16] Socialism heralds the final collapse of civilization into anarchy, when "To each according to his needs" will give way to "Every man for himself."

Despite his foreboding, he clings to hope and to life itself with the inflexible grip of a man who has lived strenuously, who exults and has substantially triumphed in the struggle of life, and who therefore is loath to die. And because his belief in the afterlife has faltered, he finds his continuance in his sons, in the fortune he will leave them, and in the treasury of wisdom preserved in his autobiography, which he confidently hopes will enable them to surmount the degrading restraints of ordinary life as he has done.

Here too is a man whose history cannot be disentangled from that of Pittsburgh. For though his memoir chronicles his family's origins and rise to power, it also bears witness to the vaulting energy, accumulative genius, and acquisitive ethics of a city that was dramatically transforming itself from a somnolent river town into the blast furnace of industrial America, the incomparable Iron City of destiny. This was a triumph of will over destiny, and so was the life of Thomas Mellon.

Three figures stand out in bold relief in the Judge's life story. Of these, Benjamin Franklin is the most significant, for his totemic autobiography guided Mellon's passage through life and served as the model for his own memoir. Herbert Spencer also stands out: the pitiless sociology so trenchantly expressed in his catchphrase "survival of the fittest" eloquently confirms the Judge's view of life as a do-or-die struggle. And finally, there is Robert Burns, whose folksy verses lend a romantic glow to worldly striving and enable Mellon to view his life as an odyssey rather than merely a lengthy, arduous, and baldly acquisitive trek from rags to riches.

Among the founding fathers of American industry, many left us their personal chronicles. All but a few of these sagas are either ghostwritten or unreadable. Some are both. I have yet to discover a single one that can stand beside *Thomas Mellon and His Times*.

On August 22, 1885, the Judge concluded his dictation. The manuscript in which he had bared his heart and mind to every living and unborn descendant—the chronicle of struggle, victory, and residual wisdom for which his descendants remember him as much as for the fortune he made—was complete.

He had much to celebrate. Coincidentally, that very day was also his wedding anniversary. "The luckiest event of my life," he calls it.[17] But, curiously, after an engaging description of their courtship, his memoir is silent about the woman who had accompanied him on the journey of life for forty-two years. Similarly, in Franklin's autobiography, the wife is neglected almost to the point of obliteration. Mellon makes frequent mention of his sons, their education, and early business careers. But if Ma was more to Pa than merely a breeder and housekeeper, he has precious little to say about it. Did the two take each other completely for granted? Did they have no interests in common? Did they come to bore or irritate one another, or both? Did they converse at meals? Did they not even keep each other company at home, as their nephew William A. Mellon claims?[18] That the aged Judge and Sarah Jane would receive their great-grandchildren in different rooms hints at aloofness between the elderly couple. Rebutting this view, their son James writes that "in their last days I recall seeing them sitting one at each side of the fire-place in the evenings like two doves, quiet and lovable."[19] A photograph shows the couple sitting precisely as James describes, but it appears to be posed.

*Thomas Mellon and His Times* was first privately printed in late 1885. Reaction to the opinions it contained could not have caused the Judge much anxiety. He had no fear of political repercussions, for he had decided not to run for a sixth term on the Pittsburgh city councils. Moreover, by limiting the distribution of his memoir to family members and a few close friends, he had sheltered himself from most public comment. Still, his more controversial opinions caused some eyebrows to be raised.

Andrew, a stickler for propriety whose instinct was to conceal, is said to have initially attempted to buy and destroy copies of the autobiography that had slipped from family ownership. We know, however, that he later presented a copy to President Calvin Coolidge and

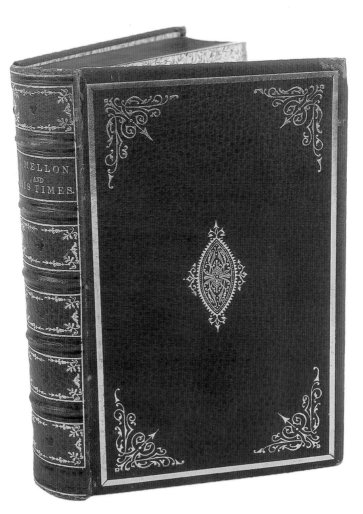

*Presentation copy of* Thomas Mellon and His Times.

Presented
By the author
To
Mr Andrew Carnegie
in acknowledgment of
his literary Taste, business
ability, and wise use
of wealth.

*Book inscription to Andrew Carnegie.*

*Thomas Mellon in 1882; photograph by Frederick Gutekunst.*

another to Alexander McMullen, whose daughter he was courting.[20] Not surprisingly, the book persuaded McMullen that the Mellons must be "a strange family," and he probably held to that view when his daughter's ill-starred marriage to Andrew foundered in horrific and protracted scandal.

Several variations of the Judge's memoir have survived. The first edition was privately printed by William G. Johnston of Pittsburgh. It opens with a bust portrait by the Judge's favorite photographer, Frederick Gutekunst of Philadelphia, and includes four additional photogravures that bear his imprint. The decorative presentation copies, bound in dark-brown calfskin embossed with gold configurations, belong to this edition. The Pittsburgh lawyer and banker William Wallace Patrick received a gift copy inscribed as follows: "Please don't mention this to my acquaintances. I haven't distributed the book among them: not even to the judges. It won't interest outsiders, and I don't want the notoriety of authorship." But in truth, the Judge had already slipped numerous copies to other nonrelatives.

His apprehensions about discussing the four revealing personal lawsuits in which he refers to his opponents as simply A, B, C, and D caused the Judge to commission a supplementary printing from which the intriguing chapter "Vexatious Litigation" was omitted. This abridged edition was apparently intended for readers outside the family circle.

In 1969, the Kraus Reprint Company of New York made the unabridged version of *Thomas Mellon and His Times* publicly available for the first time. And in 1970, a drastically edited version was privately printed for the Mellon family by the Judge's great-grandson, Matthew T. Mellon. Finally, in 1994, the University of Pittsburgh, published an attractive, generously advertised, and efficiently distributed commercial edition of the Judge's memoir. Though he had ruled that the book would "not be for sale in the bookstores, nor any new edition published," his grandson, Paul Mellon, wisely decided to permit republication.[21] That his life's story contains "nothing which it concerns the public to know" is clearly no longer true. And that it contains "much which if writing for [the public] I would have omitted" is something that the deceased need not worry about.[22]

With an abridgment of 26 percent, the University of Pittsburgh edition achieves a compactness of form that the original conspicuously lacks. In addition, the material has been rearranged in a more logical sequence, and the genealogical information, which is of interest only to the Mellon family, has been placed at the end. But the abridged edition suffers from one serious defect: the omission of Mellon's diatribes against the native Irish projects a sanitized impression of him that I have bent over backward to correct.

# XX

————◆————

## The Short Life and Long Death
## of George Mellon,
## Odyssey of the *Glen Eyre,*
## Richard Is Given Half of T. Mellon & Sons

*I could not bear to see so bright and valuable a life, so dear to me, and just
merging into manhood, going down gradually but surely to the grave. It
is hard enough for those who have borne the burdens of life past middle
age, and have found out how little of unalloyed pleasure or happiness
there is in it, to leave the world; but it is doubly hard for the young in the
bloom of hope and ambition, and anticipating long years of pleasure here,
to see themselves rapidly approaching a sure and certain end.*

EARLY IN 1881, THE JUDGE'S YOUNGEST SON, twenty-year-old
George had developed a debilitating infection in the left lung,
which at first was dismissed as merely a bad cold. Typically, his father
had terminated George's education the previous year and, instead of
sending him to college, had assigned him to supervise the construction
of fifteen or twenty row houses in Pittsburgh. But while the work
was in progress, George's strength began to ebb, and his family felt the
first chill of alarm. In September, George went to Philadelphia and
was examined at Jefferson Medical College. He was diagnosed with
tuberculosis.

In the concentric circles of Thomas Mellon's concerns, his family
had always occupied the center. He had sheltered it against every
material want and had ringed the family redoubt at 401 Negley with

twenty-five acres of fruit trees, vegetable gardens, and lawns, all of which served to distance the besieging hordes of morally flawed humanity from the Mellon family. And so his dread was perhaps suffused with irony as he pondered the ease with which a deadly sickness had breached these defenses, bringing him once more face to face with the uninvited guest who had carried off Selwyn, Rebecca, and Emma. "Was the pain and sorrow of Selwyn's loss to be repeated?" he plangently queries in his memoirs four years later, when George was still alive.[1]

In October George's parents accompanied him to Aiken, South Carolina, and placed him in the care of Dr. William Geddings, a specialist who had served on the medical staff of General Robert E. Lee. George's fight for life continued in a private house where his father had rented rooms for the family. There were "good days," when he could take a carriage ride or go for a short walk, and "blue days," when he was "feverish and unable to go out of his room."[2] George read insatiably about tuberculosis and rejoiced or agonized whenever his condition took a slight turn. Father and son pored over the same literature, tirelessly interrogated the doctor, and suffered the same antipodal mood swings whenever George's weight rose or fell by a pound. "When you write," the Judge confides to James, "say nothing discouraging, for poor George is so easily depressed. He watches and construes for bad or good every word the doctor or any one else says."[3]

Unable to conceal his pessimism, hardly daring to believe that George might recover, the father, by his mere presence, did much to thicken the gloom that settled over his son. That he understood this, and could admit it in a family letter, is to his credit:

To you all                                      Aiken, Nov. 22, 1881.
Sons and daughters:
    This was to have been my last day in Aiken, but it had such a depressing effect on George and he worried so much about my going that I have concluded to defer it for another week at least, and yet I believe I am the worst companion he could have. I

sympathize so much with him, he can read my innermost thoughts. Every downward move of his depresses me so much it has a still further depressing effect on him. . . . He clings to the hope of recovery, and I encourage him in it all I can, but he knows too much. He watches the slightest change or symptom either way, and is elated or depressed accordingly. He thinks and talks about nothing else . . .

Your father,
Thomas Mellon[4]

After six weeks at Aiken, the Judge returned to Pittsburgh. Sarah Jane stayed on with George until the spring, and his brothers came to visit and give support—Richard in December, James later that winter. But Andrew remained in Pittsburgh, where he and Henry Clay Frick had recently acquired the Pittsburgh National Bank of Commerce. This was the first of several major acquisitions that would vastly expand the Mellon business interests, and the Judge's presence at home was probably required in connection with it.

George, as we have seen, recovered sufficiently to travel to Ireland with his father in August 1882. For a while thereafter his condition remained stable, and the following spring the Judge decided to send him to Bismarck, in Dakota Territory, with Richard for company. Once again, the father hoped that a change of climate and moderate exercise would facilitate George's recovery. His excessive belief in the therapeutic effects of weather may appear naive in hindsight, but almost everyone shared this view in 1883. More important, to leave the polluted air of a nineteenth-century industrial city could only be beneficial for anyone with a lung disease.

"None of us, Dick included, believed that George could ever return to Pittsburgh for a long stay," recalls William L. Mellon. "Consequently, should George have to live in exile, some one of us would need to share that exile. Dick had been chosen—and Dick accepted this situation. That's the kind of a family we were."[5] He notes further:

"The feeling of loyalty in the family was always noted. I think it was kind of a tradition. We never had any disputes."[6] All for one, and one for all. The unqualified loyalty that bound the father to his sons and the sons to one another—the solidarity that had helped save the family from financial shipwreck in 1873—was now being marshaled to save George.

Because no son of Thomas Mellon's could be permitted to remain idle, there was also a business angle in the move to Dakota. The Northern Pacific Railway had been completed in 1883, and that year Bismarck had become the capital of Dakota Territory. With land speculation spiraling out of control, the Judge and his sons might have suspected that they were witnessing a classic real estate "blow-off." Instead they concurred with the conventional wisdom, which held that Bismarck would become the new Chicago.

For twenty years the Judge had been investing in real estate along the Western railroads, especially in Kansas and Missouri. Not all of these speculations had paid off, but he clung to his vision of a prosperous future for the West and, apparently, for Dakota in particular. With their father's backing, Richard and George opened a small bank at Fourth Street and Broadway in Bismarck and named it Mellon Brothers. They attracted a heartening flow of deposits at first and opened a lively speculation in bonds and railroad stock. They began to deal in building lots and other real estate. In addition, they acquired a 1,000-acre farm on the edge of town, planted it with wheat, bought cattle, and engaged their fifteen-year-old nephew, William L. Mellon, as a cowherd.

Richard was in overall charge of these enterprises, and it was to him that the Judge frequently wrote, pouring out a stream of advice as he had done twenty years earlier to James during his sojourn in Milwaukee. Now, however, the father's tone was mellower. He no longer ranted against acquiring bad habits, keeping low company, or showing an extramarital interest in girls. He wanted to know the plans and opinions of his sons, demanded from Richard frequent and detailed information about the family businesses at Bismarck, and limited his advice to mortgages, cattle, investing in town lots, and the like. But while managing these enterprises from day to day, Richard now corresponded less with the Judge than with Andrew, who had remained in Pittsburgh, ensconced at T. Mellon & Sons.[7] This portended the resumption of their former partnership, which had been scuttled by the Panic. Moreover, in 1883, Andrew acquired the Union Insurance Company, thus extending the family fortune into yet another sphere of business. His stature within the family was steadily growing, while that of his father continued its gradual decline.

Andrew was also anchored to Pittsburgh for another reason: he had fallen in love with Fanny Jones. She was a niece of James Mellon's wife, Rachel Larimer, and also of B. F. Jones, whose family owned the giant American Iron Works. Fanny's credentials must have swamped the Judge with satisfaction, and his ruling, that "she was of good family, and every way worthy" of Andrew was, if anything, an understatement.[8] He therefore acquiesced in his son's proposal to marry Fanny; but no sooner had the two become engaged than rumors began to circulate that Fanny was critically ill. With typically covert inquiries, the Judge learned from her physician that she was afflicted by the same disease that had once caused him to break off an engagement and was currently holding George at death's door—tuberculosis. With a heavy heart, but doubtless at his father's insistence, Andrew broke off his engagement to Fanny, who died, heartbroken, in October 1883.

As for George, periodic bouts of illness sapped his energy, leaving him despondent. But even at his best, he lacked enthusiasm for the nascent businesses that he and Richard were managing. The Judge attempted to interest him in managing the Sioux Falls Waterworks or the Idaho and Oregon Land Improvement Company, which the Mellons and Senator Alexander Caldwell had invested in. Failing that, he could return to Pittsburgh and sell real estate lots.[9] But these offers lit no fires in George. He also exhibited the symptoms of a second affliction which, in his father's eyes, was scarcely less menacing than tuberculosis: he seemed to be a spendthrift. Here, for once, was a young Mellon temperamentally ill suited for the hawking and haggling of business, who cut a rakish figure as he strode along, wearing his unbuttoned overcoat like a cloak, a nonpuritan who must have balked at memorizing bits of doggerel from *Poor Richard's Almanac*.[10] While his brothers labored ecstatically to accumulate, like fastidious beavers building their dams, George sowed the wind with his income and sank into debt.

He had bravely limped through six years of illness, passing repeatedly from false recovery to ensuing crisis, from euphoria to hopes cruelly dashed. Now—miracle of miracles—it seemed that he had conquered tuberculosis. Perhaps to celebrate, he embarked on a lengthy, perilous journey, hoping to experience the Wild West of song and story before it disappeared. The Indians were already entombed on reservations; train and telegraph had replaced the prairie schooner, and cattle now grazed among the whitened bones of the massacred buffalo. But George was determined to see what remained of General Custer's world. In 1884 he fastened a compass onto his buckboard, hitched up the mules, and navigated through the Badlands of Dakota. He crossed Wyoming and detoured into the Rockies en route to Colorado. Thus he experienced the land of which Owen Wister wrote, "The mountains are there, far and shining, and the sunlight, and the infinite earth, and the air that seems forever the true fountain of youth."[11]

Returning to Bismarck, George resumed his spendthrift ways: he spent his income as fast as it came in and then borrowed and dissipated even more. Before long, his accounts at Mellon Brothers Bank had to be closed, and though he was still permitted to draw modestly on his father's account, any overdrafts were to be deducted from his inheritance. In January 1883 the Judge wrote to Richard that George was furious because Tom was cutting his salary from the Ligonier Valley Railroad to $1,000 a year and wanted him out of the enterprise.[12]

These studied humiliations were acts of desperation, and when they produced no effect, the Judge may have admitted to himself that in George he had finally met his match—that all the vaunted Mellon training, the calculated manipulation that had worked such wonders with his elder sons, could not form this maverick into a businessman. In January 1885, with mingled bitterness and despair, he wrote a letter to Richard, which he must have known would be shown to George: "It is doubtful, however, even if [George] does get well, whether his long idleness won't take all the sand out of him for business. I hope not. A man has a poor excuse to this world who could spend all his life as a dude."[13]

Meanwhile, the vaunted Dakota land boom was showing itself to be the flimsiest of bubbles. In 1883, just as the Mellon businesses were being launched at Bismarck, a three-year depression began to deflate the U.S. economy. The crucial price of wheat started to tumble, and farmland bought on speculation began to shed its bloated worth. Far from becoming the new Chicago, Bismarck stubbornly remained Bismarck—a backwater of muddy streets and dashed hopes. It took three years of losses to convince the Mellons that their collective judgment in business had for once given them faulty signals. Decades later, Richard would ruefully reflect on having rejected the alternative of launching his ventures at Winnipeg, Manitoba, by then a town of 300,000 inhabitants.[14]

The Mellons responded to these looming setbacks by embarking on a grand tour of the United States and Mexico. On September 7, 1886, they glided out of Pittsburgh in a chartered private railroad car named *Glen Eyre* and journeyed across the continent. James and Tom and their wives and children, including eighteen-year-old William L. Mellon, were part of the initial party. Tom's in-laws and the former U.S. senator Alexander Caldwell, his wife, and two daughters joined the party at Chicago. Richard Mellon came aboard at St. Paul and George at Bismarck. As the train stopped to pick up or drop off relatives, the party numbered between twelve and seventeen.[15]

The Judge did not join this junket, and Andrew, who set out with the others, disembarked at Bismarck and returned to Pittsburgh. But Sarah Jane remained aboard for the whole journey, and her lively, articulate travel log gives us our only firsthand encounter with the woman who shared Thomas Mellon's life for sixty-four years. Ma emerges from the page as an uncanny observer and accomplished story-teller. She writes with authority and conviction about landscape, history, the people she encounters, and their customs. Her observations on geology and agriculture reveal a startling command of these subjects, reinforced by a vocabulary that extends even to Latin names.[16] Clearly, some of her schoolbook learning at Edgeworth Seminary had not faded.

With Bismarck receding behind them, Ma and her extended family chugged up the Missouri River into Montana, marveled at the geysers of Yellowstone Park, then pressed on to Spokane and down the Columbia River to Portland. From there, they proceeded to Idaho, visited the town of Caldwell (named for the senator who was aboard), and pressed on to Hailey, where there were additional Mellon and Caldwell holdings.[17]

After sixty-nine years in Pittsburgh, Ma was an enthusiastic tourist: Rivers, prairies, coastlines, waterfalls, and mountain ranges spring to life in her pictorial descriptions. Without replicating her husband's diatribes against the Mormons, she sardonically notes that their unfinished temple, which her party visited at Salt Lake City, had been so long in the making that it might ultimately be put to better use. In sloping San Francisco, she was intrigued by the ingenious streetcar system and the teeming exoticism of the Chinese quarter. From Los Angeles the wayfarers steamed across Arizona and New Mexico to Texas, where Ma describes the sprawling railroad yards at El Paso. Time and again, she ponders the significance of inventions and must have marveled at the recent proliferation of railroads that had made her transcontinental excursion possible.[18]

In Mexico City, the Mellons and Caldwells visited the "grand and beautiful" cathedral, among numerous historic sites, and dismissively declined an audience with the dictator, Porfirio Díaz, because the proposed hour would have been inconvenient. They inspected the Chapultepec Castle and were shown by Senator Caldwell the precise spot near the Belén Gate where his father had received a mortal wound on the last day of the Mexican War.[19] Reflecting on Mexico, Ma regrets the damper that Catholicism has placed on communal and individual

*Sarah Jane Mellon in later life.*

progress and reports with notable lack of censure the government's recent suppression of monasteries and nunneries.[20]

The excursionists steamed on to Puebla, where they saw the sights and met Prince Iturbide, a grandson of the ill-fated emperor. After a brief sojourn at Orizaba, they returned to Texas, retracing the route by which they had come.[21] Somewhere south of the Rio Grande, these innocents discovered that the southern border of the United States is also a cultural frontier. The Mexicans "were having little revolutions all the time," recalls William L. Mellon. "One day . . . I was in the washroom. There was a hell of a jolt in our car. The ties had been pulled out from under the track—about four or five ties—and the rails sagged right down, but somehow the train didn't go off the track. We looked out and we saw these fellows running—the bandits. The reason they were running was we had a carload of soldiers on the train, and they drove 'em off."[22]

Stopping in Denver, they visited Larimer Street, named for James's father-in-law, General William Larimer, who had effectively sited the city by building a log cabin there in 1858. The Caldwells were subsequently dropped off at Leavenworth, Kansas, and the Mellons pressed on to Pittsburgh. They reached home on November 1, after fifty-six days of hectic rubbernecking.[23]

Ma's *Glen Eyre* travel log, though composed from notes some two years after the events, reflects her surprising erudition and impressive facility with words. Far from withering with time, her superior education had come to support a growing edifice of knowledge, under the stimulus of an alert and enquiring mind. Ma had become a vastly more imposing spouse and parent than the malleable helpmate that Pa had angled for.

In December 1886, Thomas Mellon decided to "make the best of a bad bargain," cut his losses, and exit from the family's Dakota investments.[24] He had come to perceive a cycle in the post–Civil War economy—"about ten years from one extreme to the other—five up and five down"—and though he had redeemed his initial missteps in the previous depression by subsequently accumulating land at distressed prices, he was now compelled to admit that the Mellon investments at Bismarck, made precisely when wheat and real estate were peaking, had been catastrophically ill-timed.[25] Mellon Brothers Bank was therefore liquidated and the other investment gradually slewed off. That year he also sold the Pittsburgh, Oakland, and East Liberty Passenger Railway but rebalanced his investment in public transportation by building the St. Clair Incline "railway," which hauled heavy loads up Coal Hill in Pittsburgh on giant, steam-driven elevator platforms. At the same time, Andrew Mellon, in league with Henry Clay Frick, founded the Fidelity Title and Trust Company, which would metamorphose into Union Trust. He also acquired the City Deposit Bank and installed his brother James as its president.

The most pressing question was what to do with Richard. "You have had a rather worse start than the rest [of your brothers] in money making," the Judge had written a year earlier, tincturing his concern with a hint of ironic reproach. "Two declines: one at each start you made, and I hope to see you overcome it all eventually."[26] The two declines were Richard's failed development and construction partnership with Andrew, at Mansfield, Pennsylvania, and the most recent debacle at Bismarck. But the Judge had plans for his son: "After you do all that can be done to get things in a safe condition to leave, it seems to me the thing to do is to go into the Bank here with Andy. There ought to be two in it. His outside business keeps him too busy to give it sufficient attention. I have not spoken to him, but know how he would be pleased. He is nowise selfish and this would give you a regular business, and you could take advantage of any outside matter that should turn up."[27]

The Judge's remark "There ought to be two in it" is significant, for he had met with strikingly mixed results in his various partnerships. One of his coal partners and two of his law partners had bitterly disappointed him. James's partnership with Tom and Andrew's with Richard had worked well initially, but both had been aborted by the Panic of 1873—the former temporarily, the latter with finality. Still, the Judge continued to believe in the partnership principle. That his sons should work in pairs, each one contributing his wisdom and particular talents, was surely "safer" than being "entirely alone."[28] He was now prepared to let Andrew and Richard work as partners once again, and this time without overbearing parental oversight.

In the spring of 1887, when Richard returned to Pittsburgh from Bismarck, he was installed as vice president of T. Mellon & Sons. Andrew would retain the presidency, but he and Richard would own the bank jointly, as equal partners. Fortunately for Richard, this arrangement took effect just in time for him to share Andrew's investment in the Pittsburgh Reduction Company, which would become Alcoa. The Judge's grandson William L. Mellon erroneously gives Andrew undivided credit for his striking generosity to Richard: "A.W. gave Dick a marvelous welcome home. By this time A.W. was well off, while Dick's affairs out West had shriveled. What Andrew did was to take his brother into the bank as full partner. There was never a scratch of the pen to bind this bargain."[29] In Andrew's own words, "I said to him [Richard] that if he would come into the bank as a partner, I would give him half interest.... It was an outright gift.... I just said to come in, and he came in, and then we were partners."[30]

Andrew was certainly gracious about accepting Richard as half owner of T. Mellon & Sons. If he had done so only grudgingly, the two could not have collaborated amicably for forty-six years. Nonetheless, it was not Andrew but Thomas Mellon who decided that Richard should have half of the bank. And this fact points to a further truth: that in 1887 the Judge's authority in matters that crucially affected the family's destiny was still respected.

The wrenching chronicle of George Mellon's existence was now drawing to a close. After crossing the continent with his family on the *Glen Eyre,* George spent the winter of 1887 in Denver, hoping that the dry climate would prevent a recurrence of tuberculosis. But he was also fighting erysipelas, a hemolytic infection of the skin; and thus weakened, he contracted spinal meningitis, for which there was no known cure. His faithful companion in adversity, Richard, rushed to

*George Mellon (1860–87), circa 1885.*

Colorado and arrived at his brother's side in time to help him through the final agony, which ended on April 15.

The years of George's manhood—so pitifully few—had been blighted by a near-incessant struggle for life. He had lost his father's respect and had won the contempt of his brother Tom. Every form of fulfillment had eluded him. Yet we of a later day, living in the shadow of AIDS and cancer, can draw strength from the example of a man who, year after year, faced the prospect of a painful, lingering demise with courage, resolution, and irrepressible hope.

George's brutally truncated life also serves to illustrate the signature juxtaposition of hardness and love in Thomas Mellon's character. For while the father had initially hovered, week after week, at the bedside of a son whom he suspected was dying, he also wrote into the permanent record of his memoirs a bruising indictment that must have made George wince when he read it: "I still retain the hope that robust health and vigor will restore [George's] desire and capacity for regular employment. But however that may be, or should his health not be so fully restored, I rely upon his good common sense to restrain him at all times within the bounds of his income."[31] Readers who are not familiar with the background of this passage have taken it to mean that Judge Mellon's sons were expected to support themselves even on their deathbeds—which was not quite true.

# XXI

———•◆•———

# The Judge's Relations with
# Frick and Carnegie

*A man is never in so healthy a condition, morally or physically, as when
his natural disposition to improve is stimulated by his surroundings.*

A PRESENTATION COPY OF *Thomas Mellon and His Times* was
given by the Judge to Andrew Carnegie and now occupies an
honored place in my library. Bound in burgundy leather and embossed
with gold, it is inscribed as follows: "Presented by the author to Mr.
Andrew Carnegie, in acknowledgment of his literary taste, business
ability, and wise use of wealth."

Though the inscription characterizes Carnegie explicitly, it hints
at some of Mellon's qualities as well. It also invites reflection on the
relationship between the two. Though the Judge was twenty-two years
older than the Ironmaster, they were acquainted, sometimes met
socially, corresponded occasionally, and always remained on cordial
terms. "Andrew Carnegie was quite a friend of my grandfather's and
admired him very much," recalled William L. Mellon. "When he was
in Pittsburgh, he would come over to the house, sometimes, and talk
with Grandfather. That's where I would see him."[1]

Written in reply to a lost communication from Thomas Mellon, the
following letter is so characteristically slipshod that Carnegie can only
have typed it himself.

ANDREW CARNEGIE,
5 West 31st St.,
New York

January 11, 1897

[To Thomas Mellon]
MY DEAR FRIEND:

You may be sure that your letter . . . is kept to figure in my autobiography along with many touches from your autobiography.

Let me tell you that old Simon Cameron* said to me that he ranked your autobiography with Franklin's. I sent him a copy. Is it not a remarkable coincidence that Franklin should have inspired you to write it. If I can make the third of the trio, you will be right in the prediction as to the time I shall be remembered.

I need not tell you that I think often of you. There is a Freemasonry between characters that commonplace people cannot enter. You are always in that circle in my thoughts. There is another man here, Col. Le Grand B. Cannon, who has a history. I must ask him for a copy of it for you, and wont you please send me another of yours for him. I wish you two could meet.

Believe me that such a kind letter as you have written, gave me much pleasure this morning after I had read it, and after I read it to Mrs. Carnegie, it will be placed among those which I have preserved. With best wishes, believe me

Always
Your friend,
Andrew Carnegie[2]

More than twenty years later, Carnegie commenced his own memoir with a tribute to Thomas Mellon: "A book of this kind, written years ago by my friend, Judge Mellon, of Pittsburgh, gave me so much pleasure. . . . The story which the Judge told has proved a source of infinite satisfaction to his friends, and must continue to influence suc-

*Founder of the Republican political machine in Pennsylvania.

ceeding generations of his family to live life well. And not only this; to some beyond his immediate circle it holds rank with their favorite authors. The book contains one essential feature of value—it reveals the man."[3]

The Judge and the Ironmaster had both been born to Scottish Presbyterian families without means or position. Both had battled for financial freedom like gladiators in the great arena of unregulated business, and each respected the victories the other had won. That both were substantially autodidacts and had become habitual readers, writers, and thinkers forged an additional bond between them and distinguished them categorically from the lowbrows they were forced to consort with in business. Both adored the poetry of Robert Burns and found in Herbert Spencer a superior articulation and elaboration of their own convictions. Finally, both wrote outstanding autobiographies. But their similarities were superficial, their differences substantial.

Unlike Thomas Mellon, Andrew Carnegie felt at ease with people. He was amiable, witty, and charming, and he could befriend the mighty and famous as effortlessly as he could draw hurrahs from the sweaty stokers who coughed and sweltered in his steelworks. He appears to have perceived at an early date that steel would form the backbone of the onrushing Industrial Revolution, and he had positioned himself strategically. His gargantuan mills at Homestead, Braddock, and Duquesne, a few miles east of Pittsburgh, were as noteworthy for their pioneering technology as for their phenomenal output. They had made him unimaginably wealthy and would gain him worldwide supremacy among steel producers. More important, as he built his manufacturing organization, solving each problem as it arose, Carnegie was inventing the modern corporation, though he could not have understood it that way at the time.

His eye for picking brilliant executives was proverbial. That he made them his partners and insisted on motivating them with mind-boggling bonuses eventually caused a number of obscure individuals to be swamped with sudden wealth—hence the much-maligned

"Carnegie millionaires." Tight-fisted men with conventional Pittsburgh values—men like Thomas Mellon—chuckled incredulously at the Ironmaster's extravagant incentives, for it was obvious that his partners would have worked just as hard for much less. Carnegie himself must have known this, but the joy of putting himself in the limelight—of attracting public notice and approbation by speaking and behaving unconventionally—meant as much to him as money. In a life replete with showmanship, he was always at his best when playing the brilliant, benevolent maverick.

Born in Dunfermline, Scotland, Andrew Carnegie came from an impecunious family of weavers, whose members were nonetheless well-read and highly articulate. His uncle and grandfather, both political activists, had written and distributed pamphlets protesting the exploitation of labor. Young Andrew had felt the sting of poverty himself. After immigrating to America at the age of eleven, he had formed the commonplace ambition of achieving financial freedom and had gone on to become a Croesus. What distinguished him from the thundering herd of would-be millionaires was that he had decided early in life to eventually spend a generous portion of his wealth for improving the lives of ordinary working folk. He wanted to do well so that he could do good.

Steel was already one of America's most labor-intensive industries, yet the widespread fear of industrial workers found no echo in Carnegie's speeches, writings, or conversation. On the contrary, he noisily trumpeted his benevolent intentions toward labor. While rejecting revolution and claiming to abhor violence, he cheerfully tossed off innocuous antiestablishment opinions that added pepper to his dinner conversation but posed no threat to the powers that be. In dynastic Pittsburgh, where family fortunes were fiercely guarded, Carnegie inveighed against hereditary wealth and spoke of leaving his millions to educational charities. Such open defiance of Scotch-Irish values can only have distanced him from Thomas Mellon and other guardians of conventional decorum. That Carnegie decamped from Pittsburgh as soon as he was rich enough to live opulently in New

York also drew their disapproval. Flaunting these peculiarities, he was viewed by the Pittsburgh elite as a brilliant, likable, enviably successful, well-intentioned, occasionally irritating, slightly eccentric pseudoradical. Yet criticism of the Ironmaster seldom rose above a whisper or amounted to more than envious backbiting. In Pittsburgh, where money maketh the man, Carnegie was king—even if he lived in New York.

Significantly, the same disparity in values and personality that prevented Andrew Carnegie from forming more than a shallow friendship with Thomas Mellon also led to his increasingly contentious estrangement from Henry Clay Frick, whom the Mellons idealized. A slight digression suffices to highlight the intriguing triangular relationship between these totemic figures of old Pittsburgh.

Because the steel and coke industries dovetailed so neatly, Carnegie Brothers and the Frick Coke Company became linked in a partnership that obligated Frick's business to furnish Carnegie's steel mills with coke. The two industrialists bought heavily into each other's companies, and by 1883 Carnegie held the controlling interest in both. Frick subsequently served for long periods as chairman and manager of the two concerns, while Carnegie, who spent months vacationing abroad, sporadically attempted to rule by interference. This uneasy collaboration steadily deteriorated into recurrent clashes and fitful reconciliations. The ballooning egos and incongruous personalities of these two found no shortage of irritants to feed on.

Two conflicting identities grappled for control of Carnegie's life. He was inventing himself as a mighty benefactor of working people, but the expedient of improving their lot simply by raising wages found no favor with him. Giveaway charity, he insisted, was demeaning. Instead, by spending millions on free educational facilities, especially libraries, he would help the less fortunate to help themselves. While enjoying his wealth to the full, he insisted on viewing himself as merely the custodian of a fortune that would have to be donated to philanthropies of proven usefulness. To leave one's wealth to undeserving and unqualified relatives was not only illogical but immoral. What had been wrested from the public domain would have to be returned. "The man who dies rich dies disgraced."[4]

What Carnegie was proposing amounted to a new, revolutionary morality for the emerging industrial world. But that placed him in a painful quandary. He would be able to fund his libraries and other philanthropies only if his company prospered in the face of cutthroat competition. If other steel producers hired security guards to drive strikers from the work site, evicted them from company housing at gunpoint, and shot them dead at the least hint of violence, could he afford to do otherwise? Was it possible to be a benefactor of humanity and also a nineteenth-century industrialist? His initial answer was yes.

When wildcat strikers incapacitated the coke companies in 1887, Carnegie curb-reined his manager, Frick, and compelled him to compromise with the union. But when a second strike broke out at Morewood in 1891, events took a different turn. Frick, who viewed organized labor as a conspiracy against private property, insisted on enforcing the company's rights with armed security guards. That blood was certain to be spilled must have sickened Carnegie, for violence of any kind appalled him. But this time he resorted to moral anesthesia, kept his head in the sand, and left Frick to manage the crisis as he chose. Eleven strikers were shot dead and forty-six wounded.[5]

In the ferocious Homestead Strike of 1892, while Carnegie loitered on an extended fishing trip in Scotland, conveniently out of harm's way, his flagship mill at Homestead was besieged by four thousand striking steelworkers. Negotiations for the renewal of their contract had collapsed, and they were grimly determined to bar replacement labor, already known as scabs, from taking their vacant jobs.

Carnegie had cunningly placed no binding restrictions on Frick's handling of the impending showdown. Moreover, he had seen how his manager preferred to solve labor problems and must have known what to expect. On July 6, Frick sent three hundred Pinkerton security guards up the Monongahela River on barges to take possession of the giant mill prior to reactivating it with replacement workers. As the guards were approaching Homestead, thousands of strikers brandishing firearms, explosives, and any weapons that came to hand burst into the mill and occupied it. For almost twelve hours the two sides clashed in desperate battle. Volleys of gunfire thundered between the mill and the beleaguered barges. Groups of strikers hurled dynamite, lit the river ablaze with flaming oil, and attempted to fire on the Pinkertons with an outmoded cannon, which they stuffed so full of gunpowder that it exploded. Outnumbered fourteen to one, the security guards at last surrendered. Ten combatants lay dead, and sixty more had been wounded.

Frick and the sheriff of Allegheny County now demanded that Governor Robert Pattison enforce the law with troops. Politically beholden to labor, the governor stalled as long as he could but was finally compelled to dispatch eight thousand National Guardsmen to restore order. The news that they were coming was enough: the strikers backed off, and Carnegie officials reentered the mill unopposed.

With a growing force of replacement workers, Frick swiftly reactivated the bullet-riddled steelworks. He ousted the strikers and their families from company housing and rehired only a handful when their strike finally collapsed four months later. Still loitering abroad, Carnegie was profoundly upset by these events, but he would find a way to indulge his remorse. Oozing sweetness and light, he proceeded to build a free library for the survivors of Homestead.

The bone-crushing defeat that Frick had inflicted on organized labor was one that he would pay for with his blood. On July 23, just seventeen days after the fighting at Homestead, he was repeatedly shot and knifed in his own office by Alexander Berkman, a Russian anarchist. With the crisis of his life suddenly thrust upon him, Frick steeled himself to act magnificently. As blood streamed from his wounds, he walked to his desk, concluded a loan agreement, and cabled his daily report to Carnegie. A doctor arrived and began to probe for one of the bullets, but Frick was beyond pain. Whether he lived or died no longer mattered: either way, this would be his finest hour. Brushing all entreaties aside, he finished his correspondence, walked to the waiting ambulance, and had himself driven not to the hospital, but home. For

*Andrew Carnegie, by Théobald Chartran, 1895.*
*Courtesy Carnegie Museum of Art.*

*Henry Clay Frick, by Théobald Chartran, 1895/96.*
*Courtesy Frick Art and Historical Center, Pittsburgh.*

this show of valor, Frick was all but deified by the Pittsburgh establishment, and even his fiercest enemies grudgingly acknowledged their admiration. Amid the groundswell of supportive letters that reached his sickbed as he tottered at death's door and then clawed his way back to health was one which he would carefully preserve:

T. Mellon & Sons' Bank,
Pittsburgh, Pa.

July 25, 1892.

H. C. Frick;

My Dear Friend:-

I write to urge on you the necessity of quiet and mental repose. Duty to yourself, your family, and the public demands it. Let Nature, the best of all doctors, have full opportunity. To do this, all business thoughts and plans should be dismissed for the present. Callers should not be admitted. You need complete rest. The public as well as your friends have a deep interest in your perfect recovery.

I never received so heavy a shock as when the sudden, startling news came over the wire to me at Ligonier.

Your sincere friend,
T. Mellon[6]

Carnegie now embarked on a grand tour of Italy but found, to his horror, that the hurricane of indignation triggered by Homestead had spread to Europe. Shunned as a pariah, Carnegie returned to America in January 1893, wearily determined to face his accusers. He journeyed to Homestead, assembled a multitude of steelworkers interspersed with journalists, and proceeded to address them. Haunted by the bloodshed of July, he called for mutually beneficial harmony between labor and management. Chairman Frick, whom he had just described in a confidential letter to the British prime minister as "my young & rather too rash partner,"[7] he now publicly showered with kudos: "I would not exchange him for any manager I know." At the same time, he cunningly limited his encomium to the Coke Baron's sterling qualities of character, conspicuously failing to endorse his draconian strikebreaking measures. Moreover, the Ironmaster's prepared remarks were littered with jarring lapses into fantasy, as when he suggested that the steelworkers themselves would eventually come to admire Frick; when he declared, without gulping, that there could be no winner in such a strike; when he claimed not to have heard of the confrontation at Homestead until much later; and when he fatuously disclaimed all responsibility for the bloodshed by citing his irrelevant retirement from all managerial positions four years earlier.[8] Was he not still the founder and overwhelming majority owner of the company? Did anyone believe that the directors of Carnegie Steel might defy Carnegie?

Thomas Mellon responded to the Ironmaster's oration with a cautiously deferential letter in which he nonetheless argued doggedly for his own one-sided view of Homestead and voiced his unequivocal support for Frick:

THOMAS MELLON,
514 Smithfield St.,
PITTSBURGH

January 30th, 1893

Mr. Andrew Carnegie,
    Dear Sir:-
    I cannot deny myself the pleasure of thanking and congratulating you for your noble utterances published this morning on the Homestead affair. It is worthy of yourself and deserved by the board of directors. You wisely say all that is needed and yet avoid such minor matters as would afford carping labor agitators and anarchists the opportunity of unfair criticism.
    The recognition of Mr. Frick's good qualities shows remarkable discernment on your part. He is by no means the hard and arbitrary man depicted by labor parasites. I have never known one in like position who would lend more willing ear to just complaints of workingmen.

I may say here also that I have given close and interested attention to the course of events in this great strike and public sentiment regarding it, and I can say the stand taken by your company and the firmness with which it has been maintained has met the general approbation of the best and wisest of all classes. It was and is the opinion generally expressed by manufacturers and other employers of labor here that the stand taken by your firm was a necessity forced upon it, and what all will be compelled to take sooner or later. Throughout the country and among fair-minded and thinking men in the cities and towns, usurpation of the control of business of their employers by employees had to be checked or industry requiring the employment of labor would have to cease.

There has been so far no fair statement of the facts and merits of the controversy. It has all along been a tissue of misrepresentation and falsehood; and the misrepresentation has been effected by the adroitness of the labor leaders in keeping their alleged grievances constantly before the public through the medium of the press. They lay their plans and fix their ammunition under the cover of secrecy and serve it to the press by means of their press committees, giving it to the public as interviews and speeches and resolutions at public meetings. Positive falsehoods and perversions of fact have in this way been kept before the public with pernicious effect and in great measure without any adequate means of counteracting that effect. Proprietors can only make direct denial; and to do so would keep them busy and before the public all the time and, besides, would involve heavy expenses; because, while the daily papers will publish anything coming from strikers and their committees under the excuse of its being news, communications from employers must be paid for at specially high rates.

The public press has become a corrupter of public sentiment in this respect and a promoter of socialism and anarchy. The laws and constitution and established principles regulating the relations of employer and employee are thus directly antagonized by the views and sentiments constantly kept before the public by the representatives of organized labor and without the slightest expression of dissent in the papers presenting them. Privately, the managers of the paper will freely denounce what they publish; but, regarding journalism from a business stand point, they will say they cannot afford to express their private opinions in their paper. Its income and success depends on advertising; and advertising depends on circulation; and circulation depends on distribution to the greatest number of readers, irrespective of character; and the more ignorant and vicious and lower the character, the stronger the prejudice and feeling against any opposition against their policy and practices. Hence newspaper men conceive it to be their best policy to cater to the worst element, as tending to increase the number of their readers and thereby increase their advertising patronage; cost of paper and press work being so insignificant as scarcely to be a factor in the expense.

Time however will purify the public mind of the aspersions so unfairly cast upon your firm and its management. The best people of all classes understand the situation already, and your prediction as to the vindication of Mr. Frick and his companions in the management is well founded and will be fully realized, if truth and right prevail as they always do in the end.

Excuse me for inflicting this lengthy communication upon you, which is rather for my own gratification over your just and characteristic views on the subject which has for so many months agitated this community and with which you are so closely connected.

Yours respectfully,
Thos Mellon[9]

In congressional testimony given at Homestead in late November, Judge Mellon would express the view that during a strike the proper enforcement of law tended to be hampered by "too much politics" and that the use of private security guards was therefore necessary.[10] Arguably this view had been borne out by events at Homestead, where the governor of Pennsylvania had, for political reasons, hesitated to enforce the law until he no longer had a choice.

Frick went on to recover his health and resume his managerial position, but he and Carnegie continued to drift apart. What brought their escalating animus to final combustion was the Coke Baron's refusal to continue supplying the Ironmaster with coke at less than half the market price. On the memorable morning of January 8, 1900, Carnegie came to Frick's office and demanded that he pledge himself to seek no legal redress for the laughable price that he had been compelled to accept for his coke. If Frick refused, Carnegie threatened to invoke the infamous "Ironclad Agreement," which entitled Carnegie Steel to repurchase Frick's shares at book value, a mere accounting figure that amounted to about a third of the market price. Appalled by the prospect of losing most of his fortune at one stroke, Frick flew into a towering rage, and while the horrified office staff looked on incredulously, he blasted Andrew Carnegie with a firestorm of vilification: "For years I have been convinced that there is not an honest bone in your body," Frick roared at the richest man in the world. "Now I know that you are a god damned thief."[11] Carnegie fled Frick's office as though he were running on live coals, and Frick slammed the door after him with a crash that could be heard all over the building.

When the "Iron Clad Agreement" was invoked against Frick, he sued Carnegie and charged him with a laundry list of broken agreements, deliberate misrepresentations, and damaging, erratic behavior. Moreover, he threatened to expose his partner as a hypocrite by revealing the secret expressions of full support that Carnegie had communicated to him while Frick was engaged in crushing the Homestead Strike with gunfire and starvation. Among other considerations, the fear of being exposed as a two-faced, dissembling opponent of labor so mortified the Ironmaster that he caved in and bought Frick's shares at market value. Years later, Carnegie, who by then was prepared to forgive and forget, informed Frick through a mutual friend that he would like to see him again. Frick famously replied, "I'll see him in Hell."[12]

Because he had no stake in the Ironmaster's mills or in the Coke Baron's ovens, Thomas Mellon was able to avoid involvement in their wrangles. But his sympathies clearly lay with the suspicious, obdurate Frick, who had spilled his own blood to defend private property, rather than with the mercurial Carnegie, who waffled between playing the hard-nosed, self-made industrialist and posturing as an avant-garde philanthropist whenever he was lecturing, writing for publication, or addressing journalists. The limitless admiration and loyalty that the whole Mellon family felt for Frick can only have caused tension between the Judge and Carnegie, which was probably still aggravated by their memorable clash over the Ironmaster's proposed library in Pittsburgh. They would continue to correspond from time to time and would always remain on cordial terms, but one is left with the impression that they were never quite friends.

The concentration of Mellons at Frick's funeral in 1919 confirms that they regarded him as almost a family member. His pallbearers included two of Thomas Mellon's sons—Andrew, whom Frick had also named as his executor, and Richard—as well as "old Mellon men," such as President Henry McEldowney of Union Trust and U.S. Senator Philander Knox. They carried the Coke Baron to within a stone's throw of the Mellon mausoleum in Homewood Cemetery and laid him to rest beneath a ponderous marble cenotaph on which a single word proclaims, with Napoleonic thunder, "FRICK." By contrast, at Carnegie's funeral, which occurred the same year, the Mellons were conspicuous by their absence.

In truth, the Judge had come to dread Carnegie's world, with its mills and factories—beehives of anonymity, where the individual counted for nothing and free men were viewed as numbers on lists that would later be lost. Though he is known to have generously

*Pittsburgh in 1817, the year before Thomas Mellon arrived in America.*
*Courtesy Heinz History Center, Pittsburgh.*

*Industrial Pittsburgh, toward the end of Thomas Mellon's life.*
*Courtesy Heinz History Center, Pittsburgh.*

complimented the Ironmaster for his stellar accomplishments in a lost letter written early in 1897, he cannot have failed to recognize him as the master architect of a dehumanizing world order that had pulverized the reassuring certainties of preindustrial America and had degraded human dignity.

Mellon could remember a day when the carpenter, the mason, the shoemaker, the blacksmith, and the wheelwright were free, self-employed individuals who owned their own shops, stocked their own materials, and lived in a diverse population of farmers, artisans, tradespeople, and other professionals. A healthy competition for patronage required small proprietors to be good citizens—honest, thrifty, hard-working, and well behaved. They were independent mini-capitalists who owned and frequently worked in their own homes and had no employers to resent. But the Industrial Revolution had ushered in a new system of economic and social organization: Millions of workers were no longer self-respecting, independent individuals impelled by the hope of improving their lives. Instead they lived on top of each other in squalid urban ghettos, worked for subsistence wages, owned nothing, resented their employers, envied the rich, and tended not to acknowledge social responsibilities. They viewed themselves as trapped in a fixed underclass that could not improve its lot except by strikes, agitation, and occasional violence.[13]

Mellon's alarm and dismay at what industrial America had become caused him to look wistfully back on the rural world of his boyhood, with its predictable cadences. But had he not struggled to escape from precisely that world? Did his numerous coal mines not form an integral part of the new industrial order that he now dreaded but continued to benefit from?

In his memoirs, he understands that the Industrial Revolution is irreversible and accepts that on balance it has been beneficial. But he hastens to add that "there is no unmixed good in this world" and that the "evil tendencies" of industrial America "may create serious trouble before entirely eradicated, as doubtless they will be, if civilization and the progress of true social science continue."[14]

# XXII

———•◦•———

## False Spring at Kansas City,
## Divestiture of the Fortune

*I never desired wealth on its own account but for the accomplishment of some ulterior purpose. . . . While throughout my business life my main purpose was the acquisition of wealth to make me independent, after the necessary wealth was acquired, I voluntarily parted with wealth to promote my freedom from the care and responsibility requisite for retaining it, until nature should grant me the final divorce.*

A S THE 1880S WERE DRAWING TO A CLOSE, Thomas Mellon found himself in semiretirement. He retained an interest in some of the family businesses, exercised a casual supervision over their management, and continued to own a varied portfolio of real estate investments and coal properties. But by placing his sons in daily charge of these enterprises, he had substantially retreated from the hurly-burly of business to a life of reading and study. His intellectual curiosity was still focused in fields that interested him, but an infatuation with the supernatural had begun to compete for his attention. As he meditated by the fire in his somber library, a parade of subjects presented themselves for his philosophical musings. But he found himself surprisingly ill at ease.

For one thing, his eyesight was now failing so badly that reading, which he had counted on to sustain him in old age, had become a torment. Even with electricity, Franklin's gift to the world, which the teenage William L. Mellon had installed at 401 Negley, the patriarch could only read by scanning laboriously with a heavy magnifying glass. Two other grandsons, Alec and Ed Mellon, earned pocket money by reading him editorials from the Pittsburgh papers. But they soon learned that Grandpa took a lively interest in their own reading. "We were never allowed to read the sporting notes of newspapers," recalls Ed, "because nobody ever amounted to anything that ever read a sporting note in a newspaper. And we were never permitted to read novels, because nobody amounted to anything who ever read novels."[1]

But what may have irritated Thomas Mellon as much as his fading eyesight was that he had misjudged himself. Anyone who has lived actively must make the critical decision when and at what pace to withdraw from the arduous pursuits of life. Why had he lacked the self-knowledge to make that decision correctly? With heart, soul, mind, and strength, he had yearned to see his sons ably in command of the family businesses. Could that yearning have blinded him to his own resulting boredom? Had he failed to recognize that a man whose dreams still outweigh his memories is not yet old?

A more fundamental factor may also have figured: That at seventy-five his judgment in key areas of life had been imperceptibly slipping is as poignantly suggested by his mounting preoccupation with spiritualism as by the missteps that were to mar his final foray into business.

His nephew William A. Mellon, who worked for the Judge in several capacities from 1889 to about 1895 and saw him almost daily, summarizes his uncle's dilemma: "Having retired to his library with his reading and writing—his dream through all the past—he had put himself in prison. . . . He was already a railroad builder and owner, a coal and coke magnate, an owner of tenements, mortgages, lots, lands, buildings, streetcar lines, incline planes, coal lands and mines, a big iron foundry, farms. . . . He was done with building fortune, but he did want to be away—away and free to achieve for achievement's sake. . . . He did want life over again. . . . He was now for some new life."[2]

The false spring that Thomas Mellon yearned for began in 1888 with the arrival in Pittsburgh of Louis Irvine, a lawyer and promoter with experience in solving transportation problems in the Midwest. That Irvine's hometown of Kansas City, Missouri, had been built on rather uneven terrain presented both a problem and an opportunity. The problem was how to move heavily laden wagons and their teams from the Bottoms, a low-lying area of freight yards, factories, and warehouses, to the upper city, which was situated on a plateau. The most direct route switchbacked up a steep gradient known as the Bluff. The switchbacks made for a more gradual ascent, but they added to the distance. Additional time was lost as the exhausted mules and horses that hauled wagonloads of merchandise up this gradient stood panting to catch their breath.

Pittsburgh had solved the same problem by raising horse-drawn wagons, and even streetcars filled with passengers, up the steepest slopes on enormous, mechanized elevator platforms known as incline planes. By 1890, thirteen of these inclines were operating in the Iron City. They were impressive contraptions: The St. Clair Incline, which Thomas Mellon had built in 1886 and continued to control, connected 22nd Street with Salisbury Street, 370 feet above. It could raise a 50,000-pound load over 654 yards of track up a 12-degree gradient. It was to raise money for building a similar system in Kansas City that Louis Irvine had journeyed to Pittsburgh and was spreading his wares before the Judge.[3]

Irvine envisioned an extensive system of inclines, the largest and most important of which would haul from the Bottoms, at 11th Street, up the Bluff and across Lincoln Street to the upper city. He proposed that this incline should be built first. If all went well, others could be built at 8th and 17th Streets, and two more in the lower city. He called for the formation of a company, chartered in Missouri, to build, own, and operate these conveyances. As legal counsel for the company, he would obtain a transit franchise from the state government and would remove any legal obstacles on the municipal level. He had befriended the Kansas City politicians and was certain he could win their collaboration, but he neglected to mention just how he proposed to do it. His belief in the project was so firm that he insisted on investing in it himself. But, of course, a far greater sum would be required. Would Thomas Mellon be interested in this safe, high-return investment?

We can imagine the promoter delivering himself of this solicitation with apprehension, and after some mirror practice, for he knew that the stony old banker who sat quietly listening to him could, with a thumb signal, give life to the project or consign it to oblivion.

Irvine's proposal presented Mellon with a familiar quandary. On the one hand, he found himself once more face to face with an apparently bright, dynamic man hawking a business proposal that he ardently believed in but lacked the wherewithal to implement. Had not Frick been just such a man? But the Judge also knew that glib promoters with road maps to riches were a dime a dozen. When the grain was sifted from the chaff, which pile would Irvine fall in?

Incline planes offered a dependable yield, required minimal maintenance, and enjoyed comparative immunity from odious labor problems. Streetcar lines offered the same advantages, and the Judge's investments in both during the 1870s and '80s had made transportation the final pillar of his multifaceted fortune. Such enterprises attracted him with their sheer simplicity. That they amounted to unavoidable bottlenecks on travel and commerce, like ferryboats or toll bridges, went far toward dispelling his insuperable wariness and aversion to risk.

He also believed in the West—that unfathomable pool of untapped resources into which a widening river of fortune seekers kept pouring. He himself had played a bit part in westward migration when, as a boy, he had crossed the Alleghenies by Conestoga wagon. And now he read of Chicago pork barons and railroad tycoons, of land booms, of mining fortunes in Minnesota, of millions made and lost overnight in wheat futures. All this wafted a final glow from the dying embers of his ambition—not because he needed more money, but because he still needed excitement, or perhaps just a reason to live.

Did Mellon fail to subject Irvine's proposal to his usual rigorous scrutiny because it appealed to him subliminally as a tunnel of escape from the gilded cage that he had unwittingly crafted for himself by retiring prematurely? "A man in prison relates any idea to the chance of escape," reflects his nephew William on the Judge's ill-considered but firm decision to build the Kansas City inclines.[4]

In business, Mellon had never been a regional chauvinist; he had never limited his investments to the narrow confines of greater Pittsburgh. Like any veteran, he preferred to fight on familiar terrain, but if the probable reward vastly outweighed the estimated risk, he would invest elsewhere. Time and again, he had bought land along the Western railroads, in Kansas, Missouri, Wisconsin, and the Dakota Territory, and even in Colorado and Idaho. He had lived to regret a number of his forays into terra incognita, as when the seed money he had sown at Bismarck to accommodate his pioneering sons had sprouted only a harvest of weeds, and when the rebels had impounded his coal barges during the Civil War. But these had been minor setbacks. As a rule, his gains had comfortably exceeded his losses.

Early in 1889, he journeyed to Kansas City, familiarized himself with the municipal transportation system, and studied the proposed sites for the inclines. He neglected, however, to make independent inquiries about the city's corrupt political system. James, who came along to keep him company and perhaps to prevent him from giving away the farm, took a dim view of the incline project and counseled against it.[5] But the Judge remained stubborn. He summoned to Kansas City the noted engineer Samuel Diescher, who had designed a number of the Pittsburgh inclines. Diescher endorsed the project, but only from an engineering standpoint. All consideration of franchises, rights-of-way, easements, and possible resorts to eminent domain—in a word, the whole sordid politico-bureaucratic underbelly of the venture —was blindly entrusted to Irvine, who after all was a Kansas City lawyer, an experienced incline promoter, the company's legal counsel, and a would-be investor in the project.

On April 24, 1889, the Kansas City Incline Plane Company was chartered by the State of Missouri "to construct, maintain, and operate a system of incline railways in that city."[6] Its principal owner was Thomas Mellon, but there were five other investors: Louis Irvine, Richard B. Mellon, William H. H. Larimer (James Mellon's brother-in-law), Walter Mitchell (of T. Mellon & Sons), and Alexander Caldwell (Tom Mellon's brother-in-law).

The company began its life with a catastrophic blunder: on Irvine's crack-brained advice, or at least with his acquiescence, the Judge rushed in and bought a number of properties, costing, in all, $60,000 —enough land to build the entire 11th Street incline and most of the one at 8th Street. But he had stepped into a well-concealed trap: Lincoln Street, which cut across the projected route of the 11th Street incline, was legally still a public cattle trail. In this cow path, a clique of corrupt aldermen in the Lower House of the Kansas City Common Council espied an opportunity to extort money from "Banker Mellon," as he was coming to be known. They allied themselves with an ad hoc group of property owners from the vicinity of 11th Street who had been alarmed into opposing the incline project and had also been alerted to the possibility of juicy damage awards by the lawyer L. K. Thatcher, the political boss Tom Corrigan, the sergeant at arms Joseph Glynn of the Lower House, one Victor Bell, and others.

The ink had scarcely dried on Mellon's real estate acquisitions when these schemers, who had known about his project for weeks but had cunningly remained silent, broke from cover and attacked. They derided the inclines as noisy, noxious, unnecessary, monopolistic eyesores. There were garrulous public meetings, vituperative petitions, and dec-lamations against ruthless out-of-state investors. That Mellon at once agreed to sufficiently elevate the 11th Street incline so that cattle and all other traffic on Lincoln Street could pass beneath it did nothing to appease his opponents.[7]

As counsel for the company, Louis Irvine had been obliged to make a routine search for conflicting rights-of-way before approving any property acquisitions. He may simply have neglected to do his homework; but we cannot exclude the Machiavellian possibility that he deliberately failed to inform his client about the Lincoln Street obstacle. For if councillors had to be bribed into clearing a legal path for the incline project, Thomas Mellon's collaboration might have to be extorted from him. And what better way for Irvine to leverage his control over the disquietingly principled old Judge than to lure him into a number of major real estate purchases from which he could retreat only with heavy losses?

What Irvine needed was a special ordinance that provided for the 11th Street incline to cross Lincoln Street on an overpass. He quickly discovered that five city councillors, all from the Lower House, would have to be bribed to support the required legislation. That wads of Mellon money would have to be distributed as boodle was obvious. But, at what point should Mellon be informed? Fearing the aged banker's integrity, Irvine decided to postpone his dreaded request for funds until he had done his horse-trading with the recalcitrant councillors and could present the Judge with a comprehensive bribery package. This would subject the crusty old rectitudinarian to maximum temptation.

Irvine was determined to deal with the existing council, whose mandate would expire within days. His irrational fear that the next council might not be for sale lent an air of desperation to his bargaining. He nonetheless persuaded the five councillors to sell their votes for $500 each.[8]

In May 1889, Irvine sent Mellon, who had briefly returned to Pittsburgh on business, a nebulously worded telegram asking for $2,500 "to insure the success of the project."[9] Simultaneously he wrote him a letter which left no doubt that the money would be used to bribe "merchantable" councillors. Later, while testifying before a grand jury, Mellon would swear that he thought the money might be used to buy off property owners who were threatening lawsuits.[10] But there is another possibility. That he wired the money to Irvine without demanding to know its intended use makes one wonder whether he suspected or knew what Irvine was up to but decided to avert his gaze.[11]

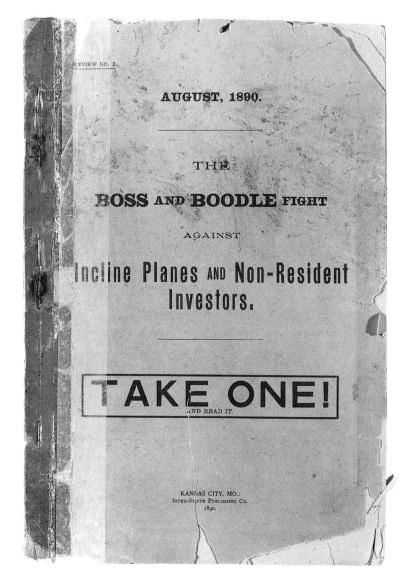

AUGUST, 1890.

THE

BOSS AND BOODLE FIGHT

AGAINST

Incline Planes AND Non-Resident
Investors.

# TAKE ONE!
AND READ IT.

KANSAS CITY, MO.:
INTER-STATE PUBLISHING CO.
1890.

*Pamphlet published anonymously by Thomas Mellon in 1890.*

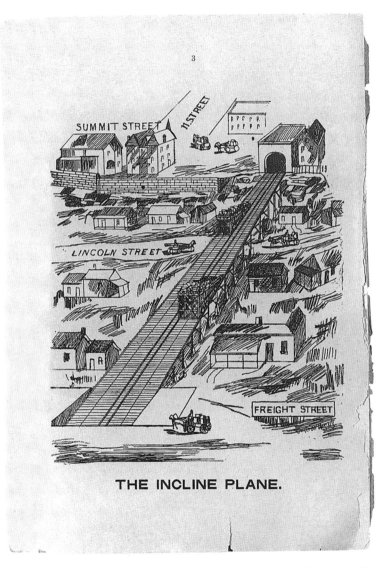

*Sketch of the initial incline plane that Thomas Mellon proposed for Kansas City.*

The swiftness with which Irvine notified the venal councillors that their bribe money was already in the bank and would now be ladled out caused two of them to reconsider their price tags. Speaker Fred Hayes of the Lower House and Councilman Dennis Bowes now doubled their demands to $1,000 each.[12]

By then, Mellon had received Irvine's letter explaining what the $2,500 was intended for.[13] The moment of truth had therefore arrived: Mellon would have to repudiate Irvine's bribery effort immediately or endorse it. But could he bring himself to repudiate it when he stood within an inch of getting what he wanted from the council? This was precisely the corner into which Irvine may well have intended to drive him.

The telegram that flew back to Kansas City must have made Irvine wince. "Your letter received. Stop payment. Not a cent for boodle."[14] After a lifetime of fighting the boodlers, Mellon had decided it was too late to sleep with them. When in Rome, insist on converting the Romans. The councillors drew back their extended palms and consigned the incline project to burial in the Committee for Public Improvements, a kind of elephants' graveyard for stalled legislation.

In the year that followed, Mellon must have reflected bitterly on the jungle of venality into which he had rushed with so little circumspection. His nephew William recalls the frontier town where their enterprise was now mired in political offal: "Kansas City, as I knew it, . . . was the center of a wide circle reaching to the northern line of the state, in which there was thickly integrated a nameless element of the damnedest splotchy character in social and business dealing to be found anywhere . . . , a heteroclitic genesis that grew horse traders, mule buyers, and sharpers. . . . I saw doubles of all these among bankers, boodlers, promoters and politicians. The region was the stamping ground of Jesse James . . . a slum of genre which has never risen high enough to decline."[15]

But the city was also a booming frontier metropolis, awash in new wealth and sparkling with opportunities: it was a city of stockyards, packinghouses, and factories, where rail lines converged to form a swinging door between East and West. All this commerce appealed to Thomas Mellon, whose heart beat faster amid scenes of vibrant accumulation. Writing from Kansas City, which would be his home for five years, he jubilantly informed his abandoned family: "I feel able to make a fresh start in the world with as good health as ever I had in my life." Letters to "Dear Ma," who had remained at 401 Negley to tend the hearth, ring with vigor and optimism but contain no hint that he misses his home, his sons, or his wife. "I hear nothing about business," he complained to his forsaken spouse. "Keep me posted on all business matters," he directed Richard. And when his sons did report to him, he belabored them with his views on T. Mellon & Sons, Waverly Coal, and the St. Clair Incline Company. These enterprises were all that rooted him to Pittsburgh, and he would return there on extended business trips several times a year. But Kansas City was now the place where he ate well, slept well, felt healthy, enjoyed life, and wanted to be.[16]

During the months of uneasy stalemate that followed his initial clash with the Kansas City politicians, Thomas Mellon steeled himself to make a major divestiture of his wealth. Whether he arrived at this decision entirely on his own or succumbed to gentle persuasion from his sons remains conjectural. But it does appear likely that the deadlock at Kansas City had raised some filial doubts about his residual capacity for business.

"The wonder is that Thomas Mellon went all his life without a will," reflects his nephew William. "This was not done through policy, so called; but it shows an instinct for holding to himself and holding his own, . . . it being against his nature to alienate a thing he held."[17] He had nonetheless initiated a gradual process of transference in the 1860s by assigning to his eldest sons, Tom and James, the income from lumber, coal, construction, and banking enterprises that he had helped them to found and continued to own at least partially.

Though not prepared to retire from T. Mellon & Sons completely, he had relinquished its day-to-day management to Andrew in 1875 and had assigned him 20 percent of the bank's income. Whatever anguish the gradual divestiture of his business interests may have caused him was mitigated by his delight at observing his sons as they ably conducted themselves in the roles he had trained them for and had once played himself. Hence it may not have surprised Andrew when he received from his father a communication that vastly strengthened the son's grasp on the once-floundering bank that he had done so much to resuscitate from the Panic of 1873 and which, under his able direction, had again become the family's flagship enterprise:

T. Mellon & Sons, Bankers.

Pittsburgh January 5, 1882.
Proposition to son Andrew for
services past and future.
He to have the entire net profits
of the Bank from January 1, 1881, includ
ing my salery  The books to be readjusted
accordingly. From 1st January instant.
He to have entire net profits of bank
and pay me an annual salery of
two thousand dollars as its attorney
and fifteen hundred per annum
rent for the banking room; and
I to allow him forty five hundred
per annum for attending to my
private affairs and estate—selling
lots collecting rents etc as done heretofore
    This arrangement to last till
supersceded by another or annulled by
either party

Thos Mellon[18]

The oddity of this weighty instrument is revealing. The misspellings, incomplete sentences, and omitted punctuation immediately define it as an informal rather than legal document. The father appears to feel no need for a binding agreement with his son but then decides to put something on paper, almost as an afterthought. Not until the last five words does a note of caution creep into the wording.

Andrew would later refer to this typically informal memo as the instrument by which his father had "given" him the bank. However, nothing could be more conspicuous here than the Judge's failure to cede ownership. He carves in stone his right to rescind the agreement unilaterally, at any time and for whatever reason. In fact, he never formally bequeathed the bank to anyone, and this eventually caused a number of his descendants to wonder whom the bank lawfully belonged to. However, the above document does persuasively imply that the Judge wanted Andrew to be the eventual owner of T. Mellon & Sons, just as Mellon Brothers was to belong to James and Tom.

Five years later, another giant step was taken toward settling the family fortune when Andrew graciously agreed to his father's request that he give Richard a half interest in the bank, after he returned with empty pockets from Bismarck.[19] Richard B. Mellon's descendants owe the bulk of their wealth to this most generous redistribution of the family fortune.

A more dramatic transfer of wealth occurred on February 3, 1890, which was Thomas Mellon's seventy-seventh birthday and Sarah Jane's seventy-third. After their birthday dinner at 401 Negley, the Judge announced that he and Sarah Jane were divesting themselves of all their real estate. Any presents that they received must have paled beside what they gave away. Eight years later, looking back on his bestowal, the eighty-five-year-old Judge took pencil in hand and scratched out a typically informal memorandum, from which the following is excerpted:

> August 25, 1898
>
> I never desired wealth on its own account but for the accomplishment of some ulterior purpose; and as the advance of the times and the occasion referred to show, the use and control of wealth was not a dominating control in my nature. . . .

*Andrew W. Mellon, circa 1880.*

Possession and ownership involve cares and responsibilities inconsistent with the entire freedom I had enjoyed in my youth when I was impecunious and my main care and desire was centered in the acquisition of knowledge; so, while throughout my business life my main purpose was the acquisition of wealth to make me independent, after the necessary wealth was acquired, I voluntarily parted with wealth to promote my freedom from the care and responsibility requisite for retaining it, until nature

*With reservations, Thomas Mellon assigned the income
from T. Mellon & Sons to Andrew in January 1882.
Courtesy Heinz History Center, Pittsburgh.*

should grant me the final divorce. I had, in my long and active
business life, acquired a very considerable estate in real and personal property. I was regarded as a man of wealth by the public; and
my wife had inherited considerable rentable property both from her
father and mother, which she still possessed, although after our
marriage I had always treated it as, and managed it with, my own.

So matters stood on the 3rd day of February, 1890, when she and I transferred and absolutely relinquished all title to our property and estate, real and personal, to our children, reserving nothing but their obligation for our fair and reasonable maintenance and support during our respective lives. Now I admit this act on the part of parents at our time of life, or indeed at any time, was a most unusual and reckless one, and in all ordinary cases unwise and unsafe, and involved risk too great to be incurred, and it would not have been done by me, who had acquired a high character for conscientiousness in all my transactions, and my only excuse in this instance of an apparent departure from it was my full confidence in the sound judgment and the other good qualities of our children.

But four of them were left to us—"boys" whose natural abilities and common sense I had admired from their infancy, and indeed for whom I had spent the most of my business life to place them in the power which wealth affords, and who, already in their business lives, had acquired wealth about equal with my own, and so far my contribution to their wealth has caused no change in their conduct or habits of life, and I am confident now, as before, that when I am gone, the confidence I had in them will show I was not mistaken in doing what to outsiders would bear the mark of imprudence.[20]

On two points the memorandum is misleading. First, the Judge insists that the father and mother gave "all title to our property and estate, real and personal, to our children," on their double birthday in 1890. But theirs was not a total divestiture. In December 1891, the Judge testified under oath, while defending himself in a lawsuit, that his personal fortune totaled "several hundred thousand" dollars.[21] He had given the real estate away but had clearly retained other forms of wealth.

Second, the aged couple did not transfer their wealth directly and equally to all of their children. The properties were given in their

*Thomas and Sarah Jane Mellon with their sons (left to right) James Ross, Andrew William, Richard Beatty, and Thomas Alexander, circa 1895.*

entirety, and absolutely, to Andrew W. Mellon, but "that was for convenience solely," insists the Judge's grandson William.[22] "The proceeds from rentals, or sales, were regularly divided in four parts."[23]

As to the total amount of wealth shed by the Judge and his wife on their double birthday, William gives a precise audit: "Official appraisals and inventories of the time fix the value of the real estate of both Judge and Mrs. Mellon at $861,986.77; and the rest—mortgages, coal lands, bills receivable, and other wealth—at $1,595,562.02. Therefore the total assets turned over to the sons by their parents amounted to a little more than $2,450,000. If the Judge's appraisal of his sons' affairs at the time he deeded away his property is sound, then each previously had gathered for himself about $600,000 and had, as well, a little more than $600,000 received from the old folks. Actually, in my opinion, the market value of the Judge's property was slightly in excess of $4,000,000" (approximately $95.7 million today).[24]

Although here "the Judge's property" appears to include the individual fortunes amassed by his four surviving sons, the *New York Tribune* may have been correct when it placed these five Mellons and grandson William on its list of American millionaires in May 1892.[25]

That one son should have received all of his parents' real estate outright and free of any legally binding obligation to share with his brothers may appear to be unfair or at least illogical; but in fact it was neither, and none of the brothers objected. Andrew Mellon's biographer Burton Hendrick explains:

> The Mellon fortune would inevitably fare better in Andrew's hands than split up into several ownerships. T. Mellon & Sons, the foundation on which it all rested, was a private bank. The personal assets of Thomas and Andrew, which stood back of its obligations—that is, its deposits—constituted its strength. By 1890, the ownership of this institution rested in Andrew and Richard. To have responsibility for the management in one quarter, and the property which gave this responsibility whatever validity it possessed in another, was not a healthy situation. The endowment of Andrew with all the Mellon properties put everything upon a business basis.
>
> Still, the obligation to the other sons remained. Thomas Mellon was not the man to ignore it, and on this same day, February 3, 1890, Andrew Mellon executed a document of his own called "A Declaration of Trust." But despite its title, it did not create a trust in the strict sense. More properly described, it was a form of promise—the program the sole owner pledged himself to follow, in managing the property:
>
> 1. It set forth Andrew's purpose to manage the estate in consultation with his three brothers, and to sell none of it without their consent.

2. The family homestead [401 Negley] was not to be disposed of in the lifetime of the mother or father.

3. At any time, the father or mother could demand the income [from the real estate]. . . . Otherwise, all four brothers were to share on equal terms in the revenue. As often as the balance on hand exceeded $20,000, this cash was to be divided in four equal parts and distributed to Thomas A., James, Andrew, and Richard.[26]

Apart from real estate, Thomas and Sarah Jane Mellon also owned other forms of wealth, and Hendrick informs us that "four years later all the 'bills receivable,' bonds, all the personal assets similarly passed into his [Andrew's] individual control. By 1895, Andrew Mellon had become the unquestioned autocrat of the family estate."[27]

The foregoing transfers and accompanying "Declaration of Trust" produced interesting results. Under Andrew's stewardship, from 1890 until 1905, the Judge's provisionally relinquished fortune increased from nearly $2,500,000 to almost $4,200,000. Over these fifteen years, it yielded approximately $330,000 in income, of which about $100,000 was remitted to his four sons jointly, providing about $1,600 per year to each of them. These figures are adjusted for two substantial losses: $50,000 in Kansas real estate and an additional $42,000 in the Idaho and Oregon Land Improvement Company.[28]

The Judge and his wife did withdraw money from the family fortune that Andrew was managing. Sarah Jane's withdrawals, over fifteen years, amounted to $13,000 for personal expenses, and the Judge requisitioned a further $44,000 for household costs. But the paramount withdrawal was $186,000 for his personal expenses. This sum must have included the drain of his five-year stay in Kansas City, as well as the outlay for his abortive incline project and the related legal expenses.[29] Clearly, the principal beneficiary of Thomas Mellon's divestiture was Thomas Mellon. Though they had now shed all of their wealth, the Judge and Sarah Jane took back from Andrew as much money as they wanted. Only the remainder was left for their sons to divide.

The incorporation of T. Mellon & Sons as the Mellon National Bank in 1902 occasioned a further significant change. As Andrew's statutory ownership of his parents' former assets was no longer required as bank collateral, he executed a formal deed of trust in October 1905 that extended his control over the same wealth, but only as a fiduciary.[30] When the subsequent trust was terminated in June 1919, the Judge's heirs drew lots for the family real estate and other assets, which had been divided into equal parcels.[31]

That Thomas and Sarah Jane Mellon made no will and shed their wealth by a succession of divestitures that were in most cases informal and unenforceable points to the granite loyalty and trust that held these early Mellons together. Is there a family today with two living parents, four grown sons, two daughters-in-law, and six grandchildren that would unanimously approve such a slipshod and by all appearances perilous transfer of wealth?

Perhaps with trepidation, but irrevocably, the wary old Judge had cut himself adrift from the moorings of his worldly dignity and had divested himself of all his material wealth. Released from financial restraint, would his sons continue to treat him fairly and with kindness? That was the gamble. And his sons did not disappoint him. They continued to uphold his ideals, cheerfully sustained him in the style of life that he chose, and never ceased to regard him as their ceremonial patriarch and beloved father. Where King Lear had lost, Thomas Mellon won.

# XXIII

## The Inclines Abandoned, The "Boodlers" Routed, Judge Mellon Sued for Slander

*Foley asked me if I did not know it was customary, where a corporation came here with money bags to obtain a valuable franchise, to pay something for such a favor.*

WITH THE CATHARSIS OF DIVESTITURE substantially behind him, the Judge returned in early 1890 to Kansas City, where his incline project continued to molder in the Committee for Public Improvements. Dining with him the night he arrived from Pittsburgh were his nephew William A. Mellon and his wife, Lillian. "He came back light and cheerful," recalls the nephew, alluding to his uncle's divestiture. "Deeper than this, we saw that he was relieved —satisfied."[1]

William and Lillian worked for the Judge and studied law on the side. They assisted him with correspondence, read to him, dined with him, and kept him company. They also edited the *Penny Press,* a diminutive Kansas City periodical that looked more like a handbill than a newspaper. Richard B. Mellon was the absentee publisher of this little sheet, and the Judge himself had founded it, for his showdown with the Common Council was now fast approaching, and he needed a voice in public affairs.

On April 1, 1890, John Nier, an engineer for the Mellon incline company, approached Councilman Fred Hayes, speaker of the Lower House, and asked for his support. Hayes had agreed a year earlier to approve the inclines but had demanded $3,500 for doing so. He now dropped his price to $2,000.[2] At a meeting with Nier on June 15, Councilman Dennis Bowes, who was famous for trumpeting his venality, also came down from $3,500 to "just $2,000" but warned that he was "not out for his health" and, referring to the franchise, added that "she will sleep until we get our stuff."[3]

Meanwhile, the Judge had also been lobbying. In a sworn affidavit that would be placed before the council six months later, he recalls, with surprising equanimity, his audience with Speaker Hayes:

> He received me affably and listened attentively. My object was to impress on him, and through him on others over whom he was supposed to have influence, that money was out of the question; that it could be used under no circumstances. We thought that if this was positively and definitely understood, the Committee [for Public Improvements] would let [the Lincoln Street franchise] go, and if it was likewise understood outside, we would have a good show in the [Lower] House. I informed Mr. Hayes that . . . we wanted his opinion as to whether our plans would have the desired effect.
>
> After some hesitation, he replied that he was in favor of the [incline] plane himself, and that of course he did not look for or expect any reward for favoring it, but some councilmen were in the habit of expecting recognition and receiving some compensation for their services in such cases, and . . . he thought they had tact and influence enough to defeat us, unless we used a little money on them.
>
> I replied to this that apart from the moral question involved neither the members of the company nor the councilmen could take the risk of paying or receiving money in such [a] case, as it

constituted a criminal offense. This was in reply to a remark of his that such a thing was customary, and if the franchise was valuable it was a better business policy to comply with the custom, although wrong. He then went on to explain that none of the parties he referred to took money for their votes or as a bribe; that they only accepted it as a fair compensation for their services and influence in canvassing with other members; that they never pledged their own vote one way or the other but left themselves free to vote as they pleased.

I should say further that these opinions were not peculiar to Mr. Hayes. Similar opinions were expressed to me by many other businessmen who were not councilmen.[4]

So Banker Mellon had finally learned what Kansas City politics was about. Better late than never.

The same day, two of his acquaintances, Peter Coign and J. McNall, introduced him to Councilman Andrew Foley at the latter's saloon on Delaware Street. "Foley said . . . he knew all about the [incline] scheme," Mellon would later testify in court,

and appreciated that it would be a good thing for the public.

Foley said, "I will give you a pointer. You want to get rid of Irvine, who has been attending to this matter for you. He has raised expectations among the boys which he failed to fulfill."[5]

The *Kansas City Star* had printed an earlier account by Mellon of this conversation:

I then explained to Foley that Irvine was not to blame in the matter, as it was my fault the boys had been disappointed. . . .

I told Mr. Foley that I wanted to know if, like some of the other councilmen I had heard of, he was controlled by bossism or boodle.

He told me that [political boss] Tom Corrigan had no influence over him and that for his own vote he did not want a cent, but needed something to exert his influence among the boys. Foley asked me if I did not know it was customary, where a corporation came here with money bags to obtain a valuable franchise, to pay something for such a favor. He told me that for half the amount demanded by Irvine he would get the matter through the Council, and on my refusal to accede to this he reduced his demands to three hundred dollars. For this three hundred dollars Foley promised to obtain three votes, but said that none of the money was for his own vote.

I told him that for such action we would be both liable for a penitentiary offense and could not consent. On this, he walked away and left me, so I said "good bye" and took my departure.[6]

McNall later testified that after Mellon left the saloon, Foley remarked, "That's a chilly old man to come in here and not say nothing. He must think people out here are fools. He expects to come out here and get a franchise that will make him money all his life and no one else get nothing. I can give him one pointer: he can put me down on his list for five hundred dollars."[7] Foley's price had again risen.

At a hearing in the Council on June 27, Irvine made a spirited defense of the incline project before the joint Committees for Public Improvements of the Upper and Lower houses, but he had found himself hopelessly outgunned and outnumbered by his opponents. That a claque of prominent homeowners from 11th Street and thereabouts introduced a petition that blasted the inclines as ugly, dirty, unnecessary, fatal to property values, and intended only for the superfluous enrichment of uncaring nonresident investors was perceived as the work of Tom Corrigan, the political boss of Kansas City, and his confederate, the lawyer L. K. Thatcher. The prospect of lucrative damage suits against Banker Mellon and his company still ranked high among the motives of these obstructers. Even the parish priest,

Father Glennon, was inveigled into producing a petition against the inclines.[8]

As his final effort, Irvine proposed a ruse: A detective posing as a paving contractor would approach the venal councillors, attempt to bribe them under circumstances permitting of verification, and then send them all to the penitentiary. But Mellon rejected this ploy. He was fed up with covert endeavors, had decided to fight his enemies publicly, and would go for the jugular.[9]

Secluded at the Coates House hotel, he now dictated to his nephew William the substance of a pamphlet that would send seismic waves through Kansas City politics. "Uncle enjoyed it all," recalls William. "He sat in his big rocker with his big palm fan, as we chatted and wrote."[10] The Judge was determined to defend the incline project and to smoke out the skunks that were holding it up for ransom. His pamphlet was of pocket size, ran to seventeen thousand words, and included a single illustration of the 11th Street incline. For maximum effect, he published it anonymously and refrained from naming the nefarious councillors. But predictably, everyone's identity was revealed in the uproar that followed.

Privately printed by the Inter-State Publishing Company of Kansas City, Missouri, *The Boss and Boodle Fight against Incline Planes and Non-Resident Investors* was to have been issued by early September 1890, but the Judge delayed its distribution until a day after the November elections to emphasize that party politics had not influenced its composition.

"I had the pamphlet printed," continues William.

Printed twenty thousand copies. Distributed them in person, with the help of a young man who was one of our [*Penny Press*] reporters. We each took a bundle and delivered each book by hand into the very hand of a recipient—to heads of stores, banks, offices. About the third day, we were halted in streets and buildings by some who wanted a copy or an extra. The third or fourth day, the cat was out and yowling through the town. Two papers had it, and the others rushed in. All front page, and in the spirit of "down with the boodlers."[11]

Under immense public pressure, both houses of the Common Council were now compelled to launch a joint investigation into the Judge's accusations. If any doubts remained as to who had authored the celebrated pamphlet, they were quickly dispelled. At the hearings, which opened on December 1, Mellon's lawyer, H. E. Colvin, submitted an affidavit in which his client admitted having authored *Boss and Boodle* and confirmed under oath the incendiary charges he had made in it. Moreover, three of the accused councillors were now identified: Fred Hayes, Dennis Bowes, and Andrew Foley. That confidential letters from Louis Irvine, which incriminated the writer as much as the councillors whose votes he had bargained for, were placed in evidence by Mellon raises the question of whether, by then, anything remained of their friendship. Was Mellon finally throwing Irvine to the wolves?

One thing is certain: between bouts of frustration, Mellon was having fun. "I rather enjoy the opposition," he admitted in a letter to Andrew.[12] To Ma he confided, "It affords me amusement."[13]

When the Judge returned to Pittsburgh, claiming illness, and refused to attend the council hearings, there was consternation and dismay in Kansas City. But, as William points out, his uncle's absence was planned for effect.[14] Every day that he absented himself and watched events from afar added drama to the hour when he would return like Ulysses.

On December 3, the council concluded its investigation and decided to hand over all evidence of wrongdoing by its members to a grand jury for possible criminal prosecution. Here at last was the opportunity that Mellon had been waiting for—the moment when he, as the star witness, could present his damning evidence in open court, under oath, and with the press and public looking on.

"MR. MELLON WILL BE HERE," boomed the *Kansas City Star* on December 17 and, three days later, "BANKER MELLON HERE."

Arriving at his hotel, the seventy-seven-year-old financier was waylaid and interviewed by reporter John Rush:

Thomas Mellon of Pittsburgh, the man who was seeking from the Council a franchise for the much-talked-of incline plane, whom Alderman Foley designated as "de chilly old mark" [prick], and who has become locally famous since the commencement of the Council investigation, arrived in the city this morning and, with a hand trembling from the weakness of age, traced the blotted signature "T. Mellon" upon the Coates House register.

Mr. Mellon is a feeble old gentleman with smooth face, scant white hair and a necktie like Andrew Jackson wore. Although showing his age more, on account of recent illness, he reminds one very much of John I. Blair. He talks easily, although slowly, in a low tone of voice, and notwithstanding his age shows by his conversation that he is still a bright man of business.[15]

Another description comes from William, who notes that Uncle Thomas, when walking "about the streets and places of Pittsburgh and of Kansas City or anywhere[,] was a closely wrapped-in figure and personality. He walked carefully, his face forward, circumspect but indecisive; his left hand across his stomach, clasping his coat or overcoat, which were never buttoned."[16] Timid, cautious, innately aware that to decide is often to gamble, Thomas Mellon walked as he lived.

On Monday, December 22, 1890, William accompanied his uncle to the grand jury hearing: "Eighth Street was jammed from Main to Walnut to get a glimpse of the Pittsburgh banker who was routing the Kansas City . . . boss-and-boodle gang. The police cleared a narrow way for us through the middle, and the county marshal, Stewart, squeezed us through the entrance and hallway. . . . Uncle wore his big seal cap with visor and ear flaps."[17]

Thomas Mellon was grilled by the grand jury for most of one day. Louis Irvine had already been questioned, and John Nier's interrogation would follow shortly. All three incriminated Councilman Fred Hayes,

*Thomas Mellon in later life.*

speaker of the Lower House, and he was indicted for having solicited bribes. Nier's and Irvine's testimony enabled the jurors to bring a similar charge against Councilman Dennis Bowes, and Irvine himself was indicted for attempted bribery. Councilman Andrew Foley miraculously escaped being charged. Emboldened by luck, he brought a $50,000 lawsuit against Thomas Mellon, charging him with two counts of libel and slander. The case would be tried a year later.

Mellon had lost a battle, but not the war. As William recalls, "Marcy K. Brown, a good double for Jesse James . . . arch slicker in county-state politics, drew the indictment, which, at the call for trial, was found to have a smoothly-edged round hole through which the accused slipped like quicksilver beads."[18] The "hole" was a recent Missouri Supreme Court decision that limited the charge of bribery to cases in which a bribe had actually been accepted. In short, the boodlers, who had solicited bribes but had then refused them because they were too small, could no longer be prosecuted.

The indictments against Irvine, Hayes, and Bowes were dismissed on February 23, 1891. But where justice had failed, the people succeeded. "Merchants' Association, civic bodies and newspapers," recalls William, "carried on the fight, and the boodle city council and its boss, the notorious Tom Corrigan—big blistery Irishman with bee-sting lips and jaws—were put down and out, and a new and decent council body was elected, to the exultant satisfaction of the town and its gratitude to the Pittsburgh banker who was bold enough to fight the gang. Leading merchants, publishers and other citizens, at every casual contact with us, expressed congratulations and gratitude."[19]

That he had become a white knight to honest folk of every stripe in Kansas City may, however, have brought Thomas Mellon only cold consolation. For during his two-year clash with the boodlers, rising interest rates, declining property values, a dimmer economic outlook, and the probably the mounting disenchantment of his partners had forced him to reconsider the ill-starred venture into which he had charged with such uncharacteristic rashness. His bitter decision to admit failure and cut losses became final on February 2, 1891, when he notified the Common Council, through Colvin, that the Kansas City Incline Plane Company was withdrawing its request for a franchise to trestle over Lincoln Street.[20] Its properties were then gradually sold off—most of them probably at a loss—and the company itself was eventually liquidated. Publication of the *Penny Press* was also discontinued.

Councilman Andrew Foley's $50,000 suit for libel and slander was now the one remaining skirmish that awaited Thomas Mellon in Kansas City. It was tried during Christmas week of 1891, and William A. Mellon leaves an eyewitness account of his uncle's trial. Col. Michael Boland was "a shrewd and secretive lawyer" whom rumor associated with the Clan nae Gael, a daring and lawless Irish secret society. Allegedly ousted from the legal community in Chicago, he had come to Kansas City and allied himself with John O'Grady, "the most astute and vitriolic barrister in the courts, and a galling nuisance to every judge presiding." One of the first cases that Boland contrived for his partnership with O'Grady was that of Andrew Foley, who was persuaded to make use of his grand jury escape to sue Thomas Mellon for slander. A third attorney, Col. John W. Wofford, was also enlisted to join the case.[21]

Prominent among Thomas Mellon's lawyers was Col. Charles O. Tichenor, "a tall, bent, longheaded supreme court practitioner, practicing alone with only a boy stenographer," recalls William, "the proverb, among lawyers, for depth and thoroughness, in all that region of the Middle West . . . a lawyer after my ideas and after Uncle's. Uncle was a lone worker and he admired most a plodding genius." Mellon's team had also been searching for "a big gun criminal lawyer of popular strength" and engaged Major William Warner, a friend of Tichenor's. "Warner was a national figure most of his life, a mighty warrior in army and civil life," recalls William. "He fought for good government in his town and state all the time, and in the Congress. At the time of our troubles—or fun—in Kansas City, he was Commander-in-Chief of the Grand Army of the Republic."[22]

The case of Foley versus Mellon began on December 22 under the direction of Judge John W. Henry, a former chief justice of the Missouri Supreme Court. The thirty-two-year-old plaintiff, Foley, was seated behind two of his lawyers, Boland and Wofford.

Mellon sat in a semicircle with his three defenders, Tichenor, Warner, and a British barrister named Dean. William A. Mellon, who was studying law, also accompanied his uncle. Foley, who had sneeringly referred to farmers as "a hay seed gang," now discovered that six of them sat on his jury.[23]

Wofford opened the case by reading the plaintiff's petition. It charged Mellon with having slandered Foley in grand jury testimony by alleging that he had offered to sell his vote in favor of the incline ordinance for $300, and with maligning the Common Council in the *Boss and Boodle* pamphlet and thus libeling Councilman Foley without actually naming him. For each of these counts, the plaintiff demanded $25,000.

On the stand, Foley admitted that Peter Coign had brought Thomas Mellon to his saloon but vehemently denied having offered to sell his vote. In a cross-examination that the *Kansas City Star* described as "merciless," Tichenor extracted from Foley that he had fled to Kansas City because a young woman in Pennsylvania had sued him for "betrayal," and that after jumping bail he had never repaid the signer of his bail bond. Pandering to "dry" sentiment, Tichenor elicited from Foley that he had been a bartender and saloon owner for all of his mature life. With lethal sarcasm, he probed for Foley's political motives: "Did you want to represent the saloons?" Whereupon Foley blurted with suicidal honesty, "No, I was simply ambitious."[24]

Reading from testimony taken by the council investigating committee, Tichenor asked Foley what he had meant when he said that "Mellon thinks we are all chumps, and he can put me down on his list." Conscious of the farmers on the jury, he also asked what Foley had meant when he referred to farmers as "Reubens" and to rural Missouri as "a whistling station."[25]

Fur continued to fly as Tichenor battered his caged victim with questions that sounded more like accusations: Had Foley not intimated to his partner, John Dwyer, that he received money for his vote? Had he not told George Payne of the local gas company that it would take money to get a certain measure through the council? Wasn't it common knowledge that bribes were required to get *anything* important through the council?[26]

On the second day, Mellon took the stand. Questioned by Wofford, he declared that Louis Irvine had furnished him with a list of councilmen who were demanding $500 apiece and that Mr. Foley's name was on it. "I understood Foley was a boodler," Mellon affirmed, "but did not know whether he was a bossism boodler or a money boodler. I felt exultant over the matter and wanted to shake Foley's hand, when he said he was on my side, but I changed my mind when he asked for money for his influence."

"Did you treat his offer with scorn and contempt?" demanded Wofford.

"Well I made no demonstration. I wanted to convert Mr. Foley from his evil ways."

"Was it not a fact, Mr. Mellon, that you withdrew the $2500 you had sent to your agent, Irvine, because one thousand dollars more was demanded, and not on account of any conscientious scruples against bribing councilmen?"

"No, sir, that is not true."

"Did it not excite you a little, Mr. Mellon, to have a city officer solicit a bribe from you?"

"No, sir. I am too well used to that sort of thing."[27]

The third and final day of the trial began with an acknowledgment of defeat from Foley: his lawyers withdrew the first count of his complaint. That left only the charge of libel, based on *Boss and Boodle,* for the court to rule on. Twenty-five thousand dollars that Foley and his team had hoped to extract for slander had just flown out the window. "MELLON WINS FIRST BLOOD," proclaimed the *Star*.

In another setback for Foley, Judge Henry now decided, over Wofford's objections, to admit a number of character-damaging depositions from Foley's hometown in Pennsylvania. To mask the rotten aftertaste of this evidence, Foley attempted to trot in Mayor Benjamin Holmes of Kansas City as a character reference; but by the time Holmes arrived, the trial was over.[28]

With the court jammed to standing room only, Foley's principal attorney, Michael Boland, a man of about sixty with full, graying moustaches, swept himself to the front of the jury. "He paraded with the stiff legs of a bobcat, his nape arched like a cobra," recalls nephew William. "It was thrilling entertainment." Towering over Thomas Mellon as he sat, and gesturing hatefully, Boland lashed out: "See him where he sits—the rich banker—greedy for profits—his incline plane —slandering our citizens. See his pale thin lips. Read the avarice in his features. Avarice—a-v-a-r-i-c-e—AVARICE."[29]

"I looked at Uncle and saw that he was suppressing smiles instead of anger," recalls William Mellon, but he adds that the whole court was "frozen in the stillness of disapproval." Still blindly wrecking his own case, Boland now singled out Major William Warner, one of Mellon's defenders, and blasted him with impermissible personal insults. Warner rose, and facing Boland, intoned with pain, pardon, and disbelief, "Oh!—Colonel Boland!" And when Judge Henry had added a reprimand of his own, Boland meekly apologized to Warner and to the court. Such was the final, disastrous effort made in Foley's behalf.

It was now Warner's turn to conclude Mellon's defense. He was a favorite stump speaker and assembly orator all over the country, and the crowd had waited for him patiently. "Andy Foley is well represented here," intoned Warner, "but where are his compatriots of the boodle gang? They are not here. . . . The wicked flee when no man pursueth!"[30] Applause.

"Warner spoke for an hour and a quarter," recalls William. "The publicity in the incline matter and its political and civic bearing furnished our orator broad wings for soaring. . . . But it was trying on the court. No power of command could stop the applause at those frequent climaxes. . . . Judge Henry pleaded but became despaired."[31]

With Christmas Eve only hours away, Foley's misbegotten suit went to the jury, both sides having slung all the mud that was in their pails. At 4:15 p.m. the jurors retired to deliberate, and an hour later they returned with their verdict, which was unanimous. On Christmas morning, a front-page article in the *Kansas City Star* chortled:

FOLEY GETS NOT A CENT.
Banker Mellon Knocks Him Entirely Out on Both Counts.

But laughable, bumptious Foley retained his council seat in the next election. No disclosure, however demeaning, could wean the voters away from their feisty, outspoken champion, though his inanities had been raucously chronicled by every paper in town and he had recently made the front page again by slugging an off-duty judge.

In the same election, Speaker Fred Hayes and alderman Dennis Bowes lost their council seats. Altogether, seven of the "Memorable Nine" whom Thomas Mellon had blasted in the *Boss and Boodle* pamphlet were turned out of office. From the sullied names and dashed careers of his opponents the acerbic old Judge must have drawn a brimming measure of satisfaction.

# XXIV

—◆—

## Selwyn and George "Return"

*As George's tears and my own violent emotion had produced a slight sensation and interrupted the proceeding temporarily, I turned to the medium and company present and exclaimed, "Oh, gentlemen! This is a sad condition for a father to be placed in—to meet a beloved son from beyond the grave, and meet him in such evident pain and sorrow, brought upon him by my own neglect of the usual religious forms of Christian worship."*

IT IS CURIOUS THAT THOMAS MELLON, old and almost blind, married for half a century, the patriarch of a close-knit family, a wealthy prominent Pittsburgher with a large and comfortable home, should have chosen to live in a Kansas City hotel room for three additional years after his incline project had foundered and his lawsuit was won. Was the indomitable eighty-year-old still hunting for business opportunities on the Frontier? Had he made investments there that are no longer known? Was he stubbornly determined to remain there until the incline properties could be liquidated without loss? Was his isolation softened by friendship with the families that Tom and James had intermarried with, the Larimers and Caldwells of nearby Leavenworth? Or was it just that he recoiled from returning to a home life that amounted to terminal boredom?

One reason for his extended sojourn at Kansas City is known. His nephew William A. Mellon and grandson William L. Mellon agree that the old Judge had a restless infatuation with the supernatural, precisely when Kansas City was a Mecca of spiritualism and was crawling with people who professed to be mediums.

In America, the golden age of spiritualism, the fad years of the occult, commenced around 1850 and persisted until the end of the century. It was a time when truth was stranger than fiction. Frowsy, cadaverous hags, plastered with makeup and barmaids posing as Russian princesses held séances in gloomy parlors cluttered with dust-covered fake antiques. They read palms, sought "guidance" from the stars, interpreted tarot cards, foretold the sexes of unborn babies, advised women on how to ensnare men, offered investment advice, touted wart cures, and claimed to grow hair on bald heads. A few of these impostors were cunning and brazen enough to achieve nationwide renown. The carriages of the rich and famous stood double-parked in front of their ramshackle parlors.

"Years back, before he was in Kansas City," William A. Mellon recalls of the Judge, "he became curious about spiritism, as many thinkers did. Out there with us, he had opportunity to witness some startling demonstrations. . . . On his trips home [to Pittsburgh], he innocently broached it to folks. Of course, there was some revolt, but not by Andy. . . . James R. and Dick became articulate, in mild but hateful breaths, because their father had slighted traditions and turned to a sideshow which was fascinating scientists and kings. But, with Andy mute and tolerant, the sage of all the Mellons went on smiling, with his back towards them all."[1]

Writing in 1898, the eighty-five-year-old Judge traces his obsessive interest in spiritualism to the influence of a young servant girl, Mary McLean, who had worked in his household. Sometime between 1856 and 1862, Mary had begun to hear unaccountable raps on the walls of the Mellon home.

Mary began to grow greatly alarmed. She knew so little about spirits at first that she was not much disturbed; but as the rapping occurred so frequently and in any part of the house when she was alone, and constantly increased in loudness and rapidity, all the inmates were annoyed and the effect began to show itself on Mary's health and appearance. Matters continued in this way until it became insufferable, when my wife took Mary to the office of Doctor John Dixon for advice or treatment. . . . His advice was to move her from our house, as the spirits had taken possession of every part of it. . . . He considered change of residence and change of acquaintances and surroundings as essential, but it would be [useless], he said, if she did not banish entirely and continuously from her mind all thoughts about spirits, ghosts or hobgoblins of any kind.

Mary was [by] then so frightened and apprehensive of the spirits that she gladly accepted any conditions that might relieve and protect her forever from what had become a great affliction.

So her sisters found another place for her at considerable distance from the city, and she seems to have fulfilled the prescribed condition of excluding spirits from her thoughts as she was never disturbed by the raps or other spirit manifestations after she left us, and in a few years became the wife of a kind and good husband and mother of several children.[2]

Thomas Mellon's memoirs reveal no preoccupation with mediums. Possibly he shrank from linking his name forever with a dubious science that has always exerted its strongest appeal on undereducated females. But he does mention an episode that helps us to trace the germination of his belief in spiritualism. Recalling the death of his nine-year-old son Selwyn in 1862, he writes: "A remarkably strong affection had existed between him and his brother Thomas. . . . An inexplicable circumstance in regard to [Selwyn's death] was that Thomas, without any knowledge of his illness whatever, had an irresistible impression that a terrible calamity was happening at home, and obtained leave of absence [from military service] to solve the mystery, a day too late to see him alive."[3]

*Mary McLean, the servant whose reports of mysterious rappings in the Mellon home piqued Thomas Mellon's interest in spiritualism. Courtesy Heinz History Center, Pittsburgh.*

Further evidence is proffered by William L. Mellon:

In my own home I was kept immune from this contagion by my parents [James and Rachel Mellon]. They had no faith in the phenomena reported from séance parlors nor in the good faith of those who conducted séances. They believed there was a catch in it some place and were satisfied to let it go at that. Nevertheless, I sometimes accompanied my grandfather to a séance.

What finally took Judge Mellon to the railroad station to get a ticket for Kansas City was word from there about a medium that made spirits not only audible but visible. It took a clever man to keep Grandfather fooled for more than a day or so about a business transaction. . . . But this was not business. This was something which found him, with his strong will, disposed to believe. After all, he had two sons and two little daughters in the next world. . . .

At different periods during my grandfather's five years in Kansas City, some member of the family was out there looking after him. A.W. [Mellon] was one of them, and he had a startling experience: They were in a parlor gathering. When they had seated themselves in a circle, they had been asked to cross their arms in front of them and in that position to "close" the circle by grasping the hands of their neighbors. They were warned of dire consequences if the chain should be broken. This imposed on the timid a disposition to clutch almost fiercely, so that any bolder ones present were really being restrained by the fearful. The medium went into a trance. From beyond some heavy portieres suddenly came cries, as from a child: "Father! Father!"

The Judge for a time was sure he recognized the voice of his little dead son, Selwyn. Then, abruptly, in a ghastly illuminated area between the portieres a little boy appeared, holding the handles of a toy wheelbarrow. The clothing worn by the apparition was in the style of that worn by little Selwyn in the pictures of him in our family albums.

For me, there is no mystery about it. The medium had been touted to Grandfather by that woman [Mary McLean]. . . . Probably through someone's treachery, hers or another's, the medium had been in a position to try to impose on Grandfather by dressing some little actor in his ménage in clothes of a style resembling those which had been worn by Selwyn.

Possibly that performance was just a little too good, because it was while he was in Kansas City that Grandfather told me that he had come to a final conclusion about spiritualism. He said: "There's nothing to it."[4]

Writing to his niece Lillian Bell Mellon, in 1897, the Judge quipped, "I am not a confirmed spiritualist any more than a socialist."[5] But this was only half true. Long after leaving Kansas City, he admitted that spiritualism was "unscientific" but still clung to the belief that there was "something in it,"[6] as the conclusion to his memorandum of August 25, 1898, unequivocally demonstrates:

> I had from childhood a strong desire to [learn] the secrets of nature, especially so in regard to mysteries of a mental, theological or psychological nature, and this desire was entirely different from the opinion formed of me by outsiders. By them, throughout the business period of my life, I was regarded as a hard practical man, disposed to acquire wealth by every fair means. This was true to a certain extent, and I have never discovered its wrong. . . .
>
> It was not until 1890 that I witnessed any material or other actual spirit manifestations. . . . After attending several general séances at St. Louis, Leavenworth and Kansas City, I had occasion to visit Cincinnati, where I was told some of the best and most reliable mediums resided at the séance room of Mr. Miller. . . .
>
> The size of the room . . . was about fifteen by twenty-four feet, and [there were] from twelve to sixteen persons present. . . . Mr. Miller was seated in an arm chair, at one side, near the middle of the room. . . . When the hour arrived, he arose and darkened the windows to the extent of reducing the glare of light to a plain room in a subdued but adequate condition for the accurate distinction of colors and personal features.
>
> Mr. Miller made no remarks and was not off his seat during the performance and seemed perfectly composed, and did not interfere in anywise with what transpired. Those awaiting manifestations, of whom I was one, sat quietly for some fifteen minutes looking around them, as if to see what might turn up. They did not seem acquainted with each other and certainly did not know me. I was an entire stranger, at the time, in Cincinnati, knowing no one there, and had not given my name or introduced myself to the medium.
>
> We had been waiting not over fifteen minutes when something seemed to take place on the vacant part of the floor, some

ten or twelve feet in front of where we and the medium were seated, but nothing visible appeared at first.

I was seated at the one side and twelve or fourteen feet from the place of the motion, which soon became visible. Its first appearance was that of a light streak or a pillar of light discon-nected, then steadily aggregating.... In a very short time it really took human shape, and I was startled by its approach across the floor directly towards myself. With three or four steady steps, it arrived immediately before me and looked steadily in my face, when I virtually recognized my dearly beloved son George whom I had lost only a few years before in the prime of his young man-hood. It rendered me speechless for a moment or two, and [then he] burst into a flood of tears and in a spiritual whisper, as if from his throat, exclaimed, "Father! Father! Father!" three times in a loud enough sound to be heard by all in the room. He was as bright and good looking and in the same suit he had worn a short time before his death, when we had visited Europe together on account of his failing health. I was dumbfounded and my feel-ings overcame me. As soon as he had uttered the above words, he retired or rather disappeared—I was too far overcome to see how—and silence unusual prevailed in all present for perhaps half a minute, and I was, myself, the first to break the spell.

It seemed to me my dear boy was in great sorrow and distress in the other world, and I was perhaps most to blame, because, as his life and mind had always been pure, I must have become accountable for leading him astray from the established method of Christian salvation by faith alone, in the Sanctified Atone-ment of Jesus.

As George's tears and my own violent emotion had produced a slight sensation and interrupted the proceeding temporarily, I turned to the medium and company present and exclaimed, "Oh, gentlemen! This is a sad condition for a father to be placed in—to meet a beloved son from beyond the grave, and meet him in such evident pain and sorrow, brought upon him by my own neglect of the usual religious forms of Christian worship."

To the astonishment of all present and my own great comfort, immediately after utterance of the last word of the foregoing sentence, George reappeared in composed form and gratified condition and spoke the following words: "No, Father! No! Not in pain and sorrow, but for joy my tears come, finding I could manifest myself again to you and that you so readily recognize me!"

He then gradually disappeared the second time before all present. Every movement, although of the most startling character, occurred in a perfectly natural manner, and his words in the last sentence uttered were distinct in the clear sound of his own voice.

If there is a future life for man, it is natural there should be spirits, and, if there are spirits of the deceased there, I have no more doubt that he was my son in the life he now enjoys than I have of my own present existence, or his former existence, on earth.

His eyes and shape were perfect and his ardor perfect, as in the best time of his life. Even his clothes were exact in every respect, with the suit he had worn when I was his traveling companion. . . .

I had so many repetitious meetings with George and others afterward to remove all doubt as to the possibility and reality of spirit forms. On one occasion I obtained permission to lay my hand on the spirit form and found it was the face of a natural being, with the loving nature and the head and hair the same in all respects as in the loving subject.

At the same meeting, above narrated, with my son George, after it was over, several other spirit forms appeared in like manner to others of those attending the same séance, but none of them so wonderful and peculiarly suggestive in its incidents as ours.[7]

Thomas Mellon's business career, and indeed his involvement in public life, was over. The long succession of his worldly triumphs had ended, surprisingly, with two lamentable missteps. If a life can be viewed as a work of art, his misbegotten incline project and his demeaning infatuation with the supernatural are the only incongruous brushstrokes in an otherwise consistent, admirably integrated portrait. What makes them the more regrettable is that they mar the crucial conclusion of his active life.

# XXV

———— ◦•◦ ————

## The Long Twilight

*If asked the sources from which I derived most happiness I would name but two: the free interchange of thought and implicit trust and confidence between me and my children in their youth, and unity of sentiment and opinion between us after they grew up; there was a deep satisfaction derived from it exceeding that from the closest friendship in any other relation of life. This was my chief source of happiness; and the next to it was the achievement of success in my plans and enterprises, and prosperity in my affairs.*

IN 1894, THOMAS MELLON RETURNED TO Pittsburgh forever. At eighty-two, the hunter was home from the hill; but unbeknownst to him, twelve long years of twilight lay ahead. In his high-ceilinged, wood-paneled study, where the gloom was deepened by his progressive blindness, the patriarch creaked rhythmically in the black rocker inherited from his mother and mused, as his grandchildren, other relatives, the secretary, and a male nurse took turns reading to him. He may have been suffering from Parkinson's disease or a related disorder, for his hands had become shaky, his writing grotesque. When answering personal correspondence, he scratched out enormous words, four or five to a line, and formed letters that looked like chicken tracks.

*Thomas Mellon in his study at 401 Negley.*

Age had at last fixed its grip on him, and his final business project—to found a Pittsburgh newspaper that would disseminate his trenchant political views—remained only a pipe dream. As the century was ending, his visits to T. Mellon & Sons became increasingly rare. But every so often, people walking on Smithfield Street would espy, amid the tangle of carriages, drays, and pedestrians, a formidable-looking old man, with stern, finely chiseled features, silver hair, and a knotted hickory cane, cautiously picking his way toward the bank he had founded decades earlier. He would be wearing outmoded Civil War clothing: a black frock coat like President Lincoln's, a starched, upright collar, and a forgotten style of bow tie. Was he aware that he had become a fashion dinosaur? If so, he accepted the judgment with scathing indifference. Appearing at the bank without warning, he would take his place in line before one of the tellers, like any other customer, to withdraw a few dollars for pocket money.

His daily life was increasingly governed by rote. When in Pittsburgh, he would eat his lonely, absent-minded lunch at the Hotel Henry, on Fifth Avenue, a few steps from the bank. He had sworn long ago not to pay more than 25 cents for his meal, and he would never break that pledge. Prices continued to climb, but he still placed his quarter defiantly on the table at Henry's, got up, and walked out. When the management quietly complained to Andrew, he told them to accept the old man's quarter and to bill T. Mellon & Sons for the rest.

The calendar of family feasts, which continued to be rigorously observed, could not have afforded him much relief from boredom. On Sundays, when the incongruously named Rev. J. Prophet Elijah Kumler had mercifully fallen silent, Mellons old and young would troop out of East Liberty Presbyterian Church and struggle through a stuffy lunch at one or another of the family homes. Matthew T. Mellon, the Judge's eldest great-grandchild, remembered fidgeting through these formal repasts in his hated Sunday suit. Eighty-five years later, he could still envision the long table lined with uncles, aunts, and cousins. He could close his eyes and taste the roast beef, watery peas, lumpy mashed potatoes, or sticky, caky rice, and see the grownups and children eating with napkins stuffed into their collars and everyone drinking ice water—except for tots, who were given milk. He could recall the snippets of conversation about business and politics and the serious tones in which his elders discussed the anesthetic sermon that had just ended. Still more memorable were the vast deserts of silence that prevailed when the conversation lapsed and only the clinking of knives and forks could be heard. Wine was conspicuous by its absence on these arid occasions. It was viewed as a wicked French concoction, unfit for God-fearing Presbyterians. But a fine cigar and a hefty slug of whiskey before or after the meal did nothing to provoke God's anger. Though a lifelong teetotaller himself, Mellon had to tolerate the heavy drinking and cigar smoking of his male friends.

*Thomas and Sarah Jane Mellon at 401 Negley, in 1900.*

Every year, on February 3, the traditional double birthday party for the Judge and Sarah Jane was celebrated at their home, which now bore the address 401 North Negley Avenue. Christmas, Thanksgiving, birthdays, baptisms, and funerals were scrupulously observed by the whole family. Retired now from every active pursuit, Thomas Mellon still served as the family's ceremonial center of gravity, the venerable architect of its prominence, the sine qua non of its existence.

Sarah Jane continued to preside over the household and to participate in charitable activities. The *Pittsburgh Dispatch* describes her as an active supporter of the Home for Aged Protestant Couples (Catholics need not apply) and as vice president of the Home for Aged Women in Wilkinsburg.[1] Swathed in black like her fashion model, Queen Victoria, Ma now spent hours by the fireplace, her generous bulk flooding an easy chair, a conspicuous wig at once hiding and advertising her baldness. So accoutered, she pored over the illustrated magazines that had become her windows on the world and snipped out items that caught her fancy. A scrapbook of hers is cluttered with sentimental pictures of dogs and small children, pithy bits of doggerel, excerpts on religion and fashion, photos of British and European royalty, Teddy Roosevelt's advice to schoolboys, Andrew Carnegie on his philanthropic giveaway policy, and a curriculum vitae of George Westinghouse.[2]

Because the Mellons had come to view themselves as an established Pittsburgh family, they now felt the urge to record for posterity their history, their faces, and their daily lives. In May 1894, they recorded their voices on a number of Edison cylindrical records. Photographs featuring four generations of the family were taken at intervals of several years, and artists were engaged to paint their portraits.

With a nose for impressionable new money, the flamboyant Parisian portrait painter Théobald Chartran, a protégé of Henry Clay Frick and the New York art dealer Roland Knoedler, descended on Pittsburgh in 1895 and '96. Andrew Carnegie himself submitted to Chartran's brush, and his delightful likeness, with its alert, focused gaze, may have helped persuade Thomas and Sarah Jane Mellon, among other Pittsburgh notables, to pose for the Frenchman.

That Frick was instrumental in arranging these commissions is confirmed by a letter to Knoedler in which the Coke Baron wrote on November 11, 1895: "Mr. Chartran can have the use of [Joseph Woodwell's] studio to paint Judge Mellon's portrait. . . . I do not want this portrait rushed through as rapidly as Mr. Carnegie's. While I think Mr. Carnegie's portrait is a very good one, yet it might have been better if more time had been taken."[3]

Chartran's portrait of Judge Mellon was appropriately presented by Frick to the Bar Association of Allegheny County. More important, David Cannadine dates Andrew W. Mellon's earliest interest in art from the painting of this portrait. It apparently delighted the Judge's other sons, too, for they commissioned the artist to paint a copy, and also a pendant likeness of Sarah Jane, and they presented these canvases to their parents.

Leaves continued to fall from the family tree. The Judge's sister Margaret had died in 1889 on her farm at Alviso, in Santa Clara County, California. As a young woman, she had crossed the Great Plains by covered wagon with her husband, Robert Shields, and their children. But Shields had become a drunken, abusive spendthrift, and with Thomas's assistance Margaret had secured the first divorce (but not the last) in Mellon family history.

Her death left the Judge with only one surviving sibling, the widowed Elizabeth Mellon Bowman. Known as Eliza or Lizzie, she was an occasional sojourner at the Mellon home, during the 1880s and '90s, and sometimes stayed for a week. She would read to her brother, offering him the priceless gift of her eyesight as his own continued to fail. They kept each other company. She died in 1898.

The next death was for him the most heartbreaking since that of Selwyn. It occurred because all four of his cigar-smoking sons had chosen to disregard the thinly veiled warning he had aimed at them fifteen years earlier in *Thomas Mellon and His Times:*

I have all my life avoided late hours and excesses, and exercised full control over my appetites; and have been a light eater of plain food, seldom using any stimulating beverage, and no tobacco. The injury resulting from stimulants is manifest to everyone, but that resulting from tobacco, though less manifest, is not less certain. I have just been to see an esteemed friend, Hon. Edgar Cowan [former U.S. senator from Pennsylvania], at his home in Greensburg, who has been suddenly compelled to abandon his worldly pursuits, and prepare for death by the lingering torture of a cancer in the tongue, produced by smoking.... Similarly has ex-president Grant's life been shortened of late by the same habit. Whilst we know that every unnatural appetite is necessarily injurious, yet strange it is that our godlike reason and boasted intelligence do not protect us against such pernicious habits as are shunned even by the lower animals.[4]

By 1898, the Judge's eldest son, fifty-four-year-old Tom, was terminally afflicted with cancer of the mouth and throat. He had been chain-smoking Juan Fortunado cigars for decades, and they had done their work thoroughly. With Tom's death the following year, after months of excruciating torment, his eighty-five-year-old father suffered the loss of a fifth child out of eight.

The Judge had long been bedeviled by a recurring nightmare: that through folly, neglect, rascality, or disaster, the fortune that proclaimed his gift for acquisition and justified a lifetime of striving might yet be lost. In 1885, he had written:

> According to my experience, it is more difficult to keep wealth when you have it than to accumulate it. Fluctuations in value, panics, unjust laws, maladministration of justice, frauds, accidents, and the constant importunity of schemers, as well as grinding taxation and other influences, tend constantly to the disintegration of wealth. More especially so at a period of life when the masterly spirit is weakened and the stimulus of success no longer allures to renewed exertion and we are more inclined to repose than activity. In that condition we are more likely to lose than gain. . . . Without prudent children, or others competent to guard it, it is a natural consequence that a man's wealth will begin to waste away with his mental and physical energies.
>
> This reflection has a saddening effect, and sometimes the heart sinks. But when we look abroad on nature, we see the autumn has its place in the animal as well as the vegetable kingdom, and is not without its tranquil beauty. Leaf and fruit must fade and drop to make way for a new and fresh crop in its turn. Man is as the grass. There need be no regret: it is the way; and the way of nature is a revelation of God.[5]

But as usual, his dark prognostications were not realized. By managing the family fortune adroitly, his sons, particularly Andrew, succeeded in dispelling their father's funereal pessimism. Far from revealing any fear of impending disaster, his letter to James on March 6, 1897, expresses only soporific discontent:

Time lies heavy on one's hands when we cease to need it. After spending as long a life-time as I have done, in its profitable use, then ceasing to make any valuable use of it at all is too radical a change to be agreeable. . . . I am no longer interested very much in any usual course of life; my chief interest . . . relates mostly to those of my blood who are to succeed me. . . . I have such thorough confidence in their good qualities that reference to them, or any of them, in thought always tends to increase my satisfaction.[6]

At the age of seventy-two, he had expressed an opinion in his memoirs that must have held true to the last: "If asked the sources from which I derived most happiness I would name but two: the free interchange of thought and implicit trust and confidence between me and my children in their youth, and unity of sentiment and opinion between us after they grew up; there was a deep satisfaction derived from it exceeding that from the closest friendship in any other relation of life. This was my chief source of happiness; and the next to it was the achievement of success in my plans and enterprises, and prosperity in my affairs."[7]

There were joyous interludes, as when William L. Mellon married Mary ("May") Taylor in 1896. Frail health prevented the Judge from journeying to Palatka, Florida, for his grandson's wedding, but he lived to see three great-grandchildren from this union: Matthew Taylor Mellon and his sisters Margaret and Rachel, all three of whom treasured a few disparate recollections of their great-grandfather. The following year, a resplendent wedding joined thirty-nine-year-old Richard B. Mellon with Jennie King, daughter of the glass manufacturer Alexander King, who had once owned the Negley mansion. Judge Mellon lived to see two grandchildren from this marriage: Richard, the future general, and Sarah, later Mrs. Alan Scaife.

Andrew, who had come to be viewed as a hopeless bachelor, held out until 1900 but then married Nora McMullen. Age alone would probably have prevented the Judge from attending his son's spectacular wedding, at Hertford Castle in England, but he is also known to have opposed the match.[8] The age difference between them—Andrew was forty-five and Nora twenty-one—can only have aroused his foreboding. But he must also have doubted whether a cheerful young woman from the idyllic English countryside could be adequately marinated in Scotch-Irish prejudices, turned into a self-effacing helpmate, and accommodated to living in sooty, industrial Pittsburgh. Mercifully, the Judge would not live to see his misgivings vindicated: Andrew's marriage eventually foundered in protracted and excruciating scandal. But he would live to rejoice in the birth of two grandchildren from this marriage, however disastrous it may have been otherwise: Ailsa, later Mrs. David Bruce, and Paul Mellon, born in 1907, when his grandfather was ninety-four.

Though Thomas Mellon left no formal will because he had given away everything he owned, the following valediction contains some final wishes and reflections:

September 24, 1895

My dear Sons,

When, a few years ago, you relieved me of care and attention to my property and affairs, I felt free and as if I could leave at any time without further care for anyone; but we can't go far in this world without finding new work to be done and new wants to be satisfied.

There is a matter or two of this kind which I cannot avoid doing something for, and, of course, must depend on you for it after I am gone. And recent indications are that possibly I may be called off suddenly.

I do not leave this as a Will or legal obligation on you, because I feel that to be unnecessary, as you will cheerfully satisfy my wishes without it.

I have no obligations outstanding, legal or otherwise, and intend to make none except those I am about to mention.

# Abbreviated Descent from Thomas and Sarah Jane Mellon

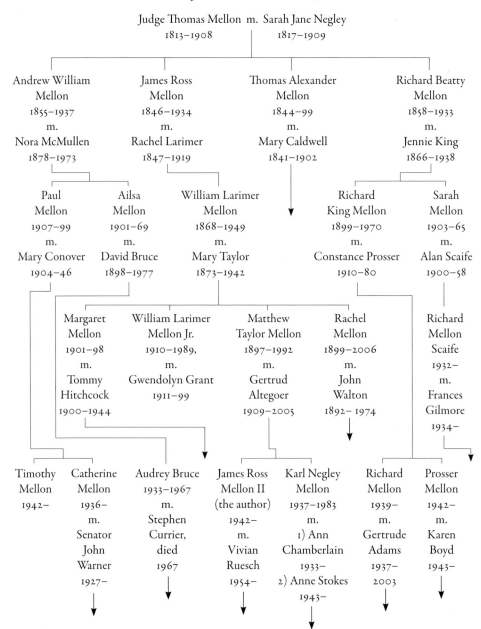

Judge Thomas Mellon m. Sarah Jane Negley
1813–1908                     1817–1909

Andrew William Mellon 1855–1937 m. Nora McMullen 1878–1973

James Ross Mellon 1846–1934 m. Rachel Larimer 1847–1919

Thomas Alexander Mellon 1844–99 m. Mary Caldwell 1841–1902

Richard Beatty Mellon 1858–1933 m. Jennie King 1866–1938

Paul Mellon 1907–99 m. Mary Conover 1904–46

Ailsa Mellon 1901–69 m. David Bruce 1898–1977

William Larimer Mellon 1868–1949 m. Mary Taylor 1873–1942

Richard King Mellon 1899–1970 m. Constance Prosser 1910–80

Sarah Mellon 1903–65 m. Alan Scaife 1900–58

Margaret Mellon 1901–98 m. Tommy Hitchcock 1900–1944

William Larimer Mellon Jr. 1910–1989, m. Gwendolyn Grant 1911–99

Matthew Taylor Mellon 1897–1992 m. Gertrud Altegoer 1909–2005

Rachel Mellon 1899–2006 m. John Walton 1892– 1974

Richard Mellon Scaife 1932– m. Frances Gilmore 1934–

Timothy Mellon 1942–

Catherine Mellon 1936– m. Senator John Warner 1927–

Audrey Bruce 1933–1967 m. Stephen Currier, died 1967

James Ross Mellon II (the author) 1942– m. Vivian Ruesch 1954–

Karl Negley Mellon 1937–1983 m. 1) Ann Chamberlain 1933– 2) Anne Stokes 1943–

Richard Mellon 1939– m. Gertrude Adams 1937– 2003

Prosser Mellon 1942– m. Karen Boyd 1943–

The chief of these relates to Henrietta [a woman raised in the Mellon family]. The other to the two grandchildren of my brother Samuel, children of William and Lillian.

Henrietta was brought up in our family, the companion and playmate of our children. . . . She has been doing all she possibly can to support herself. But the time is coming when her work won't support her. Even now her sight is failing.

. . . My request is that you make her an allowance of two hundred ($200) dollars per annum while she lives, to be paid her quarterly in payments of fifty ($50) dollars each. I perceive that she is naturally economical, and I think that ought to suffice, unless the cost of living greatly increases. If so, she might need something more to keep her comfortably in her old age, but in regard to that I leave any increase to your own discretion, knowing your feelings will lead you to be more liberal than, perhaps, I would be myself.

My other request relates to a more uncertain and difficult subject. . . . It depends entirely on future conditions and circumstances and relates more to attention and keeping an eye on those children [of William A. and Lillian Mellon], their whereabouts and condition, and prevent them to some extent from suffering the actual pain and misery of want and destitution. The children appear bright, affectionate and good-natured, but, of course, helpless, and in fact comparatively unprotected, except by the affection of a mother, herself nearly as helpless as they are. . . . The father you know, and it is doubtful whether such parents could hold and apply even a rich gold mine, if they had one, to their own and children's support. . . . I hardly expect the parents to keep together. . . . If the mother died soon, which is likely, my idea would be to put them into an orphan asylum, and what would be far better, if it could be obtained, would be to have them admitted into respectable families to be decently raised with some education and preparation for some calling to make a living when they grow up. . . . I have no idea of helping anyone, young or old, to shirk the duties and labors of life belonging to their condition. Every one should be self-sustaining. . . . The difficulty which presents itself to me so far is to help the children without helping to support the good-for-nothing father and child-like, conceited mother in comparative idleness. . . .

I have now only to mention the great comfort and happiness which I enjoy and have always enjoyed from your good qualities and uniform course of life since your infancy. I have been favored remarkably in all my immediate family relations. I was blessed in a mate and can see her good qualities in our children and grandchildren. Even our daughters-in-law have filled the place of our little daughters who left us in their childhood. In the character, ability and fidelity of those who come after me, I am surely overpaid for all their arduous care and labor of a long life.

I wish to be buried close by my parents, leaving room for your dear mother on my right, so that my very durable and serviceable old body may rest between my loving mother on one side and loving wife on the other. When the first grave is required let it be large enough for us both. . . . A rough granite block, such as those at the entrance of our home, though not so high, perhaps, with no more lettering than the name, age and date of death to be chiseled on the lower or outside face of the stone as the two compartments behind become occupied.

. . . I may say, because I feel it will comfort and give you satisfaction to know [it], that I have not the slightest fear or concern about the time or manner of going. I have very strong hope and assurance that I shall be with you all as much afterwards as before, until we all meet again face to face, and I expect also to enjoy happy communion with all my children and other loved ones who have gone before me.

Your affectionate father,
Thomas Mellon[9]

Under Spencer's influence, the Judge had veered close to atheism in his philosophical peregrinations, but he had never quite rejected traditional religion. And, now, with death dogging his heels, we find him returning to the conventional Christian fold like a homing pigeon.

When his grandchildren read to him, he frequently asked to hear the first chapter of the Gospel of John, which he had memorized for his mother when a small boy and which still worked its magic on him eighteen years later. He nonetheless continued to demur at literal interpretations of the Bible:

Pittsburgh, Pa.

December 31, 1900

Mr. J. B. Corey:

I have no friend outside of my own family whom I regard so highly as you, always sincere and true....

I am old and well stricken in years, but have hope for a future life. I believe in God and believe He is greater and better than He is usually preached or prayed to. I should not address Him as "He" or "Him," for I regard Him as the Infinite Cause of all in this and all other worlds, and that His beliefs and ways are infinitely greater than our thoughts and ways . . . [which] are but glimpses of feeble rays.

Mr. Corey, can you believe in Adam's fall, or do you believe that the wise and learned of modern times are right in disregarding the story . . . ?

Now if Adam's fall is mythical, of course there is no foundation for the redemption of sinners, on the modern plan. . . . That "in Adam's fall we sinned all" is very beautiful and comforting, [but] we feel of Adam and of his eating an apple of the wrong tree in the orchard [that it] certainly deserves a stronger proof than it has yet obtained. . . . Do not mistake me as inclined to disbelief in religion. No! . . . But mistakes or untruths in religion, if any are found to exist, should be eradicated by all religious men. If anything should be pure and eradicated of all mistakes or errors, it is religion.

I would not bother you with this kind of stuff, but know that what I get from you will be the truth as you understand it. In this life I have arrived at the outlet gate, and have no better friend than you to tell me where I am to go, when let out.

Some of my wise and pious friends have suggested to me that all such doubts are answered by faith alone. Well, but if the doubts are real, faith alone would be very inadequate support. It would be as if I came to a bridge in my journey through life that was so decayed and rotten that it must certainly break down if the weight of myself and team is placed upon it, and I should be told that it was certainly a safe crossing, [and that] if I should believe in it and trust to faith alone, I could cross it in safety.

I do not disbelieve in any alleged fact or doctrine however absurd or unreasonable, unless I know it to be untrue, and therefore I do not say that any Bible doctrine is untrue. All that I can say is that I do not know whether it is true or not. I believe in God and that God is good. I trust in him. That there is a God all nature affords full evidence, real evidence, satisfactory to the senses and mental faculties which God has supplied me with.

Your sincere old Friend,
Thomas Mellon[10]


Such were the desultory ruminations which preoccupied the patriarch as he lounged in his rocker by the hearth. Now almost totally blind, he may also have pondered John Milton's lines on his own blindness, which stoically proclaim that "they also serve who only stand and wait." And as he waited, he must have marveled at the interminable parade of history that had passed before him. That a man who had been born before the Battle of Waterloo, who had crossed the Atlantic on a square-rigger when daffy old George III was king, could have lived deep into the era of railroads, ocean liners, and telephones—

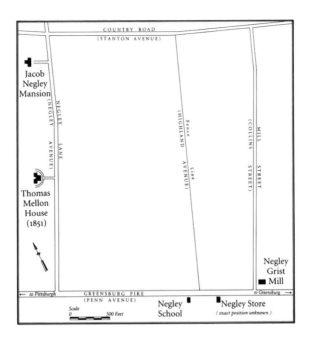

*1823*

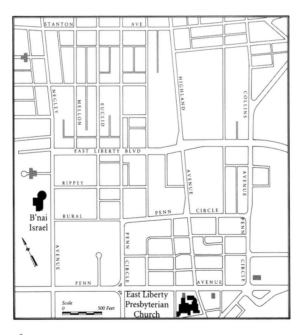

*1894*

*Two maps of the suburb of East Liberty: in 1823, when ten-year-old Thomas Mellon first walked through it; and in 1894, after he had lived there for forty years. Courtesy University of Pittsburgh Press; maps by Christopher H. Marston.*

only to find himself, at the last, in a science-fictional age of dread-nought battleships, submarines, motor cars, wireless radios, machine guns, and motion-picture shows—is simply dizzying. He may even have lived to hear the intrusive buzzing of an airplane, so long had he lingered and borne witness.

"I need hardly inform you that I am dying," he confides with stoical resignation to his niece Lillian in 1897. "It may be years before I pass out, and happily I am suffering no pain, only the decay gradually of mental and vital faculties. Mind is breaking down, especially as to recent events, and physical faculties weakening from which I had derived most pleasure in the past, and general weakness prevailing."[11]

The art of living is to grow old gracefully, and there are those who can accept with equanimity the constraints and indignities of age—who, after a life strenuously lived, find themselves peacefully at anchor on the sea of their accomplishments—those who have come to understand that no one is fit to die who has not lived, and that no one should be afraid to die who has lived. Thomas Mellon was such a man:

> Now, since I have passed through it all and experienced the reality of things, . . . I can see life and its objects and purposes in more sober colors. Whilst not what they seemed to be in pursuit, yet I am satisfied with what I found them to be in possession; and I feel that all the extra exertion, labor and deprivation expended on the various objects and projects of my life have been amply repaid.
>
> The world owes no one a living, but sooner or later rewards him fairly for his exertions in the proper direction.
>
> It is a beautiful provision of nature to make life rosy at the beginning. It develops young hope and incites to action—renders work a pleasure and lures us on. As age approaches and strength declines, the enchantment is removed and we see things differently —I will not say in their true colors, because they may be as much disguised to us in age as in youth; as much underrated in the one case as overrated in the other. It is thus, however, we are brought

gently to the point of departure. "Our little life," as Shakespeare has it, "is rounded with a sleep." And we are made to see or at least feel, with the wise man, that all is vanity. And so we are prepared to step out without regret![12]

He further reflected:

A long life is like an ear of corn with the grains shriveled at both ends. The few years at the end of an old man's life are of as little account to him or others as the few years of childhood at its beginning. But I am neither dissatisfied with life nor greatly concerned for its long continuance. And when the time comes, my hope is to depart in peace, with as little pain and suffering as possible.... My life on the whole has been a pleasant one, but my capacity for usefulness as well as for physical enjoyment is declining, and already I begin to feel desolate. On looking back, it is with a shade of sadness I find that . . . nearly all of my friends and associates whom I would feel an interest in communicating with are gone.... To the general public which surrounds me now, I am as a stranger in a strange land.[13]

On October 22, 1902, he suffered the first of several minor strokes, but with typical resilience, he was able to pose on the following day for a series of outdoor photographs. In 1907, on the seventieth anniversary of his graduation, the Western University of Pennsylvania, which had renamed itself the University of Pittsburgh, regaled its oldest living graduate and senior instructor emeritus, Thomas Mellon, with an honorary doctorate of law. That he had served with distinction as a judge and was now also the oldest living member of the Allegheny County bar must have argued for awarding him this accolade, but possibly the weightiest consideration was his passionate, lifelong interest in education. He also received a second honor from the university that year when the junior class dedicated its publication, *The Owl,* to the ninety-four-year-old jurist who had served as classics professor in 1837.

*The Judge in his last years.*

Matthew T. Mellon, who was ten years old when the Judge died, recalls a typical visit to 401 North Negley Avenue toward the end of his great-grandfather's life:

I remember the little room we sat in with its coal fire and the Swiss music box that played, among other tunes, "The Blue Bells of Scotland." He would come in with his male nurse, for he was feeble and around 95, and drink his eggnog, holding it in his long, veined hands. . . . Once he turned to me while he was drinking it and said, "Matthew, this is a wolf in lamb's clothing."[14]

While his St. Bernard dog lay snoring on the floor, Great-grandfather would sit by the fire in the rocker that had belonged to his mother. He would usually be wearing a long black Prince Albert coat, and his bedroom slippers contrasted oddly with his otherwise formal attire. His neck was skinny and shriveled, like that of a plucked chicken, and he made it look worse by wearing a starched wing collar, the ends of which did not quite meet in front, so that we could see his Adam's apple bobbing up and down, as he spoke. His receded gums showed that he had lost most of his teeth, but he could still speak intelligibly. Sometimes, he would tell us a story about his boyhood in Ireland. . . . When he fell asleep, we would tiptoe out.[15]

Early in 1908, family members received their invitations to the annual double birthday party for Thomas and Sarah Jane Mellon. But on February 3, instead of feasting and rejoicing, the Judge's relatives were shocked to learn that their chief had slipped quietly from the world early on his ninety-fifth birthday.

In the death certificate, Dr. James Macfarlane deposes that he was present at 401 North Negley Avenue when Thomas Mellon died; that "apoplexy, attended by paralysis of right arm and leg, probably due to hemorrhage" caused his death, and that the Judge breathed his last at 8:30 a.m., on February 3, 1908, after an illness of two and a half hours.[16] Whether he was in pain, or even conscious, and whether he spoke any last words, are not known. But hopefully he experienced the same solace and resignation that had impressed him forty years earlier as he stood at the deathbed of his mother-in-law, Barbara Negley, and witnessed her peaceful, fearless dissolution: "Thus nature takes us out of the world in the exercise of our ordinary commonplace thoughts and feelings, as she brought us into it unconsciously before the exercise of thought began; and, except for the interference of fellow mortals or alarmed and excited relatives and friends, we drop out again without

1813     1817

Birthday Greeting
from
Thomas and Sarah Negley Mellon
February third, nineteen hundred and eight

*Invitation to Thomas Mellon's ninety-fifth*
*birthday party. He died that morning.*

alarm into that unconsciousness from which we were awakened on coming in."[17]

His obituary in the *Pittsburgh Post* describes him as a "well-known financier" but also—incomprehensibly—as a "philanthropist." It recalls the radical changes he had once proposed in the jury system and applauds his charges to juries as "marvels of conciseness, fairness, good law and common sense."[18]

Among the shower of condolences was one from William A. Mellon, who describes his uncle Thomas as "one of those strong souls that loved life for the chance to think and do." Andrew Carnegie's letter is lost, but Andrew Mellon thanked him for his "beautiful and appreciative words."[19] A memorial meeting of the Allegheny County Bar Association commended Judge Mellon for his "honesty and common sense" in business and politics and called it an "old-fashioned doctrine."

"Stealing was stealing," the encomium concluded, "whether done by the professional pickpocket, the respectable politician, or the dishonest contractor"—words that would have caused the deceased to purr.[20]

Thomas Mellon's body was placed on view the day after his death so that friends and family members could pay final respects. The funeral service was conducted at his home on February 5 by the Rev. Frank W. Sneed of East Liberty Presbyterian Church. A choral quartet sang "Rock of Ages" and "Nearer, My God, to Thee."

"Stormy day, heavy sleet falling," wrote Mary Taylor Mellon of the burial in Allegheny Cemetery.[21] The open grave stood waiting, ringed by a huddled mass of relatives, withered by the icy touch of a dying winter day. As the light faded, the Mellon patriarch was lowered into the frozen earth near the graves of his children, his parents, and innumerable Negley in-laws. Less than a year later, on January 19, 1909, Sarah Jane Negley Mellon took her place beside him.

# XXVI

---

## In the Judge's Shadow:
## An Epilogue

THOMAS MELLON DEFTLY TRAINED HIS SONS to accumulate wealth, but, curiously, he never sought to establish a business dynasty. Because wealth had powered his upward trajectory from perceived poverty to financial freedom—for him the sine qua non of human dignity—he had drilled his sons relentlessly and from a startling early age to acquire and maintain wealth, and more important, to cope with it. But could these talents be transmitted to future generations along with the wealth itself? To that question he can have found no reassuring answer, for he had loudly proclaimed that inherited wealth engenders sloth and ineptitude in the heirs and consequently destroys both them and itself.

The Judge's aim was that each of his sons should strenuously persevere, alone or with a brother, in the lucrative occupation for which his talents and character best suited him, until he reached the plateau of financial freedom, where the demeaning restraints of the workaday world would be surmounted, and he could take control of his own destiny. But the father made no effort to form the disparate Mellon enterprises into a cohesive empire of wealth.

His was not the program of a man with dynastic aspirations, for it envisioned a dispersion, rather than a concentration, of the family fortune. Had the Judge aimed at founding an enduring business dynasty, he would have consolidated the disparate Mellon enterprises into a single holding company or partnership equally owned by all of his sons and presumably managed by the more capable ones. A measure of cohesion and continuity would then have been imposed not only on the family fortune but also on the family itself, and a more even distribution of wealth would have resulted.

But the Judge was never persuaded that wealth could be perpetuated. Nor did he want his sons to share the fortune equally. Each was to receive no more and no less than he had earned, and there is every reason to suspect that he wanted them, singly or in pairs, to compete with each other. Thus he sowed the seeds of dispersion, which, over time, have sprouted a chaotic jungle of individual fortunes, charitable foundations, and irrevocable trusts.

Raised among Ulstermen, Thomas Mellon was overdosed with the formidable Protestant work ethic that has powered America's economic growth and nurtured its competitive egalitarianism. For him, work was a moral imperative, not merely a breadwinning necessity. Success in business was a dignifying experience that called for and justified the suppression of natural frivolity and spirituality in favor of attitudes that facilitate accumulation. He nonetheless placed reasonable limits on the quest for fortune by defining his objective. "I never had any ambition to achieve fame or notoriety or great wealth or prominent public position," he wrote, once more striking an antidynastic note, "but always preferred, rather, to go on in a quiet and unostentatious way, and, having no expensive tastes to gratify, it required but little to afford me a competence and independence."[1]

In short, he refused to view wealth as an end in itself—as the scorecard in a futile rat race between plutocrats, a World Series of avarice and celebrity in which the transient winner finds that he still envies God and the Queen of England. Instead, Mellon defined his objective as "independence," though "freedom" expresses it better—freedom from what he stubbornly perceived as the degrading indigence of his plowboy youth, freedom to raise his children in a comfortable home and to educate them as he pleased, freedom to read and study, freedom to feed and exercise his hyperinquisitive mind, freedom to achieve a number of limited rational goals, freedom to do what he wanted with the one life he had—the freedom that human dignity clamors for.

At age twenty-one, he wrote that "although in some the long continued habit of acquiring money does become so strong that they seem at last to desire it for its own sake, yet no one, we presume, ever did, in his sober thoughts, regard it in any other point of view than the readiest and safest way of accomplishing his ends."[2] This remained his view. He would have agreed that one cannot be too rich, but he would have added that one can be rich enough.

Hence, as his fortune grew, he steadily disengaged from business to concentrate on the pleasurable activity of instructive reading. Similarly, with the exception of Andrew, all of his wealthy descendants, on attaining financial freedom, began to reduce their occupational commitments in favor of balanced lifestyles that included enjoyable pursuits. Richard's absences from the Mellon Bank and from Pittsburgh grew in length and frequency as he steadily reoriented his life toward Ligonier and Rolling Rock Club. James decided to travel. By the age of twenty-nine, he had sufficiently freed himself from business entanglements to embark on an extended pleasure jaunt, from Ireland across Europe to Jerusalem and the Dead Sea. Though he retained the largely honorary presidency of the City Deposit Bank and Trust Company, he was semiretired at age thirty-eight and spent his remaining winters in Florida and most summers with his children and grandchildren in the Alleghenies, at Rachelwood.

James's son, William L. Mellon, whose upbringing had been directed by the Judge, increasingly delegated his business responsibilities at Gulf Oil to surrogates, and by the age of forty-two was able to spend months with his children and grandchildren in Florida or at his summer retreat in Ontario. Eventually, even Andrew sidelined business in order to concentrate on directing the U.S. Treasury, collecting art, and building the National Gallery of Art.

Thomas Mellon's initial battle plan was to claw his way "up and out" to financial freedom. But that plan became entwined, in middle age, with an equally resolute effort to imbue his sons with the painfully acquired wisdom of a winner in a pitiless race. His sons were to steer by the stars that had guided him: ambition, discipline, honesty, education, patience, caution, thrift, and toil. Above all, they were to follow him into some profitable form of business. He deftly fashioned them into extensions of himself and subliminally into the embodiment of his immortality. But along with his fortune, he left them a more precious and durable legacy: the training to maintain financial freedom, the ennobling but elusive American Dream—and, equally important, the ability to regain it if it were lost.

What he steadfastly refused to share with them was his reading and contemplation. Intellectual cultivation had vastly enriched his own life, but for his sons he viewed it as merely a hazardous distraction from the imperative to acquire. Not until his grandson Paul Mellon forsook banking for a life of aesthetic, intellectual, and philanthropic activities and his great-grandson Matthew T. Mellon obtained a doctorate in philosophy and taught at a German university did family members appear who delighted in deep exploratory reading and the interplay of ideas.

Though Thomas Mellon came to be a powerful, established Pittsburgher, he was never satisfied with the status quo. All his life he railed against the political, economic, and legal abuses of his day. Yet his overriding aim was not to change the world but to learn how to live in it. His alarm at the present and fear for the future were always held in check by his respect for the past. His tendency in politics was to safeguard or cleanse, not to wreck and replace. For the most part, his descendants are heirs to his conservatism. Activist political programs that call for dubious radical innovations tend to rile the living Mellons. Like their ancestor, most of them are tenaciously determined to preserve the ideals and institutions that have proved their worth.

Had the Judge accumulated enough wealth to overcome his terror of losing financial freedom, he might have progressed, like John D. Rockefeller and Andrew Carnegie, from the gathering to the giving stage, as has been typical of affluent American families. How much treasure it would have taken for him to make this transformation is an intriguing imponderable.

As things were, he shunned conspicuous public philanthropy and limited his charitable giving to isolated acts of compassion, such as helping an impoverished friend or relative whose need happened to touch his sympathy. "My heart and hand was always open to relieve the actual distress of worthy objects of private charity. I have given in this way what might have been given to public charity with more praise and display, but private charity was always what attracted my feelings most."[3] It was also less expensive.

Eventually, some of his sons and grandchildren who had been raised in comfort and had accumulated or inherited fortunes far greater than his own did become givers rather than gatherers, and came to find in philanthropy an engaging ethical challenge. The Judge might even have been persuaded, by vigorous and repeated entreaties, to approve his grandson William L. Mellon's decision to build a Graduate School of Industrial Administration for the University of Pittsburgh. But he would have winced when Andrew gave the world's most valuable private art collection to the American people instead of selling it and pocketing the money.

Public service was not a calling that Thomas Mellon respected or fully understood. He engaged in it, but always with trepidation and only when he felt compelled to do so. Indeed, mistrust of government and contempt for politics form an enduring part of his legacy. Having freed himself from the economic constraints of life by personal initiative and ascendancy of character, he had little faith in collective action, viewed the run of humankind as dangerously flawed, and was viscerally alarmed by democracy. He also viewed politics as less respectable than business, for it paid less and demanded constant pretending. He may have dug deep into his bottomless bag of prejudices for these views, but time has done little to diminish their acceptance in the Mellon family.

Pressured by friends and relatives, Andrew Mellon overruled the voice of caution that whispered from within and served as secretary of

*Four generations of Mellons, July 4, 1899.*
*Left to right: William Larimer Mellon, Thomas Mellon, Mary Taylor Mellon,*
*Matthew Taylor Mellon, Lucile Mellon, Sarah Jane Mellon, Rachel Mellon,*
*James Ross Mellon, Rachel Larimer Mellon.*

the treasury under three presidents. William L. Mellon permitted himself to be drafted by his uncle Andrew as Republican Party chairman for Pennsylvania, and the Judge himself endured five consecutive terms as a Pittsburgh city councillor. But in their awkward political forays, these Mellons do not appear to have been motivated primarily by a civic-minded urge to improve the quality of life, much less by a longing for public acclaim; rather, they were moved by the fear that others whom they viewed as opponents, scoundrels, or simply fools might obtain power over taxation, commerce, and tariffs. These were the spheres of government control that directly affected business, and the founders of the Mellon fortune had convinced themselves that the interests of business and those of the human community are not only compatible but inseparable.

It was Thomas Mellon's fate to live in the undertow of a sinking religious faith. Christian dogma challenged him philosophically but made no controlling ethical demands. He steered by secular stars. His attendance at church was irregular and reluctant. Organized religion served him as a proof of class identity and gave him a forum for social and business contacts. For his descendants, the golf course and tennis court perform these functions.

That such a worldly man resorted, in the winter of his life, to an aberrant infatuation with the supernatural may indeed have been occasioned as much by a life of relentless materialism and consequent spiritual desiccation as by a pathetic yearning to communicate with his dead sons and daughters. Be that as it may, this geriatric flirtation with the occult amounted to more than a sideshow, for it came to modify the adamantly mundane orientation toward life that resonates so forcefully in his memoirs, written five years earlier.

Among living Mellons, conventional church attendance has dwindled to the verge of extinction, but, happily, so have Thomas Mellon's intractable prejudices. On present-day family occasions, nominal Presbyterians sit amicably at table with nominal Catholics, nominal Episcopalians, cocktail-party Buddhists, uncloseted atheists, and befuddled observers of life. What holds the overall Mellon family together is plain friendship reinforced by a ponderous awareness of history.

Thomas Mellon was a well-lopsided rather than a well-rounded man. Like the ancient Greeks, he paid lip service to moderation—"meliorism," he calls it—but was selectively immoderate; he trumpeted his biases and blotted out whole areas of human interest and achievement. Visual art meant little or nothing to him. His appreciation of poetry and of fictional, rather than instructive, literature was limited to the narrowest of slivers, and his sensitivity for music remained undeveloped.

He engaged in no form of recreation. With the exception of Andrew, his sons were hunters and fishermen, yet their uncommonly predatory father cared for neither rod nor gun. From early manhood, his lifestyle had been sedentary—unhealthy, by the standards of a later day—yet he was never overweight, retained his mental faculties arguably to the last, and lived to be ninety-five. That he ate only simple food in sparing portions and effortlessly shunned both drink and tobacco may have done much to offset the debilitation of inactivity.

But whatever he did to discourage his sons from the whiskey bottle and cigar box had little effect. Andrew drank temperately, Tom and Richard heavily; only James was a teetotaler. They all smoked cigars—James and Richard moderately, Andrew heavily, Tom like a chimney. Similarly, their taste in architecture was influenced by prevailing fads, not by their father's booming condemnation of "shoddyocracy." They built gloomy, hulking imitation Tudor or Victorian mansions like Richard's Baywood, which resembled a misshapen chocolate wedding cake; James's candy castle, Rachelwood, which came to have a pagoda roof; and William's Ben Elm. These were precisely what the austere, unpretentious Judge would have shrunk from.

The steady unraveling of family ties since Thomas Mellon's day has been persistently bewailed by senior family members. The Judge, his parents, grandparents, uncles, and aunts—all born in Ireland—had arrived on these shores as immigrants and, typically, had clung to one another like castaways. As long as their patriarch lived, and even for some time afterward, the Mellons remained a close-knit family or clan who attended church together and shared the ritual family feasts. But inevitably, as their snowballing wealth and consequent power dissolved the immigrant insecurities that had welded them together, they drifted apart.

Then too, their numbers have increased geometrically. In 1900, Thomas Mellon presided over a family that totaled fewer than twenty descendants and spouses, all of whom lived in three adjacent houses on North Negley Avenue or a short ride away. Now, with more than 150 family members scattered from coast to coast, the clan continues to proliferate. Yet each emerging branch of the family tree is free to recreate a semblance of the close-knit ties that unified the original immigrant clan, and some of them have done this.

Notwithstanding their spiraling numbers, the Judge's descendants have been stamped with an unambiguous historical identity. In the court of public opinion, from which there is no appeal, the Duponts are forever linked to Wilmington, the Cabots to Boston, and the Biddles to Philadelphia. The Mellons are similarly linked to Pittsburgh, where their ancestors have left tracks in granite and concrete. The epicenter of the city is Mellon Square. William L. Mellon's Graduate School of Industrial Administration is an adjunct to the University of Pittsburgh, and the Mellon Institute of Industrial Research has been subsumed into Carnegie-Mellon University. The nickname "Mellon's Fire Escape" clings tenaciously to Pittsburgh's most imposing house of prayer, East Liberty Presbyterian Church. The list goes on and on. Some family members sighed with relief when the airport was named for Carnegie.

These monuments, all built by four generations of the Judge's descendants, have forged an indissoluble bond between the Mellons and Pittsburgh. This is not to say that the Judge would have approved of so much largesse, much less paid for any part of it himself. But his affection for the city where fortune had favored him ran so deep, and his life was so densely intertwined with its history, that he taught his children and grandchildren to view themselves as inalienable

*Four generations of Mellons, in 1897.*
*Left to right: the Judge, great-grandson Matthew,*
*grandson William, and son James.*

Pittsburghers. Hence, the cloudburst of philanthropy that they eventually unleashed came to be disproportionately showered on the Iron City rather than thinly scattered over the rest of America. Hence also, they kept a number of the family's principal businesses headquartered in Pittsburgh.

That the Mellon name is permanently associated with business must also be credited to the Judge. His was a program of rigorous early training, brilliant supervision, and generous inducements that led two of his sons and three of his grandsons to heap up fortunes. That some Mellons have compiled Medician art collections, built palatial yachts, won innumerable horse races, and ladled out philanthropy has lent a veneer of celebrity to the family name. But Mellons are profoundly aware that it will never be easy to make a fortune, nor difficult to give one away; that without the power of wealth, there would have been no yachts or African safaris, no foundation grants, no victories at Ascot, no National Gallery of Art, and no Albert Schweitzer Hospital in Haiti. Not surprisingly, they continue to view themselves as scions of a business family—which is what Thomas Mellon wanted—and only those who engage in business can experience the satisfaction of living in full continuity with the family's history.

If we could devise a test for happiness using the criteria of good health, satisfying human relationships, fulfilling work, and a nourishing spiritual life, Thomas Mellon would receive an A on the first three but only a C on the last. There was, moreover, an admirable equilibrium between the elements of his personality—a harmony of psychic faculties that contributed heavily to his effectiveness. Though generously endowed with common sense, he was nonetheless completely at home in the realm of ideas. Because their values are geared to production, most Americans define themselves by what they do, and they recoil at the mere thought of living a contemplative life. Thomas Mellon was certainly an activist and producer, but curiously, he was not afraid to live the life of the mind and longed for the opportunity to do so.

While often succumbing to ferocious preconceptions, he more often amazes us by challenging the conventional wisdom: hence the flashes of brilliance and unexpected echoes of modernity that repeatedly surprise us in his autobiography. Already in 1848 he resettled in rural East Liberty to escape the increasingly polluted air of Pittsburgh. In 1885 we find him agonizing over crime in the cities, political corruption, the quality of public education, and excessive taxation. Do these problems agitate the public mind any less today? Are we not also still fighting his fight for identity and equilibrium amid the dehumanizing tendencies of an increasingly regimented, mechanized, impersonal, and elaborately dire industrial world?

Just as the unexamined life is not worth living, the unlived life is not worth examining. And what especially endears Thomas Mellon to this particular scion is the urgency with which he struggled to share with his descendants the lessons of a life strenuously lived and fearlessly examined—a life in which action and reflection were ingeniously counterpoised. The passion to share one's treasury of wisdom with posterity is, after all, an expression of love.

# Abbreviations

| | |
|---|---|
| AA | Author's archive. |
| ABF | Franklin, Benjamin. *The Autobiography of Benjamin Franklin*. New York: Modern Library, 2001. |
| ACML | Archive of Charles Mellon Lockerby. |
| APM | Archive of Paul Mellon, National Gallery of Art, Washington, D.C. |
| BB | Mellon, Thomas. *The Boss and Boodle Fight against Incline Planes and Non-Resident Investors*. Kansas City, Missouri: Inter-State, August 1890. |
| BH | Hersh, Burton. *The Mellon Family: A Fortune in History*. New York: William Morrow, 1978. |
| BHA | Hendrick, Burton J. "Andrew William Mellon." Unpublished manuscript, APM. |
| BHC | Hendrick, Burton J. "A. W. and R. B. [Mellon] Contrast." Unpublished manuscript, AA. |
| BHS | Hendrick, Burton J. "Hendrick's Summary." Unpublished manuscript on Andrew W. Mellon, from the papers of Boyden Sparkes, AA. |
| CEP | Pearce, Charles E. *The Jolly Duchess*. New York: Brentano's, n.d. |
| CHM | McCullough, C. Hax, Jr. *One Hundred Years of Banking:* |

|  | *The History of Mellon National Bank and Trust Company.* Pittsburgh, Pennsylvania: Herbick & Held, 1970. |
| CHS | Sipe, C. Hale. *Fort Ligonier and Its Times.* Harrisburg, Pennsylvania: Telegraph Press, 1932. |
| CMS | Centre for Migration Studies, Ulster-American Folk Park, Omagh, Northern Ireland. |
| CTM | "The Courtship of Thomas Mellon." Unpublished manuscript, APM. |
| DC | Cannadine, David. *Mellon: An American Life.* New York: Alfred A. Knopf, 2006. |
| DK | Koskoff, David E. *The Mellons: The Chronicle of America's Richest Family.* New York: Thomas Y. Crowell, 1978. |
| HCF | Sanger, Martha Frick Symington. *Henry Clay Frick: An Intimate Portrait.* New York: Abbeville Press, 1998. |
| HHC | Heinz History Center, Pittsburgh, Pennsylvania. |
| JBC | Corey, James B. *Memoir and Personal Recollection of J. B. Corey.* Pittsburgh, Pennsylvania: Pittsburgh Printing Company, 1914. |
| JGL | Leyburn, James G. *The Scotch-Irish: A Social History.* Chapel Hill: University of North Carolina Press, 1962. |
| JMS | Mellon, William Larimer. *Judge Mellon's Sons.* Pittsburgh, Pennsylvania: Privately printed, 1948. |
| JRM | Mellon, James R. *Letters.* Pittsburgh, Pennsylvania: Privately printed, 1928. |
| JWJ | Jordan, John W. *A Century and a Half of Pittsburgh and Her People.* New York: Lewis, 1908. |
| KCS | *Kansas City Star.* |
| KP | Phillips, Kevin. *The Cousins' Wars.* New York: Basic Books, 1999. |
| LS | Steffens, Lincoln. *The Shame of the Cities.* New York: Hill and Wang, 1988. |
| MK | Mintz, Steven, and Susan Kellog. *Domestic Revolutions: A Social History of American Family Life.* New York: Free Press, 1988. |

MR        *Municipal Record* (Proceedings of the Select and Common
          Councils of the City of Pittsburgh).
MS        Sadleir, Michael. *The Strange Life of Lady Blessington.*
          Boston: Little, Brown, 1933.
NLT       *National Labor Tribune.*
PBS       Papers of Boyden Sparkes, AA.
PK        Krause, Paul. *The Battle for Homestead, 1880–1892:
          Politics, Culture and Steel.* Pittsburgh, Pennsylvania:
          University of Pittsburgh Press, 1992.
PPG       *Pittsburgh Post-Gazette.*
RSS       Mellon, Paul, with John Baskett. *Reflections in a Silver
          Spoon.* New York: William Morrow, 1992.
RUP       Records of the University of Pittsburgh.
SF        Foote, Shelby. *The Civil War: A Narrative.* New York:
          Random House, 1963.
SSM       Mellon, Sandra Springer, ed. *Dear Sons: Letters from
          Thomas Mellon, 1882–1886.* Ligonier, Pennsylvania:
          Mellon Rolling Rock Museum, 2005.
TMT       Mellon, Thomas. *Thomas Mellon and His Times.*
          Pittsburgh, Pennsylvania: William. G. Johnston, 1885.
UPE       Mellon, Thomas. *Thomas Mellon and His Times.* Ed. Mary
          Louise Briscoe. Pittsburgh, Pennsylvania: University of
          Pittsburgh Press, 1994.
WAC       *Warranty Atlas of Allegheny County,* reproduced by Joel
          Fishman for the Western Pennsylvania Genealogical
          Society, Pittsburgh, Pennsylvania, 1982.
WAM       Mellon, William A. Letters to Burton Hendrick. Archive
          of Charles Mellon Lockerby, Lusby, Maryland.
WCW       Last will and testament of Conrad Winebiddle, September
          3, 1795, HHC.
WLM       William Larimer Mellon, interviewed by Boyden Sparkes,
          1944–45, AA.

# Notes

## Chapter I

Unless otherwise noted, all chapter epigraphs are taken from Thomas Mellon's memoir, *Thomas Mellon and His Times* (hereafter TMT).

1 TMT, 47, 52–54.
2 Mountjoy and Abercorn estate records, CMS.
3 TMT, 64.
4 TMT, 77–78.
5 Mountjoy estate records, CMS.
6 JGL, 83–98.
7 JGL, 83–98.
8 JGL, 99–107.
9 JGL, 99–107.
10 JGL, 120–32.
11 JGL, 125; also TMT, 47, 52.
12 JGL, 297–316.
13 Paul Mellon, "The Irish Cottage Where an American Dream Was Born," *Architectural Digest,* August 1993.
14 TMT, 99, 143.
15 TMT, 461.
16 TMT, 140–41.
17 TMT, 54.
18 Mountjoy estate records, CMS.
19 Letter from Robert Graham to Thomas Mellon, November 9, 1900, JRM, 205; also TMT, 87.
20 TMT, 145.
21 TMT, 145.
22 Peter M. Toner, "The Mellon Ship," unpublished report prepared for the author, 1944, AA; letter from Eric Montgomery to the author, June 24, 1996, AA.
23 JGL, 174–76.
24 TMT, 145.
25 TMT, 148.
26 Toner, "The Mellon Ship."
27 TMT, 148.
28 TMT, 148.
29 TMT, 150–51.
30 TMT, 60–61.
31 TMT, 63.
32 TMT, 153–54.
33 TMT, 155.
34 TMT, 159–62.
35 TMT, 168–69.
36 TMT, 163.
37 TMT, 161.
38 TMT, 162.
39 TMT, 149–203.

40 CTM, 27–28.

41 TMT, 155.

42 Conveyance of a lease, December 16, 1800, Registry of Deeds, Dublin.

43 Indenture of a lease, dated April 7, 1780, and deed of assignment, April 27, 1781, Registry of Deeds, Dublin.

44 TMT, 195, 200.

45 TMT, 195, 200.

46 TMT, 563–64.

47 TMT, 98.

48 TMT, 179.

49 TMT, 563.

50 TMT, 131.

51 TMT, 174.

52 TMT, 175.

### Chapter II

1 TMT, 184.

2 TMT, 185.

3 TMT, 187–88.

4 TMT, 187–88.

5 TMT, 165.

6 TMT, 165–66.

7 Dell Upton, ed., *America's Architectural Roots: Ethnic Groups That Built America* (New York: Preservation Press, 1986).

8 TMT, 200.

9 TMT, 169.

10 TMT, 169–70.

11 ABF, 91–92.

12 ABF, 96.

13 ABF, 88–89.

14 ABF, 65.

15 TMT, 203.

16 TMT, 204.

17 TMT, 204.

18 TMT, 102.

19 TMT, 103.

20 Archive of Wilbur Samuel Mellon Jr., of Sarasota, Florida.

21 TMT, 213.

22 TMT, 203.

23 TMT, 204, 171.

24 Letter from Thomas Mellon to his uncle Thomas Mellon, March 23, 1833, APM.

25 TMT, 231.

26 TMT, 206–8.

27 TMT, 209–10.

28 TMT, 216.

29 TMT, 217.

30 CTM, 19.

31 APM.

32 APM.

33 CTM, 28.

34 TMT, 221.

35 TMT, 221.

36 TMT, 221–22.

37 Letter from Thomas Mellon to John Coon (Kuhn), August 16, 1834; see also letters from Thomas Mellon to his uncle Thomas Mellon, December 25, 1831; March 23, 1833; and May 17, 1834, APM, and letter from Thomas Mellon to Coon, August 23, 1834, APM.

38 TMT, 223–24.

39 APM.

40 TMT, 230–31.

### Chapter III

1 APM.

2 TMT, 231–32.

3 TMT, 237.

4 TMT, 238.

5 TMT, 238.

6 TMT, 238–39.

7 TMT, 239.

8 TMT, 60, 96.

9 TMT, 159.

10 TMT, 243.

11 TMT, 244–45.

12  TMT, 247.

13  TMT, 643.

14  TMT, 250–51.

15  TMT, 251–52.

16  TMT, 252.

17  TMT, 252.

18  TMT, 252.

19  TMT, 250.

20  TMT, 253.

21  TMT, 256.

22  TMT, 253.

23  ABF, 88

24  TMT, 252–53.

25  TMT, 253.

26  TMT, 255.

27  TMT, 122.

28  Sarah H. Killikelly, *The History of Pittsburgh: Its Rise and Progress* (Pittsburgh, Pennsylvania: B. C. & Gordon Montgomery, 1906), 278.

29  Manuscript list of schoolbooks used by Thomas and Sarah Jane Mellon, HHC.

30  TMT, 269.

31  Benjamin Franklin, *Poor Richard's Almanac,* January 1740.

32  TMT, 256–57.

33  TMT, 257–58.

34  TMT, 261.

35  TMT, 264–65.

36  TMT, 265.

37  TMT, 266.

38  TMT, 267–68.

39  TMT, 269.

40  ABF, 75.

41  TMT, 256.

42  TMT, 268.

43  TMT, 255.

44  TMT, 275.

45  TMT, 277.

46  TMT, 311–13.

47  TMT, 268–69.

## Chapter IV

1  Annie Clark Miller, *Chronicles of Families, Houses and Estates of Pittsburgh and Its Environs* (Pittsburgh Pennsylvania: privately printed, 1927), 95–96.

2  JWJ, 24; C. Hax McCullough Jr., "The Surnames of Pittsburgh: Conrad Winebiddle, 18th Century Patriot, Landowner," *Bimonthly Newsletter of the Historical Society of Western Pennsylvania,* vol. 9, no. 2 (March–April 2000).

3  Ibid.; see also Ella Chalfant, *A Goodly Heritage* (Pittsburgh, Pennsylvania: University of Pittsburgh Press, 1955), 185; JWJ, 243.

4  Chalfant, *A Goodly Heritage,* 187.

5  See WCW.

6  See bill of sale by Elizabeth Winebiddle and Jacob Negley (Nigly), recorded November 4, 1795, Allegheny County Deed Book 4, 361.

7  WCW.

8  KP, 134–35.

9  C. Hale Sipe, *Fort Ligonier and Its Times* (Harrisburg, Pennsylvania: Telegraph Press, 1932), 436.

10  Ibid.

11  Ibid., 426.

12  Ibid., 333.

13  Ibid., 435–39.

14  KP, 134–35.

15  John W. Jordan, *Encyclopedia of Pennsylvania Biography* (New York: Lewis Historical Publishing, 1915), 5:1633; see also TMT, 117.

16  TMT, 117.

17  TMT, 118.

18  *The East Liberty Presbyterian Church* (Cleveland, Ohio: Caxton Company, 1935), 5.
19  Ibid., 5.
20  Ibid., 1.
21  TMT, 123.
22  TMT, 122–23.
23  TMT, 122.

## CHAPTER V

1  TMT, 361.
2  TMT, 248.
3  TMT, 313.
4  Quoted in Joel A. Tarr, *Devastation and Renewal* (Pittsburgh, Pennsylvania: University of Pittsburgh Press, 2003), 15.
5  Ibid., 15.
6  TMT, 313.
7  TMT, 134, 276.
8  TMT, 361–62.
9  TMT, 363.
10  TMT, 363.
11  TMT, 365.
12  TMT, 255.
13  TMT, 365.
14  Recalled by the author's father, Matthew T. Mellon.
15  WLM.
16  JMS, 1.
17  JMS, 4, 6, 8.
18  TMT, 369.
19  TMT, 52.
20  TMT, 369–70.
21  TMT, 370.
22  Diary of James Ross Mellon, 1857–58, HHC.
23  TMT, 82.
24  TMT, 370.
25  Letter from Thomas Mellon to his son James Ross Mellon, November 27, 1863, HHC.
26  Letter from Thomas Mellon to his son James Ross Mellon, January 22, 1864, HHC.
27  Letter from Thomas Mellon to his son James Ross Mellon, January 27, 1864, HHC.
28  TMT, 366–67.
29  TMT, 367–68.
30  Letter from Thomas Mellon to his sons Thomas Alexander Mellon and James Ross Mellon, December 25, 1862, HHC.
31  TMT, 371.
32  TMT, 371–72.
33  TMT, 259–60.
34  JMS, 22.
35  TMT, 164–65.
36  TMT, 135.
37  JMS, 29.
38  JMS, 29.
39  MK, 43.
40  WLM; scrapbooks of Sarah Jane Mellon, AA.
41  WLM.
42  TMT, 102–3.
43  TMT, 103–4.
44  TMT, 375.

## CHAPTER VI

1  JBC, 72–73.
2  TMT, 301–6.
3  TMT, 290–95.
4  TMT, 285.
5  TMT, 291, 292.
6  TMT, 294.
7  TMT, 295.
8  TMT, 296–98.
9  TMT, 280–81.
10  TMT, 288–89.
11  TMT, 45.
12  Letters from Thomas Mellon to his son James Ross Mellon, January 10, 1864, and December 11, 1863, HHC.
13  TMT, 320.

14 TMT, 321–22.

15 James Ross Mellon, "Reminiscences of the East Liberty Presbyterian Church from 1850 to 1870," manuscript, 1932, 8–9, AA.

16 Michael Fitzgibbon Holt, *Forging a Majority: The Formation of the Republican Party in Pittsburgh, 1848–1860* (Pittsburgh, Pennsylvania: University of Pittsburgh Press, 1990), 232–33; *Pittsburgh Gazette,* May 23 and June 11, 1857; *Pittsburgh Dispatch,* June 11, 1857.

17 *Pittsburgh Post,* August 27, 1857.

18 Holt, *Forging a Majority,* 257.

19 TMT, 394–95, 397–98.

20 Holt, *Forging a Majority,* 255–58.

21 *Pittsburgh Gazette,* February 17, 1859.

22 Ibid.

23 TMT, 396–97.

24 Letter from Thomas Mellon to his son James Ross Mellon, February 8, 1864, HHC.

25 TMT, 77.

26 TMT, 76–77.

27 HHC.

28 Stotler Family Archive, HHC.

29 TMT, 323–25.

30 TMT, 325.

31 TMT, 323.

32 *Pittsburgh Gazette,* October 15, 1859.

33 *Pittsburgh Post,* July 1, 1859.

CHAPTER VII

1 Letters from James Ross Mellon to Thomas Mellon, October 2, November 8, and November 27, 1862, HHC.

2 Letter from Thomas Mellon to his son James Ross Mellon, December 7, 1863, HHC.

3 KP, 548.

4 Letter from James Ross Mellon to Thomas Mellon, May 14, 1864, HHC.

5 Telegram from Thomas Mellon to his son James Ross Mellon, May 17, 1864, HHC.

6 Letter from Thomas Mellon to his son James Ross Mellon, May 17, 1864, HHC.

7 Letter from James Ross Mellon to Thomas Mellon, May 19, 1864, HHC.

8 Letter from Sarah Jane Negley Mellon to her son James Ross Mellon, May 20, 1864, HHC.

9 Letters from Thomas Mellon to his son James Ross Mellon, May 19, 22, and 29, 1864, HHC.

10 TMT, 381–82.

11 SF, 2:151.

12 TMT, 380.

13 Roy P. Basler, ed., *The Collected Works of Abraham Lincoln* (New Brunswick, New Jersey: Rutgers University Press, 1953), 7:233.

14 Letter from Thomas Mellon to James Ross Mellon, July 16, 1864, HHC.

15 Letter from Thomas Mellon to James Ross Mellon, July 30, 1864, HHC.

16 TMT, 353–56.

17 BH, 58.

18 TMT, 46.

19 TMT, 286.

20 JRM, 154–63.

21 JRM, 154–63.

22 TMT, 379.

CHAPTER VIII

1 TMT, 348.

2 TMT, 348–49.

3 Quoted in Susan Jacoby, "On Faith," *Washington Post,* February 12, 2009.

4 Charles Darwin, *The Descent of Man,* in *From So Simple a Beginning: The Four Great Books of Charles Darwin,* ed. Edward O. Wilson (New York: W. W. Norton, 2006), 873–74.

5  TMT, 100.

6  TMT, 132.

7  TMT, 250.

8  TMT, 132.

9  Thomas Mellon, memorandum,
   August 25, 1898, APM.

10  TMT, 349.

11  TMT, 349–50.

12  TMT, 350–51.

13  TMT, 351–52.

14  Letter from Thomas Mellon to his
    son James Ross Mellon, November
    22, 1881, HHC.

15  TMT, 292–93.

16  TMT, 461–62.

17  TMT, 459–60.

18  TMT, 531.

19  TMT, 531–32.

20  TMT, 532–33.

21  TMT, 533–34.

22  TMT, 534.

23  TMT, 527–28.

24  TMT, 528–29.

25  TMT, 530.

26  TMT, 534.

### CHAPTER IX

1  *Pittsburgh Legal Journal,* January 28,
   1860.

2  Ibid., May 14, 1860.

3  TMT, 330.

4  TMT, 327.

5  TMT, 327.

6  TMT, 329.

7  TMT, 345–46.

8  TMT, 346.

9  James R. Mellon, "Reminiscences
   of the East Liberty Presbyterian
   Church from 1850 to 1870," signed
   manuscript, 1932, AA.

10  TMT, 337.

11  TMT, 337.

12  TMT, 337.

13  TMT, 330–32.

14  TMT, 333–34.

15  TMT, 340–41.

16  *Biographical Review* (Boston:
    Biographical Review Publishing
    Company, 1897), 24:213.

17  TMT, 632–33.

18  Negley K. Teeters, *Scaffold and
    Chair: A Compilation of Their Uses
    in Pennsylvania, 1682–1962*
    (Philadelphia: Pennsylvania Prison
    Society, 1963).

19  *Pittsburgh Gazette,* November 12,
    1862.

20  Ibid.

21  *Pittsburgh Daily Post,* March 2, 1863.

22  Ibid.

23  *Pittsburgh Gazette,* December 2, 1865.

24  *Pittsburgh Gazette,* October 7, 12,
    and 13, 1865; January 13, 1866.

25  Ibid.

26  Ibid.

27  Ibid.

28  Ibid.

29  Ibid.

30  Ibid.

31  Ibid.

32  Ibid.

33  Ibid.

34  Ibid.

35  Ibid.

36  *Pittsburgh Gazette* and *Pittsburgh
    Daily Post,* October 23–30 and
    November 27, 1865; January 9 and 20,
    1866.

37  Ibid.

38  Ibid.

39  Ibid.

40  Ibid.

41  Ibid.

42  Ibid.

43  Ibid.

44  Charles Alexander Rook, *Western*

*Pennsylvanians* (Pittsburgh, Pennsylvania: Western Pennsylvania Biographical Association, 1923), 414.

45 *Pittsburgh Gazette* and *Pittsburgh Daily Post,* October 23–30 and November 27, 1865; January 19 and 20, 1866.

46 Ibid.

47 *Pittsburgh Gazette* and *Pittsburgh Daily Post,* January 13, 1866.

48 *Pittsburgh Gazette* and *Pittsburgh Daily Post,* January 19 and 20, 1866.

49 *Daily Pittsburgh Gazette,* May 19, 1864.

50 *Pittsburgh Gazette,* October 18, 1866.

51 *Pittsburgh Commercial Gazette,* October 26, 1866.

52 *Pittsburgh Gazette,* June 19, 1868; January 7–9 and April 30, 1869.

53 Ibid.

54 Ibid.

55 Ibid.

56 Ibid.

57 Ibid.

58 Ibid.

59 Ibid.

60 Ibid.

61 *Pittsburgh Gazette,* February 4, 1867.

62 *Pittsburgh Daily Gazette,* January 31, 1868.

63 *Pittsburgh Gazette,* February 1, 1869.

64 "Half a Century of the Allegheny County Bar Association," *Western Pennsylvania Historical Magazine* 4, no. 3 (July 1921).

65 TMT, 358–59.

66 TMT, 359–60.

67 TMT, 360.

## CHAPTER X

1 Stefan Lorant, *Pittsburgh: The Story of an American City* (Lenox, Massachusetts: Author's Edition, 1975).

2 Agnes Dodds Kinard, *Celebration of Carnegie in Pittsburgh: The Man, the Institute, and the City* (Pittsburgh, Pennsylvania: Carnegie Museum of Art, 1982).

3 Remark by the British writer James Parton in 1868, quoted in Franklin Toker, *Pittsburgh: An Urban Portrait* (University Park: Pennsylvania State University Press, 1986), 189.

4 TMT, 592.

5 TMT, 310.

6 TMT, 357.

7 TMT, 287.

8 TMT, 357.

9 TMT, 384.

10 JMS, 45–49.

11 John W. Jordan, *Colonial and Revolutionary Families of Pennsylvania* (New York: Lewis Publishing, 1911), 3:1509–12.

12 Herman S. Davis, compiler, *Reminiscences of General William Larimer* (Lancaster, Pennsylvania: New Era Printing Company, 1918), 87.

13 Jordan, *Colonial and Revolutionary Families,* 3:1512.

14 TMT, 377.

15 TMT, 377.

16 TMT, 378.

17 TMT, 379.

18 Recorded February 15, 1867, in the Plan Book for the 20th [later 7th] Ward of Allegheny County, 74–75, HHC.

19 See: last will and testament of Barbara A. Negley, February 23, 1867, recorded in the Registry of Wills for Allegheny County, vol. 12, no. 200, 371.

20 *Pittsburgh Press,* April 18, 1976.

21 See: "Plan of Building Lots in East Liberty," recorded August 20, 1867, of the Plan Book for Allegheny County, HHC, 3:194–95.

22 TMT, 379.

23 WLM.

24 WLM.

25 Related by the elder James R. Mellon to his grandson, Matthew T. Mellon.

26 TMT, 378.

27 TMT, 379–80;

28 JMS, 134–35.

29 Edward Mellon, interviewed by Boyden Sparkes, October 25, 1944, AA.

30 CHM, 9.

31 Samuel A. Schreiner Jr., *Henry Clay Frick* (New York: St. Martin's Press, 1995), 18.

32 James B. Corey, *Memoir and Personal Recollection of J. B. Corey* (Pittsburgh, Pennsylvania: Pittsburgh Printing Co., 1914), 73.

33 Letter from Thomas Mellon to his son James Ross Mellon, January 21, 1864, HHC.

34 CHM, 5.

35 JMS, 32.

36 CHM, 10.

37 CHM, 5.

38 TMT, 387.

39 TMT, 9.

40 TMT, 9.

41 TMT, 8.

42 WLM.

43 CHM, 11.

44 BH, 60.

45 Harvey O'Connor, *Mellon's Millions: The Life and Times of Andrew W. Mellon* (New York: John Day, 1933), 35.

46 WLM.

47 Recalled by Matthew T. Mellon, who served as a messenger at the Mellon National Bank, in 1913.

48 WLM.

49 Photograph of 512–514 Smithfield Street, AA.

50 CHM, 9.

51 George Harvey, *Henry Clay Frick: The Man* (New York: Charles Scribner's Sons, 1928), 40.

52 Ibid., 69.

53 Ibid., 38.

54 HCF, 43–44.

55 Harvey, *Henry Clay Frick,* 42.

56 HCF, 44–45.

57 HCF, 45.

58 HCF, 44.

59 TMT, 642–43.

60 Letter from Thomas Mellon to his son James Ross Mellon, July 16, 1864, HHC.

61 WLM.

62 *Pittsburgh Millionaires* (Pittsburgh, Pennsylvania: Breen & Ramsey, 1886).

63 Henry A. Phillips, Andrew W. Mellon's accountant, interviewed by Boyden Sparkes, September 30, 1944, AA.

64 TMT, 385.

65 TMT, 376.

66 Information supplied by the U.S. Military Academy at West Point.

67 TMT, 384–85.

68 TMT, 385.

69 BHA, 11.

70 JMS, 48–49.

## Chapter XI

1 TMT, 409–13.

2 WLM.

3 TMT, 411–12.

4   TMT, 409–13.

5   TMT, 414.

6   Quoted in *Bartlett's Familiar
    Quotations, Seventeenth Edition*
    (Boston: Little, Brown and Company,
    2002), 320.

7   TMT, 414.

8   TMT, 287.

9   TMT, 414–15; Erasmus Wilson, ed.,
    *Standard History of Pittsburgh,
    Pennsylvania* (Chicago: H. R.
    Cornel, 1898).

10  TMT, 418.

11  TMT, 419.

12  TMT, 419.

13  Edward White, *A Century of
    Banking in Pittsburgh* (Pittsburgh,
    Pennsylvania: Index Company, 1903).

14  WLM.

15  CHM, 41–42.

16  CHM, 41–42.

17  WLM.

18  WLM.

19  WLM.

20  JMS, 61.

### Chapter XII

1   TMT, 585.

2   UPE, xiv, xv.

3   TMT, 585–88.

4   TMT, 585.

5   TMT, 588–616.

6   BH, 41–42; UPE, 464.

7   JBC, 262.

8   "Adsectum Index to Appear Docket,
    Court of Common Pleas No. 1 for
    the County of Allegheny," vol. 10,
    case no. 837, December term, 1876,
    141, Felix C. Negley and Graham
    Scott, plaintiffs, and Thomas Mellon,
    defendant.

9   TMT, 616–21.

10  Letter from Thomas Mellon to his
    son Richard B. Mellon, January 27,
    1883, APM.

11  TMT, 621–31.

12  "Adsectum Index to Appear Docket,
    Court of Common Pleas No. 1 for
    the County of Allegheny," vol. 11,
    130, case no. 177, December term,
    1879, Thomas Scott, plaintiff and
    Thomas Mellon, defendant; see also
    Supreme Court of Pennsylvania,
    Western District, Paper Book of
    Plaintiff in Error, filed January 19,
    1884, *Thomas Scott v. Thomas Mellon*.

13  TMT, 589.

14  TMT, 634.

15  TMT 634–35.

16  TMT, 635–37.

### Chapter XIII

1   JMS, 26.

2   JMS, 26–27.

3   BH, 56.

4   JMS, 27–28; also WLM.

5   BH, 58.

6   JMS, 28.

7   JMS, 27.

8   TMT, 374–75.

9   TMT, 385–86.

10  Quoted in Philip Kopper, *America's
    National Gallery of Art* (New York:
    Harry N. Abrams, 1991), 43.

11  Letter from Thomas Mellon to his
    son James Ross Mellon, November 8,
    1862, HHC.

12  WLM.

13  Robert C. Alberts, *Pitt: The Story of
    the University of Pittsburgh, 1787–
    1987* (Pittsburgh, Pennsylvania:
    University of Pittsburgh Press, 1987),
    23–31.

14  RUP.

15  APM.

16  APM.

17  APM.

18  APM.

19  APM.

20  TMT, 228–29

21  JMS, 29.

22  JMS, 29.

23  WLM; TMT, 406–7.

24  WLM.

25  Letter from Thomas Mellon to his son James Ross Mellon, January 21, 1864, HHC.

26  CHM, 13

27  WLM.

28  WLM; also BH, 72.

29  George Harvey, *Henry Clay Frick the Man* (New York: Charles Scribner's Sons, 1928), 70.

30  JMS, 117.

31  HCF, 394.

32  RSS, 25–26.

33  DC, 168–82.

34  HCF, 43–45.

35  BHA, chapter 2.

36  BHA, chapter 2.

37  DC, part 1, chapter 1, 25.

38  RSS, 28.

## Chapter XIV

1  TMT, 422–23.

2  JMS, 70.

3  WLM, 72–73.

4  TMT, 425.

5  CHS, 436.

6  JMS, 75.

7  TMT, 425–26.

8  WAM, July 8, 1940.

9  William A. Mellon, "Notes for Biography of Andrew Mellon," unpublished manuscript, 1940, ACML.

10  Letter from William A. Mellon to Burton Hendrick, July 8, 1940, WAM.

11  William A. Mellon, "Notes for Biography."

12  Letter from William A. Mellon to Burton Hendrick, August 1, 1940, WAM.

13  Letter from William A. Mellon to Burton Hendrick, July 8, 1940, WAM.

14  John Gabbert Bowman, interviewed by Boyden Sparkes, University of Pittsburgh, August 3, 1944, AA.

## Chapter XV

1  TMT, 541–63.

2  Harvey O'Connor, *Mellon's Millions* (New York: John Day, 1933), 33; Sarah H. Killikelly, *The History of Pittsburgh: Its Rise and Progress* (Pittsburgh, Pennsylvania: B. C. & Gordon Montgomery, 1906).

3  TMT, 527.

4  *Pittsburgh Commercial Gazette,* July 25, 1877.

5  *Independent* (New York), July 26 and August 2, 1877.

6  PK, 149.

7  PK, 149–50.

8  NLT, February 28, 1881.

9  Andrew Roy, *A History of the Coal Miners of the United States* (Columbus, Ohio: J. L. Trauger, 1902), 191.

10  NLT, February 19, 1881.

11  NLT, November 18, 1880.

12  PK, 159.

13  PK, 159

14  NLT, January 13, 1883.

15  NLT, November 27, 1880.

16  NLT, February 12, 1881.

17  NLT, February 12, 1881.

18  *Pittsburgh Commercial Gazette,* February 21, 1881.

19  Ibid.

20  Ibid.

21 Ibid.

22 Ibid.

23 NLT, February 19 and 28, 1881.

24 PK, 158.

25 PK, 158.

26 NLT, February 28, 1881.

27 NLT, February 28, 1881.

28 NLT, February 28, 1881.

29 NLT, February 28, 1881.

30 NLT, March 5, 1881.

31 NLT, October 29, 1881.

32 *Pittsburgh Commercial Gazette,*
   November 18, 1881.

33 TMT, 549.

34 TMT, 551.

35 NLT, February 4, 1882.

36 TMT, 535–63.

37 NLT, January 13, 1883.

38 TMT, 561.

39 TMT, 549–50.

40 NLT, November 20, 1880.

41 Letter from Thomas Armstrong to
   Terence Powderly, January 1, 1880,
   Terence Vincent Powderly Papers,
   Columbia University Library.

42 PK, 88.

43 TMT, 550.

44 NLT, October 29, 1881.

45 William B. Weeden, *The Social Law
   of Labor* (Boston: Roberts Brothers,
   1882), AA.

### CHAPTER XVI

1 TMT, 442.

2 TMT, 16.

3 TMT, 16.

4 TMT, 32–33.

5 TMT, 443–45.

6 TMT, 447.

7 TMT, 448.

8 TMT, 443.

9 TMT, 449.

10 TMT, 450–51.

11 TMT, 39.

12 TMT, 33–34.

13 TMT, 453.

14 TMT, 455–56.

15 TMT, 456.

16 TMT, 457.

17 TMT, 464.

18 TMT, 464–65.

19 TMT, 465–66.

20 TMT, 466–68.

21 TMT, 479.

22 TMT, 35.

23 TMT, 481–82.

24 TMT, 488–89.

25 TMT, 489–90.

26 TMT, 490.

27 TMT, 492.

28 TMT, 495.

29 TMT, 497.

30 TMT, 497–98.

31 TMT, 503.

32 TMT, 504–5.

33 TMT, 41.

34 TMT, 41.

35 TMT, 512.

36 Letter from Thomas Mellon to his
   son James Ross Mellon, August 6,
   1864, HHC.

37 WLM.

### CHAPTER XVII

1 TMT, 393.

2 Peri E. Arnold, "Democracy and
  Corruption in the 19th Century
  United States: Parties, Spoils, and
  Political Participation," essay
  contributed to the Working Group
  on the History of Administration
  of the International Institute of
  Administrative Sciences, University
  of Notre Dame, n.d.

3 LS, 106–7.

4 Ibid., 105.

5  Ibid., 116.

6  Lincoln Steffens, "Pittsburg: A City Ashamed," *McClure's Magazine,* May 1903.

7  LS, 119–20.

8  Steffens, "Pittsburg: A City Ashamed."

9  Carmen DiCiccio, *Social Biographies of Select and Common Council Membership of Pittsburgh from 1879 to 1906* (Pittsburgh, Pennsylvania: Privately printed, 1990).

10  MR.

11  MR, April 7, 1879.

12  MR, November 10, 1879, and February 26, 1881.

13  MR, October 13, 1879.

14  MR, 1879–87.

15  DK, 47.

16  MR, April 28, 1879.

17  MR, June 30 and September 15, 1879.

18  MR, April 12, 1880.

19  MR, April 5, 1880.

20  MR, April 5, 1880.

21  MR, April 11, 1881.

22  MR, April 11, 1881.

23  MR, September 20, 1881.

24  Letter from Andrew Carnegie to the Hon. Robert W. Lyon, mayor of the city of Pittsburgh, November 25, 1881, in MR, December 5, 1881.

25  MR, February 6, 1883.

26  MR, February 6, 1883.

27  MR, February 6, 1883; DK, 45.

28  Letter from Andrew Carnegie to the mayor and councils of Pittsburgh, February 6, 1890, in Robert M. Lester, *Forty Years of Carnegie Giving* (New York: Charles Scribner's Sons, 1941), 104.

29  William A. Mellon, "Notes for Biography of Andrew Mellon," unpublished manuscript, 1940, ACML; WLM.

30  PK, 274–83.

31  MR.

32  MR.

33  MR.

34  Letter from Andrew Carnegie to the Mayor and Councils of Pittsburgh, February 6, 1890, in: Lester, *Forty Years of Carnegie Giving,* 104.

35  County Commissioner Charles H. McKee, quoted in *Pittsburgh Commercial Gazette,* February 1, 1884.

36  *Pittsburgh Commercial Gazette,* August 27, 1884.

37  Ibid.

38  *Pittsburgh Commercial Gazette,* September 11, 1884.

39  Ibid.

40  Ibid.

41  Ibid.

42  Ibid.

43  MR.

44  TMT, 550.

45  TMT, 643.

46  TMT, 535.

47  TMT, 541.

CHAPTER XVIII

1  BHC, 4.

2  BHS, 1.

3  BHS, 1.

4  Recalled by the author's father, Matthew T. Mellon.

5  JMS, 395.

6  RSS, especially 147–56.

7  BHC, 3; JMS, 126.

8  John Gabbert Bowman, interviewed by Boyden Sparkes, August 3, 1944, PBS; JMS, 128–29.

9  Ibid.

10  Ibid.

11  William Donner, interviewed by Boyden Sparkes, June 25, 1945, PBS.

12  Newsreels of Andrew W. Mellon, AA.
13  Ibid.
14  BH, 276.
15  BHC, 260.
16  BHC, 1.
17  BHC, 4.
18  BHC, 2.
19  BHC, 2.
20  Henry Phillips, interviewed by Boyden Sparkes, 1944–45, PBS.
21  BHC, 2–3.
22  BHC, 2.
23  Bowman interview.
24  Ibid.
25  BHC; also BHS.
26  BHC, 3.
27  WLM; also recalled by Matthew T. Mellon.
28  BHC, 4.
29  BHC, 4.
30  Recalled by Matthew T. Mellon.
31  BHC, 3.
32  Bowman interview.
33  BHC, 3.
34  DK, 68–69; BHC, 3.
35  BHA, chapter 5, 31–32.
36  Letter from William A. Mellon to Burton Hendrick, July 8, 1940, WAM.
37  BHC, 5.
38  Willard M. Kiplinger, *Washington Is Like That* (New York: Harper & Brothers, 1942).
39  JMS, 32.
40  DC.
41  Letter from Andrew W. Mellon to Nora McMullen Mellon, March 13, 1923, APM.
42  David Finley, interviewed by Boyden Sparkes, March 1, 1945, PBS.
43  BH, 278.
44  Andrew W. Mellon, *Taxation: The People's Business* (New York: Macmillan, 1924).
45  WLM.
46  *World* (New York) June 15, 1926.
47  BHS, 2–3.
48  Andrew W. Mellon, Letter Books, vol. 8, series, 2, p, 67, APM.
49  Paul Krause, *The Battle for Homestead, 1880–1892* (Pittsburgh, Pennsylvania: University of Pittsburgh Press, 1992), 273–83.
50  TMT, 326.
51  Donner interview.
52  Ibid.; Krause, *The Battle for Homestead,* 273–83.
53  BHA, chapter 11, 3–6; also Burton J. Hendrick, interview with John Galey, March 10, 1941, AA.
54  DC.
55  Letter from Henry A. Phillips, Andrew W. Mellon's accountant, to Boyden Sparkes, September 30, 1944, AA.
56  JMS, 220.

CHAPTER XIX

1  TMT, 106.
2  TMT, 110–11.
3  TMT, 2.
4  TMT, 55, 219.
5  TMT, 1.
6  TMT, 1–2.
7  TMT, 1–2.
8  TMT, 648.
9  TMT, 3.
10  TMT, 541.
11  TMT, 643–44.
12  TMT, 249.
13  TMT, 3.
14  TMT, 2.
15  TMT, 517.
16  TMT, 542.

17  TMT, 648.
18  Letter from William A. Mellon to Burton Hendrick, July 8, 1940, WAM.
19  JRM, preface.
20  WLM; RSS, 27.
21  TMT, 3.
22  TMT, 2.

### Chapter XX

1  TMT, 436.
2  Letter from Thomas Mellon to his son James Ross Mellon, November 17, 1881, HHC.
3  Ibid.
4  HHC.
5  JMS, 97.
6  WLM.
7  Letters between Andrew W. Mellon and his brother Richard B. Mellon, 1882–87, APM.
8  TMT, 646.
9  Letters from Thomas Mellon to his son Richard B. Mellon, January 16 and May 20, 1885, and December 9, 1886, APM.
10  Letter from William A. Mellon to Burton Hendrick, August 1, 1940, WAM.
11  Owen Wister, *The Virginian* (London: Macmillan, 1928).
12  Letter from Thomas Mellon to his son Richard B. Mellon, January 9, 1883, APM.
13  Letter from Thomas Mellon to his son Richard B. Mellon, January 15, 1885, APM.
14  Richard King Mellon, interviewed by Boyden Sparkes, October 18, 1944, PBS; JMS, 97.
15  Letters from Richard B. Mellon to William H. H. Larimer, October 17 and 24, 1886, Colorado Historical Society, Denver.
16  Sarah Jane Mellon, "Glen Eyre," manuscript travel log, n.d., Archive of Seward Mellon, Ligonier, Pennsylvania.
17  Ibid.
18  Ibid.
19  Ibid.
20  Ibid.
21  Ibid.
22  WLM.
23  Sarah Jane Mellon, "Glen Eyre."
24  APM.
25  Letter from Thomas Mellon to his son Richard B. Mellon, December 14, 1884, APM.
26  Letter from Thomas Mellon to his son Richard B. Mellon, January 16, 1885, APM.
27  Letter from Thomas Mellon to his son Richard B. Mellon, December 9, 1886.
28  Letter from Thomas Mellon to his son Richard B. Mellon, May 20, 1885, APM; BHA, chapter 3, 29–30.
29  JMS, 129.
30  *Official Report of the Proceedings Before the U. S. Board of Tax Appeals, A. W. Mellon, Petitioner, vs. Commissioner of Internal Revenue, Respondent.* Docket no. 76499, 4420–22, 4610–12, National Archives, Washington, D.C.
31  TMT, 647.

### Chapter XXI

1  WLM.
2  APM.
3  Andrew Carnegie, *The Autobiography of Andrew Carnegie* (Garden City, New York: Doubleday, Doran, 1933), 1.

4  Andrew Carnegie, "The Gospel of Wealth," *North American Review,* June 1889.

5  HCF, 132.

6  Frick Art and Historical Center, Pittsburgh, Pennsylvania.

7  Letter from Andrew Carnegie to William Gladstone, September 24, 1892, Gladstone Papers, vol. 437, Adds. Ms. 44,522, fol. 302, British Museum, London.

8  *Pittsburgh Post-Gazette,* January 30, 1893.

9  Andrew Carnegie Papers, Library of Congress, Washington, D.C.

10  Arthur G. Burgoyne, *The Homestead Strike of 1892* (Pittsburgh, Pennsylvania: University of Pittsburgh Press, 1979), 234–35.

11  HCF, 282.

12  HCF, 311.

13  TMT, 522–24.

14  TMT, 524.

## CHAPTER XXII

1  Edward Mellon, interviewed by Boyden Sparkes, October 25, 1944, AA.

2  Letter from William A. Mellon to Burton Hendrick, August 1, 1940, WAM.

3  Ibid.

4  Ibid.

5  Ibid.

6  BB, 4.

7  BB, 7–10.

8  BB, 8.

9  KCS, December 20, 1890.

10  KCS, December 2, 1890.

11  BB, 8–9; KCS, December 20, 1890.

12  BB, 8–9; KCS, January 1, 1891.

13  BB, 8–9; KCS, December 20, 1890.

14  BB, 9.

15  Mellon to Hendrick, August 1, 1940.

16  Letters from Thomas Mellon to "all at home," February 17, 1890; to Sarah Jane Mellon, February 28, 1890; to his son Andrew W. Mellon, February 25 and March 29, 1890, APM.

17  Letter from William A. Mellon to Burton Hendrick, July 8, 1940, WAM.

18  HHC.

19  Letter from Thomas Mellon to his son Richard B. Mellon, December 9, 1886, APM.

20  Thomas Mellon, unpublished memorandum, August 25, 1898, APM.

21  Letter from William A. Mellon to Burton Hendrick, August 1, 1940, WAM.

22  See volume 678 of the Allegheny County book of deeds.

23  JMS, 183.

24  JMS, 186.

25  *New York Tribune,* May 1, 1892.

26  Burton J. Hendrick, manuscript, PBS.

27  BHA, chapter 4, 4; Transfer of Assets from Thomas Mellon to Andrew W. Mellon, 1875–94: Assignment by Thomas Mellon of certain bonds and mortgages to Andrew W. Mellon, December 26–29, 1894, APM.

28  APM, Box 15, Folder "Miscellaneous Financial Records, 1892–1917."

29  Ibid.

30  Trust agreement, October 16, 1905, APM.

31  Henry Phillips, interviewed by Boyden Sparkes, 1944–45, PBS; Trust dissolution document, June 19, 1919, APM.

## Chapter XXIII

1. Letter from William A. Mellon to Burton Hendrick, August 1, 1940, WAM.
2. KCS, January 1, 1891.
3. KCS, January 1 and December 24, 1891.
4. KCS, December 2, 1890.
5. KCS, December 23, 1891.
6. KCS, December 2, 1890.
7. KCS, December 2, 1890.
8. BB, 14–16, 19–23, 31–32; *Kansas City Globe,* June 28, 1890.
9. KCS, December 2, 1890; BB.
10. Mellon to Hendrick, August 1, 1940.
11. Ibid.
12. Cited in Thomas Mellon, *Thomas Mellon and His Times,* ed. Mary Louise Briscoe (Pittsburgh, Pennsylvania: University of Pittsburgh Press, 1994), 391.
13. Burton J. Hendrick, "Andrew William Mellon," unpublished manuscript, chapter 4, 13, APM.
14. Mellon to Hendrick, August 1, 1940.
15. KCS, December 20, 1890.
16. Mellon to Hendrick, August 1, 1940.
17. Ibid.
18. Ibid.
19. Ibid.
20. KCS, February 2, 1891.
21. Mellon to Hendrick, August 1, 1940.
22. Ibid.
23. Ibid.
24. KCS, December 22, 1891.
25. KCS, December 22, 1891.
26. KCS, December 22, 1891.
27. KCS, December 24, 1891.
28. KCS, December 24, 1891.
29. Mellon to Hendrick, August 1, 1940.
30. Ibid.
31. Ibid.

## Chapter XXIV

1. Letter from William A. Mellon to Burton Hendrick, July 8, 1940, WAM.
2. Thomas Mellon, unpublished memorandum, August 25, 1898, APM.
3. TMT, 375.
4. JMS, 189–91.
5. Letter from Thomas Mellon to Lillian Bell Mellon, May 20, 1897, ACML.
6. UPE, 391.
7. Thomas Mellon, memorandum, August 25, 1898.

## Chapter XXV

1. *Pittsburgh Dispatch,* January 20, 1909.
2. Scrapbook of Sarah Jane Negley, AA.
3. *Collecting in the Gilded Age: Frick Art and Historical Center, Pittsburgh* (Hanover, New Hampshire: University Press of New England, 1997), 215.
4. TMT, 642.
5. TMT, 644–45.
6. Letter from Thomas Mellon to James Ross Mellon, March 6, 1897, HHC.
7. TMT, 366–67.
8. Charles D. Marshall, interviewed by Burton J. Hendrick, April 8, 1940, 6, APM.
9. Letter from Thomas Mellon to his sons, September 24, 1895, HHC.
10. JBC, 262–64.
11. Letter from Thomas Mellon to Lillian Bell Mellon, May 20, 1897, ACML.
12. TMT, 218–19.
13. TMT, 647–48.
14. Matthew T. Mellon, *The Private Collection of Matthew Taylor Mellon*

(Miami, Florida: Privately printed, 1985), 4, AA.

15 Recorded by the author from conversation with his father, Matthew T. Mellon.

16 Death certificate of Thomas Mellon, Bureau of Vital Records, New Castle, Pennsylvania.

17 TMT, 136.

18 *Pittsburgh Post,* February 9, 1908.

19 Andrew W. Mellon to Andrew Carnegie, February 8, 1908. Andrew Carnegie papers, container 148, Library of Congress, Washington, D.C.

20 "Memorial meeting of the Allegheny County Bar Association, the Tenth day of February Nineteen Hundred Eight," Archive of the Allegheny County Bar Association, Pittsburgh, Pennsylvania.

21 Diary of Mary Taylor Mellon, AA.

CHAPTER XXVI

1 TMT, 379.

2 Thomas Mellon, essay on wealth, written during his studies at the Western University of Pennsylvania, 1834, APM.

3 Letter from Thomas Mellon to his son James R. Mellon, September 24, 1895, HHC.

# Bibliography

Adamson, Ian. *The Identity of Ulster: The Land, the Language and the People.* Northern Ireland: W. & G. Baird, 1982.

———. *The Ulster People, Ancient, Medieval and Modern.* Belfast: Universities Press, 1991.

Albert, George Dallas. *The History of Westmoreland County, Pennsylvania.* Philadelphia: L. H. Everts, 1882.

Alberts, Robert C. *Pitt: The Story of the University of Pittsburgh, 1787–1987.* Pittsburgh, Pennsylvania: University of Pittsburgh Press, 1987.

Alexander, Edwin P. *On the Main Line: The Pennsylvania Railroad in the 19th Century.* New York: Clarkson N. Potter, 1971.

"Annual Report of the Secretary of Internal Affairs of the Commonwealth of Pennsylvania." *Industrial Statistics* 9 (1882–83).

*Atlas of the City of Pittsburgh, Pennsylvania, 1911.* Pittsburgh: Western Pennsylvania Genealogical Society, 1992.

Baron-Wilson, Mrs. Cornwell. *Memoirs of Harriot, Duchess of St. Albans.* 3rd ed. London: Henry Colburn, 1844.

Barr, Robert M. *Pennsylvania State Reports, Containing Cases Adjudged in the Supreme Court.* Philadelphia: T & J. W. Johnson, 1849.

Basler, Roy P., ed. *The Collected Works of Abraham Lincoln.* 8 vols. New Brunswick, New Jersey: Rutgers University Press, 1953.

Beers, Paul B. *Pennsylvania Politics Today and Yesterday.* University Park: Pennsylvania State University Press, 1980.

Bell, Albert H. *Memoirs of the Bench and Bar of Westmoreland County, Pennsylvania.* Batavia, New York: Batavia Times, 1925.

*A Biographical Congressional Directory, 1774–1911.* Washington, D.C.: U.S. Government Printing Office, 1913.

*Bituminous Coal Annual.* Washington, D.C.: Bituminous Coal Institute, National Coal Association, 1950.

*Bituminous Coal Fields of Pennsylvania.* Commonwealth of Pennsylvania Department of Forests and Waters, 1928.

Blanchard, Charles, ed. *The Progressive Men of the Commonwealth of Pennsylvania.* Logansport, Indiana: A. W. Bowen, 1900.

Bothwell, Margaret Pearson. "Some Pioneers and Some of Their Descendants." *Western Pennsylvania Historical Magazine,* 53 (April 1970).

——. *Old Ligonier Valley and Rachelwood.* Privately printed, c. 1925.

Brownson, James I. "The Life and Times of Senator James Ross." Washington, Pennsylvania: Washington County Historical Society, 1910.

Burgoyne, Arthur G. *All Sorts of Pittsburghers.* Pittsburgh: Leader All Sorts, 1892.

——. *The Homestead Strike of 1892.* Pittsburgh, Pennsylvania: University of Pittsburgh Press, 1979.

Burke, Sir Bernard. *A Genealogical and Heraldic Dictionary of the Peerage and Baronetage of the British Empire.* London: Harrison and Sons, 1863.

——. *A History of the Dormant, Abeyant, Forfeited, and Extinct Peerages of the British Empire.* London: Harrison, 1883.

*Burke's Peerage and Baronetage, 106th Edition.* Ed. Charles Mosley. Crans, Switzerland, 1999.

Byington, Margaret F. *Homestead: The Households of a Mill Town.* Pittsburgh, Pennsylvania: University Center for International Studies, University of Pittsburgh, 1974, originally published in 1910.

Cannadine, David. *Mellon: An American Life.* New York: Alfred A. Knopf, 2006.

Carnegie, Andrew. *The Autobiography of Andrew Carnegie.* Garden City, New York: Doubleday Doran, 1933.

Chapman, T. J. *Old Pittsburgh Days.* Pittsburgh, Pennsylvania: J. R. Weldin, 1900.

Cohen, Josiah. "Half a Century of the Allegheny County Bar Association." *Western Pennsylvania Historical Magazine* 4, no. 3 (July 1921).

Collins, John Stuart Fulton, Jr. *Stringtown on the Pike.* Ann Arbor, Michigan: Privately printed by Edwards Brothers, 1966.

Corey, James B. *Memoir and Personal Recollection of J. B. Corey.* Pittsburgh, Pennsylvania: Pittsburgh Printing Company, 1914.

Couvares, Francis G. *The Remaking of Pittsburgh.* Albany: State University of New York Press, 1984.

Crawford, Margaret E. *The Hungry Stream: Essays on Emigration and Famine.* Belfast: Nicholson & Bass, 1997.

Darlington, Mary Carson. *History of Colonel Henry Bouquet.* Privately printed, 1920.

Darwin, Charles. *The Descent of Man.* In *From So Simple a Beginning: The Four Great Books of Charles Darwin,* ed. Edward O. Wilson. New York: W. W. Norton, 2006.

Daughters of the American Revolution of Allegheny County, Pennsylvania, compilers. *Fort Duquesne and Fort Pitt: Early Names of Pittsburgh Streets.* 4th ed. Pittsburgh, Pennsylvania: Reed & Witting, 1914.

DiCiccio, Carmen. *Coal and Coke in Pennsylvania.* Harrisburg: Pennsylvania Historical and Museum Commission, 1996.

——. *Social Biographies of Select and Common Council Membership of Pittsburgh from 1879 to 1906.* Pittsburgh, Pennsylvania: Privately printed, 1990.

*Dictionary of American Biography*. Ed. Allen Johnson and Dumas Malone. New York: Charles Scribner's Sons, 1958.

Duncan, Clarence Barclay. "Evolution of the Government of Pittsburgh." M.A. thesis, University of Pittsburgh, 1929.

Eastman, Frank M. *Courts and Lawyers of Pennsylvania: A History*. New York: American Historical Society, 1922.

Eavenson, Howard N. *The First Century and a Quarter of American Coal Industry*. Pittsburgh, Pennsylvania: Privately printed, 1942.

Edwards, Richard, ed. *Industries of Pittsburgh: Trade Commerce and Manufactures; Historical and Descriptive Review*. Pittsburgh, Pennsylvania: Richard Edwards, 1879.

*Encyclopedia of Contemporary Biography of Pennsylvania*. New York: Atlantic, 1890.

*Encyclopedia of Pennsylvania Biography*. Ed. John W. Jordan. New York: Lewis Historical, 1921.

*Encyclopedia of Pennsylvania Biography*. Ed. Alfred Decker Keator. New York: Lewis, 1948.

Evans, Henry Oliver. "The Penns' 'Manor of Pittsburgh.'" *Western Pennsylvania Historical Magazine* 27 (March–June 1944).

"The First Convention of the American Federation of Labor, Pittsburgh, Pennsylvania, November 15th–18th, 1881." *Western Pennsylvania Historical Magazine* 7 (January 1924).

Fitzsimons, Gray, and Rose Fitzsimmons, eds. *Westmoreland County, Pennsylvania: An Inventory of Historic Engineering and Industrial Sites*. Washington, D.C.: National Park Service, 1994.

Fleming, George Thornton. *History of Pittsburgh and Environs*. New York: American Historical Society, 1922.

———, ed. *Pittsburgh: How to See It*. Pittsburgh, Pennsylvania: William G. Johnston, 1916.

———, compiler. *Views of Old Pittsburgh: A Portfolio of the Past*. Pittsburgh, Pennsylvania: Crescent Press, 1932.

Foote, Shelby. *The Civil War: A Narrative*. New York: Random House, 1963.

Fox, Arthur B. "The Ups and Downs of Pittsburgh's Inclines." *Pennsylvania History* 22, no. 4 (July–August 1999).

Franklin, Benjamin. *The Autobiography of Benjamin Franklin*. New York: Modern Library, 2001.

Gangewere, R. Jay. "The Origins of the Carnegie." *Carnegie Magazine* 61, no. 6 (November–December 1992).

Grant, Benjamin. *Reports of Cases Argued and Adjudged in the Supreme Court of Pennsylvania*. Philadelphia: William J. Campbell, 1889.

Gray, James H. "Allegheny County Common Pleas Court Law Judges, 1791–1939." *Western Pennsylvania Historical Magazine* 24 (September 1941).

Hall, J. Morton. *Pittsburgh's Great Industries*. Pittsburgh, Pennsylvania: William G. Johnston, 1891.

Harper, Frank C. *Pittsburgh: Forge of the Universe*. New York: Comet Press, 1957.

————. *Pittsburgh of Today: Its Resources and People.* New York: American Historical Society, 1931.

Harvey, George. *Henry Clay Frick the Man.* New York: Charles Scribner's Sons, 1928.

Hays, Samuel P., ed. *City at the Point.* Pittsburgh, Pennsylvania: University of Pittsburgh Press, 1989.

Henderson, James A. "The Railroad Riots in Pittsburgh." *Western Pennsylvania Historical Magazine* 11, no. 3 (July 1928).

Hendrick, Burton J. "Andrew William Mellon." Unpublished manuscript, Archive of Paul Mellon, National Gallery of Art.

————. "A. W. and R. B. [Mellon] Contrast." Unpublished manuscript, author's archive.

————. "Hendrick's Summary." Unpublished manuscript, papers of Boyden Sparkes, author's archive.

————, ed. *Writings of Andrew Carnegie.* 10 vols. New York: Doubleday, Page, 1933.

Hersh, Burton J. *The Mellon Family: A Fortune in History.* New York: William Morrow, 1978.

*History of Allegheny County, Pennsylvania.* Philadelphia: L. H. Everts, 1876.

*History of Allegheny County, Pennsylvania.* Chicago: A. Warner, 1889.

Hofstadter, Richard. *Social Darwinism in American Thought.* Boston: Beacon Press, 1959.

Holmberg, James C. "The Industrializing Community: Pittsburgh, 1850–1880." PhD diss., University of Pittsburgh, 1981.

Holt, Michael Fitzgibbon. *Forging a Majority: The Formation of the Republican Party in Pittsburgh, 1848–1860.* Pittsburgh, Pennsylvania: University of Pittsburgh Press, 1990, first published in 1969.

Hudson, William Henry. *Philosophies Ancient and Modern: Herbert Spencer.* New York: Dodge, n.d.

Huff, William S. "Richardson's Jail." *Western Pennsylvania Historical Magazine* (Spring 1958).

Ingham, John N. *Making Iron and Steel.* Columbus: Ohio State University Press, 1991.

Isaacson, Walter. *Benjamin Franklin: An American Life.* New York: Simon & Schuster, 2003.

James, Alfred P. "General James Scott Negley." *Western Pennsylvania Historical Magazine* 14, no. 2 (April 1931).

Jones, Mrs. Edw. C. *A Brief History of Pittsburgh, 1728–1927.* Pittsburgh, Pennsylvania: Vanity Press, 1927.

Jordan, John W. *A Century and a Half of Pittsburgh and Her People.* New York: Lewis, 1908.

————. *Genealogical and Personal History of Western Pennsylvania.* New York: Lewis, 1915.

Jordan, Wilfred, ed. *Colonial and Revolutionary Families of Pennsylvania.* New York: Lewis, 1954.

Josephy, Alvin M., ed. *The American Heritage History of American Business & Industry.* New York: American Heritage, 1972.

Jucha, Robert J. "The Anatomy of a Streetcar Suburb." *Western Pennsylvania Historical Magazine* 62, no. 4 (October 1979).

Katarincic, Joseph A. "The Allegheny County Bar Association, 1870–1960." *Western Pennsylvania Historical Magazine* 43, no. 4 (December 1960).

Kelly, George B., ed. *Allegheny County: A Sesqui-Centennial Review, 1788–1938.* Pittsburgh, Pennsylvania: Allegheny County Sesqui-Centennial Committee, 1938.

Kidney, Walter C. *Pittsburgh's Landmark Architecture.* Pittsburgh, Pennsylvania: Pittsburgh History & Landmarks Foundation, 1997.

Killikelly, Sarah H. *The History of Pittsburgh: Its Rise and Progress.* Pittsburgh, Pennsylvania: B. C. & Gordon Montgomery, 1906.

Kinard, Agnes Dodds. *Celebration of Carnegie in Pittsburgh: The Man, the Institute, and the City.* Pittsburgh, Pennsylvania: Carnegie Museum of Art, 1982.

———. *Celebrating the First 100 Years of the Carnegie in Pittsburgh.* Pittsburgh, Pennsylvania: Carnegie Museum of Art, 1995.

Kiplinger, Willard M. *Washington Is Like That.* New York: Harper & Brothers, 1942.

Kleinberg, S. J. *The Shadow of the Mills: Working-Class Families in Pittsburgh, 1870–1907.* Pittsburgh, Pennsylvania: University of Pittsburgh Press, 1989.

Kopper, Philip. *The National Gallery of Art: A Gift to the Nation.* New York: Harry N. Abrams, 1991.

Koskoff, David E. *The Mellons: The Chronicle of America's Richest Family.* New York: Thomas Y. Crowell, 1978.

Krause, Paul. *The Battle for Homestead, 1880–1892: Politics, Culture and Steel.* Pittsburgh, Pennsylvania: University of Pittsburgh Press, 1992.

Lester, Robert M. *Forty Years of Carnegie Giving.* New York: Charles Scribner's Sons, 1941.

Leyburn, James G. *The Scotch-Irish: A Social History.* Chapel Hill: University of North Carolina Press, 1962.

"Life Sketches of Leading Citizens of Pittsburgh and the Vicinity." *Biographical Review,* vol 24. Boston: Biographical Review, 1897.

Lorant, Stefan. *Pittsburgh: The Story of an American City.* Lenox, Massachusetts: Authors Edition, 1975.

Love, Philip H. *Andrew W. Mellon: The Man and His Work.* Baltimore, Maryland: F. Heath Coggin, 1929.

Loyd, William H. *The Early Courts of Pennsylvania.* Boston: Boston Book Company, 1910.

McCullough, C. Hax, Jr. *One Hundred Years of Banking: The History of Mellon National Bank and Trust Company.* Pittsburgh, Pennsylvania: Herbick & Held, 1970.

———. "The Surnames of Pittsburgh: Conrad Winebiddle, 18th Century Patriot, Landowner." *Bimonthly Newsletter of the Historical Society of Western Pennsylvania* 9, no. 2 (March–April 2000).

———. "The Surnames of Pittsburgh: Judge Charles Shaler and Shaler Township." *Bimonthly Newsletter of the Historical Society of Western Pennsylvania* 8, no. 8 (December 1999).

———. "The Surnames of Pittsburgh: Ross Street and James Ross." *Bimonthly Newsletter of the Historical Society of Western Pennsylvania* 4, no. 1 (January 1995).

McCusker, John J. *How Much Is That in Real Money?* Worcester, Massachusetts: American Antiquarian Society, 1992.

Mellon, James Ross. *Letters.* Pittsburgh, Pennsylvania: Privately printed, 1928.

———. "Reminiscences of the East Liberty Presbyterian Church from 1850 to 1870." Unpublished manuscript, 1932.

Mellon, Paul. "The Irish Cottage Where an American Dream Was Born." *Architectural Digest,* August 1993.

Mellon, Paul, with John Baskett. *Reflections in a Silver Spoon.* New York: William Morrow, 1992.

Mellon, Rachel Hughey Larimer. *The Larimer, McMasters and Allied Families.* Philadelphia: J. B. Lippincott, 1903.

Mellon, Sandra Springer, ed. *Dear Sons: Letters From Thomas Mellon, 1882–1886.* Ligonier, Pennsylvania: Mellon Rolling Rock Museum, 2005.

Mellon, Thomas. *The Boss and Boodle Fight against Incline Planes and Non-Resident Investors.* Kansas City, MO: Inter-State, August 1890.

———. *Thomas Mellon and His Times.* Pittsburgh, Pennsylvania: William G. Johnston, 1885.

———. *Thomas Mellon and His Times.* Pittsburgh, Pennsylvania: Murdoch-Kerr Press, 1885.

———. *Thomas Mellon and His Times.* New York: Kraus Reprint Company, 1969.

———. *Thomas Mellon and His Times* Ed. Matthew T. Mellon. Belfast: Brough, Cox and Dunn, 1970.

———. *Thomas Mellon and His Times.* Ed. Mary Louise Briscoe. Pittsburgh, Pennsylvania: University of Pittsburgh Press, 1994.

Mellon, William Larimer. *Reminiscences of General William Larimer.* Lancaster, Pennsylvania: New Era, 1918.

Mellon, William Larimer, with Boyden Sparkes. *Judge Mellon's Sons.* Pittsburgh, Pennsylvania: Privately printed, 1948.

Miller, Annie Clark. *Chronicles of the Houses and Estates of Pittsburgh and Its Environs.* Pittsburgh, Pennsylvania: Privately printed, 1927.

———. "Old Houses and Estates in Pittsburgh." *Western Pennsylvania Historical Magazine* 9, no. 3 (July 1926).

Mintz, Steven, and Susan Kellog. *Domestic Revolutions: A Social History of American Family Life.* New York: Free Press, 1988.

Morse, Jedidiah. *The American Gazetteer.* Boston: S. Hall and Thomas & Andrews, 1797.

Muller, Edward, ed. *Atlas of the County of Allegheny, Penna.* Repr. Historical Society of Western Pennsylvania, 1988.

*Municipal Record.* Proceedings of the Select and Common Councils of the City of Pittsburgh.

Murray, Lawrence L. "Andrew W. Mellon, the Reluctant Candidate." *Pennsylvania Magazine of History and Biography* 97, no. 4 (October 1973).

———. "The Mellon Family, Making and Shaping History: A Survey of the Literature." *Western Pennsylvania Historical Magazine* 62, no. 1 (January 1979).

———. "The Mellons, Their Money, and the Mythical Machine: Organizational Politics in the Republican Twenties." *Pennsylvania History: Quarterly Journal of the Pennsylvania Historical Association* 42, no. 3 (July 1975).

Myers, Gustavus. *History of the Great American Fortunes.* New York: Modern Library, 1936.

Myers, James M. "The Ligonier Valley Railroad as It Touched the Life of Latrobe." *Western Pennsylvania Historical Magazine* 38 (Spring–Summer 1955).

O'Connor, Harvey. *Mellon's Millions: The Life and Times of Andrew W. Mellon.* New York: John Day, 1933.

*Palmer's Pictorial Pittsburgh and Prominent Pittsburghers Past and Present, 1758–1905.* Pittsburgh, Pennsylvania: R. M. Palmer, 1905.

Parrington, Vernon. *The Colonial Mind, 1620–1800.* New York: Harcourt, Brace, 1927.

Pearce, Charles E. *The Jolly Duchess.* New York: Brentano's, n.d.

*Pennsylvania Historical Review: Cities of Pittsburgh and Allegheny.* New York: Historical Publishing Company, Publishers, 1886.

Phillips, Kevin. *The Cousins' Wars.* New York: Basic Books, 1999.

*Pittsburgh and Allegheny Illustrated Review, Historical, Biographical and Commercial.* Pittsburgh, Pennsylvania: J. M. Elstner, 1889.

*Pittsburgh Millionnaires.* Pittsburgh, Pennsylvania: Breen & Ramsey, 1886.

Powderly, Terence Vincent. Terence Vincent Powderly Papers, 1864–1937. Columbia University Library, New York.

Reed, George Edward, ed. *Pennsylvania Archives.* Harrisburg, Pennsylvania: Commonwealth of Pennsylvania, 1902.

Rishel, Joseph F. *Founding Families of Pittsburgh.* Pittsburgh, Pennsylvania: University of Pittsburgh Press, 1990.

Roberts, Thomas P. *Memoirs of John Bannister Gibson, Late Chief Justice of Pennsylvania.* Pittsburgh, Pennsylvania: Jos. Eichbaum, 1890.

Rook, Charles Alexander, ed. *Western Pennsylvanians.* Pittsburgh, Pennsylvania: Western Pennsylvania Biographical Association, 1923.

Roy, Andrew. *A History of the Coal Miners of the United States.* Westport, Connecticut: Greenwood Press, 1970.

Ruvigny, Marquis of. *The Titled Nobility of Europe.* London: Harrison & Sons, 1914.

Sadleir, Michael. *The Strange Life of Lady Blessington.* New York: Farrar, Straus, 1947.

Sanger, Martha Frick Symington. *Henry Clay Frick: An Intimate Portrait.* New York: Abbeville, 1998.

Schreiner, Samuel A., Jr. *Henry Clay Frick: The Gospel of Greed.* New York: St. Martin's, 1995.

Schwennicke, Detlev. *Europäische Stammtafeln.* Marburg: J. A. Stargardt, 1984.

Seaman, Ezra C. *Essays on the Progress of Nations.* Detroit: M. Geiger, 1846.

Serrin, William. *Homestead: The Glory and Tragedy of an American Steel Town.* New York: Times Books, 1992.

Shetler, Charles William. "The Evolution of the O'Hara-Schenley Properties in Allegheny County to 1880." M.A. thesis, University of Pittsburgh, September 1948.

Sipe, C. Hale. *Fort Ligonier and Its Times*. Harrisburg, Pennsylvania: Telegraph, 1932.

Smith, Percy F. *Memory's Milestones*. Pittsburgh, Pennsylvania: Murdoch-Kerr, 1918.

———. *Notable Men of Pittsburgh and Vicinity*. Pittsburgh, Pennsylvania: Pittsburgh Printing Company, 1901.

Sparkes, Boyden. Papers of Boyden Sparkes. Author's archive, New York City.

Spencer, Herbert. *First Principles*. Akron, Ohio: Werner, 1900.

Starrett, Agnes Lynch. *Through One Hundred and Fifty Years: The University of Pittsburgh*. Pittsburgh, Pennsylvania: University of Pittsburgh Press, 1937.

Steffens, Lincoln. *The Shame of the Cities*. New York: Hill and Wang, 1988.

*The Story of Pittsburgh and Vicinity*. Pittsburgh, Pennsylvania: Pittsburgh Gazette Times, 1908.

Swetnam, George. *The Bicentennial History of Pittsburgh and Allegheny County*. Hopkinsville, Kentucky: Historical Record Association, 1955.

Tarr, Joel A. *Devastation and Renewal: An Environmental History of Pittsburgh and Its Region*. Pittsburgh, Pennsylvania: University of Pittsburgh Press, 2003.

Taylor, E. J., ed. *The Book of Prominent Pennsylvanians*. Pittsburgh, Pennsylvania: Leader, 1913.

Taylor, Matthew, and Wood, Sarah. *A History of the Taylor Family*. Pittsburgh, Pennsylvania: Privately printed, 1938.

Teeters, Negley K. "Public Executions in Pennsylvania, 1682 to 1834." *Journal of the Lancaster County Historical Society* 64, no. 2 (Spring 1960).

———. *Scaffold and Chair: A Compilation of Their Use in Pennsylvania, 1682–1962*. Philadelphia: Pennsylvania Prison Society, 1963.

Thrasher, Eugene. "The Magee-Flinn Political Machine." M.A. thesis, University of Pittsburgh, 1951.

Thurston, George H. *Allegheny County's Hundred Years*. Pittsburgh, Pennsylvania: A. A. Anderson & Son, 1888.

———. *Pittsburgh and Allegheny in the Centennial Year*. Pittsburgh, Pennsylvania: A. A. Anderson & Son, 1876.

———. *Pittsburgh's Progress, Industries and Resources*. Pittsburgh, Pennsylvania: A. A. Anderson & Son, 1886.

Toker, Franklin. *Pittsburgh: An Urban Portrait*. University Park: Pennsylvania State University Press, 1986.

*The Twentieth Century Bench and Bar of Pennsylvania*. Chicago: H. C. Cooper, Jr., Bro., 1903.

Upton, Dell, ed. *America's Architectural Roots: Ethnic Groups that Built America*. New York: Preservation Press, 1986.

U.S. Bureau of the Census. *Historical Statistics of the United States: Colonial Times to 1957*. Washington, D.C.: U.S. Department of Commerce.

*Vale Pennsylvania Digest, 1682 to date, Covering Pennsylvania Supreme and Superior Court Reports and All Other Courts of Record, Etc.* St. Paul, Minnesota: West, 1938.

Van Doren, Carl. *Benjamin Franklin*. New York: Viking Press, 1938.

Van Trump, James D. *Majesty of the Law: The Court Houses of Allegheny County*. Pittsburgh, Pennsylvania: Pittsburgh History & Landmarks Foundation, 1988.

Van Trump, James D., and Arthur P. Ziegler Jr. *Landmark Architecture of Allegheny County, Pennsylvania.* Pittsburgh, Pennsylvania: Pittsburgh History & Landmarks Foundation, 1967.

Vexler, Robert I., ed. *Pittsburgh: A Chronological and Documentary History, 1682–1976.* New York: Oceana, 1977.

Volwiler, Albert T. *George Croghan and the Westward Movement, 1741–1782.* Cleveland, Ohio: Arthur H. Park, 1926.

Waddell, Louis M. *The Papers of Henry Bouquet.* Harrisburg: Pennsylvania Historical and Museum Commission, 1994.

Wainwright, Nicholas B. *George Croghan, Wilderness Diplomat.* Chapel Hill: University of North Carolina Press, 1959.

Wall, Joseph Frazier. *Andrew Carnegie.* Pittsburgh, Pennsylvania: University of Pittsburgh Press, 1970.

Ware, Susan. *Forgotten Heroes.* New York: Free Press, 1998.

*Warranty Atlas of Allegheny County,* reproduced by Joel Fishman for the Western Pennsylvania Genealogical Society, Pittsburgh, Pennsylvania, 1982.

Warren, Kenneth. *Triumphant Capitalism.* Pittsburgh, Pennsylvania: University of Pittsburgh Press, 1996.

Watts, Isaac. *The Improvement of the Mind.* New York: N. Bangs and T. Mason, 1822.

Wauchope, Gladys M. *The Ulster Branch of the Family of Wauchope.* London: Simkin Marshall, 1929.

Webb, James H. *Born Fighting: How the Scots-Irish Shaped America.* New York: Broadway Books, 2004.

Weeden, William B. *The Social Law of Labor.* Boston: Roberts Brothers, 1882.

White, Edward. *A Century of Banking in Pittsburgh.* Pittsburgh, Pennsylvania: Index, 1903.

Wilson, Erasmus, ed. *Standard History of Pittsburgh, Pennsylvania.* Chicago: H. R. Cornell, 1898.

## *Acknowledgments*

MY SPECIAL THANKS TO Dr. Michael O'Malley for encouraging Yale University Press to accept *The Judge* for publication.

A brimming measure of thanks to Professor Carmen DiCiccio for discovering and mining a vast number of sources that yielded valuable information, much of it original, for this book. As I do not live in Pittsburgh, it was essential for me to engage an energetic, discriminating researcher with an encyclopedic knowledge of Pittsburgh's history, and in Carmen I found him.

I'm indebted to Herb Schaffner for his incisive editing of my manuscript, and for having helped me through the painful process of converting this work from a privately printed family chronicle to a published biography.

An equal measure of thanks to my team at Yale University Press, which included editor Margaret Otzel, Piyali Bhattacharya, Niamh Cunningham, Maureen Noonan, and designer Mary Valencia.

The boiler-room job of actually piecing this book together was masterfully performed by Peter Strupp and his team at Princeton Editorial Associates.

I'll always be grateful to Gary Cohen for having retrieved the voluminous transcripts of my grandfather William Larimer Mellon's conversations with the journalist Boyden Sparkes. These transcripts encompass much of the original material that makes this book relevant.

My cousins Prosser and Sandy Mellon also deserve a generous acknowledgment for making a number of historic family photographs and portraits available for reproduction in this book.

While I was laboring on *The Judge,* Professor David Cannadine was writing his biography of Thomas Mellon's son Andrew, entitled *Mellon.* That we read and discussed each other's manuscripts and shared our sources of information had, I feel, a salubrious effect on both books —especially on mine. That David and I became friends in the course of our related endeavors was particularly gratifying.

Ironically, the Carnegie Library of Pittsburgh, which was established as a publicly supported institution over Thomas Mellon's strident opposition, provided a greater fund of useful information for his biography than any other research facility. The Hunt Library at Carnegie Mellon University also proved useful, as did the Hillman Library and the Archives of Industrial Society, both at the University of Pittsburgh.

David Grinnell, curator of the Heinz History Center in Pittsburgh, rendered laudable service in locating and making available a number of previously lost family photographs and original documents. The Allegheny County Legal Library, at the City-County Building, and the Allegheny County Bar Association, both in Pittsburgh, were of service, as was the Carnegie Library of Homestead. The public library, courthouse, and City-County Buildings at Greensburg also yielded useful information.

I must also acknowledge my gratitude to the National Gallery of Art, and to curator Maygene Daniels in particular, for having preserved the archives of my late cousin Paul Mellon, which contain a vast treasury of material relevant to Thomas Mellon's life.

The illustrations for this book, which included many antique photographs, were scanned with superlative precision and expertise by Tom Palmer.

As always, the New York Public Library was indispensable, and my visits to the Library of Congress proved rewarding.

Finally, I'm grateful that during the writing of this book, my wife, Vivian, cared enough to be irked by my mental absences, instead of covertly enjoying them.

Unless otherwise noted, illustrations were supplied by the author.

# Index

Mellon, Andrew William (*continued*)
—as banker and businessman (*continued*)
371–74, 411, 417–18, 451; on science in
business, 388–89; on speculation, 374–75;
start of career, 111, 268–69, 273–74; strategy of, 383–87; transfer of family business
to, 418, 449–51. *See also specific companies*
—birth of, 121
—childhood and youth of, 156, 208, 265–73
—children of, 491
—education of, 109, 111, 265, 267, 269–73
—marriage of, 276, 278, 363, 379, 405,
490–91
—personal characteristics of, 275–78,
362–63; self-sufficiency, 265, 278, 362–63;
sense of humor, 369; shyness, 265, 269,
278, 362
—physical appearance of, 269, 362, 368, 371
—in politics: machine, 359, 380–83, 511;
views of, 379–80
—portraits and photos of, 364, 368, 452, 455
—relationships of: engagement to Fanny
Jones, 411; family deference in, 286; with
Frick, 275–77, 362, 435; interactions with
other people, 269, 272, 275–78, 362–69;
parenting skills in, 363; in social life, 275,
276, 363, 366; with TM, 267, 268, 274–75,
278; with wife, 276, 278, 363, 379, 405,
490–91
—religious views of, 379
—residence of, 267, 275
—and *Thomas Mellon and His Times,* 401–5
—transfer of family leadership to, 285–86,
411
—transfer of family wealth to, 451–58
—travels of: foreign, 276; in grand tour of
U.S., 413
—as treasury secretary, 247, 361, 380, 509–11
—wealth of, 234, 376, 377–78, 387–88, 389
Mellon, Annie (aunt), 12
Mellon, Archibald (ancestor), 2, 8
Mellon, Archibald (grandfather), 11, 12, 16
Mellon, Archibald "Archy" (uncle), 12, 16,
25, 51, 392

Mellon, Armour (uncle), 12
Mellon, Edward (grandson), 219, 440
Mellon, Elinor (sister). *See* Stotler, Elinor
Mellon
Mellon, Elizabeth (ancestor), 2, 122
Mellon, Elizabeth (sister). *See* Bowman,
Elizabeth Mellon
Mellon, Elizabeth Armour (grandmother),
11, 12, 16
Mellon, Eliza Toby (aunt), 35
Mellon, Emma (daughter), 87, 105, 121
Mellon, George Negley (son), 407–20;
birth of, 121; death of, 121, 418–20; education of, 111, 407; health problems of,
313, 332, 407–13, 418–19; in Mellon
Brothers Bank, 410, 412; portrait of, 419;
relationship with TM, 268; spending
habits of, 411–12; start of career of, 111,
407; TM's frustration with career of,
412–13, 419–20; and TM's interest in
supernatural, 479–80; travels in U.S.,
412, 413; trip to Ireland (1882), 313–19,
332, 409
Mellon, James Ross (son): as adolescent,
TM's advice to, 111–13; anti-Catholic
views of, 26; balance of work and personal life, 507; birth of, 87, 121; birth of
children of, 213, 235; in City Deposit
Bank, 417; in Civil War, desire to enlist,
149–54; confidence in TM, 113–16; in
construction business, 97, 102; education
of, 108–11, 265, 267, 269, 270; farm work
by, 110; foreign travels of, 244, 311–13;
and George Mellon's illness, 409; in
grand tour of U.S. and Mexico, 413;
health problems of, 149; on Kansas City
inclines, 443; on Leavenworth real estate,
158; Ligonier Valley property of, 284–85;
in Ligonier Valley Railroad, 281–82; marriage of, 158, 210–13; on marriage of Sarah
Jane and TM, 401; in Mellon Brothers,
111, 213, 215–19, 234, 248; namesake of, 87,
99, 121; Oceola Coal Works leased by, 111,
211–13, 215; after Panic of 1873, 248; in

Mellon, Richard King (grandson), 372, 490

Mellon, Samuel (brother): birth of, 17; career of, 391–92; in Civil War, 155; death of, 122, 391–92; land abandoned by, 158

Mellon, Samuel (great-grandfather), 22

Mellon, Samuel (uncle), 16

Mellon, Sarah (granddaughter). *See* Scaife, Sarah Mellon

Mellon, Sarah Jane Negley (wife): children of (*See* children); on Civil War, 152; courtship by TM, 73–80; death of, 503; domestic role of, 119–20; education of, 74–75, 76; family life of, 76; finances of, TM's role in, 119; and George Mellon's illness, 408, 409; in grand tour of U.S. and Mexico, 413–16; history of family of, 89–99; inheritance of, 99, 215–18; introduction to TM, 73–74; in later life, 486–87; in Ligonier Valley Railroad, 282; marriage of, 81–84, 87, 120, 278, 287, 401; personal characteristics of, 84, 87, 120–21; physical appearance of, 74; portraits and photos of, 83, 415, 455, 486, 487, 510; religious views of, 172; social status of, 76, 77; in *Thomas Mellon and His Times,* 120, 401; transfer of wealth to sons, 451–58; wealth of family of, 76, 89, 93–99, 102

Mellon, Selwyn (son): birth of, 105, 121; death of, 121, 122–23, 265, 267–68, 408, 475; education of, 109, 265; portrait of, 122, 266; and TM's interest in supernatural, 475, 477

Mellon, Thomas (TM)

—as banker, 219–35; approach to risk, 207, 233–34, 240, 375–76; customers of, 229–33, 236, 245, 262, 275, 359; disillusionment of, 243–44; early experience as, 67; employees of, 223–24, 227–28; establishment of first bank, 219–23; in Panic of 1873, 240–46, 279; power of, 222; respectability of, 222. *See also* Mellon National Bank; T. Mellon & Sons

—birth of, 1–2

—burial of, 494, 503

—as businessman, 213–36; breadth of work as, 376; cards of, 68, 222; integrated business strategy of, 97, 219; vs. lawyer, choice between work as, 209–10; legacy of, 514–15; missteps in later years, 440, 441; partnerships in strategy of, 137, 213–15, 234, 417–18; vs. politician, choice between work as, 358; transfer of family businesses to sons, 418, 449–51. *See also* *specific companies and types of business*

—career of: during college years, 56; early plans for, 41–42; vs. family life, importance of, 101, 507; parents' views on, 42–43, 46, 48–50, 54, 63; rejection of farming as, 41–51; wealth in choice of, 63–64, 209–10. *See also specific companies and jobs*

—character and values of: accumulation of wealth in, 156–57, 451–52, 506–7; ambition in, 29, 30, 36, 42, 64, 506; conservatism in, 508; development of, 18–28; influence of farm life on, 1, 20–21; influence of Franklin on, 36–42; moderation in, 512; pessimism in, 18, 208, 358–59, 398, 399–400; sense of humor in, 54, 204, 369; sentimentality in, 20, 288; work ethic in, 506. *See also* prejudices

—childhood and youth of, 16–54; career plans in, 41–42; development of values in, 18–28; farm work in, 17–19, 22, 33, 48, 51–52; financial status in, 17–19, 30, 33; first visit to Pittsburgh in (1823), 29–33; happiness of, 19–20; in Ireland, 1, 10; religious views in, 24–26, 40–41; romantic interests in, 52–54

—children of (*See* children)

—on Civil War, 149–57, 207–8

—death of, 501–3

—education of: college, 48, 54–61; at County Academy, 43–48; elementary, 21–22; legal, 64–66; religious, 22–26; self, through reading, 33–40; theoretical vs. practical, 60–61; at Tranquil Retreat Academy, 51–52

National Guard: in Great Uprising of 1877, 290–91; in Homestead Strike of 1892, 427

*National Labor Tribune,* 297, 299, 301–4

Native Americans. *See* Indians

Negley, Alexander (ancestor), 91–93, 282, 284

Negley, Barbara Winebiddle (mother-in-law): children of, 73; death of, 122, 213, 218, 501; after death of husband, 84, 97–99; history of family of, 90–99; marriage of, 90, 93; portrait of, 214; relationship with TM, 104–5; Sarah Jane and TM living with, 84, 213; will and testament of, 215–18

Negley, Daniel (brother-in-law), 79–80

Negley, Elizabeth, 91

Negley, Felix Casper, 214–15, 254

Negley, George (brother-in-law): death of, 392; as executor of Barbara Negley's will and testament, 215–18; on marriage of Sarah Jane and TM, 79–80; TM's son named for, 121

Negley, Isabella. *See* Beatty, Isabella Negley

Negley, Jacob (father-in-law): children of, 73; death of, 84, 97; history of family of, 90, 91–99, 284; library of, 161; marriage of, 90, 93; mechanical gristmill of, 30–31, 95; TM's first encounter with, 30–31; wealth of, 31, 93–97

Negley, James S., 142, 291

Negley, Johann, 91

Negley, Sarah Jane (wife). *See* Mellon, Sarah Jane

Negley, William B.: on Carnegie library, 349; as law partner of TM, 138, 214; as member of Common Council, 341, 342–44

Negley family: history of, 89–99; mansion of, 31, 94–95, 96; vs. Mellon family, 75–76; as Presbyterians, 95–96; social status of, 76; TM's first encounter with, 30–31, 73; wealth of, 31, 76, 89, 93–99, 102. *See also specific members*

Negley Lane house (Pittsburgh), 105–8; Barbara Negley living at, 213; construc-

tion of, 105; demolition of, 107; electricity installed at, 440; holiday celebrations at, 248, 486; layout and style of, 105–7; photo of, 107; staff of, 108, 248–49; telephone of, 249; TM's children living at, 213, 218, 247–48, 249; TM's children living next to, 248; visitors to, 286; William A. Mellon living at, 285–86

Negleytown (Pittsburgh): development of, 95–97; location of, 95; TM's first visit to (1823), 30–31. *See also* East Liberty

Nell (slave), 91

Nelson, Nathaniel, 138, 214

*New England Primer,* 22–24

New York, Carnegie's move to, 424–25

New York *Independent,* 293

New York Shipbuilding Company, 386

*New York Times,* 377

*New York Tribune,* 456

New York *World,* 381

Nier, John, 460, 465, 467

Norcross Brothers, 354, 356

Northern Pacific Railway, 238, 410

Obey, John, 186–88

Oceola Coal Works, 111, 211–13, 215

O'Connor, Harvey, 227

O'Grady, John, 468

O'Hara, Michael, Jr., 257

Ohio & Pennsylvania Railroad, 140

*Ohio Valley Boycotter,* 302

oil industry: Andrew W. Mellon's entry into, 386–87; in Pennsylvania, 208, 386–87

Oliver, Mary Gould, 74

Omagh (Ireland), 2, 319

*On the Origin of Species* (Darwin), 137

orchards, 17, 104

Ord, John, 351

organized labor. *See* labor unions

Otis, Bass, 36

Overholt, Abraham, 230

Overholt, Elizabeth, 230

*Owl, The* (student publication), 499

public education, TM's views on, 173–75
public service, by Mellon family, 509–11
puritanism, of TM: in advice to children, 109, 112–13; in childhood, 24; in romance, 53, 71

Queenstown (Ireland), 313–14

Rachelwood estate, 285, 512
railroads: bonds funding, 140–43, 293; built by Mellon family, 244, 279–83, 285; corruption in, 140–41; establishment in Pittsburgh, 139–40; Great Uprising of 1877 in, 290–93; in Panic of 1873, 238, 239, 240, 244; TM's land acquisition along, 157–58, 159, 410
reading, by TM: in childhood and youth, 33–42, 51–52; in college, 56–57; on economic theory, 304, 305; with failing eyesight, 439–40, 483, 488; during judgeship, 161, 172–73; motivation for, 172; passion for, 41–42; time for, as judge vs. lawyer, 161
real estate: accumulation of wealth through, 93; in Negley family, 93–99; in Panic of 1873, 244–45; Pennsylvania law on, 128–33
real estate development: by Andrew W. and Richard Mellon, 273–74; by Tom and James Mellon, 215–19, 220–21, 234, 248
real estate investments, of TM. See under Mellon, Thomas
real estate taxes: increases in, 140–43, 336; TM's views on, 140–43, 344
reason, conflict between religion and, 24–25
reasonable doubt, 196–97
Reconstruction, 336–37
religion: of Andrew W. Mellon, 379; in Castletown society, 9–10; conflict between reason and, 24–25; creation myths in, 162; in education of TM, 22–26; emotion in, 327–28; and evolution, 162, 168; of Franklin, 40–41; freedom of, 6; influence on TM, 171–72; of Mellon

family, 2, 9–10, 25, 511; of Negley family, 95–96; of Sarah Jane Mellon, 172; Spencer on, 163; TM's views on, 24–26, 40–41, 168–72, 392, 495–96. See also specific religions
religious conflict, among Irish Catholics and Protestants, 2, 3, 6–8, 9–10, 26
Remington, Frederick, 374
Republicans: Andrew W. Mellon in political machine of, 380–83, 511; in Common and Select councils of Pittsburgh, 341, 342; in presidential election of 1872, 337–38; on railroad bonds, 141; TM's affiliation with, 144–45, 337; TM's views on political machine of, 338–40, 344, 359
reputation, of TM, 244
residences, of TM. See Camp Hill Cottage; Pittsburgh residences; Poverty Point farm
respectability, TM's views on, 76–77, 171, 222
retirement, of TM. See under Mellon, Thomas
Revolutionary War. See American Revolution
Richardson, Henry Hobson, 350–57
ringism, 342–44, 345
risk: Andrew W. Mellon's approach to, 233–34, 375–76; TM's approach to, 207, 233–34, 240, 375–76
Roberts, David, 200
Rockefeller, John D., 234, 376
Rodgers, John, 22–24
Rolling Rock Club, 283–84, 285, 374
Rolling Rock Farms, 283
romantic interests: of TM during college, 57–60; TM's advice to children about, 112–13; TM's first, 52–54; in TM's search for wife, 70–80. See also marriage
Roosevelt, Franklin D., 246, 247
Ross, James: death of, 87; Mellons named after, 87, 99, 121; Negley family wealth saved by, 97–99; portrait of, 98
Roundhouse Riot of 1877. See Great Uprising

sociology, 174

South Carolina, 408–9

speculation, TM's views on, 233, 374–75

Spencer, Herbert: on education, 173, 174; on evolution, 162–67; *First Principles,* 366; vs. Franklin, 175–76; on individualism, 164–65, 358; on labor, 304, 305; and Panic of 1873, 245; in *Thomas Mellon and His Times,* 400; TM's study of, 41, 162–67, 172

spinal meningitis, 418

spiritualism, TM's interest in, 474–81, 511

spoils system, 336–37

Standard Steel Car Company, 386

Stanton, Edwin, 155–56

St. Clair Incline, 417, 441

steam power, 30–31

Steele, Mrs. Joseph, 321–22

steel industry: Bessemer process in, 237; Carnegie's approach to, 423–24; coke industry links to, 425; Homestead Strike of 1892 in, 426–35; immigrant workers in, 289; Mellons' entry into, 385–86; working conditions in, 289. *See also* coke industry

Steffens, Lincoln, 338, 339, 340–41

Stein, Andrew, 200

Stein, Charles, 200

Sterrett, David, 51

Sterrett, James P.: in Boyd's Hill murder case, 191–92, 197–98; as chief justice of Pennsylvania Supreme Court, 182; in civil cases, 203; in Grinder case, 195–97; in Keenan case, 189; in Lane case, 202; personality of, 198; relationship with TM, 182; TM as associate law judge under, 182–84

stock prices, in Panic of 1873, 244

Stockton, J., 22, 75

Stotler, Elinor Mellon (sister), 17, 19, 122, 267, 392

Stowe, Edwin H.: in civil cases, 203; in Grinder case, 195, 197; in judicial elections, 145, 146, 184; in Keenan case, 189; in Lane case, 202; personality of, 198

streetcars, 234, 340

strikes. *See* labor strikes

Sullivan, Anna, 194

Sunday dinners, 485

supernatural, TM's interest in, 439, 474–81, 511

Supreme Court. *See* Pennsylvania Supreme Court

"survival of the fittest." *See* fitness

Swartzwelder, Marshall, 189, 200

Tarr, Joel, 103

Taub, Casper, 89–90, 93, 96

Taub, Elizabeth. *See* Winebiddle, Elizabeth Taub

taxation: by Common and Select councils of Pittsburgh, 336; of Irish farms, 11, 143–44; Lafayette Hall convention against (1859), 141–42; on real estate, 140–43, 336, 344; Spencer on, 165; TM's aversion to, 140–44

teaching career, of TM, 60, 64, 66–67

telephones, 249

Texas, 386–87

Thatcher, L. K., 444, 462

*Thomas Mellon and His Times* (Mellon), 391–406; on ABCD lawsuits, 251, 254, 405; Andrew W. Mellon on, 401–5; on Burns, 400; Carnegie's copy of, 403, 421, 422; completion of, 400–401; on criminal sentencing, 180; decision to write, 392; editing of, 397; on Franklin, 400; on Industrial Revolution, 437; on labor, 304; legacy of, 515–16; length of, 397; on life in Ireland, 1, 9; on military service, 153; pessimism in, 398, 399–400; photographs of, 402, 403; Pittsburgh in, 400; private publication of, 401–5; reasons for writing, 393–97; on religion, 171; on Sarah Jane Mellon, 120, 401; on Spencer, 400; subjects covered in, 397–400; on supernatural, 475; timing of, 392–93; on tobacco, 488; versions of, 405–6; writing style of, 397

against, 294–95; TM as investor in, 137, 295

*Way of All Flesh, The* (Butler), 324

wealth: of Andrew W. Mellon, 234, 376, 377–78, 387–88, 389; of Carnegie, 387–88, 424; and evolution of families, 166–67; from industrialization, 208–9; from integrated businesses, 97; in legal profession, 63–64; luck in, 389; military draft avoided with, 154; of Negley family, 31, 76, 89, 93–99, 102; origins of TM's pursuit of, 18, 21, 25, 27, 31; in Pittsburgh, rise of, 208–9, 237–38; as primary motivation in life, 156–57, 171; purpose of accumulating, 156–57, 451–52, 506–7; as sign of merit and ability, 209–10; as sign of religious fitness, 25; in Spencer's philosophy, 164–65; TM on inheritance of, 166–67, 505–6; in TM's choice of profession, 63–64, 209–10; transfer from TM to sons, 451–58

weapons: in Civil War, 207; production in Pittsburgh, 208; revolver in TM's trip to Ireland, 314, 315, 316

Webster, Daniel, 155, 271, 337

weddings: of James and Rachel Mellon, 213; of Sarah Jane and TM, 81

wedding tour, of Sarah Jane and TM, 81–84

Weeden, William B., 309

West: Mellon family's grand tour of, 414; TM's real estate investments in, 157–59, 236

*Western Calculator* (Stockton), 22, 75

Western University of Pennsylvania: Andrew W. Mellon at, 270–71; location of, 55; Richard Mellon at, 111; size of, 55; TM as professor at, 60, 64, 66–67; TM's decision to attend, 55; TM's education at,

55–61; TM's preparatory study for, 51–52. *See also* University of Pittsburgh

Westinghouse, George, 237

Westmoreland County (Pennsylvania): emigration of Mellons to, 12, 15–16; Ulster influence in, 28

Whig Party, 43, 144, 337

White, James, 203

White Star Line, 313

will and testament, TM's lack of, 449, 458, 491

Williams family, 47–48

Wilson, John, 355

Winebiddle, Barbara. *See* Negley, Barbara Winebiddle

Winebiddle, Conrad, 90–91

Winebiddle, Elizabeth Taub, 90–91

Wisconsin, James Mellon in, 149–52

Wister, Owen, 412

Witherow, James, 382

Wofford, John W., 468–71

women, Andrew W. Mellon's views on, 272. *See also* romantic interests

Woodbridge, William, 47

Woods, George, 271

workers: Carnegie's views on, 424; Catholic, 289, 293; effects of Industrial Revolution on, 437; in Great Uprising of 1877, 290–93; immigrant, 289–90; TM's views on, 305–9. *See also* labor unions

work ethic, of TM, 506

World War I, 387

World War II, 388–89

Wuth, Otto, 194

Wylie Street, TM's residence and office on, 87, 104

Young, Mary, 79

ML                    ?/11